AF782319

Situated Communication

Trends in Linguistics
Studies and Monographs 166

Editors

Walter Bisang
Hans Henrich Hock
Werner Winter

Mouton de Gruyter
Berlin · New York

Situated Communication

edited by

Gert Rickheit
Ipke Wachsmuth

Mouton de Gruyter
Berlin · New York

Mouton de Gruyter (formerly Mouton, The Hague)
is a Division of Walter de Gruyter GmbH & Co. KG, Berlin.

∞ Printed on acid-free paper which falls within the guidelines
of the ANSI to ensure permanence and durability.

Library of Congress Cataloging-in-Publication Data

Situated communication / edited by Gert Rickheit, Ipke Wachsmuth.
p. cm. – (Trends in linguistics. Studies and monographs; 166)
Includes bibliographical references and index.
ISBN-13: 978-3-11-018897-4 (hardcover : alk. paper)
ISBN-10: 3-11-018897-X (hardcover : alk. paper)
1. Context (Linguistics) 2. Cohesion (Linguistics) 3. Reference (Linguistics) 4. Psycholinguistics. 5. Computational linguistics. I. Rickheit, Gert. II. Wachsmuth, Ipke. III. Series.
P325.5.C65S57 2006
410–dc22
2005034470

ISBN-13: 978-3-11-018897-4
ISBN-10: 3-11-018897-X
ISSN 1861-4302

Bibliographic information published by Die Deutsche Bibliothek

Die Deutsche Bibliothek lists this publication in the Deutsche Nationalbibliografie; detailed bibliographic data is available in the Internet at <http://dnb.ddb.de>.

© Copyright 2006 by Walter de Gruyter GmbH & Co. KG, D-10785 Berlin
All rights reserved, including those of translation into foreign languages. No part of this book may be reproduced or transmitted in any form or by any means, electronic or mechanical, including photocopy, recording or any information storage and retrieval system, without permission in writing from the publisher.
Printed in Germany.

Contents

Introduction

Gert Rickheit and Ipke Wachsmuth

This volume contains a selection of studies from the Collaborative Research Center (CRC) "Situated Artificial Communicators". The Research Center (Sonderforschungsbereich 360) was established in 1993 and has been funded by grants from the German Research Foundation (Deutsche Forschungsgemeinschaft) for more than twelve years. The research initiative has brought together computer scientists, linguists, psycholinguists, and psychologists in an endeavor to investigate human-human and human-machine interaction in situations which closely model everyday workplace demands.

The Collaborative Research Center comprises a number of basic research projects and several projects of a more applied character. While the basic research projects have dealt with the study and explanation of linguistic and cognitive characteristics of communication, the applied projects have pursued the transmission and implementation of cognitive principles and their utilization in artificial information processing systems. In the course of the scientific collaboration, a strong interaction between projects in these two strands of research has evolved. The starting point of the empirical research has been the attempt to corroborate or refute theoretically derived hypotheses by means of systematic experimentation. Results from the experiments have then been validated in computer simulations of cognitive processing. These models have led to more specific hypotheses which have been put to test in further experiments, and so on. In this way – on the basis of what we have termed the experimental-simulative method – we have successfully developed information processing systems with cognitively adequate application functionalities.

In the CRC, phenomena such as flexibility and robustness, the situation and knowledge dependence of language and image processing, and their integration in communication have been examined in much detail. In doing so, questions like the following have been pursued:

- How can irregular, fragmented, and distorted information be so easily and adequately assigned to definite states?
- What are the cognitive criteria in the organization and selection of domain knowledge relevant to the situation in question?

- What is the role of the situational and cognitive context in the processing of information?
- How can the interaction between perception and knowledge be organized in order to facilitate adequate understanding?
- Which recommendations for the design of integrated communication systems can be derived from experimentation and simulation?

Within the framework of the Collaborative Research Center, these questions have been investigated in an interdisciplinary fashion in thematically representative projects which support and complement each other in terms of theory and methodology. In recent years, diverse research efforts in cognitive science have made clear that, while interdisciplinary cooperation is vital for the development of theoretical and formal models; scientific progress has as prerequisites a close coupling to a particular problem area and a solid empirical foundation. Drawing on this experience, all the projects in the CRC are tied to a common scenario and subscribe to a joint methodological basis. Such a research strategy does not only foster the establishment of a common empirical basis for the participating projects; it also allows for the results to be systematically related to one another.

The innovation potential of cognitive science arises from the cooperation of the various disciplines. A truly interdisciplinary approach will bring about synergy, and thus give rise to highly creative solutions in terms of theory formation and methodology. In contemporary cognitive science, theoretical conceptualizations which yield progress in several disciplines are being proposed with increasing frequency. Within the scope of these developing theories, empirical and formal methods are increasingly interlinked. Building on this, computer simulation can be applied for the purpose of validating theory. Such an interweaving of experimental and simulative work is the hallmark of the CRC: Here, the experimental-simulative method is systematically applied and further developed with respect to situated communication.

The technological relevance of research in knowledge-based language and image processing stems from its application potential in the areas of information, communication, and education. In fact, natural language systems – to some extent – have already transcended the experimental stage. The mission behind this is the advancement of human-machine communication in natural language. Since most of the information in mass media is language coded, adequate design will make available various computer services to society. The information overflow which we are likely to encounter in the near future brings along a growing need to handle, as adequately and efficiently as possible, the knowledge accrued and to be conveyed.

The volume in hand comprises thirteen contributions which focus on special aspects of situated communication. The first chapter, "The constitution of meaning in situated communication" by Gert Rickheit, the CRC coordinator, introduces the concept of situated artificial communicators as jointly developed by the members of the research initiative. In the chapter, the basic scenario of the CRC is outlined: During the cooperative accomplishment of assembly tasks, different participants with different competences use verbal and non-verbal means in order to coordinate their sensorimotor activities. Since situated artificial communicators are a reconstruction of natural communicators interacting in specific situations, the characteristics of situatedness, integration, and robustness of the artificial systems have been systematically examined.

The chapter "Processing instructions", authored by Petra Weiß, Thies Pfeiffer, Hans-Jürgen Eikmeyer, and Gert Rickheit, presents a closer look at the processing of instructions in the context of an assembly task domain. The results of pertinent experiments show that and how the interpretation of instructions is determined by the intricate interplay of linguistic information and the visual context. Comparing the performance of both systems, human and machine, they found that the performance depends partly on the structure of the problem domain and partly on the structure of the conceptual knowledge and the processes working therein.

In their account of "Visually grounded language processing in object reference", Constanze Vorwerg, Sven Wachsmuth, and Gudrun Socher describe how representations of verbal and visual information are mapped onto each other in human communicators and how such a mapping can be achieved by artificial systems communicating with humans. At that, categorization principles play a major role since categorization constitutes the connecting link between vision and language. Categorization includes the assignment of a given perceptual input to a category that is associated with a linguistic term. So, when referring to visual object attributes, a speaker deploys at least two kinds of processes within conceptualization: the selection of an attribute dimension, and the categorization of dimension values on the basis of a reference system.

Helmut Flitter, Thies Pfeiffer, and Gert Rickheit show that „Psycholinguistic experiments on spatial relations using stereoscopic presentation" yield results that differ from those of 2½D experiments which make use of perspectival pictures. Proceeding from the assumption that the processing of 3D pictures requires different and possibly higher cognitive demands than the processing of 2½D pictures, the authors have observed a wider variety of answers for descriptions of spatial locations given under 3D presentation conditions, although the instructions had been identical in both presentation modes. In particular, the authors report that the deictic referential system (which requires relatively little cognitive effort) is used with almost the same frequency under 2½D and 3D presentation conditions. In contrast, the intrinsic referential system (which requires considerably more cognitive effort) is used less frequently in the 3D presentation mode.

The paper "Deictic object reference in task-oriented dialog" by Alfred Kranstedt, Andy Lücking, Thies Pfeiffer, Hannes Rieser, and Ipke Wachsmuth presents a collaborative approach towards a detailed understanding of the usage of pointing gestures accompanying referring expressions. This research has been undertaken in the context of human-machine interaction integrating empirical studies, the theory of grammar and logics, and simulation techniques. The authors classify the role of pointing in deictic expressions and present a model of the focused area of pointing gestures, the so-called pointing cone. This pointing cone serves as a central concept in a formal account of multi-modal integration at the linguistic speech-gesture interface as well as in computational models of processing deictic expressions.

Marc Pomplun, Elena Carbone, Hendrik Koesling, Lorenz Sichelschmidt, and Helge Ritter have developed "Computational models of visual tagging" that account for strategies which people employ in browsing complex visual stimuli. Two experiments on scanning strategies – as evidenced by human eye gaze movements during the viewing of spatial object distributions – are reported in this chapter. The results of both experiments indicate that a simple scan path minimizing algorithm, the so-called "traveling salesman strategy", is most effective in reproducing human scan paths. The authors have also found an influence of color information on empirical scan paths and successfully adapted the traveling salesman based model to this finding.

In the seventh chapter, Horst M. Müller discusses "Neurobiological aspects of meaning constitution during language processing". He describes three accounts of the efficiency of language processing: categorization in the sense of evolutionary epistemology, functional anatomy of language perception and comprehension in the brain, and neurolinguistic observations of the time course of the constitution of meaning.

In their contribution "Neuroinformatic techniques in cognitive neuroscience of language", Matthias Kaper, Peter Meinicke, Horst M. Müller, Sabine Weiss, Holger Bekel, Thomas Hermann, Axel Saalbach, and Helge Ritter show that the calculation of coherence allows to investigate communication between cell assemblies of the human brain, thus providing deeper insights into psychophysiological information processing. The authors give detailed overviews of the analysis of activation patterns in electroencephalography

(EEG) data sets by using Principal Component Analysis and Machine-Learning classification techniques, in order to investigate which information contrasts which conditions and how well they can be separated from each other on the basis of single trials.

The chapter "Situated interaction with a virtual human – perception, action, and cognition", authored by Nadine Leßmann, Stefan Kopp, and Ipke Wachsmuth, introduces the virtual humanoid agent "Max". As an embodied face-to-face collaboration partner, Max can assist the human by combining manipulative capabilities for assembly actions with conversational capabilities for mixed-initiative dialog. During the interaction, Max employs speech, gaze, facial expression, and gesture; also, he is able to initiate assembly actions. The authors present the underlying model of Max's competence for managing situated interactions and show how the required faculties of perception, action, and cognition are realized and connected in the cognitive architecture of an artificial agent.

Christian Bauckhage, Gernot A. Fink, Jannik Fritsch, Nils Jungclaus, Susanne Kronenberg, Franz Kummert, Frank Lömker, Gerhard Sagerer, and Sven Wachsmuth have investigated „Integrated perception for cooperative human-machine interaction". They present a perceptive system that integrates automatic speech processing with image understanding. The system, which is capable of learning. is intended to be an intelligent interface for a robot that is able to follow verbal instructions to manipulate objects in its surroundings. By combining statistical and declarative methods for inference and knowledge representation, this perceptive system reaches a performance superior to common-style human-machine interaction.

In a chapter on "Architectures of situated communicators: From perception to cognition to learning", Gernot A. Fink, Jannik Fritsch, Nadine Leßmann, Helge Ritter, Gerhard Sagerer, Jochen J. Steil, and Ipke Wachsmuth focus on three fundamental aspects of system integration: perception, cognition, and learning. Technically, the results obtained have been combined in a common demonstrator system that works at a realistic level of complexity. Conceptually, the ideas developed here constitute an essential advancement in the research on architectures of artificial cognitive systems.

Hans-Jürgen Eikmeyer, Walther Kindt, Yvonne Rittgeroth, and Hans Strohner present "A systems framework of communicative understanding". The authors conceive of the dynamics of cognitive systems in communication as constrained-based, interactive, and parallel. A high degree of flexibility is attained by equipping the cognitive system with special knowledge units which process any external influences in order to produce an adequate discourse response comprising both verbal and non-verbal information. Such an architecture emphasizes the fact that in communicative understanding the impact of the social situation must be taken into account, not only as an additional factor but as an indispensable precondition for many cognitive and communicative processes.

In their contribution "System theoretical modeling on situated communication", Hans-Jürgen Eikmeyer, Walther Kindt, and Hans Strohner outline a methodology for the theoretical, empirical, and simulative research in cognitive science. They argue that the successful study of the complex subject of natural language communication requires a systematic integration of notions and methods from the various disciplines that have a share in this endeavour. Such a systematic integration is possible on the basis of a system-theoretical conception of cognitive science. The authors argue that the adequate method for an investigation of the intricate interaction processes in situated communication is the extended experimental-simulative method which, accordingly, is described in detail in this chapter.

The editors would like to thank Lorenz Sichelschmidt for critical comments on earlier drafts of some of the chapters of this book, Gráinne Delany and Vivian Raithel for their assistance in proofreading and translating some of the contributions, and Anke Weinberger for the preparation of the final copy.

All of the contributors to this volume would be pleased if the book in hand were to stimulate further discussion and research in the complex domain of situated communication.=

The constitution of meaning in situated communication

Gert Rickheit

Abstract. The idea connected with the concept of "Situated Artificial Communicators" is the modeling of communicatively supported action in a real-world setting. In order to enable such action, the artificial communicator must be equipped with numerous highly complex capabilities for information processing, not all of which can be topics of the Collaborative Research Center (CRC) in the same way. Therefore, the CRC focuses on three central characteristics of situated artificial communicators, namely situatedness, integratedness, and robustness. These characteristics more or less strongly affect all behavior areas and processing phases of an artificial communicator's interaction with its environment. Thus, the situative conditions exert a substantial influence on any kind of communication designed for mutual understanding. A prerequisite for mutual understanding is the appropriate constitution of meaning.

1. Introduction

Both phylogenetically and ontogenetically, communication in concrete situations is of fundamental importance (Campbell and Wales 1970). The evolution of language took place, for the most part, in the management of certain everyday tasks (Müller 1990), with language serving as a tool for interaction (Herrmann 2005). A prerequisite for the ontogenesis of language is a child's sensorimotor development, which also takes place within different situational contexts (Piaget 1975).

More than seven decades ago, Bühler (1934: 23) spoke of a "situation theory of language" in contrast to "situation-distant speaking"; in doing so, he proceeded from a "concrete language experience", explained through his "Organon" model in which the referential field (Zeigfeld) plays a prominent role. Building upon Bühler's ideas and on Wittgenstein's conception of language games, according to which the meaning of language is its use, Hörmann (1976: 501) has come to the conclusion that "language, together with the activities in which it is involved, constitutes a whole: the language game that encompasses speaker, listener, and situation". Therefore, language can be considered a versatile tool for situation management (Fiehler 1980). With the help of language, humans can bring everyday problems closer to a solution by mutually directing each other's ideas or by exerting direct control over actions.

Throughout his writings, Herrmann (1972; 2001) has emphasized the importance of the functional context of verbal communication: "In order to understand something verbal, one must consider the sender, the receiver, and the situation in which they find themselves" (Herrmann 1972: 17). In the same vein, Clark (1992: 372) has pointed out that "what a word signifies depends not only on generic properties of the conceptual domain, but on the situation being described at the moment".

In psycholinguistic experiments, the influence of the current situation on the meaning of a word or an utterance has been well established. For instance, Hörmann (1983) has demonstrated the varying meanings of quantifiers like *some*, *several*, and *a few* within different situational contexts. Above all, Clark (1992; 1996) has extensively examined the role of situational factors in communication by means of experimentation, thus influencing research by showing, e.g., the importance of *shared knowledge* and *common ground*. These play a fundamental role in communication in that they lay the basis for the constitution of meaning and, along with that, for mutual understanding between interlocutors.

In a critical appraisal of the development of Artificial Intelligence (AI), primarily discussing the relationship between human knowledge (especially the workings of the human brain) and computer programs, Clancey (1997) has developed the "situated cognition" approach. In this approach, the role of feedback, mutual organization, and the emergence of intelligent behavior is emphasized (Clancey 1997: 1–2): "The theory of situated cognition [...] claims that every human thought and action is adapted to the environment, that is, *situated*, because what people *perceive*, how they *conceive of their activity*, and what they *physically do* develop together." The interaction between the internal and external organizations is characteristic for this notion of situatedness. "Being situated involves a casual, in-the-moment, coupling *within* internal organizing (forming new coordinations) and *between* internal and external organizing (changing stuff in the world)" (Clancey 1997: 344). Of central importance for situated cognition is the availability of feedback – both about the interaction of internal processes with each other and about the interaction of internal processes with the environment – so that actions are coordinated in their execution. With that, the concept of knowledge acquires a dynamic aspect (Clancey 1997: 4): "This shift in perspective from knowledge as *stored artifact* to knowledge as *constructed capability-in-action* is inspiring a new generation of cybernetics in the fields of situated robotics, ecological psychology and computational neuroscience." Similar to humans, future robots should have at their disposal some means of conceptual coordination that organizes the different aspects of cognition, perception, and motor activity in parallel, so that such systems are as efficient and flexible as possible – according to each situation – in solving certain problems within an appropriate time frame. In order to meet the high demands, such systems will have to be equipped with a dynamic memory (Schank 1999).

The CRC "Situated Artificial Communicators" has concentrated on those situational restrictions that apply to communication in a scenario in which two interlocutors exchange instructions for the accomplishment of an assembly task. Against this background, it has been examined, on the one hand, which capabilities of a human (referred to here as a natural communicator) make his or her verbal and non-verbal behavior adequate and thus justify to describe it as intelligent. On the other hand, it has been attempted to utilize the insights on intelligent human behavior for the construction of hardware or software systems (referred to here as artificial communicators). Such artificial communicators should, in the long term, have the ability to assume the role of a human's partner in accomplishing assembly tasks. In the shorter view, they allow a more thorough investigation of the workings of human cognition. Since cognitive processes cannot be observed directly, and many of these processes likely occur automatically, only after attempting an artificial reconstruction is may become clear which elements of intelligent behavior are pertinent to the solution of a complex assembly task.

Part of this is that a human acoustically perceives the interlocutors' utterances, i.e. hears; visually perceives the situation (including the partner, the scene, and the ongoing procedures), i.e. sees; cognitively processes the available information, i.e. understands; formulates his or her own utterances, i.e. speaks; and plans and executes purposeful, goal-directed object manipulations, i.e. acts. Such accomplishments are attained in a certain situation, so that human communicators can be said to be situated. In a way, this situatedness constrains a human communicator's potential; however, it also creates the preconditions both for a close investigation of the workings of cognition and action as well as for a successful transmission to artificial systems. Beyond this, humans also produce the above accomplishments when the available information is incomplete or distorted; an ability which is referred to as robustness. Unlike humans, many artificial systems lack a similar degree of robustness. Finally, humans can relate information from different sources or input channels to each other and process the information as an integrated whole. So, humans are able to integrate the relevant information in a given situation in order to create, or construct, or constitute meaning – which is fundamental to each kind of successful communication.

2. The concept of Situated Artificial Communicators

Under "Situated Artificial Communicators", we understand formal systems that reconstruct the behavior of natural communicators in relevant aspects. The conception of the Collaborative Research Center is based on the idea that, in certain natural language coordinated interactions, the role of human communicators can at least partly be assumed by automated systems. Some of the capabilities that an artificial communicator must have at its disposal in a real application situation are addressed in the following questions:

- Which kinds of activities and communicative tasks are to be performed by the artificial communicator?
- Which restrictions apply regarding the artificial communicator's knowledge about the task and the situation?
- Is the action planning already precisely definable at the beginning of the interaction, or does it develop during the interaction?
- To what extent must artificial communicators be able to negotiate meaning in the situation in question?
- To what extent does the artificial communicator have to cope with disturbances that may occur in the situation?

Depending on the answers to these and similar questions, situated artificial communicators must be conceived of as processing systems capable of performing highly complex processes or of simulating, in one way or another, the corresponding abilities of natural communicators. Within the CRC, gradual complexity reduction, necessary for the stepwise development of simulations, is not to be based upon the one-sided modeling of certain abilities. Rather, an integrated approach has been taken where the interaction of sensorimotor, cognitive, and linguistic abilities has been studied from the beginning. This approach is in line with recent research developments, for example, with research on the effects on processing of a situation that can be modified through actions (Dretske 1988). Similarly, in the philosophy of mind, arguments have been brought forward in favor of approaches which model "minds", "persons", or "agents" including intentionality, rational reasoning, information management, situated action, or the like (Pollock 1990). Of importance here is that these ventures proceed in close contact with Artificial Intelligence research on rational cooperating agents for one, and theories of intentionality for another (Cohen and Levesque 1990).

These arguments motivate a research concept for situated artificial communicators which exhibits, as its essential characteristic, the integration of the verbal communication level with a perception-action component, and which regards discourse as a synergetic interaction of both parts. Correspondingly, an important objective lies in the investigation and reconstruction of the conditions for such interactions and the feedback resulting from them (Gerrig and Littman 1990; Selfridge 1986). One of the advantages of such an approach is the expected gain in robustness that results from an overall increase in the efficiency of the system.

3. A basic scenario

In order to successfully tackle the development of situated artificial communicators, it appeared to be instrumental to restrict the complexity and the variability of natural communication in an appropriate manner. Such restrictions refer, on the one hand, to the choice of an interesting, manageable real-world domain and, on the other, to the modeling of only the most relevant system dimensions. In this way, artificial communicators can be devised that are controllable in concrete situations, and the handling of which is feasible.

Concretely, a basic scenario was agreed upon in which different participants with different competences coordinate their actions during the cooperative accomplishment of a logistics or assembly task by both verbal and non-verbal means. Thus, the concept of Situated Artificial Communicators has been restricted from the start to the application in task-oriented domains. An issue is not made of general discourse competence which one would have to assume for the command of all logically possible discourse situations.

As an exemplary realization of the basic scenario, a cooperative assembly task was chosen in which a toy aircraft had to be assembled from a set of wooden "baufix" parts. The basis of the procedure was a blueprint picture that showed how the individual parts were to be assembled step by step. Pairs of interlocutors were recruited who had to solve the task under specific conditions: The first communicator – the "instructor" – was to direct his or her partner – the "constructor" – according to the blueprint so that, by means of verbal exchange, the toy aircraft could be appropriately assembled by the constructor. Since the instructor could not see the supply of parts available to the constructor, and because no commonplace terms exist for many of the parts, this task could neither be solved by simple, deictic references alone, nor by the exclusive use of standard verbal means. Rather, success essentially depended on the possibility of close cooperation involving language processing and sensorimotor skills.

For one, this scenario served to collect an extensive corpus of empirical materials on task-oriented communication. For another, the scenario allowed the identification of specific abilities to be simulated in an artificial communicator – a robot that assumes the role of the constructor. A major characteristic of the scenario is that it combines language, knowledge, planning, action, and sensorimotor skills in a natural but manageable way. Each of these areas can fully unfold its complexity within the scenario. At the same time, through suitable definition of intermediate stages and starting from a minimum, the complexity level and the degree of realism can gradually be increased in the course of research.

The possibilities of the chosen scenario should become clear from the following selection of samples of authentic discourse from different dialogs (I = Instructor, C = Constructor; English translation supplied). The first three examples illustrate the variety of linguistic realizations of an instruction. For example, in (1) the grasping of an object is explicitly required; in (2), only a list of necessary objects is given, and in (3), the grasping of the object is implied by another instruction:

(1) I: Now first take the block [.].
I: *Nimm jetzt erstmal den Block [.].*

(2) I: First two bolts with yellow heads [..] two bolts with red heads [..] ah two connecting pieces with four holes.
I: *Erstmal zwei Schrauben mit gelbem Kopf [..] zwei Schrauben mit rotem Kopf [..] äh zwei Verbindungsteile mit vier Löchern [..].*

(3) I: And now put the ah orange rhombus underneath there.
I: *Und jetzt packste da die äh orangene Raute drunter.*

Occasionally, an unexpected situation is caused by unfulfilled default assumptions. In one such case, interlocutors had to cope with the fact that a certain sort of bolt, called for in the blueprint, was not available:

(4) I: And now you need [..] two orange ones.
I: *Und jetzt brauchst du [...] zwei orange.*

C: Two orange bolts?
C: *Zwei orange Schrauben?*

I: Mhm.
I: *Mhm.*

C: [..] Don't have 'em.
C: *[..] Ha'm se nicht.*

I: Don't have 'em. Well take yellow.
I: *Ha'm se nicht. Na nimm gelbe.*

Beyond that, further difficulties must be anticipated in natural situations: Instructions may not always be precisely verbalized, or elliptical and simple instructions may be linearly interconnected or hierarchically combined to form macro-instructions. The more competent the constructor is, the more successful will he or she be in the interpretation, the execution, and possibly, the anticipation of the instructor's verbal directions. Conversely, the instructor's directions can be more fragmentary, vague, or complex.

In the sense of the characteristics mentioned above, the basic scenario has been systematically varied as to the integration of verbal and visual information and to the situatedness and robustness of the processing operations. In principle, it would facilitate communication if information on which objects are relevant were available to the interlocutors as a result of their visual analysis of the scene. On the constructor's side, a narrowing of focus on relevant objects could thus be achieved. Conversely, on the instructor's side, the cognitive effort in the formulation of a serviceable instruction would be reduced if differentiating characteristics of the relevant object were visible. Example 5 illustrates the necessity for integrating verbal and visual information:

(5) I: And then there must be another [pause] there I also don't know what that is; it looks like [pause] [.] also round,.
I: *Und dann muss da noch [Abbruch] da weiß ich auch nicht was das ist; das sieht aus [Abbruch] [.] auch rund,.*

C: Mhm.
C: *Mhm.*

I: Um but on one side it looks wider than on the other.
I: *Öhm aber an einer Seite sieht's breiter aus als an der anderen.*

C: Oh yeah.
C: *Ah ja.*

Here, on the one hand, the intended object could not be focused on without a linguistic description. On the other hand, a vague description was sufficient to identify the referent object.

The interaction's dependence on the current state of knowledge becomes apparent in different performance aspects. For instance, the constructor is able to anticipate certain actions required from him, if he is already familiar with the object to be assembled. Often, the constructor's anticipations are due to the fact that the global interaction goal of the assembly task is communicated to him. In the following example (6), the constructor knew that an aircraft was to be assembled:

(6) C: This is going to be the propeller, if I'm guessing right
C: *Das wird der Propeller, wenn ich das richtig ahne.*

Moreover, knowledge of communication rules and technical terminology is of great importance. It is useful, for example, that the interlocutors master the rules of conversational organization to the extent that the constructor can signal his or her understanding of utterances as well as the progress of associated actions and is able to request the continuation of the communication (7):

(7) I: And the whole thing is now [.] uhm fixed with a cube. [.] Underneath this cube ...
I: *Und das Ganze wird jetzt [.] äh mit einem Würfel befestigt. [.] Unter diesen Würfel ...*

C: Hold on, [.] hold on, hold on, [.] I must align this first [...] yes.
C: *Moment, [.] Moment, Moment, [.] ich muss das erst ausrichten [...] ja.*

I: ... you put another cube.
I: *... setzt du einen anderen Würfel.*

With natural dialog partners, communication ability includes knowledge of the rules of metacommunication in order to make communication problems discussable and resolvable (8):

(8) I: it'll probably fit then.
I: *dann passt es wahrscheinlich.*

C: then it would have [pause] that's why it didn't fit before. We were talking around each other before.
C: *dann hätt' es ja [Abbruch] deswegen hat es vorhin nicht gepasst. Wir haben vorhin nebeneinander hergeredet.*

Furthermore, knowledge that is based on information acquired in the interaction is important (9):

(9) I: And now comes the [pause] it's best if you take a blue bolt again.
I: *Und jetzt kommt die [Abbruch] am besten nimmst du nochmal eine blaue Schraube.*

C: And a rhombus too, probably.
C: *Wahrscheinlich auch ne Raute.*

In this example, the constructor had learned from a previous, similar assembly step that for the desired action a diamond shaped nut was required.

The dependence of communicative processing operations on the situation manifests itself in a very high variance of the verbal expressions used and in the recipient's ability to also understand implicitly formulated expressions. Knowledge of the constructor's visual context results in a reduction of the formulation effort and permits the production of elliptical expressions, as in example (10):

(10) C: Well, but then I can't fasten it. Look, I still have three here.
C: *Naja, dann kann ich sie aber nicht befestigen. Guck mal, ich hab hier jetzt noch drei.*

Here, the constructor refers to three holes in a bar, visible to both interlocutors.

Also, the choice of relative or absolute object localizations (11) and the choice of a definite or an indefinite description (12) strongly depend upon which objects currently are in the field of vision:

(11) I: Then fasten that – the one closer to – to the yellow bolt, with the orange rhombus.
I: *Dann die - das, was näher zum - zur gelben Schraube hin ist, mit der orangenen Raute festmachen.*

(12) I: And that is now connected with the block – with one of the blocks.
I: *Und der wird jetzt mit dem Block verbunden - mit einem der Blöcke.*

In the latter example, the instructor, possibly only in a second step, realizes that, relative to the constructor's field of vision, an indefinite description is to be used.

In our data, one can find many expressions with deictic aspects that illustrate the effectiveness of an interaction involving linguistic and visual information (13):

(13) I: Ah, that would have to be placed one further to the back.
I: *Äh, das müsste doch einen noch weiter nach hinten versetzt sein.*

C: This here?
C: *Das hier?*

I: Yep. Exactly, the whole thing there.
I: *Ja. Genau, das Ganze da.*

The dynamic nature of communicative processes is, finally, based on knowledge resources that not only originate from the visual context. Mental models of the object to be constructed may guide the interlocutors' expectations at crucial points in communication and assembly (14):

(14) I: Now we can start.
I: *Jetzt können wir starten.*

C: The wheels are still missing!
C: *Da fehlen noch die Räder!*

I: No, don't have 'em.
I: *Ne, ha'm die nicht.*

C: Okay. So this is right, then? [.] Good. [.] No wheels at the back?
C: *Ach so. So ist es dann richtig? [.] Gut. [.] Keine Räder hinten?*

I: No wheels at the back.
I: *Keine Räder hinten.*

C: Mhm
C: *Mhm*

The diversity of robustness phenomena becomes particularly evident in the processing of syntactically not well-formed expressions (15) and corrected utterances (16):

(15) I: Ah, two [.] yes, dark violet [.] don't know, this is so – so circles, so [pause]
I: *Äh zwei [.] ja, dunkelviolette [.] weiß nicht, das ist so - so Kreise, so [Abbruch]*

(16) I: mounted at a right angle to each other [.] in front of the green block – ah of the red block, in front
I: *Im rechten Winkel zueinander versetzt [.] vorne an den grünen Block vor - äh an den roten Block vor.*

Furthermore, inclusion in the visual and action contexts permits a toleration of utterances which, although semantically deviant (17) or incomplete (18), are pragmatically successful:

(17) I: So the whole thing is fastened with a rhombus.
I: *Denn das Ganze wird mit einer Raute gekontert.*

(18) I: Yeah, and now place that …
I: *Ja, und jetzt leg das mal ...*

C: Yeah?
C: *Ja?*

I: … ah, right away onto this double, the spare one peeking out there yet [.]
I: *... äh, gerade auf dies Zweier drauf, das da jetzt noch übrig runterguckt [.]*

Here, "this double" referred to a bar with five mounting holes, of which, in the given assembly situation, only two were relevant for the next assembly step.

The preceding examples also show a set of prosodic attributes which have discourse structuring and steering functions, for instance in contrastive and deictic contexts, in echoic questions, dialog idioms, and hesitation and confirmation vocalizations. Taken together, the examples given above illustrate that an artificial communicator acting in the basic scenario must dispose of many visual, cognitive, and linguistic abilities in order to yield the same achievements as a natural communicator. This underscores the importance of the integrative research approach chosen.

4. Theoretical orientation of the Collaborative Research Center

The modeling of agents sensibly communicating and interacting in a world requires that the agents dispose of intentional states, goals, and plans; it further requires that the agents are able to perceive their world and, in principle, to modify it. Perceptions enter cognitive processing, which in turn effects changes of intentional states and initiates actions. Within the world, communication is a special, mostly verbal, form of action, the goal of which lies, above all, in the mutual modification of agents' intentional states. If situated artificial communicators are to reconstruct natural communicators who interact both verbally and non-verbally, then the characteristics of situatedness, integratedness, and robustness must be systematically examined.

4.1. Situatedness

Artificial communicators, like natural communicators, operate in situational contexts. Thus, on-going processes are directly affected by the context. This concerns relevant processing mechanisms such as focus and reference, inference and planning, resources (e.g. knowledge and motor skills) and also regulating systems (e.g. conventions and rationality postulates). Contextualization is closely linked to integration, since one processing channel may contain context information for another (Rickheit and Vorwerg 2003).

Modeling contextual dependency has a long tradition in linguistics. It constitutes a branch of pragmatics concerned with indexicality. However, theories and models in the field of pragmatics – in contrast, for example, to psycholinguistics – usually remain structuralistic. The relation between context and a verbal expression is largely examined in a unilateral fashion since expressions are widely viewed as being dependent on context. For dynamic theories of language processing, the question of context dependency arises anew, specifically with respect to the dynamics of the interrelations between context and verbal expression during the progression of discourse (Eikmeyer and Rieser 1985; Kindt 1984; Pereira and Pollack 1991).

In the research on language processing in Artificial Intelligence, it was recognized in the design of dialog systems that the natural language abilities of such a system suggest a communicative competence leading the user to expect cooperative system behavior. Modeling of central aspects of cooperative behavior has been carried out in dialog systems as partner modeling or, more generally, user modeling. Wahlster and Kobsa (1989) distinguish three types of user models of rising complexity: models with a-priori knowledge, models with stereotypical attributes for a class of users, and dynamic user models which are constructed during dialog and which are causally affected by speech acts. So far, the issues addressed in the context of user modeling include the violation of presuppositions (Kaplan 1984), over-answering (Wahlster et. al. 1983), the discovery and recovery of misunderstandings and false assumptions (Carberry 1990; McCoy 1989), and partner oriented object localization (Herrmann 1990). In comparison to the concept of the Situated Artificial Communicator, it should be noted that the very concept of a user model is already based on a non-symmetrical relation between the system and its user.

In image processing, context-related system modeling still runs into difficulties since, at the current state of research, the necessary data structures cannot yet be sufficiently and reliably generated from the images. For a successful transfer of these models to geometrically or topologically defined scene and object relations, it must be a priority for the objects of a scene to recognize the respective "device topology" of their mechanical components. Frequently, there is no straightforward coupling of objects through connection elements. Rather, combinations often occur loosely, through shared presence in the same environment, as a consequence of movements or actions. This emphasizes the importance of taking into account the spatio-temporal context, i.e. the processing of dynamically changing images. Only then is a solid foundation laid for the examination of causality and context, both of which are indispensable to the formation of mechanical or mental models. The intensive utilization of redundant information, e.g., by employing analogous models after an initial interpretation, leads to a substantial increase in the robustness of understanding.

Dependency on context is also featured in the theory of situated planning, or "plan-as-communication" (Agre and Chapman 1990; Suchman 1987). Here, action plans are used along with other sources of information for the handling of constellations in the world. It appears that actions can be partially planned; however, they must be dynamically adapted to the requirements of the current situation. World knowledge, visual analysis results, intentions, computed or verbally supplied plans, assumptions about the co-operating partners etc., are considered as resources that are utilized by a central cognitive processing unit to determine the behavior which is most appropriate for the current information state. The concept of situated action planning, like situated speech act planning, should be understood as a special instantiation of the general postulate of situatedness. For example, an assembly instruction in natural language is generated in situ like an underspecified plan: Very often, parts of the verbal instruction are only comprehensible if the current assembly state, the nominal state as visualized in the blueprint, and possibly the capabilities and knowledge acquired in the course of assembly help to supplement the underspecified instruction. Hence, in an architecture that corresponds to the general conditions of this framework, there is no need to separate the areas of action and text planning.

Systems permitting situated planning, in this sense, must exhibit an architecture in which the various sensorimotor, cognitive, and verbal components have direct and mutual access to one another. The central execution component is assigned the task to optimally use the available resources for action control by establishing a flexible measure of cross-connections between the underspecified representations of the different components. The visual and verbal information given in a situation, inferences triggered by the situation, local plans, and the like are therefore to be considered as constraints on a general action competence.

4.2. Integratedness

Situated artificial communicators reconstruct abilities for communicative as well as for non-communicative action. This is accomplished not through an isolated treatment of single abilities but rather, under the perspective of mutual dependence and support of such abilities. Accordingly, the processing of information from different channels (visual, verbal) and for different actions (verbal, manual) is taken to be closely intertwined. Only in this way, is it ensured that planning of actions, cognitive processes, and language processing proceed in an integrated manner, building on the overall information pool available .

So, situated artificial communicators consist of a multitude of units that intricately interact with each other, thus constituting an integrated whole in which cognition is of central importance. Nonetheless, these units must be differentiated in terms of structure, function, and processes. Sensorimotor activities, cognition, and language are closely related to each other, with the relations between perception and conception depending on requirements of the current situation.

Integration of image and language processing provides the opportunity to devise semantic components which are realistic in that they are pragmatically oriented and that they build on, amongst other aspects, the exploitation of the available information, situatedness, and robustness as basic theoretical principles. This approach introduces novel ways of putting semantic components to test. One of these, the successful use of a deviant expression in the context of robotics, e.g., in order to identify a referent object, provides clues as to the pragmatic adequacy of a specification of meaning.

In an instruction dialog, the various verbal realizations depend, among other factors, on whether the information to be conveyed can be assigned to shared knowledge, private knowledge, or to mutual assumptions. Without doubt, one will have to expect a complex interaction when choosing one particular type of knowledge as a reference point for utterances and context. The boundaries between the diverse knowledge types may shift through actual use in speech acts and speech act sequences: Mutual assumptions may be "de-problemized" after repeated usage and assigned to shared knowledge; private knowledge may become public in communicative use and turn into mutual assumptions.

From the perspective of computer vision systems, such an integrative approach facilitates the incremental constitution of meaning in that it is no longer based solely on the visual information but makes available further constraints from the discourse context. Such constraints can originate from several sources, e.g., from the focus and purpose of a conversation, from conventions regarding actions, interpretations, and reference, and from "common ground" knowledge. This offers the chance to reduce uncertainty in the recognition process along several important dimensions: What to look for first in a scene? Which relations between objects must be captured? How can vague references be interpreted?

The realization of an integration of language and cognition essentially depends on how and how well correspondences between concepts and visual description primitives can be established. Answers to these questions strongly depend on the internal design of the language and vision components. On the side of the vision components, this mainly relates to the question of which visual description primitives are to be chosen.

In situated artificial communicators, knowledge about the execution conditions of actions can be associated with the world to varying degrees. On the one side, some action competence could be conceived which would be based on a world model reduced to essential traits. The execution of planned actions would then occur on the basis of tacit postulates about the predictability of change in the world and about the stability of world states, similar to the postulates of rationality assumed for the planning of speech acts. On the other side, artificial communicators could be exposed to the world, totally, without any model construction. Here, actions would be regarded as system responses that are exclusively triggered by external stimuli.

In the modeling of knowledge and the constitution of meaning, the processing and representation of visual and verbal information play a central role. The paramount question here is whether the mental representation of information is to be conceived of as modality specific or as independent from the modality of the sensory input (e.g., on the basis of abstract propositional units). In cognitive science, two theoretical approaches are currently being discussed: the symbol processing approach and the connectionist approach. For the modeling of knowledge, an obvious way to go would be to consider both approaches so as to be able to utilize their respective advantages for the development of a hybrid system architecture (Anderson 1990; Eikmeyer and Schade 1993) as well as to meet the demands of the processes to be modeled.

4.3. Robustness

By no means, situated artificial communicators are regarded as ideal systems operating free from any disturbances. On the contrary: Disturbances, being particularly manifest cases of incoherence, are highly informative and should thus be accounted for systematically. An artificial communicator should at least be able to communicate with a partner who is subjected to disturbances.

The complex environment in which artificial communicators operate requires that they dispose of a high degree of robustness. In this way, they can more or less successfully cope with disturbances; they are, e.g., able to process irregular and fragmentary information, or resolve incoherence of various sorts. The resolution of incoherence is ensured by two mechanisms: First, the availability of rich information from different sources; and second, cooperation mechanisms at the object level and the meta-communicative level.

One of the most important cognitive properties effecting robustness is modularity. Modularity, in the domain of cognition, is to be understood in the sense of a differentiation of internal states into functional units that interact (Newell 1990) and compete with each other (Wachsmuth 1989). To be sure, this conception of modularity does not imply that the respective subsystems are isolated, autonomous instances (Fodor 1983). Rather, the division of cognitive processing to diverse units permits a more fine-grained analysis of the working of a system and goes along with a certain redundancy of the activated information. This enables compensatory information processing strategies in the case of certain disturbances.

Besides modularity, human cognition avails of a high degree of flexibility through self-referentiality, the ability to partially model its own states. Self-referentiality is a necessary condition for an adequate representation of subject-object-relations, e.g., in verbal deixis. This again is an aspect of representation that provides solutions to several problems of situatedness.

As experimental research in cognitive linguistics has shown since the beginning of the 1970s, a highly important factor for robustness is inference formation (Graesser and Bower 1990; Rickheit and Strohner 1985). Inferences are particularly important because, in relation to the amount, the diversity, and the complexity of verbal and non-verbal information to be processed, only a small part of the information is complete and unambiguous. Much of what is to be conveyed, therefore, is not explicitly stated by the speaker; it is only implicitly "co-meant" (Clark 1992: 78; Sperber and Wilson 1986). However, relying on common knowledge, the speaker can safely assume that the listener will infer, from the utterance and its context as well as from his or her knowledge, the information required for comprehension.

In a context of vision and action, more kinds of incompleteness and deviance and a higher degree of deviance of linguistic forms than would be possible in a purely verbal context can be tolerated. Indeed, reference and predication are often pragmatically successful, in spite of semantic deviance. Such deviance percolates to propositions and inferences, the premises of which it enters. As a consequence, a concept of inference, which builds on the concept of pragmatic adequacy, will have to be established in the long run. Pragmatic adequacy of operations with simultaneous structural incoherence further relates to an important compensatory property of information processing in discourse: Inferences are not drawn dependent on a static set of premises, but rather on the basis of a dynamic conceptual space.

5. Methodological orientation of the Collaborative Research Center

In addition to the orientation towards a shared theoretical conception of Situated Artificial Communicators, another principle of research hallmarks the work of the Collaborative Research Center – the orientation towards a common methodology. In the CRC, an experimental-simulative method has been advanced (Eikmeyer, Kindt and Strohner, this volume; Eikmeyer and Schade 1993; Rickheit and Strohner 1993). According to this, the investigation of artificial communicators proceeds on the basis of empirical data which serve as a starting point for the simulation of specific aspects that, in turn, are subjected to closer experimental analysis, and so forth. In summary, work in the Collaborative Research Center has been guided by a methodological orientation towards empirical foundation, system development, and hybrid representations.

5.1. Empirical foundation

If artificial systems communicate only with each other, it is questionable whether natural language should be employed at all. If, however, a natural communicator is involved, it is desirable that the artificial system adapt to the greatest extent possible to the capabilities, habits, expectations, etc., of the natural communicator. However, these have to be empirically investigated in greater depth yet.

An empirical study of the cognitive and linguistic foundations of Situated Artificial Communicators can resort to a variety of different empirical methods – from comparatively unconstrained observation (as, e.g., in ethnomethodology) to highly controlled procedures (such as experiments or simulations). It stands to reason that, for the empirical analysis of task-oriented interaction against the background of the basic scenario, the empirical methods of choice – along with the resources available – are determined by the particular research question. Thus, a methodological approach would have to be taken which balances the degree of internal and external validity so that it optimally corresponds to both the specific research question and the theoretical interest pursued. To warrant the ecological validity of the methodological approach, it would be necessary, on the one hand, to precisely specify the observations made under poorly controlled conditions (e.g., corpus analyses), and, on the other hand, to closely tie the observations made under highly controlled conditions (e.g., experiments) to the basic scenario.

This already suggests different possibilities for the empirical exploitation of the scenario. Psycholinguistic research comprises numerous studies that meet these considerations rather closely and thus represent appropriate departure points for the empirical investigation of the linguistic and cognitive foundations of Situated Artificial Communicators. Related studies comprise, among other aspects, the processing of directions, object naming, verbal object localization, the description of static scenes, and the description of spatio-temporal actions (Graf et al. 1991; Herrmann 1990; Herrmann and Grabowski 1994). For specific linguistic research questions, it is sensible to direct the focus of the investigations primarily to the relationship between the scenario and the verbal behavior of the interlocutors. Aspects of nonverbal communication can be added by taking into account certain states of the assembly task. In this way, sequences of speech acts can be studied as to their dependence on the situation as it develops. If the research interest is primarily oriented towards semantic-pragmatic processing, it seems advisable to put the methodological problems related to spoken communication into perspective through the consideration of written communication. Starting from the communicative framework supplied by the scenario, the focus of the investigations could be placed on questions of language production and comprehension. In doing so, investigations of causal relationships that hold in spoken and written exchange could also be of interest.

Apart from verbal conversation, special aspects of non-verbal communication – including its relationship to verbal communication – could be studied in an analogous fashion. This also comprises the interaction of the interlocutors' sensorimotor activities with language processing.

5.2. System development

To reiterate, situated artificial communicators are formal systems which reconstruct relevant aspects of natural communicators. Accordingly, implementations that model various selected aspects have been developed in the Collaborative Research Center. Such implementations serve several functions: First, in the work of the CRC, the realization of hardware and software systems constitutes an important goal in itself. Second, the implementations are being employed as tools for the evaluation of the models. And finally, more refined hypotheses are deduced from the evaluation results and, in subsequence, put to empirical test. This approach helps to ensure the step-by-step development of an overall system that integrates the particular aspects investigated and the implementations developed within the various projects. Thus, the full complexity of a Situated Artificial Communicator is reached by the gradual integration of single functions.

5.3. Hybrid representations

In view of the plethora of information processing abilities that must be mastered by an artificial communicator, including sensorimotor and language skills, it is essential to employ a broad range of different formalisms representing the information to be processed. Accordingly, hybrid approaches that permit the handling of several representation formalisms are of great importance.

In this context, it is useful to reconsider the distinction between symbolic and connectionist methods. A lively discussion on the relative strengths and shortcomings of the two approaches has been going on in cognitive science for quite some time – often under the hardly helpful aspect of an "in-principle realizability" (a sort of virtual implementation, so to speak) of single functions on the basis of one or the other of the two representation formalisms (Graubard 1989). Since both approaches are sufficiently powerful, in principle, to realize any computable function, ultimately only questions of efficiency and utility can matter. With respect to the data complexities to be mastered by situated artificial communicators, theoretically founded predictions concerning these questions are no longer possible (Winograd and Flores 1986). Instead, practical experience with the employment of symbolic or connectionist representations in systems of a realistical level of complexity must primarily foster further development.

The experience gained so far indicates that connectionist approaches are more promising for the early stages of sensory processing whereas symbol-based formalisms appear to be more suitable at higher system levels. At the state of research to date, symbol-based approaches usually offer better possibilities for control and specification since they mostly operate on the basis of an explicit knowledge representation. When sufficiently precise insight into the processes to be realized exists, this will be a substantial advantage over connectionist methods. In contrast, representations in connectionist systems are typically highly implicit; they can, in all but a few cases, only be directly generated from a specification. It is, however, possible to formulate learning procedures that generate connectionist representations from a series of examples. Thus, such formalisms can be employed where reasonable modeling through symbol-based methods is no longer, or not yet, possible – a situation that arises particularly easily with the integration of several system functions (Schade 1990, 1999). Therefore, the two representation paradigms can well be considered as complementing each other.

Acknowledgements

From 1 July 1993, to 31 December 2005, the CRC 360 "Situated Artificial Communicators" has been funded by grants from the German Science Foundation (Deutsche Forschungsgemeinschaft; DFG). We are grateful to DFG for their support. As the coordinator of the CRC, I would like to thank everyone involved in the projects for their constructive cooperation and hard work. Without such a cooperation, neither the Collaborative Research Center nor this text would have been possible.

References

Agre, P., and D. Chapman
1991 What are plans for? *Robotics and Autonomous Systems* 6: 17–34.
Anderson, J. A.
1990 Hybrid computation in cognitive science: Neural networks and symbols. *Applied Cognitive Psychology* 4: 337–347.

Bühler, K.
1934 *Sprachtheorie. Die Darstellungsfunktion der Sprache*. Jena: Fischer.
Campbell, R., and R. Wales
1970 The study of language acquisition. In *New Horizons in Linguistics,* J. Lyons (ed.) 242–260. Harmondsworth: Penguin.
Carberry, S.
1990 *Plan Recognition in Natural Language Dialogue.* Cambridge, MA: MIT Press.
Clancey, W. J.
1997 *Situated Cognition. On Human Knowledge and Computer Representations.* New York: Cambridge University Press.
Clark, H. H.
1992 *Arenas of Language Use.* Chicago: The University of Chicago Press.
1996 *Using Language.* New York: Cambridge University Press.
Cohen, P. R., and H. L. Levesque
1990 Intention is choice with commitment. *Artificial Intelligence* 42, 213–261.
Dretske, F. J.
1988 *Explaining Behavior: Reasons in a World of Causes.* Cambridge, MA: MIT Press.
Eikmeyer, H.-J., and H. Rieser
1985 A procedural grammar for a fragment of black English discourse. In *Dynamic Linguistics,* T.T Ballmer (ed.), 85–178. Berlin: de Gruyter.
Eikmeyer, H.-J., and U. Schade
1993 The role of computer simulation in neurolinguistics. *Nordic Journal of Linguistics* 16, 153–169.
Fiehler, R.
1980 *Kommunikation und Kooperation. Theoretische und empirische Untersuchungen zur kommunikativen Organisation kooperativer Prozesse.* Berlin: Einhorn.
Fodor, J. A.
1983 *The Modularity of Mind.* Cambridge, MA: MIT Press.
Gerrig, R. J., and M. L. Littman
1990 Disambiguation by community membership. *Memory and Cognition* 18, 331–338.
Graesser, A. C., and G. H. Bower (eds.)
1990 *Inferences and Text Comprehension.* San Diego: Academic Press.
Graf, R., S. Dittrich, E. Kilian, and T. Herrmann
1991 *Lokalisationssequenzen: Sprecherziele, Partnermerkmale und Objektkonstellationen. Drei Erkundungsexperimente.* Research Report 35; CRC „Sprechen und Sprachverstehen im sozialen Kontext“. Mannheim: Universität Mannheim.

Graubard, S. (ed.)
1989 *The Artificial Intelligence Debate: False Starts and Real Foundations.* Cambridge, MA: MIT Press.
Herrmann, T.
1972 *Einführung in die Psychologie.* Bern: Huber.
1990 Vor, hinter, links, rechts: Das 6H-Modell. *Zeitschrift für Literaturwissenschaft und Linguistik* 78, 117–140.
2001 Sprache und Komplexitätsbewältigung. In *Sprache, Sinn und Situation,* L. Sichelschmidt and H. Strohner (eds.), 13–28. Wiesbaden: Deutscher Universitäts-Verlag.
2003 Kognitive Grundlagen der Sprachproduktion. In *Psycholinguistik. Ein internationales Handbuch,* G. Rickheit, T. Herrmann and W. Deutsch (eds.), 228–244. Berlin: de Gruyter.
2005 *Sprache verwenden. Funktion – Evolution – Prozesse.* Stuttgart: Kohlhammer.
Herrmann, T., and J. Grabowski
1994 *Sprechen. Psychologie der Sprachproduktion.* Heidelberg: Spektrum.
Hörmann, H.
1976 *Meinen und Verstehen. Grundzüge einer psychologischen Semantik.* Frankfurt: Suhrkamp.
Kaplan, J. S.
1984 Cooperative responses from a portable natural language database query system. In *Computational Models of Discourse,* M. Brady and R. Berwick (eds.), 167–208. Cambridge, MA: MIT Press.
Kindt, W.
1984 Dynamische Semantik. In *Dynamik in der Bedeutungskonstitution,* B. Rieger (ed.), 95–141. Hamburg: Buske.
McCoy, K. F.
1989 Highlighting a user model to respond to misconceptions. In *User Models in Dialog Systems,* A. Kobsa and W. Wahlster (eds.), 133–254. Berlin: Springer.
Müller, H. M.
1990 *Sprache und Evolution. Grundlagen der Evolution und Ansätze einer evolutionstheoretischen Sprachwissenschaft.* Berlin: de Gruyter.
Newell, A.
1990 *Unified Theories of Cognition.* Cambridge, MA: Harvard University Press.
Pereira, F. C., and M. E. Pollack
1991 Incremental interpretation. *Artificial Intelligence* 50, 37–82.
Piaget, J.
1975 *Sprechen und Denken des Kindes.* Düsseldorf: Schwann.
Pollock, J.
1990 Philosophy and Artificial Intelligence. *Philosophical Perspectives* 4, 462–497.

Rickheit, G.
2001 Situierte Kommunikation. In *Spektren der Linguistik,* S. Anschütz, S. Kanngießer and G. Rickheit (eds.), 95–118. Wiesbaden: Deutscher Universitäts-Verlag.

Rickheit, G., and H. Strohner
1993 *Grundlagen der kognitiven Sprachverarbeitung. Modelle, Methoden, Ergebnisse.* Tübingen: Francke.

Rickheit, G., and H. Strohner (eds.)
1985 *Inferences in Text Processing.* Amsterdam: North-Holland.

Rickheit, G., and C. Vorwerg
2003 Situiertes Sprechen. In *Psycholinguistik. Ein internationales Handbuch,* G. Rickheit, T. Herrmann and W. Deutsch (eds.), 279–294. Berlin: de Gruyter.

Schade, U.
1990 *Konnektionismus. Zur Modellierung der Sprachproduktion.* Opladen: Westdeutscher Verlag.
1999 *Konnektionistische Sprachproduktion.* Wiesbaden: Westdeutscher Verlag.

Schank, R. C.
1999 *Dynamic Memory Revisited.* New York: Cambridge University Press.

Selfridge, M.
1986 Integrated processing produces robust understanding. *Computational Linguistics* 12, 89–106.

Sperber, D., and D. Wilson
1986 *Relevance. Communication and cognition.* Cambridge, MA: Harvard University Press.

Suchman, L. A.
1987 *Plans and Situated Actions. The Problem of Human Machine Communication.* Cambridge, UK: Cambridge University Press.

Wachsmuth, I.
1989 *Zur intelligenten Organisation von Wissensbeständen in künstlichen Systemen.* Stuttgart: IBM Deutschland, IWBS Report 91.

Wahlster, W., H. Marburger, A. Jameson, and S. Busemann
1983 Over-answering yes-no questions: Extended responses in a NL interface to a vision system. In *IJCAI'83 Proceedings,* 643–646.

Wahlster, W., and A. Kobsa
1989 User models in dialogue systems. In *User Models in Dialogue Systems,* A. Kobsa and W. Wahlster (eds.), 4–34. Berlin: Springer.

Winograd, T., and F. Flores
1986 *Understanding Computers and Cognition: A New Foundation for Design.* Norwood: Ablex.

Processing instructions

Petra Weiß, Thies Pfeiffer, Hans-Jürgen Eikmeyer, and Gert Rickheit

Abstract. Instructions play an important role in everyday communication, e.g. in task-oriented dialogs. Based on a (psycho-)linguistic theoretical background, which classifies instructions as requests, we conducted experiments using a cross-modal experimental design in combination with a reaction time paradigm in order to get insights in human instruction processing. We concentrated on the interpretation of basic single sentence instructions. Here, we especially examined the effects of the specificity of verbs, object names, and prepositions in interaction with factors of the visual object context regarding an adequate reference resolution. We were able to show that linguistic semantic and syntactic factors as well as visual context information context influence the interpretation of instructions. Especially the context information proves to be very important. Above and beyond the relevance for basic research, these results are also important for the design of human-computer interfaces capable of understanding natural language. Thus, following the experimental-simulative approach, we also pursued the processing of instructions from the perspective of computer science. Here, a natural language processing interface created for a virtual reality environment served as basis for the simulation of the empirical findings. The comparison of human vs. virtual system performance using a local performance measure for instruction understanding based on fuzzy constraint satisfaction led to further insights concerning the complexity of instruction processing in humans and artificial systems. Using selected examples, we were able to show that the visual context has a comparable influence on the performance of both systems, whereas this approach is limited when it comes to explaining some effects due to variations of the linguistic structure. In order to get deeper insights into the timing and interaction of the sub-processes relevant for instruction understanding and to model these effects in the computer simulation, more specific data on human performance are necessary, e.g. by using eye-tracking techniques. In the long run, such an approach will result in the development of a more natural and cognitively adequate human-computer interface.

1. Introduction

Instructions play an important role in everyday communication, especially in the context of education or at work where they are often embedded in task-oriented dialogs. Research on instruction processing is, among other things, also particularly relevant for the design of human-computer interfaces capable of understanding natural language. The development of such an interface can be the objective only of an interdisciplinary approach undertaken as a joined effort of (psycho-)linguistics and computer science.

1.1. Instructions in the research line of the CRC

Our research follows the experimental-simulative approach. Based on the theoretical background in psycholinguistics, we conduct experiments in order to collect empirical evidence on the performance of human instruction processing. At the same time we approach our research questions constructively from the perspective of computer science and human-computer interface design. The natural language processing interface created for a virtual reality environment is the basis for the simulation of our empirical findings. Using virtual reality techniques allows us to employ a broad range of interaction between human and machine while still being able to concentrate on the higher levels of communication and not being overwhelmed by sensory and motor control problems. Comparing the performance of both systems, the human vs. the machine constructor, leads to further insights into the complexity of the problem of instruction processing and the processes involved in human instruction understanding, which will finally lead to a more natural human-computer interface.

Communication is about contexts. In our setting we placed the scenario of the Collaborative Research Center (CRC) 360, where a human instructor directs an artificial robot constructor, in an immersive virtual environment (cf. Fig. 1). In a collaborative construction task the human instructor guides the system in building a toy airplane from a (virtual) wooden toy kit consisting of a set of generic parts, such as bolts, cubes, or bars. Thus the roles of the interlocutors are not equal, as the instructor is assumed to know how to build the desired object, and the constructor is expected to realize the instructor's directions. The system is represented visually by "Max" (Kopp et al. 2003), a human-sized virtual agent. He provides the human instructor with a conversational partner to attend to instead of addressing the void. This is important in order to establish a more natural communicative situation.

In the research presented in this chapter, we are interested in the role of the constructor and the way she interprets the verbal instructions given by the instructor. In doing so, we concentrate on basic single sentence instructions such as *Connect the red bolt with the cube*, and do not permit full games with several turns. This allows us to focus on the effects of verb- and object-specificity, prepositions, and the influence of the visual context.

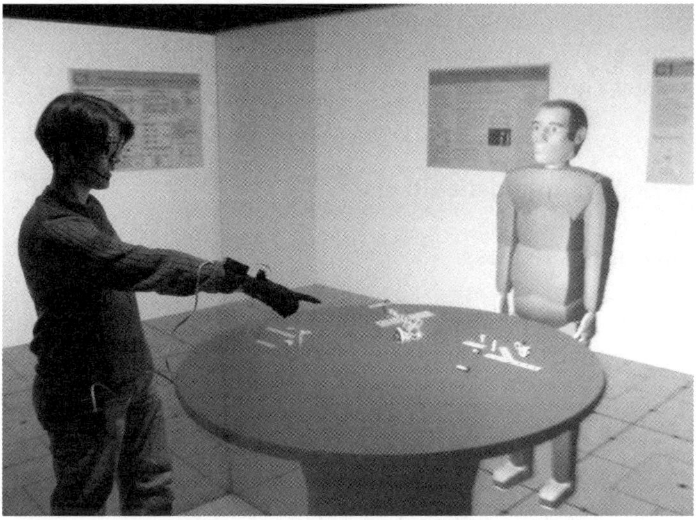

Figure 1. In the virtual reality setting, the user instructs the system, represented by the virtual agent "Max", in building an airplane from toy building blocks. The human-computer interface supports both speech and gestures, as in the example: *Nimm die ↘ rote Schraube! – Take the ↘ red bolt!* (↘ indicates the stroke of the pointing gesture).

1.2. The structure of this chapter

In the first part of this chapter we relate instructions to their theoretical background in linguistics, especially speech act theory, as well as in psycholinguistics and identify important components of instructions. In the second part we present experiments undertaken to investigate how humans perform when processing instructions under different linguistic and contextual conditions. In part three we present the human-computer interface for a situational understanding of instructions. This presentation will mainly focus on reference resolution where the conceptual information conveyed by the instruction and interpreted by a speech-processing system is used to identify the intended objects in the virtual environment. In part four we will develop a local performance measure for instruction understanding in the simulation. This measurement will then allow us to relate the simulative approach to the results of the psycholinguistic experiments. Using selected examples we will show that the visual context has a comparable influence on the performance of both systems, human and machine. However, this approach is limited when it comes to explaining some effects evoked by variations of the linguistic structure. We will conclude with a discussion and outline our plans for further research.

2. Instructions in linguistic theory

2.1. Instructions as requests

Instructions can be subsumed into the class of utterances called requests (Carroll and Timm 2003; Hindelang 1978). Requests are speech acts with which a speaker wants to prompt his or her partner to do something or to behave in a special way intended by the speaker (Graf and Schweizer 2003; Herrmann 1983: 112–151, 2003), e.g. to take a further step in the assembly of the toy airplane. Based on speech act theory (Austin 1962; Searle 1969, 1976) requests in turn can be assigned to the class of directives (e.g. to command, to request, to permit, to advise, etc.). The basic assumption in speech act theory is that language use is not only information transfer but a special kind of acting with language. In speech act theory, the actions performed with language are categorized according to their communicative function, the illocution (Rolf 1997). This means that utterances are accounted for by their intended or achieved effectiveness.

The realization of the illocutionary act of requesting does not depend on a special grammatical sentence form (Wunderlich 1984). Requests can be formulated using an explicit performative utterance like *I call on you to take the red bolt*, or a declarative sentence with a modal verb such as *You should take the red bolt*, and of course using an instruction with an imperative: *Take the red bolt!* Imperative sentences are prototypical realizations of requests (Wunderlich 1984). Thus, it is not possible to identify an utterance as a request solely from its linguistic form. As a consequence, in speech act theory conditions were formulated that have to be fulfilled in order to identify an utterance as a request (cf. Herrmann and Grabowski 1994: 163; Rolf 1997):

(i) The action will be conducted in the future.
(ii) The speaker wants the partner to conduct the action.
(iii) The speaker believes that the partner is able to conduct the action.
(iv) The speaker believes that the partner is willing to conduct the action.

(v) The speaker presumes that the partner will not conduct the action anyway.

The identification of an utterance as a request depends on the interpretation of a complex combination of linguistic and non-linguistic situational factors and of para-verbal (e.g. smiling) and non-verbal components (e.g. pointing) accompanying the verbal utterances (Grabowski-Gellert and Winterhoff-Spurk 1988). So far, in psycholinguistics there exists no comprehensive or even exhaustive theoretically well-funded systematization of possible variants of requesting. Primarily, two dimensions emerge for the classification of requests: politeness and directness.

With regard to requests, the concept of politeness is closely connected to the idea of "face-work" or "face-management" (Goffman 1989). In a communicative situation interlocutors want to be respected and accepted ("positive face"), and they are afraid of being degraded or losing their reputation ("negative face"; Blum-Kulka, House, and Kasper 1989). For requesting, this means that a speaker has to prompt his or her interlocutor to conduct the intended action and at the same time has to minimize the threatening of the "face" of both (Meyer 1992). Thus, politeness is a possible form of successful "face-work".

Requests can also be either very direct or indirect. Explicit performative utterances and utterances with an imperative verb are direct forms of requests, whereas formulations as questions or as subtle cues are more indirect forms, e.g. by saying *It's very cold in here*, in order to get the partner to close the window. Furthermore, the directness of requests correlates with the degree of politeness (Brown and Levinson 2004). Usually more direct requests are less polite. But very indirect requests are not per se also very polite (Blum-Kulka 1987; Herrmann 1983). Additional factors like cultural norms and situational factors determine whether a special form of requesting is judged as being polite or not (Graf and Schweizer 2003; Herrmann 2003).

2.2. The classification of requests according to AUFF

Especially the dimension of directness with regard to situational factors led to the psycholinguistic classification of (verbal) requests, AUFF, developed by Herrmann (1983: 112-126; Herrmann and Grabowski 1994: 166-174). The acronym AUFF is derived from the German word "*Auff*orderung" [request]. In AUFF five variants of requests are distinguished (cf. Graf and Schweizer 2003; Herrmann 2003):

- Imperative and performative requests (I): The partner is directly committed to do something (e.g. *Take the red bolt! – I call on you to take the red bolt*).
- Requests referring to the legitimation of the speaker (V): The speaker is authorized to commit the partner to do something (e.g. *You must take the red bolt! – I can demand from you to take the red bolt*).
- Requests referring to the secondary goal of the speaker and to conditions concerning the partner (A): The speaker wants the partner to do something and the partner is able and willing to do so (e.g. *Can you take the red bolt?*).
- Requests referring to the primary goal of the speaker and to the conditions concerning the speaker (E): The speaker wants to reach a special target state through the action of the partner (e.g. *I want you to take the red bolt*).
- Requests without referring to the speaker, the partner, deontic conditions (conditions concerning social conventions or norms), or to the action the speaker wants the partner to conduct; "hints" (H): The speaker only refers to conditions of the intended target state (e.g. *A red bolt is missing in the assembly*).

AUFF is a (partial) structure of implications. In this system requests are classified with respect to situational factors like legitimation of the speaker, his primary goals or the intended actions. These factors are interrelated in different and complex ways. In AUFF, the directness of requests is defined by the implicational relations between facts different kinds of requests refer to. Direct and indirect requests can be considered as being polite or not, in dependence on the communicative situation and different verbalizations.

Furthermore, AUFF is not only a descriptive psycholinguistic taxonomy of requests but rather it is conceived as a cognitive scheme represented mentally by an individual. This implies that, given the actual communicative situation, verbalizing of only a few components is sufficient to activate the entire AUFF system – following the principle of "pars pro toto" (Herrmann and Grabowski 1994: 349). As regards directness, the speaker is confronted with a tradeoff between communicative clarity (very direct requests) and the risk of misunderstanding or reactance by the partner. In this respect, requests with medium directness hold a small communicative risk and are used most frequently (Blum-Kulka, House, and Kasper 1989).

Aside from the question of how to classify requests, there is also the problem of which factors determine what kind of request is chosen by a speaker in a specific situation. Following Herrmann and Grabowski (1994;

see also Graf and Schweizer 2003; Herrmann 2003) essentially four factors, as conceived by the speaker, determine his or her choice:

(i) the willingness and
(ii) the ability of the partner to conduct the intended action;
(iii) the speaker's legitimation to request the partner to conduct the action;
(iv) the urgency to reach the primary goal connected with the intended action.

In a couple of experimental and field studies it was possible to identify systematic relations between the four factors mentioned above and the kind of request being produced (Herrmann 2003; Herrmann and Grabowski 1994: 186–205; Hoppe-Graff et al. 1985; for a critical discussion cf. Engelkamp and Mohr 1986).

2.3. Instructions relevant for the CRC scenario

With respect to the communicative situation of the scenario under consideration here, the interlocutors show a clear role allocation. As both share a common goal, their willingness is expected to be high. The instructor, who knows the plan of the model, has the legitimation to give directions and typically takes the role of the speaker. The partner is the constructor and her task is to follow the speaker's instructions by conducting the intended actions. The communicative situation can therefore be considered a standard situation in which normally simple and direct requests are produced (Herrmann and Grabowski 1994). Under this assumption we will concentrate in the following on simple and direct verbal instructions (basic single sentences). Furthermore, we restricted our experiments to instructions related to actions requiring the connection of parts, as these are most frequently used in the corpus of the CRC (cf. Brandt-Pook 1999).

2.4. Linguistic components of instructions for construction processes

Verbal instructions like *Schraube die rote Schraube in den grünen Würfel* (*Screw the red bolt in the green cube*) consist of several linguistic components which have to be processed in order to identify the action to be performed.

2.4.1. Semantic components

At first, the hearer has to interpret the construction verb (*schrauben*, i.e. *to screw*). To interpret a verb in an instruction means to get to know what to do. But the verb on its own does not convey sufficient information to understand an instruction. The constructor also has to know which objects to use in order to carry out the intended action. Therefore she has to interpret the object names (*Schraube*, i.e. *bolt*; *Würfel*, i.e. *cube*). Interpreting the names of the objects does not only mean to understand the literal meaning of the words registered in a kind of mental lexicon, but also to identify the correct objects for conducting the intended action. With action-related instructions this can only be achieved by taking into account the communicative situation. In addition to the linguistic information, especially the visual object context can be consulted for reference resolution and for the identification of the required actions.

Particularly for instructions, verbs and object names cannot be interpreted in isolation. Only the correct interpretation of the combination of object referents and verb admits the processing of the instruction in the intended way. The specificity of verbs and object names plays an important role. A verb like *to screw* specifies a highly specific action, screwing, which in turn imposes further requirements for the objects to be chosen. Whereas an unspecific verb like *to connect* is less restrictive. The same holds for the object naming. Almost all the objects in the context can be referred to by *part*, whereas the name *bolt* matches only with a few objects.

Aside from verbs and object names, prepositions can be important for the adequate interpretation of an instruction. In the example mentioned above, the preposition *in* implicates the direction of the action: The bolt has to be screwed *into* the cube and not, vice versa, the cube *into* the bolt (the "baufix" cubes have six mounting holes, some with a thread and some without). This is different when combining *to screw* with the preposition *an* (*on*). While the established connection is the same, both directions of action are possible: The bolt can be screwed on the cube and the cube can be screwed on the bolt respectively. Hence, the preposition *in* is more specific than the preposition *on*. Furthermore, this aspect is connected with the allocation of the roles of the objects. In combination with *in*, the bolt is the target object which will be chosen, moved, and connected to the reference object, which, in our case, is the cube. In combination with *on*, the role of target or reference object can be assigned to both objects likewise.

2.4.2. Syntactic factors

One important syntactic factor affecting especially the time course of the interpretation process is the variation of the syntactic position of the components mentioned with respect to the concrete formulation of an instruction. In the first instance the position of the verb of action in an instruction is important. There might be a great difference concerning the interpretation process if the verb of action (*schrauben*, i.e. *screw*) is in front position (e.g. *Schraube in den grünen Würfel die rote Schraube* – literally, *Screw in the green cube the red bolt*) or in final position (e.g. *In den grünen Würfel die rote Schraube schrauben – In the green cube the red bolt (is to be) screwed*). In the first case, it is easy to know right from the beginning that the intended action is to screw; in the second case, the instruction has to be processed completely in order to know which action has to be taken.

These considerations can also be applied to the naming of objects: It is possible to mention the target object (*die rote Schraube*, i.e. *the red bolt*) first and then the reference object (e.g. *Schraube die rote Schraube in den grünen Würfel – Screw the red bolt in the green cube*) or vice versa (e.g. *Schraube in den grünen Würfel die rote Schraube – Screw in the green cube the red bolt*). This variation may affect especially the availability of the information about the object referents. Of course, these aspects also interact with the naming of the objects and with context factors.

3. Psycholinguistic experiments on the processing of instructions

In this section we report on a series of experiments in which we investigated the influence of the linguistic components explicated above on the interpretation of simple and direct instructions to conduct assembly actions (connection of parts) within the scope of the scenario of the CRC.

In Experiment 1, we addressed lexical-semantic factors like the specificity of verbs and of object naming in interaction with factors of the visual object context. In Experiment 2, we examined the influence of a syntactic factor, the position of the verbs in the instructions, in combination with the specificity of the verbs and a variation of the visual context. In Experiment 3, we also varied the order of target and reference object (sequence of arguments) in the instructions with regard to the direction of the intended action mediated by the specificity of the prepositions.

Before reporting these experiments in greater detail, we give a brief description of the general method applied in the experiments.

3.1. General procedure in the experiments

In all experiments we used a cross-modal presentation technique in combination with the reaction time paradigm in order to test the influence of the linguistic and the contextual factors on the processing of simple and direct oral instructions.

Participants were presented pictures with arrangements of objects on a computer screen. In a first step, the participants could see the potential target object in combination with contextual objects in the upper half of the screen. Then they were presented an instruction acoustically, and at the same time another object appeared at the bottom of the screen. We will call this object the reference object because the target object has to be moved and fitted to this object depending on the interpretation of the instruction, especially of the construction verb (see Fig. 2; for a terminological discussion cf. Weiß 2005: 31–33).

Participants had to choose one of the objects presented in the upper row as the appropriate target object by pushing the appropriate button on the keyboard or by a mouse click as fast and correctly as possible. Thus the participants had to conduct an action-related decision task. The selection of the target object indicates how they interpret an instruction. Additionally, reaction times were taken as a measure for the processing complexity of the instructions under consideration.

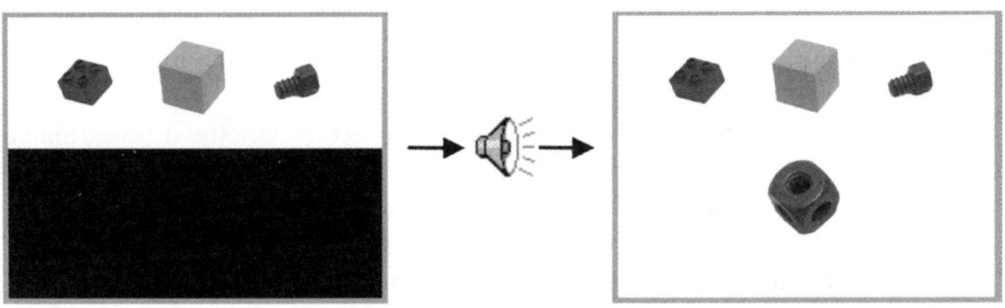

Figure 2. Example of the presentation of an experimental item: First the potential target object (TO) and context objects (CO) are presented (TO top right: red bolt, CO top left and mid: blue LEGO brick, yellow block), then the reference object (RO) (below: green cube) appears, and at the same time an instruction referring to the arrangement of objects is presented acoustically. A sample instruction might be *Schraube die rote Schraube in den grünen Würfel* (*Screw the red bolt in the green cube*).

3.2. Experiments 1 and 2: Influence of verbs, object naming and context

In Experiment 1, we examined the influence of the specificity of verbs and object naming in visually ambiguous vs. unambiguous object contexts. The relevance of the information carried by the construction verb and the contextual information was examined in greater detail in Experiment 2 by systematically varying the position of the verbs in the instructions (Weiß, Hildebrandt, Eikmeyer, and Rickheit 1999; Weiß, Hildebrandt, and Rickheit 1999).

Based on studies that showed sentence processing – in particular, the processing of oral instructions – to take place in an incremental and interactive way (Altmann and Kamide 1999; Tanenhaus et al. 1995), we assumed that, particularly in the case of unspecific linguistic information, the visual object context helps to interpret the instructions.

In these experiments the instructions were always formulated in the following way: The reference object (e.g. *green cube*) was the first object mentioned, and the target object (*red bolt*) the second one, e.g. *Schraube in den grünen Würfel die rote Schraube* (*Screw in the green cube the red bolt*). When considered in isolation, a formulation like *Screw the red bolt in the green cube* might sound more natural. But in the context of the assembly of the toy airplane, there usually is an existing (old) part or aggregate to which a new component should be added. Therefore the constructor has to choose one of the possible objects for a target object and move it to the already determined and fixed reference object. This choice might be easier if the structure of the instruction follows the given-new contract (Clark and Haviland 1977; Hörnig, Oberauer, and Weidenfeld 2002). Also, from the preceding visual presentation of the potential target objects, these objects should already be activated prior to the visual presentation of the reference object and the acoustic presentation of the instruction. Accordingly, by mentioning the reference object simultaneously with its visual presentation, the attention of the participants should not be focused on a particular target object but on the reference object.

3.2.1. Experiment 1: Method, factors, and design

In Experiment 1, several factors were investigated in combination in an orthogonal design. The factor "verb specificity" was varied within cases at two levels (specific vs. unspecific). The factor "specificity of target object naming" was varied between cases at two levels (specific vs. unspecific). Furthermore, two variables concerning the visual "object context", i.e. color and function of the target object relative to two context objects, were varied within cases at two levels (ambiguous vs. unambiguous) each.

- *Verb specificity:* The classification of verbs depending on their level of specificity is based on a transfer of the semantic relation of hyponymy from the classification of nouns (e.g. *a sparrow is a bird*) to the classification of verbs (Miller 1998; Miller and Fellbaum 1991), in which case the relation is termed troponymy (Fellbaum 1998). Troponymy means that specific verbs like *verschrauben* (*to screw*) bear more information (i.e., have higher entropy) than less specific verbs like *verbinden* (*to connect*). Thus, with specific verbs, the possible actions mediated are more constrained than with unspecific verbs. With unspecific verbs, there is a larger amount of possible actions and objects with which these actions can be carried out (Miller 1991: 228–230). The resulting hierarchy of verbs differs from the hierarchy of nouns in that, additionally, the quality of the relation has to be supplied (e.g., "screwing is a special way of connecting"). Taken together, the hierarchy of verbs is shallower than that of nouns, with the number of hierarchy levels normally not exceeding four (Miller 1991: 230). Not in every case is there exactly one superordinate verb for a group of semantically related verbs. As a consequence, it is comparatively difficult to classify verbs based on the relation of troponymy. By using a questionnaire (cf. Weiß, Hildebrandt, and Rickheit 1999), we were able to construct eight pairs of construction verbs differing in their degree of specificity and to combine them with possible objects of action.
- *Specificity of target object naming:* This variation was obtained by using *Teil* (*part*) for an unspecific naming of the target object and a term at the basic level (Rosch 1978) in the specific case, e.g. *Schraube* (*bolt*).
- *Object context:* The referential (un-)ambiguity of color and function of the potential target object was varied in relation to the color and function of two further context objects. In the case of an unambiguous color, only the target object had the color mentioned in the instruction (red, blue, green, or yellow; see Fig. 1); in the case of ambiguous color, all three potential target objects had the same color (for an example, see Fig. 12 below). In the case of an unambiguous function, the intended action could only be carried out with the target object; in the case of functional ambiguity, each of the three objects could serve as the target object (e.g. three bolts; see Fig. 13 below). In a third experimental condition, we combined the referential ambiguity of color and function by creating a set consist-

ing of the target object (e.g. a red bolt), one context object matching the target object in color (e.g., a red cube), and one matching it in function (e.g., a yellow bolt).

In Experiment 1, the unspecific or specific verbs in the instructions were always presented in a sentence final position, as *verbinden* (unspecific) or *verschrauben* (specific) in *Mit dem grünen Teil sollst du die rote Schraube verbinden/verschrauben* (*With the green part the red bolt is to be connected* (unspecific verb) or *In the green part the red bolt is to be screwed* (specific verb).

With this kind of formulation we aimed at making the participants process the information about the object referents first and then the explicit information about the intended action mediated especially by the verb. We assumed that, particularly in combination with ambiguous object arrangements, the information conveyed by (specific) verbs would be of special importance in interpreting the instruction and in selecting the target object.

3.2.2. Experiment 1: Results

On the whole, instructions with specific verbs were processed more quickly than instructions with unspecific verbs. This result holds both in combination with an unambiguous visual object context as in combination with an ambiguous one (Fig. 3).

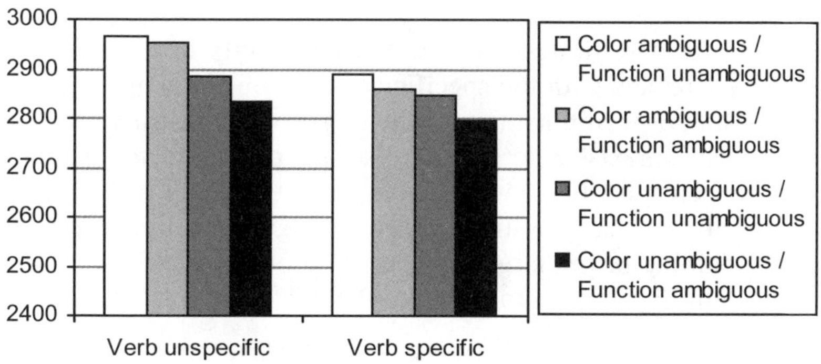

Figure 3. Experiment 1 – Average reaction times (ms) for the choice of the target object for instructions with unspecific and specific verbs in dependence on the visual object context.

Concerning the specificity of object naming of the target object we obtained a contrary result. Here instructions with a specific naming of the target object were processed more slowly than instructions with an unspecific naming (Fig. 4).

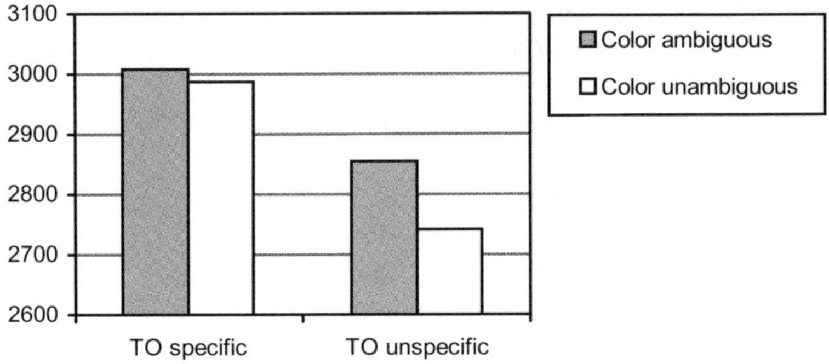

Figure 4. Experiment 1 – Average reaction times (ms) for the choice of the target object: Interaction of specificity of naming of the target object (TO) and (un-)ambiguity of the color of the target object.

With regard to the variation of the contextual factors the following results appeared: Under the condition of referential unambiguous color the instructions were processed more quickly than under the condition with ambiguous color (Fig. 3 and 4). In contrast, instructions related to an object arrangement with a functionally unambiguous target object were processed more slowly than instructions related to an object arrangement with a functionally ambiguous target object (Fig. 3).

Furthermore, the influence of the (un-)ambiguity of the color of the object context interacts with the specificity of the object naming. Especially in the case of an unspecific naming of the target object instructions referring to unambiguous contexts in terms of color are processed more quickly than instructions referring to contexts with ambiguous color. This also means that, especially in the condition with unambiguous color, instructions with unspecific naming of the target objects are processed more quickly than instructions with a specific naming (Fig. 4).

3.2.3. Experiment 1: Discussion

Specific verbs facilitate the interpretation of instructions. But contrary to our expectations, there is no interaction between the specificity of the verbs and the factors of the visual object context. With specific as well as with unspecific verbs the influence of the variation of the object context is the same (see Fig. 3). This means that the linguistic information mediated by verbs is crucial for the interpretation of the instructions. On the other hand, instructions with specific naming of the target objects are processed more slowly than instructions with unspecific naming. This effect may be due to the fact that in the current situation a specific object naming is redundant and a kind of overspecified object naming (Mangold 1987; Weiß and Barattelli 2003). Especially in the case of unambiguous color of the target object a specific naming of the target object has high entropy which leads to a rich mental representation that results in a complex reference resolution and longer processing times (Fig. 4). This may be not necessary because the correct target object could be selected correctly by its color alone. This corresponds to the main effect that instructions referring to objects in contexts with unambiguous color are processed more quickly than instructions in contexts with ambiguous color (Fig. 4).

The effect of the (un-)ambiguity of the function of the object context is a different one. Here a functionally unambiguous context leads to longer processing times than a functionally ambiguous context (Fig. 3). This rather unexpected result may be due to the fact that the information about the function of the objects is not as directly accessible as the information about their color, which is mediated linguistically (by explicit mentioning) and visually and which in general is central for reference resolution (cf. Weiß and Mangold 1997).

In the following experiment our aim was to find out more about the influence of the verb and context information by a systematic variation of the position of the verbs in the instructions.

3.2.4. Experiment 2: Method, factors, and design

As an additional factor, in Experiment 2 we also varied the position of the verbs in the instructions, aside from verb specificity and (un-)ambiguity of the color and function of the target object in relation to the visual object context. The verbs were presented at either front, mid, or final position. The specificity of the verbs and the color and function of the target object were varied at two levels along the lines of Experiment 1. All factors were varied within cases (see Tab. 1 for the experimental design and for examples of the instructions for assembly). There was no variation of the specificity of object naming.

We expected a replication concerning the effects of the specificity of the verbs and the visual object context. With respect to the factor verb position we expected an interaction with the visual object context: Especially in combination with ambiguous object arrangements, instructions with the verb in final position should be processed more slowly because the utterance has to be processed completely and the decision deferred about the correct target object until the processing of the verb. On the other hand, instructions with the verb in front position should be processed more quickly because right from the beginning on – particularly with specific verbs – it is clear what kind of action has to be conducted.

Table 1. Experiment 2: Design and examples of instructions

	Verb specificity	Verb position	Color context ambiguous / unambiguous
Function context ambig. / unambig.	specific	front	*Verschraube mit dem grünen Teil das rote Teil* *Screw in the green part the red part*
		mid	*Mit dem grünen Teil verschraube das rote Teil* *In the green part screw the red part*
		final	*Mit dem grünen Teil das rote Teil verschrauben* *In the green part the red part is to be screwed*
	un-specific	front	*Verbinde mit dem grünen Teil das rote Teil* *Connect with the green part the red part*
		mid	*Mit dem grünen Teil verbinde das rote Teil* *With the green part connect the red part*
		final	*Mit dem grünen Teil das rote Teil verbinden* *With the green part the red part is to be connected*

3.2.5. Experiment 2: Results

In Experiment 2, the results concerning the effects of the specificity of the verbs were replicated: Instructions containing specific verbs were processed faster than instructions with unspecific verbs (Fig. 5). This effect was independent of the position of the verbs (Fig. 6). Also, the effect of the color of the target object was replicated: Instructions referring to situations with unambiguous target object color were processed faster than instructions referring to a situation with ambiguous target object color (Fig. 5 and 7).

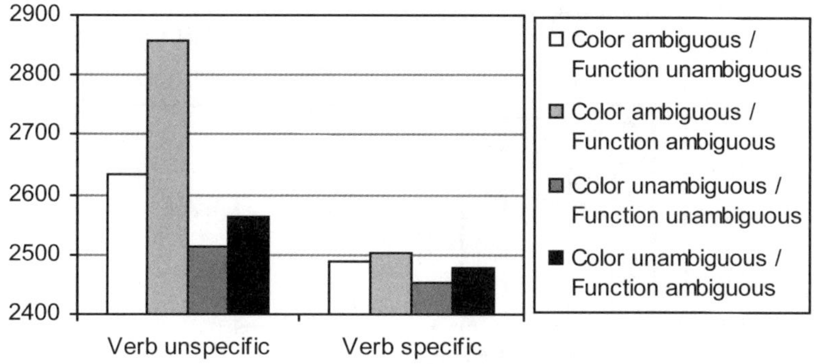

Figure 5. Experiment 2 – Average reaction times (ms) for the choice of the target object for instructions with unspecific and specific verbs in dependence on the visual object context.

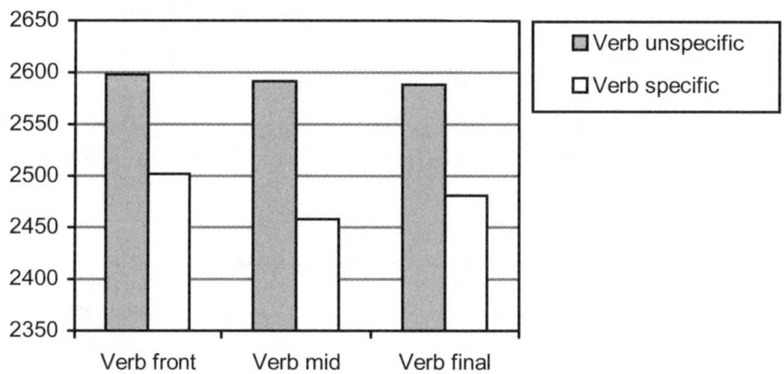

Figure 6. Experiment 2 – Average reaction times (ms) for the choice of the target object for instructions with unspecific and specific verbs in dependence on the verb position.

There was no main effect of the position of the verbs (Fig. 6), but there was an interaction with the ambiguity of the target object color (Fig. 7). As expected, in the case of unambiguous color, instructions with the verb in final position were processed fastest, whereas instructions with the verb in front position were processed slowest; instructions with verbs in the middle took an intermediate time. In the case of ambiguous target object color, the latency for instructions with verbs in front and mid position showed the same course, but contrary to the condition with unambiguous color, there was an increase for instructions with verbs in final position (Fig. 7).

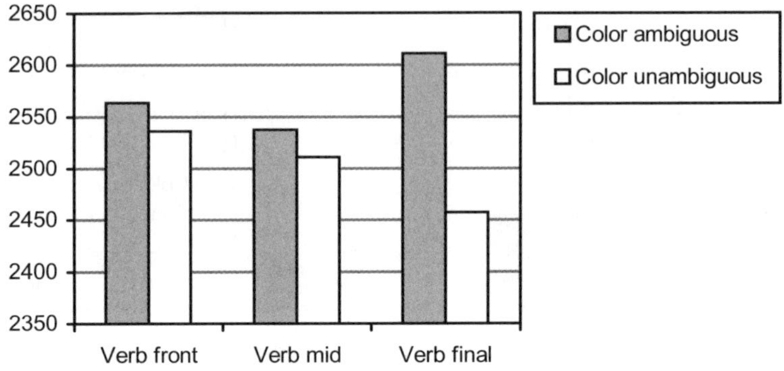

Figure 7. Experiment 2 – Average reaction times (ms) for the choice of the target object: Interaction of color of the target object and verb position.

The effect that the instructions are processed more quickly in combination with a referential ambiguous functional object context could only be replicated for instructions with the verb in final position (Fig. 8). This form of the instructions corresponds to the instructions used in Experiment 1 with respect to the position of the verb. In contrast, instructions with the verb in front or mid position related to a functionally unambiguous context were processed more quickly than instructions related to a functionally ambiguous context (Fig. 8).

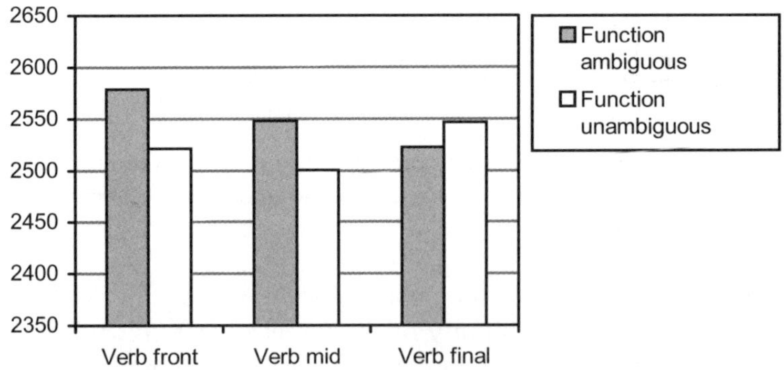

Figure 8. Experiment 2 – Average reaction times (ms) for the choice of the target object: Interaction of function of the target object and verb position.

Though there was no interaction between the factors verb specificity and verb position, we also conducted analyses separated by the verb specificity. It could be shown that the interaction between verb position and color of the target object could be put down especially to instructions with specific verbs, whereas the main effect of the color of the target object appears particularly in combination with unspecific verbs (Fig. 5).

3.2.6. Experiment 2: Discussion

With Experiment 2, we could replicate the results of Experiment 1 concerning the main effects of verb specificity and of the influence of the target object color on the processing of the instructions under consideration. Again, there is no statistically relevant interaction between verb specificity and the context variables. But by inspecting Figure 5, it becomes apparent that there are clear differences in the influence of the contextual factors on the processing of specific and unspecific verbs. In combination with unspecific verbs, particularly instructions that refer to configurations with ambiguous color and function of the target object lead to longer latencies.

This discrepancy to the result of Experiment 1 might be due to the variation of the position of the verbs in the instructions. This variation leads to differences in the temporal availability of the linguistic information conveyed by the verb on the one hand and linguistic information referring to the context on the other. When the verb is in final position, the information referring to the color of the target object is available early in the interpretation process because it is mentioned prior to the linguistic information about the action as conveyed by the verb. Thus, when the color of the target object is unambiguous, it is possible to utilize this information immediately on processing the color adjective and seeing the object arrangement, so as to directly choose the correct target object. In contrast, in cases with ambiguous color, it is necessary to wait until the verb is interpreted in order to know which action is required and to decide on which object should be chosen as target object – in particular because of the fact that the objects were named unspecifically as *part*. This interpretation is further substantiated by the difference in the reaction times concerning the interaction between color and verb position in the presence of specific and unspecific verbs.

The rather unexpected result concerning the influence of the function of the objects of Experiment 1 – instructions referring to functionally ambiguous object arrangements are processed more quickly than instructions referring to functionally unambiguous arrangements – also becomes clearer when looking at the differences resulting from the variation of the verb position. This effect could only be replicated with verbs in final position. In the case of functional unambiguity of the target object in combination with the verb in final position, it is necessary to build up more than one possible functional context of action because there are two or three different types of objects. When the verb appears in final position, the verb has to be processed first in order to determine which action has to be performed and with which of the objects this action is possible. In the case of functional ambiguity, however, only one functional context of action has to be built up. This requires less cognitive effort and leads to shorter processing times.

3.2.7. Discussion of Experiments 1 and 2

The results from these experiments show that the processing of instructions does not only depend on linguistic information but also on visual information about the object arrangements under consideration. Especially the linguistic-semantic information mediated by the verb of action as well as the information provided by the visual context (in particular the color of the objects) contributes in a significant way to the processing of the instructions. Furthermore, the syntactic position of the different information units plays an important role. These findings correspond to approaches which suppose that sentence processing or language processing in general can be regarded as an incremental and integrative process (Crain and Steedman 1985; Spivey-Knowlton et al. 1998; Trueswell and Tanenhaus 1994). We interpret these results as evidence that instructions or more generally speaking utterances are processed in a constituent based incremental way (Hildebrandt et al. 1999; Weiß, Kessler et al. 1999).

The findings of Experiment 1 concerning the specificity of the naming of the target object (unspecific naming is processed more quickly than specific naming) were accounted for at first by the fact that in the experimental setting with only three potential objects the specific name of the target object may be redundant. Thus, it might make the understanding of the instructions and the referential interpretation more difficult than an unspecific naming (cf. Weiß and Barattelli 2003).

In two follow-up studies we examined the influence of the specificity of objects naming in more detail within cases. In one experiment we varied the specificity of the naming of the target object and of the reference object. In another experiment we examined whether the number of objects in the visual context (7 vs. 2) takes an effect on the relevance of the specificity of target object naming. We expected that a specific naming of the target object facilitates the processing of the instructions, especially in the case of more than three potential objects of action.

Generally, the result of Experiment 1 concerning the specificity of object naming could not be replicated. In contrast, the reaction times tend to go in the direction expected originally: Instructions with specific naming of the target object were processed faster than those with unspecific naming. But this result only occurs in interaction with the specificity of the naming of the reference object. This effect may be attributed to the linguistic surface of the instructions: The specific naming of the reference object mentioned first in the instructions might lead to a specific naming default. When this specific naming is followed by an unspecific target naming (as in *Screw in the green cube the red part*), this default has to be revised. Such a revision is not necessary with an unspecific naming of the reference object; here, an unspecific naming and a specific naming of the following target object can be processed alike. The fact that the expected effect of the specificity of the object naming did also not occur in the experiment that varied the number of context objects might be taken to indicate that the object arrangements chosen so far are too simple and straightforward to yield clear results concerning the specificity of the object naming. Additionally, the specificity of the target object might not be very helpful because in these experiments there was no variation of the ambiguity of the function or color of the object context. So again, a specific naming in these contexts is a kind of overspecification.

3.3. Experiment 3: Influence of prepositions and sequence of arguments

In Experiment 3 (Weiß 2001), we examined how the specificity of the preposition influences the processing of instructions. We were especially interested in any effects regarding the direction of the intended action, indicated by the assignment of the roles of target and reference object.

3.3.1. Experiment 3: Method, factors, and design

Participants in Experiment 3 viewed pictures with four objects on a computer monitor (e.g. red bolt, yellow bolt, red cube, yellow cube; for an example see Fig. 14 below). At the same time, an oral instruction was presented acoustically. Participants had to choose one of the objects as the correct target object by pressing a key on the keyboard. The reaction times for their decisions were measured.

Three factors were varied within cases: the specificity of the preposition, the sequence of arguments, and the position of the verb. The specificity of the verbs was not manipulated in this experiment; however, most of the verbs that we used can be classified as specific.

- *Specificity of preposition:* At the level of the verb-argument structure, the variation in the specificity of the preposition refers to whether or not it is possible to unambiguously assign an argument like a prepositional phrase (Britt 1994). For the combination of the verb *to screw* with the preposition *in* and a visual context comprising, for example, a cube with a hole and a bolt, this assignment is specific, since only the prepositional phrase *in the cube* is possible. In contrast, the combination of *to screw* with the preposition *on* in the same context is less specific, because two corresponding prepositional phrases (*on the cube / on the bolt*) are possible (cf. Olsen 1996). – We expected instructions with specific prepositions to take more processing time than instructions with less specific prepositions because in the former case, there is only one possible assignment of the arguments. In the latter case, however, participants have to choose exactly one object as correct target object among several candidates – and such a decision process presumably takes time.
- *Sequence of arguments:* As a second factor, we varied the sequence of the naming of the objects and thus, the sequence of the arguments. In the experiments reported so far, the reference object (RO) was always mentioned first and the target object (TO) second, as in *Screw in the blue part* (RO) *the red part* (TO). In the present experiment, we varied the sequence of the arguments and also presented instructions like *Screw the red part* (TO) *in the blue part* (RO). – Based on observations on the processing of instructions for the establishment of spatial relations between objects (Harris 1975; Huttenlocher and Strauss 1968), we expected that instructions in which the potential target object is mentioned first are processed faster than instructions in which it is mentioned last (cf. the "advantage of first mention"; Gernsbacher 1991).
- *Verb position:* The third experimental factor again was the position of the verb of action in the instructions, with front, mid and final position as the factor levels. We expected a modifying influence on the processing of the instructions. This assumption was based on the results obtained so far and on the fact that the variation of the position of the verb also leads to a variation in the availability of the information about the action to be performed.

The orthogonal combination of these factors yields the experimental design which, together with examples of the instructions, is shown in Table 2.

Table 2. Experiment 3: Design and examples for instructions with the verb *schrauben* (*to screw*), comparing the prepositions *in* (*in*) and *an* (*on*)

Preposition specificity	Verb position	Argument sequence	
specific	front	TO…RO	*Schraube ein rotes Teil in ein blaues Teil* *Screw a red part in a blue part*
		RO…TO	*Schraube in ein blaues Teil ein rotes Teil* *Screw in a blue part a red part*
	mid	TO…RO	*Ein rotes Teil schraube in ein blaues Teil* *A red part screw in a blue part*
		RO…TO	*In ein blaues Teil schraube ein rotes Teil* *In a blue part screw a red part*
	final	TO…RO	*Ein rotes Teil in ein blaues Teil schrauben* *A red part in a blue part is to be screwed*
		RO…TO	*In ein blaues Teil ein rotes Teil schrauben* *In a blue part a red part is to be screwed*
un-specific	front	TO…RO	*Schraube ein rotes Teil an ein blaues Teil* *Screw a red part on a blue part*
		RO…TO	*Schraube an ein blaues Teil ein rotes Teil* *Screw on a blue part a red part*
	mid	TO…RO	*Ein rotes Teil schraube an ein blaues Teil* *A red part screw on a blue part*
		RO…TO	*An ein blaues Teil schraube ein rotes Teil* *On a blue part screw a red part*
	final	TO…RO	*Ein rotes Teil an ein blaues Teil schrauben* *A red part on a blue part is to be screwed*
		RO…TO	*An ein blaues Teil ein rotes Teil schrauben* *On a blue part a red part is to be screwed*

3.3.2. Experiment 3: Results

As expected, the reaction times were significantly longer in the case of a specific preposition than in the case of an unspecific preposition (Fig. 9). The difference in the sequence of the arguments did not take a significant main effect, but the average reaction times were on the whole longer with the sequence TO–RO than with the sequence RO–TO. This means that, contrary to our assumption, the processing of the instructions took longer when the target object was mentioned first than when it was mentioned second (Fig. 10).

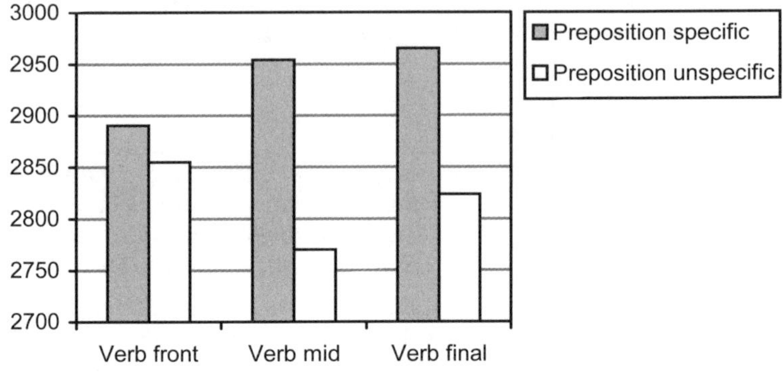

Figure 9. Experiment 3 – Average reaction times (ms) for the choice of the target object: Interaction of verb position and specificity of preposition.

Moreover, the verb position had no significant effect on its own. This factor interacted both with the specificity of the preposition and with the sequence of the arguments. Because of the quality of this interaction, it was possible to also interpret the main effect of the specificity of the preposition in its own right (Fig. 9). The interaction between verb position and sequence of arguments (Fig. 10) required a more differentiated consideration of the conditions, which yielded that only in the condition with the verb in final position there was a statistically significant difference in the reaction times with the sequence TO–RO showing a distinct increase of reaction times compared to the sequence RO–TO.

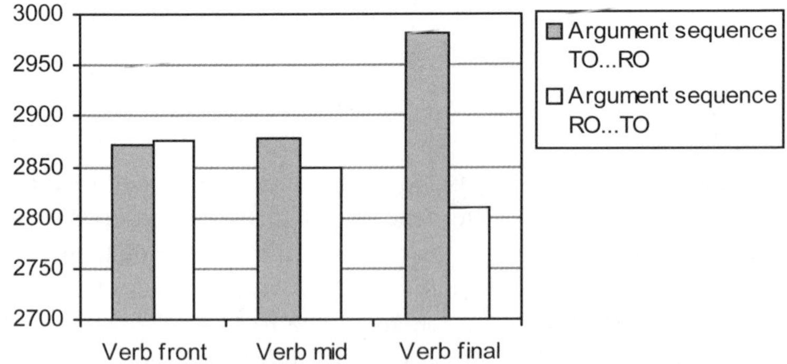

Figure 10. Experiment 3 – Average reaction times (ms) for the choice of the target object: Interaction of verb position and sequence of arguments.

3.3.3. Experiment 3: Discussion

As expected, reaction times for instructions with specific prepositions are longer than for instructions with unspecific prepositions. The processing of the instructions is more costly when participants have to choose exactly one object as the correct target object than in the case with two possible target objects. In a similar way, Chambers et al. (2002) were able to show an influence of prepositions on the processing of instructions with an eye-tracking study. Their instructions varied in the selectivity of the prepositions (specific vs. unspecific). In their setting, the information mediated by the preposition restricted the possible interpretation of the following noun phrase in a prospective way (as measured by the sequence of eye fixations). As in our experiment, the specificity of the preposition leads to a pre-selection of the resolution of the object references.

In our experiment, the sequence of the linguistic components relevant for the processing of the instructions again plays an important role. The effect of the specificity of the preposition appears only in the conditions with the verb in mid or final position (Fig. 9). When the action to be conducted is clearly specified by the verb right from the beginning of the utterance, the information contributed by the subsequent components may already have been established.

With respect to the sequence of the arguments we obtained the unexpected result that reaction times were not faster in the condition TO–RO (in which the target object was mentioned first and the reference object second). But again, the position of the action verb had a modifying influence: Only in the verb final condition, reaction times for TO–RO were significantly longer than for RO–TO (Fig. 10). Evidently, the earlier the verb information (which is relevant for acting) is available, the less influential are the other factors. However, in the condition RO–TO, the reaction time pattern is reversed (Fig. 10). Such a sequence of arguments goes along with an unusual formulation of instructions, and in order to process such instructions it is necessary to jump back and forth between the relevant information units (see Tab. 2).

On the whole, this result corresponds with findings in favor of the idea that it is easier to relate a (new) target object to a reference object already given (Oberauer and Wilhelm 2000; cf. also Hörnig, Oberauer, and Weidenfeld 2002). Furthermore, in the condition RO–TO, the target object is always the object mentioned second. As the experimental task was to choose this target object, it was possible to react immediately after processing this object reference. Thus, this result is in line with the idea of an effect of recency of mentioning (cf. Gernsbacher 1991).

3.4. General discussion of the experimental results

With our experiments we were able to show that linguistic-semantic factors such as the specificity of verbs, objects, and prepositions as well as syntactic factors such as the position of the linguistic components influence the interpretation of the kind of instructions under consideration here. Furthermore, the information conveyed by the visual object context also contributes significantly to the understanding of the instructions. And in some cases even information only on the context leads to a correct choice of the object of action and hence, to an adequate reference resolution.

Comparable results have been obtained for example by Spivey-Knowlton et al. (1998). Their examination of the processing of oral instructions showed an immediate influence of the visual context of objects as well as an important influence of the context of action and the experimental task the participants had to complete. As in our experiments, the authors used the conduction of an action as an indicator for the interpretation of the instructions. Such a procedure differs highly from the traditional ways of examining sentence processing. Here often only the linguistic reception of sentences is analyzed without or with only reduced (linguistic) contexts (e.g. Ferreira and Clifton 1986). Particularly for the processing of more complex instructions, but also for the processing of (syntactically) incomplete or underspecified and elliptical instructions – which typically occur in task-oriented communication –, we expect contextual information to become even more relevant, possibly vital for an adequate interpretation of an utterance.

4. Processing instructions in virtual reality

Having presented insights into the human side of instruction processing, we now want to switch sides and take on the machine's perspective. We present work on understanding instructions in a virtual reality construction task scenario, concentrating on the relevance of verb and object specificity and the temporal availability of information in natural language instructions. This is done under the perspective of reference resolution, i.e. the process of identifying the objects the instructions refer to. We will contrast some of the empirical results on humans with the prospects resulting from a computational approach and discuss how these results can be used to improve the naturalness of the speech understanding system.

In the following, we will concentrate on the description of the framework used for speech and gesture understanding. In doing so, we will emphasize the reference resolution process in which the effects of verb and object specificity are simulated. Then we will draw a comparison between the empirical findings and the technical approach.

4.1. Speech and gesture understanding

The central module of our system for the understanding of multimodal instructions and direct manipulative actions in virtual reality is a tATN (Latoschik 2003). This is basically an ATN (Woods 1970) specialized for synchronizing multimodal input. As an ATN, it operates on a set of states and defines conditions for state transitions. The actual state represents the context of the utterance processed so far. Possible conditions classify words, gesture content, or test the context of the application. If a condition matches, the associated state becomes the actual state. The most prominent part of the context is the set of visual objects which is represented in the world model. Whenever information about visual objects is processed, the tATN queries a module called "reference resolution engine" (RRE) in order to verify the validity of the complex object descriptions specified so far and find the matching objects in the world model (Pfeiffer and Latoschik 2004). The set of possible interpretations of a complex object description delivered by the RRE is incrementally restricted by adding new constraints in the course of the processing of the utterance by the tATN. If the parsing process finally has been successful, the tATN initiates the execution of the instruction using the prominent entries in the result set.

4.2. Reference resolution

The task of the RRE is to interpret complex demonstrations according to the current world model represented in heterogeneous knowledge bases for symbolic information such as type, color, or function, and for geometrical information. This is done using a fuzzy-logic based constraint satisfaction approach. The tATN communicates with the RRE using a query language interface. After computing the query, the RRE returns a set of possible solutions, assigning entities in the world model to the specified variables, classified according to their relevance.

To parse the instruction *Nimm die rote Schraube!* (*Take the red bolt!*), the tATN would finally end up with a query as shown in Figure 11. It searches for a single entity matching the noun phrase *die rote Schraube* (*the red bolt*).

A query consists of variable definitions, e.g., `(inst ?x OBJECT)`, and a set of constraints (**has-color**, **is-a**, **has-type**). The maintenance of temporal relations by the tATN is necessarily continued in the RRE. This is reflected by an additional parameter in the constraints associating each with a certain time during which the constraint is expected to hold. This may be not so important for the constraints over color or type used in the example, as they refer to static properties, but it will be for those constraints that refer to topological relations and arrangements of objects.

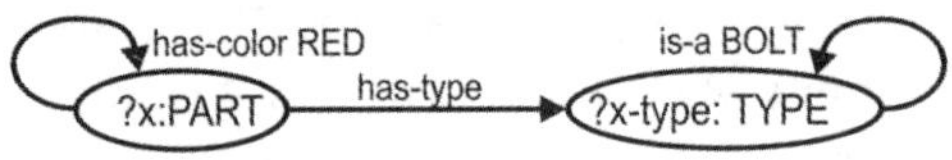


```
(inst ?x OBJECT)
   (has-color ?x RED time-1)
(inst ?x-type TYPE)
   (is-a ?x-type BOLT)
(has-type ?x ?x-type time-2)
```

Figure 11. The figure shows the constraint representation generated when processing the instruction *Take the red bolt!* The upper part depicts the constraint graph view on the textual constraints shown below.

Time is an important factor, as in the dynamic scenes of an immersive virtual environment most of the constraints can only be computed on demand. Especially, geometric constraints conveyed verbally, e.g. *Nimm die Schraube rechts vom Block!* (*Take the bolt to the right of the block!*), are computationally demanding. Even single constraints are highly ambiguous, and the fuzziness keeps adding up when several constraints are spanning over a set of variables. The RRE uses various techniques to overcome this problem: query refinement, hierarchical ordering, and incremental processing.

- *Query refinement:* The tATN only formulates queries made explicit in the utterance. In order to improve performance, the RRE refines these queries by adding constraints that define expectations or assumptions. The search space of potential reference objects, for example, is restricted to those of the toy kit by assuming `(inst ?x OBJECT)` for variables introduced by speech. In addition, the set of relevant objects is restricted to those that are located between the two interlocutors. Other constraints help in differentiating alternative solutions in the case of underspecification. So, for example, objects close to a participant (within reach of the hands) are preferred, or when connecting two objects, the pairing with minimal distance is preferred.

– *Hierarchical ordering of constraints:* Some constraints (like those that concern symbolic knowledge) are comparatively fast to compute; however, some others (like constraints on the arrangement of context objects), are computationally expensive. Some constraints are highly selective, singling out a small group of objects; some are fuzzy or too general for the context, as in the case of overspecification. In order to speed up computation, the RRE arranges the constraints in a hierarchical order, preferring faster, more selective constraints over more expensive, general ones.
– *Parameterization of the search process:* Occasionally, entities of an utterance, e.g. elements of a verbal expression, directly guide the further course of the search process. A frequently cited example is the handling of definite or indefinite articles. Experiments have shown that noun phrases with an indefinite article are processed faster than those with a definite article (Eikmeyer, Schade and Kupietz 1995). The behavior of the RRE can be changed accordingly. In the case of a definite article, the RRE can make an exhaustive search to ensure that the very best matching object is returned. When handling an indefinite article, the RRE can be requested to search for the first match rated over a specified threshold. In the worst case, this can take as long as in the case of a definite article, but on average it will be faster. – The example of the parameterization of the search process already shows that these features of the RRE do not only improve performance in terms of speed or resources; they can also be used to improve performance in terms of cognitive adequacy. Although the structures and processes used by the RRE are different from those of humans, constraints in time and capacity apply to both systems, human and machine, and the principles of coping with them might be similar.

5. Comparing instruction processing in humans and machines

Both systems, the human and the machine, have to deal with the same problem – the processing of assembly instructions in a specific context –; however, the technical premises on which the systems build are entirely different. Yet, in the end, by and large the same actions are taken on the side of human and artificial constructors. Ideally those are the actions, the instructor had had in mind – and this is, of course, the purpose the machine had been designed for in the first place. As both constructors are getting the same input and produce comparable actions, we are asking:

- How can we compare both approaches to instruction processing?
- How can results of such a comparison be interpreted?

Our idea is that we will get a deeper understanding of human instruction processing by looking at the problem from a different, a machine perspective.

5.1. Performance measurement

Before conducting an experiment and compare the two systems, we have to find an appropriate performance measure. Fortunately, for data on the human behavior we can resort to the results of the psycholinguistic experiments presented earlier in this chapter. The latencies recorded in these experiments provide a valid measure of the efforts required in the processing of instructions under varying conditions of linguistic structure and visual contexts.

Testing the performance of the machine by measuring plain processing times would be simple. However, the machine is much faster than the human, operating in the range of only a few milliseconds. This, together with the fact that the performance of the machine depends highly on the implementation and the hardware, renders this approach invalid for us.

Instead, as the reference resolution engine is based on a constraint-satisfaction technique, our measurement of its performance will use the number of constraint evaluations necessary when interpreting an instruction within a given context. This is a reliable and valid measure in that it is independent of the quality and efficiency of both the implementation and the hardware. However, it still depends on the way the knowledge of the world is modeled within the system.

In the following we will pick out representative examples of the items used in the experiments, look inside the reference resolution engine, and provide a detailed view of the constraint evaluations. For this, we will, on the one hand, make transparent the constraints created during the syntactic and semantic parsing of the instruction done by the tATN. On the other hand, we will show the progress of the RRE by stating the remaining variable assignments valid for a given context after the new constraints have been evaluated. In each step of the understanding process, the number of constraint evaluations depends on the number of variable assignments remaining after the preceding step and the number of constraints added in the current step. For our purposes each processing step can be marked by a single word or expression being actively processed.

5.2. Context effects

We start by investigating the effects of context on the performance of understanding simple noun phrases. This is a good starting point for introducing our notation.

5.2.1. The color

Experiment 1 shows, that instructions referring to color within an object context, in which the intended (target) object is in this regard identifiable unambiguously, are processed faster than in an ambiguous context. This holds at least for instructions with the verb in final position. As an example, the noun phrase *die gelbe Schraube* (*the yellow bolt*) is considered in an unambiguous and an ambiguous context (Fig. 12).

1. *die* (*the*): On encountering the article, the tATN requests the RRE to instantiate a new variable `?x` with the basic type `OBJECT` (see first cell in the "Query" column). The RRE creates the new variable and already tries to find possible assignments according to the current context. The results of this process are shown in the "Assignments" column. In this notation each assignment is represented by a tuple with a number of values corresponding to the number of variables – in our case this is a single value. In both contexts, there are initially four possible assignments for the new variable `?x` (the gender information in the German article is ignored).

2. *gelbe* (*yellow*): Verbal reference to a color is captured by the constraint **`has-color`**. The RRE evaluates this constraint for each assignment, resulting in a total of four constraint evaluations for each context. In the case of an unambiguous color context, the constraint only holds for one assignment. In the case of an ambiguous color context, three assignments pass the evaluation. Thus, verbal reference to the color was more restrictive in the unambiguous context than in the ambiguous one, as had been expected.

3. *Schraube* (*bolt*): As the type or the function of an object is of a different quality than its appearance, it is represented with an additional variable `?x-type`. This also reflects the heterogeneous design of our system, as different knowledge bases are involved for representing the visual information or the information regarding functions or types. The newly cre-

ated variable is then interlocked with the existing variable `?x` by the binary constraint **`has-type`**. Now the selectivity of the reference to color shows its consequences for the number of constraint evaluations. As for the unambiguous case the possible assignments have already been narrowed down to a single tuple, the **`has-type`** constraint has only to be evaluated once. In the ambiguous context, the constraint evaluation count is three.

Interpretation of NPs in contexts with unambiguous or ambiguous colors			
Context:	**left:** green-ball blue-knob yellow-bolt bottom: red-cube **right:** yellow-cube yellow-brick yellow-bolt bottom: red-cube		
Noun Phrase:	*die gelbe Schraube* (*the yellow bolt*)		
Surface	Query	Assignments (?x), later (?x, ?x-type)	
die (*the*)	`(`**`inst`**` ?x OBJECT)`	(green-ball) (blue-knob) (yellow-bolt) (red-cube)	(yellow-cube) (yellow-brick) (yellow-bolt) (red-cube)
gelbe (*yellow*)	`(`**`has-color`** `?x YELLOW)`	(yellow-bolt)	(yellow-cube) (yellow-brick) (yellow-bolt)

Schraube
(*bolt*)
	`(`**`inst`**` ?x-type TYPE)`
	`(`**`is-a`**` ?x-type BOLT)`
	`(`**`has-type`**
	`?x ?x-type)`
		(yellow-bolt, BOLT)	(yellow-bolt, BOLT)

Figure 12. The upper part of the figure shows the context and the noun phrase. The lower part shows results of the speech understanding process: The "Surface" column shows the fragment of speech currently being processed, the "Query" column shows the built query, and the "Assignments" column shows the possible assignments (each in parentheses) as returned by the RRE. In the case of the context with an ambiguous color, more constraint evaluations have to be processed with the last query.

Comparing the results of the constraint evaluation, we may sum up that in the ambiguous context at least two more constraint evaluations have to be computed. This reflects the fact that referencing color is more discriminative in contexts with an unambiguous constellation of colors. In this respect, the processing in the RRE conforms to the observations of the experiment.

5.2.2. The functional context

The second contextual factor varied in the experiments was function. The results of Experiment 2 show that the influence of this factor depends on the position of the verb. When the verb is in front position, processing an instruction in a functionally ambiguous context takes longer than in an unambiguous context. In contrast, with the verb in final position, the difference between the reaction times is only very small but with a slight indication which makes it seem to be the other way round, namely processing the instruction in a functional ambiguous context being slightly faster than in the unambiguous context, which has also been shown in Experiment 1.

In Figure 13, two sentences, with the verb in front position and in final position respectively, are considered within two contexts. The figure shows that the contextual factor "function" causes a large difference when the verb is in front position, thus replicating the experimental findings by positing less constraint evaluations in the functionally unambiguous context than in the ambiguous one. In contrast, an investigation of instructions with the verb in final position yields no difference, at least with the reduced representation we use for purposes of demonstration (Fig. 13).

However, the constraint (**connectable** ?target ?reference) is internally translated to:

- (**inst** ?target-type TYPE)
- (**has-type** ?target ?target-type)
- (**inst** ?reference-type TYPE)
- (**has-type** ?reference ?reference-type)
- (**connectable** ?target-type ?reference-type).

This is done because the information of connectivity is part of the conceptual knowledge about types and functions. When instantiating the variables ?target-type and ?reference-type in the context with unambiguous functions, four different values (BALL, KNOB, BOLT, and CUBE) are initially assigned, in the ambiguous context there are only two (BOLT and

Interpretation in unambiguous vs. ambiguous functional contexts			
Context:	**left:** green-ball blue-knob yellow-bolt bottom: red-cube **right:** green-bolt blue-bolt yellow-bolt bottom: red-cube		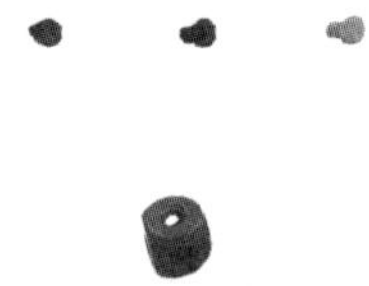
Sentence:	*Mit dem roten Teil das gelbe Teil verbinden!* (*With the red part the yellow part is to be connected!*)		
Surface	Query	Assignments (?target, ?reference)	
Mit dem roten Teil	`(has-color ?reference RED)`	(green-ball, red-cube) (blue-knob, red-cube) (yellow-bolt, red-cube)	(green-bolt, red-cube) (blue-bolt, red-cube) (yellow-bolt, red-cube)
das gelbe Teil	`(has-color ?target YELLOW`	(yellow-bolt, red-cube)	(yellow-bolt, red-cube)
verbin-den	`(connectable ?target ?reference)`	(yellow-bolt, red-cube)	(yellow-bolt, red-cube)
Sentence:	*Verbinde mit dem roten Teil das gelbe Teil!* (*Connect with the red part the yellow part!*)		
Surface	Query	Assignments (?target, ?reference)	
Verbinde	`(connectable ?target ?reference)`	(red-cube, yellow-bolt) (yellow-bolt, red-cube)	(red-cube, green-bolt) (red-cube, blue-bolt) (red-cube, yellow-bolt) (green-bolt, red-cube) (blue-bolt, red-cube) (yellow-bolt, red-cube)
mit dem roten Teil	`(has-color ?reference RED)`	(yellow-bolt, red-cube)	(green-bolt, red-cube) (blue-bolt, red-cube) (yellow-bolt, red-cube)
das gelbe Teil	`(has-color ?target YELLOW`	(yellow-bolt, red-cube)	(yellow-bolt, red-cube)

Figure 13. Two complete instructions with the verb in front respectively final position are processed. In the latter case, an ambiguous functional context leads to the processing of the most constraint evaluations.

CUBE). As the possible assignments for `?target` and `?reference` are already restricted to a single tuple, the set of assignments for both type variables are restricted to one as soon as the corresponding **`has-type`** constraints are processed. Thus, when finally processing the computationally demanding **`connectable`** constraint, the same number of constraint evaluations has to be processed in both cases. This leaves the small overhead of two evaluations of the **`has-type`** constraint (which evaluates very fast) for the unambiguous context.

5.3. Effects based on differences in the linguistic material

5.3.1. Specificity of object naming

When a variable for an object is defined by `(`**`inst`**` ?x OBJECT)`, the initial set of possible assignments for `?x` is the set of currently visible objects. This restriction reflects the fact that the instructions in our scenario are all about manipulating objects that are currently available. In the case of a specific object naming, as in *die Schraube* (*the bolt*), the variable for the visual object is tied to a newly created variable for the type: `(`**`inst`**` ?x-type TYPE)` `(`**`has-type`**` ?x ?x-type)` `(`**`is-a`**` ?x-type BOLT)`. This is different with an unspecific object naming, as in *das Teil* (*the part*). Here, the noun does not add any further type information, so the variable for the visual object is not linked with a new type variable. Therefore, fewer constraints have to be evaluated when unspecific object names are to be processed – a difference which closely corresponds to the findings from the first experiment.

However, this may only hold for sentences in which the specific variable is fully specified at the time the noun is processed, for example by some preceding reference to its unambiguous color or function. Under such circumstances, adding a specific object naming would lead to an overspecification and impose an additional processing overhead. This is not the case when dealing with underspecifications. Here, the restrictive power of a specific object naming could substantially reduce the number of possible assignments. In that case, we have a tradeoff between the additional constraint evaluations needed to select the visual objects of a given type and the constraint evaluations needed in the subsequent processing steps, which may now operate on a smaller set of remaining possible assignments. Overall, one would expect an advantage for a specific naming, unless there already is an overspecification.

5.3.2. Specificity of prepositions

So far, the observations of the RRE neatly match the data from the experiments. This also holds for the result that instructions making use of a specific preposition, such as *in*, are processed more slowly than those with an unspecific one. However, the dependence of this effect on verb position and the order of the arguments (RO–TO vs. TO–RO) is not replicated, as we will show now.

<table>
<tr><td colspan="5">Specific vs. unspecific prepositions with verb in front position</td></tr>
<tr><td>Context:</td><td colspan="4">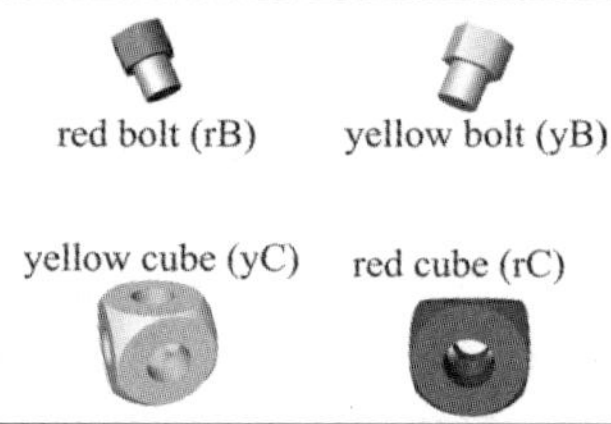
</td></tr>
<tr><td>Sentence:</td><td colspan="4">Füge ein rotes Teil in/an ein gelbes Teil!
(Put a red part in/on a yellow part!)</td></tr>
<tr><td>Surface</td><td colspan="2">Query</td><td colspan="2">Assignments (?target, ?reference)</td></tr>
<tr><td>Füge</td><td colspan="2"><code>(connectable ?target ?reference)</code></td><td colspan="2">(rB, yC) (rB, rC) (yB, yC) (yB, rC) (yC, rB) (yC, yB) (rC, rB) (rC, yB)</td></tr>
<tr><td>ein rotes Teil</td><td colspan="2"><code>(has-color ?target RED)</code></td><td colspan="2">(rB, rC) (rB, yC) (rC, rB) (rC, yB)</td></tr>
<tr><td></td><td>in</td><td>an</td><td>in</td><td>an</td></tr>
<tr><td>in/an</td><td><code>(has-port ?target 'MALE)
(has-port ?reference 'FEMALE)</code></td><td>--</td><td>(rB, rC)
(rB, yC)</td><td>(rB, rC) (rB, yC)
(rC, rB) (rC, yB)</td></tr>
<tr><td>ein gelbes Teil</td><td colspan="2"><code>(has-color ?reference YELLOW)</code></td><td>(rB, rC)</td><td>(rB, yC) (rC, yB)</td></tr>
</table>

Figure 14. The preposition *in* is more specific than *an* (*on*) adding two additional constraints. This leads to a successful reference with a single solution; not so for the preposition *an*, as it adds no further constraints. The result is ambiguous and either a pragmatic arbitrary choice or a clarifying question has to follow.

Before we present proper examples, we have to explain the mapping of the prepositions to the constraints. For an unspecific preposition this is easy as no further constraints need to be added. But in the case of a specific preposition, the following constraints are added: `(`**`has-port`**` ?target 'MALE)` `(has-port ?reference 'FEMALE)`. Ports are used in the knowledge bases to mark areas where objects can be connected (Jung 2003). There are several possible types of ports; in our case we are faced with screws ports. For these ports, two different subtypes exist, 'male' and 'female': A "baufix" bolt typically has one male port and a cube six female ports. The intended direction of the connection is then reflected by specifying the ports needed to accomplish the connection suggested by the preposition.

Figure 14 gives an example for an instruction with the verb in front position and both a specific and an unspecific preposition. After processing the instruction with the specific preposition *in*, the set of possible assignments is narrowed down to a single value. The preposition helps to select the intended order of the objects (bolt into cube). In the unspecific case, the preposition *an* (*on*) does not add any further constraints. The instruction is underspecified and two different assignments remain. In Experiment 3 the subject then had to choose one of the assignments arbitrarily. This underspecification goes along with a smaller number of constraint evaluations. This holds for all the variants of the instructions. Constraint values for different instruction variants are shown in Table 3.

Table 3. Constraint evaluations for specific vs. unspecific prepositions

Condition		Preposition	Constraint Evaluations (CE)				Total
TO–RO	verb front		Verb	NP	Prep	NP	
		- *in*	12	8	4 + 2	2	28
		- *an*	12	8	0	4	24
	verb mid		NP	Verb	Prep	NP	
		- *in*	12	6	4 + 2	2	26
		- *an*	12	6	0	4	22
	verb final		NP	Prep	NP	Verb	
		- *in*	12	6 + 3	2	1	24
		- *an*	12	0	6	4	22
RO–TO	verb front		Verb	Prep	NP	NP	
		- *in*	12	8 + 4	4	2	30
		- *an*	12	0	8	4	24
	verb mid		Prep	NP	Verb	NP	
		- *in*	12 + 6	4	2	2	26
		- *an*	0	12	6	4	22
	verb final		Prep	NP	NP	Verb	
		- *in*	12 + 6	4	2	1	25
		- *an*	0	12	6	4	22

5.3.3. Sequence of arguments

Below, we shall discuss examples that differ from the examples given above with respect to verb position and the sequence of arguments (see Figures 15 and 16).

<table>
<tr><td colspan="5">Specific vs. unspecific prepositions with verb in final position and order TO–RO</td></tr>
<tr><td>Context:</td><td colspan="4">For a picture of the context, see Figure 14</td></tr>
<tr><td>Sentence:</td><td colspan="4">Ein rotes Teil in/an ein gelbes Teil fügen!
(A red part in/on a yellow part is to be put!)</td></tr>
<tr><td>Surface</td><td colspan="2">Query</td><td colspan="2">Assignments (?target, ?reference)</td></tr>
<tr><td>Ein rotes Teil</td><td colspan="2">(has-color
?target RED)</td><td colspan="2">(rB, yB) (rB, yC) (rB, rC) (rC, rB)
(rC, yB) (rC, yC)</td></tr>
<tr><td></td><td>in</td><td>an</td><td>in</td><td>an</td></tr>
<tr><td>in/an</td><td>(has-port
?target 'MALE)
(has-port
?reference 'FEMALE)</td><td>--</td><td>(rB, rC)
(rB, yC)</td><td>(rB, yB) (rB, yC)
(rB, rC) (rC, rB)
(rC, yB) (rC, yC)</td></tr>
<tr><td>ein gelbes Teil</td><td colspan="2">(has-color
?reference YELLOW)</td><td>(rB, yC)</td><td>(rB, yB) (rB, yC)
(rC, yB) (rC, yC)</td></tr>
<tr><td>fügen</td><td colspan="2">(connectable
?target ?reference)</td><td>(rB, yC)</td><td>(rB, yC) (rC, yB)</td></tr>
</table>

Figure 15. In the condition “verb in final position and specific preposition *in*“, the correct assignment for ?target can be established as soon as the preposition is fully processed. In contrast, the instruction with the unspecific preposition is underspecified and two alternative assignments for ?target remain. These two assignments emerge when processing the first NP after 12 constraint evaluations. Thus, although the specific preposition allows a full specification, the assignment for ?target is only established after the preposition is processed.

The specific preposition increases the number of constraint evaluations in all cases, singling out one specific assignment. The unspecific preposition leads to an underspecification with two alternative assignments while evaluating fewer constraints. This replicates the results from Experiment 3 that instructions with unspecif ic prepositions are processed faster than those with specific ones. However, regarding the interaction with the position of the verb, the data from the RRE suggest that the computational effort for processing an instruction decreases the later the verb is positioned. In the experiments this only holds for the RO–TO argument order. Also, differences between specific and unspecific prepositions decrease the later the verb is positioned in the instruction. This runs contrary to the experimental results in which the instructions with the verb in mid or final position show a significant difference, whereas with a front position both variants yield quite similar reaction times.

Specific vs. unspecific prepositions with verb in final position and order RO–RO				
Context:	For a picture of the context, see Figure 14			
Sentence:	*In/an ein gelbes Teil ein rotes Teil fügen!* (*In/on a yellow part a red part is to be put!*)			
Surface	Query		Assignments (?target, ?reference)	
	in	*an*	*in*	*an*
In/an	`(has-port ?target 'MALE)` `(has-port ?reference 'FEMALE)`	--	(rB, rC) (rB, yC) (yB, rC) (yB, yC)	(rB, yB) (rB, yC) (rB, rC) (rC, rB) (rC, yB) (rC, yC) (yB, rB) (yB, yC) (yB, rC) (yC, rB) (yC, yB) (yC, rC)
ein gelbes Teil	`(has-color ?reference YELLOW)`		(rB, yC) (yB, yC)	(rB, yB) (rB, yC) (rC, yB) (rC, yC) (yB, yC) (yC, yB)
ein rotes Teil	`(has-color ?target RED)`		(rB, yC)	(rB, yB) (rB, yC) (rC, yB) (rC, yC)
fügen	`(connectable ?target ?reference)`		(rB, yC)	(rB, yC) (rC, yB)

Figure 16. The constraint evaluations for instructions with the alternative order of arguments differ only slightly from those shown in Figure 15.

The tendency for the argument order RO–TO to lead to faster reaction times than the order TO–RO is also not replicated by the study of the RRE (see Fig. 15 and 16, also Tab. 3). While both variants do not differ in the number of constraint evaluations when processing instructions with unspecific prepositions, the average number of constraint evaluations for instructions with specific prepositions is slightly higher for RO–TO.

5.4. Discussion

We compared the processing of instructions in humans with a computer science approach based on fuzzy constraint satisfaction. For this, we used the number of constraint evaluations as a measurement comparable to the reaction times collected in the psycholinguistic experiments described above. The applicability of this approach was then demonstrated on representative examples taken from the experiments.

We started our investigations with a focus on the effects of the contextual influences of color and function. Then we shifted our attention to local semantic differences, investigating the effects of specificity in naming. Finally, we had a look at the effects of the syntactic order of both arguments and verbs. In the chapter in hand, we intentionally skipped a comparison regarding the effect of verb specificity, because the presentation of the necessary knowledge structures involved would have gone beyond the scope of this chapter.

We consequently drew a line from factors regarding external visual context to factors of a structural linguistic kind. In our setting, the structure of the visual context defines the complexity of the reference problem. While it is true that the structure of the linguistic material reflects this complexity, it is mainly influenced by the interlocutors' knowledge of language use, conceptual world knowledge, and internal processes operating on that knowledge.

As both systems are able to solve the reference problem, their performance shows comparable effects with respect to changes in the complexity of the problem domain, i.e. the visual context. In contrast, the results concerning the effects of changes in the linguistic material show that the interpretation of instructions by the machine does not scale up well enough to match the human's performance. Though its capabilities already meet the pragmatic requirements of a human-computer interface, the performance is not cognitively adequate.

We are quite aware of the fact that these results might be artifacts of the measurement of the performance of the machine's processing capabilities by counting constraint evaluations. This is a linear measurement which is implicitly based on the assumption that the constraints are evaluated in a sequential fashion. The reaction time of a system always is an abstraction from the way of processing, be it sequential or parallel. Counting single evaluations also assumes that the time needed to evaluate a constraint is a constant. It has already been shown for the `connectable` constraint that its complexity matters. Some constraints pertain to easily accessible properties, such as color, which can be thought of as computing in linear time. Other constraints depend on the power of the set of contextual objects. Examples (not addressed in the present study) are constraints over relative attributes, such as size or position. The categorization of properties, e.g., when processing a specific naming of type or function, may also depend on the complexity and the structuring of the world knowledge. A more precise measurement would incorporate all these factors.

6. Conclusion

This chapter presented a closer look at instruction processing in the context of a construction task domain. Instructions can be assigned to the concept of requests in speech act theory. They can also be categorized psycholinguistically according to the system AUFF. Linguistic aspects relevant for processing the special kind of instructions in our scenario are the specificity of verbs, object naming, and prepositions and the sequence of components in the linguistic surface structure. The results of our experiments also show that the interpretation of instructions is not exclusively determined by linguistic information but also by non-verbal information pertaining to the visual context. These findings are in line with recent approaches to sentence processing, which assume that linguistic and non-linguistic information is processed in an interactive and incremental way (Ferstl and Flores d'Arcais 1999). In order to resolve object references and to get to know which action has to be conducted, any adequate information available in the actual communicative situation is pulled up immediately.

In the section on a multimodal human-computer interface for a virtual constructor, we took a computer scientist's perspective and gave an example of a speech understanding system for virtual reality environments. As the syntactic structure of the instructions under consideration is relatively simple, we concentrated on the semantic-pragmatic processing. This is realized in the reference resolution engine, which is responsible for the identification of the objects of action. The solution presented combines constraint-satisfaction algorithms with fuzzy logic in order to approach the problem of vagueness in natural speech.

Comparing the performances of both systems, human and machine, we have found that the performance depends partly on the structure of the problem domain and partly on the structure of the conceptual knowledge and the processes working thereon. While our measurement grasps the content and the order in which information is available to the processing system, it cannot disambiguate effects of parallel processing or capture the complexity of the processes needed to de-reference each chunk of information. It also neglects side effects and interactions of sub-processes, which could explain, for instance, the effects observed in the interaction of a specific naming of the reference object and the target object.

In both the psycholinguistic experiments and the computer simulation it becomes obvious that the information gathered using reaction time measurement does not yield enough information to get a deeper insight into the timing and interaction of the sub-processes relevant for the comprehension of instructions. In order to model these effects in the computer simulation, more data on human performance are necessary. Further experiments, making use of eye movement tracking or electroencephalography, could provide the necessary empirical basis for an improvement of the human-computer interface and help in making it more cognitively adequate.

The work presented here concentrated on the processing of basic single sentences by the constructor. Work is on the way to extend the studies to the investigation of more complex instructions such as *Nimm die rote Schraube und stecke sie von oben in den grünen Würfel* (*Take the red bolt and put it from above in the green cube*), or instruction sequences such as *Stecke die rote Schraube in den grünen Würfel und die gelbe in den roten* (*Put the red bolt in the green cube and the yellow [one] in the red [one]*) (Weiß, Pfeiffer, and Allmaier 2004).

References

Altmann, G. T. M., and Y. Kamide
1999 Incremental interpretation at verbs: Restricting the domain of subsequent reference. *Cognition* 73: 247–264.

Austin, J. L.
1962 *How to do Things with Words*. Oxford: Clarendon Press.

Blum-Kulka, S.
1987 Indirectness and politeness in requests: Same or different? *Journal of Pragmatics* 11: 145–160.

Blum-Kulka, S., J. House, and G. Kasper (eds.)
1989 *Cross-Cultural Pragmatics: Requests and Apologies*. Norwood: Ablex.

Brandt-Pook, H.
1999 *Eine Sprachverstehenskomponente in einem Konstruktionsszenario*. Dissertation. Bielefeld: Universität Bielefeld.

Britt, M. A.
1994 The interaction of referential ambiguity and argument structure in the parsing of prepositional phrases. *Journal of Memory and Language* 33: 251–283.

Brown, P., and S. C. Levinson
2004 *Politeness: Some Universals in Language Usage*. Cambridge, UK: Cambridge University Press.

Carroll, M., and C. Timm
2003 Erzählen, Berichten, Instruieren. In *Sprachproduktion*, T. Herrmann and J. Grabowski (eds.), 687–712. Göttingen: Hogrefe.

Chambers, C. G., M. K. Tanenhaus, K. M. Eberhard, H. Filip, and G. N. Carlson
2002 Circumscribing referential domains during real-time language comprehension. *Journal of Memory and Language* 47: 30–49.

Clark, H. H., and S. E. Haviland
1977 Comprehension and the given-new contract, In *Discourse Production and Comprehension,* R. O. Freedle (ed.), 1–40. Norwood: Ablex.

Crain, S., and M. Steedman
1985 On not being led up the garden path: The use of context by the psychological syntax processor. In *Natural Language Parsing,* D. R. Dowty, L. Karttunen, and A. M. Zwicky (eds.), 320–358. Cambridge, UK: Cambridge University Press.

Eikmeyer, H.-J., U. Schade, and M. Kupietz
1995 Ein konnektionistisches Modell für die Produktion von Objektbenennungen. *Kognitionswissenschaft* 4: 108–117.

Engelkamp, J., and G. Mohr
1986 Legitimation und Bereitschaft bei der Rezeption von Aufforderungen. *Sprache & Kognition* 2: 127–139.

Fellbaum, C.
1998 A semantic network of English verbs. In *WordNet: An Electronic Lexical Database,* C. Fellbaum (ed.), 69–104. Cambridge, MA: MIT Press.

Ferreira, F., and C. Clifton
1986 The independence of syntactic processing. *Journal of Memory and Language* 25: 348–368.

Ferstl, E., and G. Flores d'Arcais
1999 Das Lesen von Wörtern und Sätzen. In *Sprachrezeption*, A. D. Friederici (ed.), 203–242. Göttingen: Hogrefe.

Gernsbacher, M. A.
1991 Cognitive processes and mechanisms in language comprehension: The structure building framework. In *The Psychology of Learning and Motivation 27*, G. H. Bower (ed.), 217–263. San Diego: Academic Press.

Goffman, E.
1989 *Interaction Ritual – Essays on Face-to-Face-Behavior*. New York: Pantheon Books.

Grabowski-Gellert, J., and P. Winterhoff-Spurk
1988 Your smile is my command: Interaction between verbal and nonverbal components of requesting specific to situational characteristics. *Journal of Language and Social Psychology* 7: 229–242.

Graf, R., and K. Schweizer
2003 Auffordern. In *Psycholinguistik: Ein internationales Handbuch,* G. Rickheit, T. Herrmann, and W. Deutsch (eds.), 432–442. Berlin: de Gruyter.

Harris, L. J.
1975 Spatial direction and grammatical form of instructions affect the solution of spatial problems. *Memory and Cognition* 3: 329–334.

Herrmann, T.
1983 *Speech and Situation. A Psychological Conception of Situated Speaking*. Berlin: Springer.
2003 Auffordern. In *Sprachproduktion*, T. Herrmann and J. Grabowski (eds.), 713–732. Göttingen: Hogrefe.

Herrmann, T., and J. Grabowski
1994 *Sprechen: Psychologie der Sprachproduktion*. Heidelberg: Spektrum.

Hildebrandt, B., H.-J. Eikmeyer, G. Rickheit, and P. Weiß
1999 Inkrementelle Sprachrezeption. In *KogWis99: Proceedings der 4. Fachtagung der Gesellschaft für Kognitionswissenschaft,* I. Wachsmuth and B. Jung (eds.), 19–24. Sankt Augustin: infix.

Hindelang, G.
1978 *Auffordern: Die Untertypen des Aufforderns und ihre sprachlichen Realisierungsformen*. Göppingen: Kümmerle.

Hörnig, R., K. Oberauer, and A. Weidenfeld
2002 Räumliches Schließen als Sprachverstehen. *Kognitionswissenschaft* 9: 185–192.

Hoppe-Graff, S., T. Herrmann, P. Winterhoff-Spurk, and R. Mangold
1985 Speech and situation: A general model for the process of speech production. In *Language and Social Situations,* J. P. Forgas (ed.), 81–95. Heidelberg: Springer.

Huttenlocher, J., and S. Strauss
1968 Comprehension and a statement's relation to the situation it describes. *Journal of Verbal Learning and Verbal Behavior* 7: 300–307.

Jung, B.
2003 Task-level assembly modeling in virtual environments. In *Computational Science and its Applications - ICCSA 2003, Proceedings,* V. Kumar, M. L. Gavrilova, C. J. K. Tan, and P. L'Ecuyer (eds.), 721–730). Springer.

Kopp, S., B. Jung, N. Leßmann, and I. Wachsmuth
2003 Max – A multimodal assistant in virtual reality construction. *KI – Künstliche Intelligenz* 4: 11–17.

Latoschik, M. E.
2003 Designing transition networks for multimodal VR-interactions using a markup language. In *Proceedings of the IEEE Fourth International Conference on Multimodal Interfaces, ICMI 2002,* 411–416. Pittsburgh, USA: IEEE Computer Society.

Mangold, R.
1987 Schweigen kann Gold sein – über förderliche, aber auch nachteilige Effekte der Überspezifizierung. *Sprache und Kognition* 4: 165–176.

Meyer, J. R.
1992 Fluency in the production of requests: Effects of degree of imposition, schematicity and instruction set. *Journal of Language and Social Psychology* 11: 233–251.

Miller, G. A.
1991 *The Science of Words*. New York: Scientific American.
1998 Nouns in WordNet. In *WordNet: An Electronic Lexical Database,* C. Fellbaum (ed.), 23–46. Cambridge, MA: MIT Press.

Miller, G. A., and C. Fellbaum
1991 Semantic networks of English. *Cognition* 41: 197–229.

Oberauer, K., and O. Wilhelm
2000 Effects of directionality in deductive reasoning: I. The comprehension of single relational premises. *Journal of Experimental Psychology: Learning, Memory, and Cognition* 26: 1702–1712.

Olsen, S.
1996 Pleonastische Direktionale. In *Wenn die Semantik arbeitet: Klaus Baumgärtner zum 65. Geburtstag* G. Harras and M. Bierwisch (eds.), 303–329. Tübingen: Niemeyer.

Pfeiffer, T., and M. E. Latoschik
2004 Resolving object references in multimodal dialogues for immersive virtual environments. In *Proceedings of the IEEE Virtual Reality 2004* Y. Ikei, M. Göbel, and J. Chen (eds.), 35–42. Chicago: IEEE Computer Society.

Rolf, E.
1997 *Illokutionäre Kräfte: Grundbegriffe der Illokutionslogik*. Opladen: Westdeutscher Verlag.

Rosch, E.
1978 Principles of categorization. In *Cognition and Categorization,* E. Rosch and B. B. Lloyd (eds.), 27–48. Hillsdale: Erlbaum.

Searle, J. R.
1969 *Speech Acts: An Essay in the Philosophy of Language*. Cambridge, UK: Cambridge University Press.
1976 A classification of illocutionary acts. *Language in Society* 5: 1–23.

Spivey-Knowlton, M. J., M. K. Tanenhaus, K. M. Eberhard, and J. C. Sedivy
1998 Integration of visuospatial and linguistic information: Language comprehension in real time and real space. In *Representation and Processing of Spatial Expressions,* P. Olivier and K.-P. Gapp (eds.), 201–214. Mahwah: Erlbaum.

Tanenhaus, M. K., M. J. Spivey-Knowlton, K. M. Eberhard, and J. C. Sedivy
1995 Integration of visual and linguistic information in spoken language comprehension. *Science* 268: 1632–1634.

Trueswell, J. C., and M. K. Tanenhaus
1994 Toward a lexicalist framework for constraint-based syntactic ambiguity resolution. In *Perspectives on Sentence Processing* C. Clifton, L. Frazier, and K. Rayner (eds.), 155–179. Hillsdale, NJ: Erlbaum.

Weiß, P.
2001 "Schraub' in" oder "schraub' an"? Präpositionen bei der Verarbeitung von Handlungsanweisungen. In *Sprache, Sinn und Situation,* L. Sichelschmidt and H. Strohner (eds.), 75–89. Wiesbaden: Deutscher Universitäts-Verlag.
2005 *Raumrelationen und Objekt-Regionen: Psycholinguistische Überlegungen zur Bildung lokalisationsspezifischer Teilräume.* Wiesbaden: Deutscher Universitäts-Verlag.

Weiß, P., and S. Barattelli
2003 Das Benennen von Objekten. In *Sprachproduktion,* T. Herrmann and J. Grabowski (eds.), 587–621. Göttingen: Hogrefe.

Weiß, P., B. Hildebrandt, H.-J. Eikmeyer, and G. Rickheit
1999 Verb-, Objekt- und Kontextinformation bei der Rezeption von Handlungsanweisungen. In *KogWis99: Proceedings der 4. Fachtagung der Gesellschaft für Kognitionswissenschaft,* I. Wachsmuth & B. Jung (eds.), 238–243. Sankt Augustin: infix.

Weiß, P., B. Hildebrandt, and G. Rickheit
1999 Empirische Untersuchungen zur Rezeption von Handlungsanweisungen: der Einfluß semantischer und kontextueller Faktoren. *Sprache und Kognition,* 18: 39–52.

Weiß, P., K. Kessler, B. Hildebrandt, and H.-J. Eikmeyer
1999 Konzeptualisierung in inkrementell-integrativer Sprachverarbeitung. *Kognitionswissenschaft* 8: 108–114.

Weiß, P., and R. Mangold
1997 Bunt gemeint, doch farblos gesagt: Wann wird die Farbe eines Objektes nicht benannt? *Sprache und Kognition* 16: 31–47.

Weiß, P., T. Pfeiffer, and K. Allmaier
2004 Blickbewegungsmessungen bei der Verarbeitung elliptischer Konstruktionsanweisungen in situierter Kommunikation. In *44. Kongress der Deutschen Gesellschaft für Psychologie,* T. Rammsayer, S. Grabianowski, and S. Troche (eds.), 307. Lengerich: Pabst.

Woods, W.
1970 Transition network grammars for natural language analysis. *Communications of the ACM* 13: 591–606.

Wunderlich, D.
1984 Was sind Aufforderungssätze? In *Pragmatik in der Grammatik: Jahrbuch des Instituts für deutsche Sprache 1983,* G. Stickel (ed.), 92–117). Düsseldorf: Schwann.

Visually grounded language processing in object reference

Constanze Vorwerg, Sven Wachsmuth, and Gudrun Socher

Abstract. In situated communication, vision and language often have to be related to each other, for example, when talking about objects or spatial relations perceived in the communication situation. This chapter reviews previous and current research on the question of how verbal and visual representations are mapped onto each other in human communicators and how such a mapping can be achieved by a robotic system enabling it to interrelate linguistic information provided by a human instructor and the visual front-end of the system. The main focus is on visually perceivable object attributes, such as color, size, shape, and spatial location, as these seem prime candidates for a perceptual foundation of linguistic categories.

Basic conceptual processes involved in specifying an attribute for object reference are attribute selection and attribute categorization. Factors influencing these processes are considered. Different kinds of reference values are discussed and related to context effects. Furthermore, relationships between different attribute dimensions are considered. The object class statistics gained in a web-based experimental study were used to model the probabilistic relations between visual object attributes and linguistic categories in a Bayesian network.

A specific attribute used for object reference is spatial location. The choice of a spatial frame of reference has been shown to be influenced by perceptual saliency, consistency effects and verb semantics. Factors affecting spatial categorization have been identified – including a tilt effect for the apparent sagittal. A region-based 2D spatial model has been developed, which defines acceptance areas on the basis of space partitioning by the reference object. Whereas this model is employed to solve object identification and spatial reasoning, a 3D scene representation has been constructed for interactive assembly, e.g. for grasping purposes.

Based on the object class and spatial models developed, a Bayesian network model has been set up for object reference, which allows to compensate for only partially correct recognition results.

1. Introduction

The constitution of meaning in communication, among other things, involves taking-into-account visual information available for both interlocutors. Common object context and perceptual space form one of the components of the communication situation, which may influence verbal behavior (Herrmann 1983; for a review on situated speech see Rickheit and Vorwerg 2003). In object reference, the context of objects simultaneously present, for instance, influences the way an intended object is named (Herrmann and Deutsch 1976; Olson 1970).

What do words, such as *long*, *thin*, *behind,* or *round*, mean? If we are to describe their meaning, we draw on perceptually based mental representations. If these words are used for object reference in a concrete communication situation with a visual context available to both interlocutors, speaker and addressee have to link language and vision. Speakers often use perceptually based object attributes (such as color, shape, size, location) for object naming (for a review see Mangold 2003; Weiß and Barattelli 2003); listeners make use of this information for object identification (for a review see Vorwerg 2003a).

1.1. Relating vision and language

The research described in this chapter relates to the question of how linguistic and visual representations are mapped onto each other in human communicators and how such a mapping can be achieved by artificial systems communicating with human users. A key issue are categorization principles, as categorization constitutes the bridge or connecting link between vision and language (see Vorwerg and Rickheit 1998; 1999b, specifically for spatial categorization). Categorization involves the assignment of a given perceptual input (e.g. a dimensional degree) to a category which is associated with a linguistic term. Thereby, a large quantity of continuously varying input values (such as differing degrees of 'length') have to be mapped onto a small number of linguistic terms (such as *long* and *short*). Quantitative series of values of a certain kind, such as length or lightness, are referred to as perceptual dimensions. The term 'dimension' had originally been used to denote the three orthogonal characteristics of space [lat. dimensio; cf. metiri 'to measure']. However, it has come to be used as a term for any kind of perceptual continua or other measurable aspects of things or stimuli. Dimensional values (or degrees) can be quantified and assigned to categories. Therefore, attribute dimensions can be regarded as ranges of values, which are divided into few sections corresponding to attributes. These may be specified linguistically. Usually, speakers specify no more than one, two, or three attributes (see Mangold-Allwinn et al. 1995).

So, when referring to visual object attributes a speaker deploys at least two kinds of processes within conceptualization: the selection of an attribute dimension and the categorization of dimension values on the basis of a reference system. Empirically, the research presented here has addressed aspects of choice of an attribute dimension, use of reference systems, and categorization processes. Issues that have been considered include the role of visual context, characteristics of different attribute dimensions, and a comparison between them, as well as the interplay between different processes involved.

1.2. Artificial communicators

The development of systems which are capable of simulating communication between humans and computers is a research area which has been getting growing attention in the past decade. Intuitive and natural human-computer interfaces aware of their visual environment have very much been facilitated by trends in technology, computer science, and artificial intelligence. Merging digital cameras with communication devices like cell phones and PDAs as well as first toy-robots with built-in cameras have become commercially available. Emerging research areas like cognitive vision (Christensen 2003; Wachsmuth et al. 2005) or cognitive robotics (Schultz 2004) put forward the thesis that a system needs to actively explore its environment in order to understand and communicate about it. The visual grounding of meaning is a key ability in such systems.

Despite significant recent progress, still many problems need to be solved in natural human-computer communication in order to pass the robustness barrier of such systems (Oviatt 2002). Systems still suffer from spontaneous speech effects, like varying speed, shortened or abbreviated words, hesitations, or violation of syntactic constraints. Designed speech interfaces are typically very restricted because of the high selectivity of any choice of vocabulary. Furnas et al. (1987: 971) showed that for complex systems "many, many alternative access words are needed for users to get what they want". They conclude that an interface design has to "begin with user's words, and find system interpretations. We need to know, for every word that users will try in a given task environment, the relative frequencies with which they would be satisfied by various objects" (Furnas et al. 1987: 968). In the same way, computer vision systems typically suffer from cluttered scenes, ambiguous object views, occlusions, and a finite set of pre-defined object models. Anything outside this test domain will be treated as noise. This way one important measurement of a system's performance is its robustness with regard to noisy input. Therefore, the key issue for a robust system is to control the transformation of the sensory input data to a qualitative symbolic description. Temporary inconsistencies may be resolved by exploiting the redundancy in the verbal coding of the speaker's intention, the redundancy in the visual coding of referenced objects, and the redundancy in the combined auditory and visual information.

There are not many systems reported in the literature that account for these kinds of strategies in order to increase robustness. Srihari (1994) gives an overview of computational models and applications for integrating linguistic and visual information in the past. Most approaches rely on an integrated knowledge base that relates linguistic and visual concepts on a semantic level by introducing additional symbolic or fuzzyfied links (Ide et al. 1998; Jackendoff 1987; Nagel 1999; Srihari and Burhans 1994). A joint processing of text/speech and image data has been shown to be very valuable in retrieval systems (Duygulu et al. 2002; Lazarescu, Venkatesh, and West 1998; Naphade et al. 1998). Systems using cross-modal inferences in terms of error correcting strategies have been studied by Waibel and Suhm (Suhm, Myers, and Waibel 1996; Waibel et al. 1997) in the area of multi-media systems. First performance advances have been demonstrated for different modality combinations like speech and pen or speech and lip movement (Oviatt 2002).

1.3. Instructing robots by speech in the "baufix" domain

In the following, we will describe a module that interrelates information provided by a robot instructor and the visual front-end of a robotic system. The robot can be instructed by speech and gestures in a most natural way. While the communication between a human instructor and the system is constrained as little as possible, the domain setting is rather restricted. A collection of 23 different elementary "baufix" components lie on a table (Fig. 1). Most of these elementary objects have characteristic colors, e.g. the length of a bolt is coded by the color of its head. Nevertheless, the color does not uniquely define the class of an object. The scene on the table is viewed by a stereo camera head that is used for object recognition and localization. A wireless microphone system is used for speech recording. The robot constructor has two robot arms that act on the construction table. It can grasp objects on it, screw or plug them together, and can put them down again. The actions that are supposed to be performed by the robot are verbally specified by a human. In contrast to the system that has specific domain knowledge about the "baufix" world, the human instructor is assumed to be naive, i.e. he or she has not been trained on the domain.

Therefore, speakers tend to use qualitative, vague descriptions of object properties instead of precise "baufix" terms (see Fig. 1). Typically, the human instructor has a target object in mind to be constructed, for example a toy plane or a toy truck. Such a construction consists of several assembly steps and subgoals. For example, before the toy airplane can be assembled, a propeller, an engine block, a cockpit, a tail unit, and landing gear must be constructed first. The instructor will use this terminology during the construction process, e.g. *take the propeller and screw it onto the engine block.* Such terms typically denote complex objects that consist of several connected elementary objects and were constructed during the assembly process. The system has no pre-defined semantics for words like *propeller* or *engine block* and must treat them as words with unknown semantics.

Gib mir die kleine runde, den kleinen runden Holzring
(*Give me the small round, the small round wooden ring*)

Das ist ein äh flacher, äh eine flache Scheibe mit einem Loch
(*That is a er flat, er a flat disc with a hole*)

Den hellen Ring neben dem blauen Ring
(*The bright ring next to the blue ring*)

Gib mir die kleine lila Schra[ube] Scheibe
(*Give me the small purple bo[lt] disc*)

Dreilochleiste zwischen der Fünflochleiste und der [Siebenlochleiste]
(*Three-holed bar between the five-holed bar and the [seven-holed bar]*)

Ich möchte eine Dreierleiste und zwar liegt die ganz rechts
(*I would like a three-holed bar and it lies on the very right*)

Figure 1. Example scenes and spoken instructions in the "baufix" domain.

2. Naming visual object attributes

2.1. Attribute selection

Objects to be named in communication have a number of characteristics, which can be used for reference. A particular cup might be called *small*, *round*, *blue*, *porcelain*, *with a handle*, *real*, *intact*, etc. What attributes do we select for object reference? Object references are not exhaustive; speakers tend to refer to objects by specifying those attributes which permit to differentiate the intended referent from alternative objects. This idea was put forward by Olson (1970) in the context of his approach to a cognitive theory of semantics arguing that the choice of words in an utterance is not a matter of syntactic or semantic markers that belong to the language system but of the speaker's knowledge of referents. His conclusion that speakers specify those features of an object which allow to discriminate the intended object from a set of alternatives has been confirmed in various experimental studies (Ford and Olson 1975; Herrmann and Deutsch 1976; Herrmann and Laucht 1976). Usually, alternative objects are given by the (e.g. visual) context; therefore they are referred to as context objects. For example, a cup might be called *porcelain* in the context of earthen cups, it might be called *blue* to distinguish it from white and yellow cups.

Object references that comprise neither less nor more than the attributes necessary to distinguish the referent from alternatives are often referred to as 'minimally specified' (Mangold-Allwinn et al. 1995; Pechmann 1989). Underspecification (i.e. use of too few attributes) increases with successive reference to the same object (Grosser and Mangold-Allwinn 1990; Krauss and Glucksberg 1977; Krauss and Weinheimer 1964); overspecification (i.e. use of more attributes than necessary for discrimination) is a function of syntactic role, partial discriminativity and perceptual saliency (Mangold-Allwinn et al. 1995; Mangold and Pobel 1988) combined with lacking predictability (Weiß and Mangold 1997). Sometimes, incremental speech production may contribute to overspecification (Pechmann 1989).

Another aspect of context-discriminative object naming concerns the case of multiple namability. If there are two or more attribute dimensions in which the intended object differs from context objects, which one will be chosen for reference? For example, the cup meant by the speaker might differ from all other cups in color as well as size. Would it be called *blue* or *small*? Research has shown that speakers tend to prefer that attribute dimension in which the intended object differs most perceptibly from its context objects (Herrmann and Deutsch 1976; Herrmann and Laucht 1976). In the so-called "candle experiment", children aged 9 – 12 years named objects (rectangles representing candles) of varying height and breadth. The results confirmed the assumption that the dimension presenting a greater difference between intended object and context object is selected more often for object reference. This factor of attribute selection, called 'object-context distance', has been incorporated into a connectionist model for the production of referential noun phrases by varying the activation value of a corresponding gating node accordingly (Eikmeyer et al. 1996). This activation mechanism within the model also predicts a growing likelihood of an attribute dimension being specified with a growing number of attribute-dimension values present in the context; i.e. according to the model, a small red cup would be more likely to be called *red* in the context of large yellow and blue cups than in the context of large yellow cups.

The effect of a large vs. small number of values in the attribute dimensions relevant for object reference was tested in a naming experiment (Vorwerg 2006). Another question investigated with this experiment was whether this factor depended on what attribute dimensions were involved and, more generally, whether certain attribute dimensions would be preferred for object reference.

Participants were presented with five objects (on a computer screen), one of which was to be named. Each of the five objects presented together belonged to the same object class (parts of a toy construction kit, such as bolts, cubes, or wheel rims). The objects in each group differed concerning two attribute dimensions (e.g. length and brightness), with five different values on one dimension and less (two to four) values on the other dimension (see Figure 3). The following combinations of attribute dimensions were included in the material (see Figure 2):

color × location	length × brightness
color × shape	length × thickness
size × hue shades	color × size
size × brightness	thickness × saturation

Figure 2. Combinations of varying attribute dimensions used in the naming experiment.

In a first step, the referential noun phrases produced by participants were classified according to whether they contained a specification of dimension 1 (the one with more dimension levels) or dimension 2 (the one with less dimension levels) or both (an overspecification) or none of them (using another attribute for reference). An overspecification occurred in 5% of all trials. An attribute different from both dimensions in question was specified in 4.8% of all utterances; in all but one of these cases location was specified instead of one of the two dimensions which had been varied experimentally. Comparing the frequency of utterances specifying dimension 1 (five dimension levels) and those specifying dimension 2 (less than five dimension levels), we find that altogether (pooling all dimension combinations) that dimension is selected more often for object reference n which there are *less* values present in the context (245 vs. 184 utterances; $p < .01$, $\chi^2 = 8.67$).

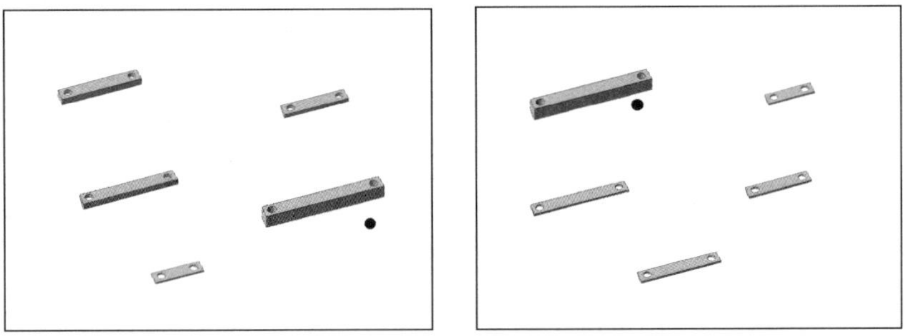

Figure 3. Examples of the material used for the combination "length × thickness" (left: 5 length levels × 2 thickness levels; right: 5 × 4 levels).

In the second step, data were analyzed separately for each combination of dimensions. Results show that for six out of eight combinations one dimension is preferred over the other regardless of the number of dimension levels in context. Dimensions preferred were color, size, and length (see Figure 4). These 'dominant' dimensions seem to be those which are perceptually salient either by preattentive processability (color; cf. Nothdurft 1993; Peeke and Stone 1973; Treisman and Gormican 1988) or by determining global extension in space (size, length).

color × location	**length** × brightness
color × shape	**length** × thickness
size × hue shades	**size** × brightness

Figure 4. 'Dominant' attribute dimensions: Dimensions whose names are printed in bold were predominantly specified for object reference within the combinations indicated.

Examples of distributions are given in Figure 5. Color was specified almost exclusively in combination with shape or with location (a variation in the number of object locations had been achieved by grouping objects). Another example is length, which was specified more often than brightness regardless of whether the number of length levels exceeded the number of brightness levels or vice versa. However, as Figure 5 (right side) shows, the dominance of length compared to brightness is modulated by an effect of number of dimension levels: The frequency of specification is augmented for the dimension in which there are comparatively less different values present.

In each of the other two combinations used (color × size; thickness × saturation of red) neither dimension was generally preferred (see Figure 6). Instead, the 'less-values' dimension was specified more often than the 'more-values' dimension. A precondition for the occurrence of this distribution pattern seems to be that either both varying dimensions are dominant dimensions (color × size) or none of them are (thickness × saturation).

A comparison of proportions of attribute specification over all the different combinations tested shows that the 'less-values' dimension is generally selected more often than the other one – i.e. even in those conditions where one dimension is preferred over the other one (Wilcoxon matched pairs test; $z = -2.52$; $p = .01$).

In sum, this means, if an object can be referred to by specifying either of two attribute dimensions (multiple nameability) and the number of levels present in the context differs between both dimensions, two factors determine which attribute is selected for object reference. First, certain attribute dimensions are preferred for object reference, namely color, size and length. Second, the dimension in which there are less levels present in the context is specified more often. Both factors act in combination in determining attribute specification, i.e. even if one dimension predominates in object references, the frequency of attribute specification tends to be a function of the number of dimension values within the context.

2.2. Attribute categorization

The main conceptual processes involved in specifying attributes for object reference besides attribute selection include those of attribute categorization. A particular level of length may be categorized as *long* or *short* or *medium-long*. A cup may be called *small* or *large*, or *medium* or even *tiny* or *huge*, etc. In order to be able to name a particular attribute currently perceived, the range of values for the attribute dimension concerned has to be partitioned

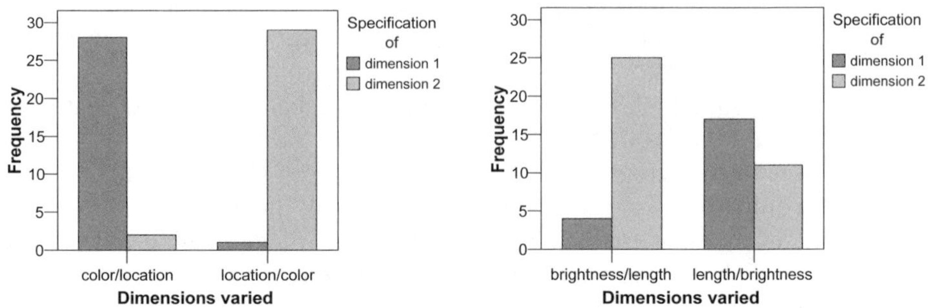

Figure 5. Examples of object-naming results with one predominant dimension. The objects to be named varied in two dimensions with one dimension having five levels (dimension 1) and the other dimension having two to four levels (dimension 2). Left side: Color is preferred to location for object reference regardless of the number of levels present. Right side: Length is specified more often than brightness regardless of whether there are more levels of length than of brightness or more levels of brightness than of length present in the object context. This effect is modulated by number of dimension levels.

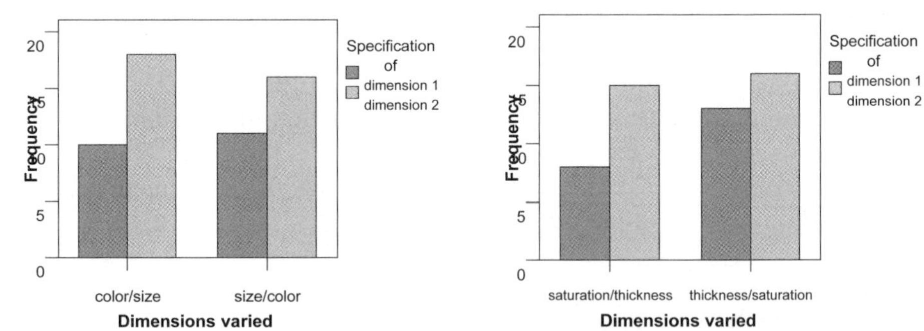

Figure 6. Object-naming results with two balanced dimensions. The preferred dimension for specification is the one in which there are less levels in the context. Left side: Both color and size seem to be dominant dimensions; this would explain why neither of them is generally preferred in this combination. Right side: Neither saturation nor thickness seem to be dominant dimensions; neither of them is generally preferred in this combination.

into a few sections or categories. In order to be able to form category judgments, a frame of reference is required in relation to which perceived values can be judged. The use of perceptual adjectives relates what is being named to an implicit frame of reference.

This frame of reference may be called implicit insofar as it is not apparent for the person judging, who is usually not aware of it and quite immediately has the impression that something is *long* or *small* or *heavy*. Accordingly, we often make "absolute" judgments. For illustration purposes this citation from a children's book ('The Borrowers') is taken: "Then it came alive once more as a *tiny* figure climbed onto the worktop. [...] Potter was *close* behind; than began to fill the wall *near* the borrowers' home with *thick* white foam." There is no explicit comparison included (such as "closer than" or "thicker than"). The understanding and production of utterances containing 'absolute' judgments seem to cause no difficulty at all; such absolute (or categorical) judgments are even an important part of reports, descriptions, and diagnostic criteria. As early as in 1899, Martin and Müller found that despite their instruction to comparatively judge weights relative to a standard weight, participants tended to make absolute judgments, i.e. instead of assessing the weight lifted by them as "heavier" or "lighter" than the standard weight, they had the tendency to denote their impression spontaneously as "heavy" or "light" – even before the standard weight was presented. Similar results concerning temporal-interval, loudness, and length estimates were reported by Titchener (1905).

Findings like these led Wever and Zener (1928) to introduce the "method of absolute judgment" into psychophysics: the requirement of a judgment in absolute terms for singly presented members of a stimulus-series. However, although categorical judgments like *heavy* or *light*, *very large* or *very very small* are absolute in terms of both perceptual appearance and linguistic form, they are relative in that they do depend on a frame of reference – usually given by context. Wever and Zener (1928: 471) already assumed that "the absolute impression is not a constant affair, but is responsive to a change in the magnitude or the range of stimuli used in a given situation". Their statement (Wever and Zener 1928: 471) that "an absolute judgment expresses a relationship between a present stimulus and a whole series of stimuli" has been confirmed by a large number of studies (e.g., Haubensak 1985; Helson 1964; Lockhead 2004; Parducci 1974; Petrov and Anderson 2005; Sarris 1971; Thomas, Lusky, and Morrison 1992; Witte 1961).

Such categorical (seemingly 'absolute') judgments relative to some frame of reference seem to constitute the interface between psychophysics and psycholinguistics, and we propose them to form the primary basis for semantic decisions regarding size adjectives, such as *long*, *short*, *wide*, *narrow*, etc. Two of the authors performed a web-based experimental study including a large sample of native speakers of German (N = 264), in order to investigate how people categorize the "baufix" construction-toy objects (see Figure 1) used in our scenario on several size and shape dimensions (Vorwerg and Socher 2006; see also Vorwerg 2001b). Aside from color (which is unsuited for web-based research, for obvious reasons), size and shape attributes have been shown to be named especially frequently in descriptive communication (Arbeitsmaterialien B1, 1994a), but also in instructive communication with either a real human (Arbeitsmaterialien B1, 1994b) or a simulated computer (Brindöpke et al. 1995). These three spoken-language corpora concerning the objects we are dealing with contain a number of size and shape adjectives of which we chose the general ones (such as *long*, but not *fingertip-long*). The 18 size and shape adjectives included in the study are shown in Table 1.

Table 1. Adjectives used in a web-based categorization study.

Size adjectives		Shape adjectives	
groß	*(big)*	*rund*	*(round*
mittelgroß	*(medium-sized)*	*länglich*	*(elongated/longish)*
klein	*(small)*	*eckig*	*(angular)*
lang	*(long)*	*viereckig*	*(quadrangular)*
mittellang	*(medium-long)*	*rechteckig*	*(rectangular)*
kurz	*(short)*	*rautenförmig*	*(diamond-shaped)*
dick	*(thick)*	*sechseckig*	*(hexagonal)*
dünn	*(thin)*		
schmal	*(narrow)*		
hoch	*(high/tall)*		
flach	*(low/flat)*		

We were interested in finding out how people would categorize all of our 20 construction-toy objects (collapsing the four differently colored cubes into one achromatic) as indicated by assignment of those attributes which, according to their view, characterize the depicted object. The objects (slats of three different lengths, bolts of five different lengths with either a circular or a hexagonal head, a cube, a rhomboid nut, and five different circular objects, namely a rim, a tire, two washers, and a socket) were presented together with all adjectives and an according number of buttons to click on. Participants were asked to select all those attributes which apply to a particular object. The specific aims of this multiple-choice study were to (1) determine what objects contribute to the frame of reference for the linguistic categorization of perceived dimension levels, (2) determine the reference values constituting such a frame of reference for size and shape dimensions, (3) explore the effects of simultaneous context on both size and shape dimensions, and (4) explore relationships between different kinds of attribute dimension.

2.2.1. What type of objects contribute to the frame of reference?

In the case of naming objects currently perceived, the basis for a reference frame is provided by the immediate context of other objects. But what objects go to make up the effective context for the judgment of a particular object attribute?

In psycholinguistic object-naming studies it is often (explicitly or implicitly) assumed that the object context consists of those objects which are simultaneously present. Mangold-Allwinn and colleagues (1995: 64) differentiate between absolute and relative attributes maintaining that absolute attributes can be identified independently from context (cf. also Herrmann and Deutsch 1976; Pechmann 1994) and that relative attributes are usually determined relative to a context; a simultaneous context is implied by their experiments as well their examples (which include even comparative judgments such as *the bigger cube*). Pechmann (1994: 146) argues that with the use of only two size levels size might possibly turn into an absolute attribute dimension due to learning processes. Therefore, the same size level had to be called *small* or *large* in different trials, depending on simultaneous context. Herrmann and Deutsch (1976: 19) explicitly define object context as the complementary set of the object to be named within a set of simultaneously given objects. The experimental set-ups in all these object-naming studies go back to the aforementioned paradigm by Olson (1970), in which an object has to be named within a variable context of alternative objects.

This restriction of context on simultaneously present objects in object-naming studies contrasts with the psychophysical results cited above, which have shown that people are able to make categorical judgments for 'relative attributes' of objects presented one by one within a series, and that they even tend to do so when instructed to judge comparatively. In order to investigate whether participants would be able to assign not only shape but also size adjectives to individually presented objects, we used two different presentation modes: In one condition each object was presented separately with no context, in the other condition objects were presented within the context of other objects. Altogether, eight different contexts were used for the context condition, of which each participant saw three. Each participant was asked to name each object once, either in isolation (no-context condition; n = 132) or in one of the three contexts (context condition; n = 132).

In either condition, an introduction was given together with an overview of typical "baufix" objects. This was done to orient the participants about the possible (or expectable) range of dimension values in this construction-toy set as a basis for a frame of reference. As Wever and Zener (1928: 471) put it, the ability to make a categorical judgment relative to a series of stimuli "presupposes some sort of knowledge of that series". However, no judgments were required on this screen page and no instruction was given.

The results of the study reveal that this basic orientation is sufficient in order to judge size and shape attributes in a categorical way without a simultaneous context. Furthermore, the psychometric functions mostly correspond surprisingly well for the categorization of singly presented objects and the mean categorization of objects presented in context. As an example, the mean length rating for bolts and slats in both experimental conditions is given in Figure 7. The mean rating of length is ascertained by computing the arithmetic mean of all length categories selected for a particular object using number 1 for *short*, number 3 for *long*, and number 2 for *medium-long*. The use of the arithmetic mean is based on the common assumption that category scales in psychophysics are interval scales and subject to linear transformations (e.g., Sarris 2000; Stevens 1975: 135). For the context condition the mean of all context means was computed.

A similarity of the general shape of function between context and no-context condition holds for all attributes and all objects, a close correspondence for most of them (with exceptions for both size and shape attributes; see also Socher 1997). Thus, the comparison between no-context and context conditions shows that (1) people are able to categorize size and shape levels with singly presented objects of an object set – at least after having an impression of the kinds of objects involved – and that (2) the categorization without simultaneous object context is strikingly similar to the mean context-specific categorization.

Another aspect of the question what objects contribute to a frame of reference is object-class specificity. There is widespread agreement that frames of reference are formed by values present in objects of the same kind or class (e.g. Haubensak 1985). We find this principle confirmed in our data (Fig. 7);

however, neither the series of bolts nor (even less so) the series of slats exhaust the full scale of length ratings. This could be explained by partial frames formed by a compromise between regarding bolts and slats as different kinds of objects and using a common frame for both of them (cf. Budde 1980, for partial reference-frames for pitch in musical instruments). Another account could be that cube and rhomb-nut are included in the same series as the slats. Indeed, the inclusion of these five object types (slats of three different lengths, cube, and rhomb-nut) yield a full scale of length rating.

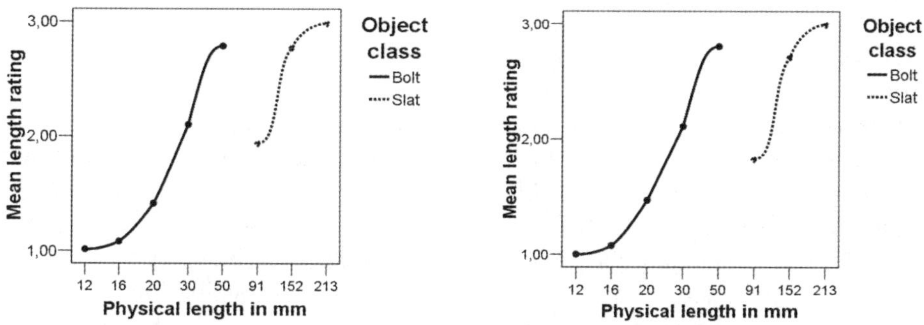

Figure 7. Objects presented for naming in isolation (left) or in context (right). The category "1" stands for *short*, "2" stands for *medium-long*, and "3" stands for *long* (see text).

To sum up, not only simultaneously presented objects but also previously perceived objects of one kind contribute to a frame of reference for attribute categorization. All in all, following a brief object-set presentation, the categorization of singly presented objects is similar to the mean categorization of objects presented in simultaneous context. Size categorizations are class specific, although so far it is an open question as to what people use as partial or supplementary bases for reference frames.

2.2.2. *What reference values constitute the frame of reference?*

The frame of reference for categorizing a size dimension is determined by an empirical distribution of size levels present in a series of objects of a particular class. However, the question is how the relationship between a presented stimulus and the whole series of stimuli is determined, which is expressed by a categorical judgment. Or, to put it differently: What characteristics of an empirical distribution within a set of objects of a given class are used as standards or reference values relative to a given value being judged?

If one regards the assignment of an attribute as a kind of comparison between all objects present in the context, one might assume that the "middle" value, the median of all values of a series, represents the medium (or "neutral") stimulus. That is, if there are bolts of five different lengths and we put them in an ascending order, the middle one then may be expected to be called *medium-long* most often – so there would be two which are longer in length and two which are shorter in length compared to the *medium-long* one.

Another possibility would be that the (arithmetic or geometric) mean of a series is used. For example, a geometric mean has been proposed in adaptation-level theory (Helson 1948), according to which a dimensional judgment (J_i is a function of the ratio of the dimension level judged (X_i) to a "neutral" adaptation level (AL): $J_i = f(X_i/AL)$ with adaptation level AL being proportionate to a weighted geometric mean of all effective stimuli. Another example is the formal-semantic analysis of dimensional adjectives put forward by Bierwisch (1987: 101; 138). It is proposed that the contrastive interpretation of dimensional adjectives is determined by a comparison of a given dimensional value with the norm NC for a contextually defined comparison class, i.e. with a mean value that could be an arithmetic or a geometric mean of all perceived dimension measures.

No matter how a mean value is determined, as long as a given value is judged relative to a mean value, the range of values cannot influence categorization for all those distributions which have the same mean. This does not only seem obviously implausible; it has also been shown that even distributions with the same mean can produce different 'medium responses' for different ranges of values (Parducci et al. 1960). A number of theories propose that the range of values within a series or set of objects plays a decisive role in the categorization of dimension. This means that the effective stimulus extremes have to be taken into account (cf. e.g. Parducci 1965; Witte 1961). Both Witte's equisection theory and Parducci's range-frequency theory assume that the categories used to judge certain levels of a particular dimension (such as length) subdivide the range of values into subranges. Each subrange corresponds to a category. As an example, suppose there were just two categories (long and short), then the midpoint between the two endpoints of the total series would form the 'neutral' value of the subjective scale. According to Witte, this is the point of equal similarity to both 'poles' of the phenomenal scale. A main difference between both theories is that Parducci's range principle refers to the psychological range (which must be inferred from the judgments) whereas Witte's equisection applies to the stimulus scale. Another difference concerns the additional frequency principle postulated by the range-frequency theory, which "asserts that the judge uses each category for a fixed proportion of … judgments" (Parducci 1965: 408). As the two principles (range and frequency) conflict, a compromise between them is maintained by the theory (for an account of frequency effect in terms of consistency, cf. Haubensak 1992).

In order to explore what kind of reference value would be used as a subjective 'medium' in our material, the distribution of *medium-long* categorizations for bolts was considered, in comparison with the *long* and *short* functions (Fig. 8).

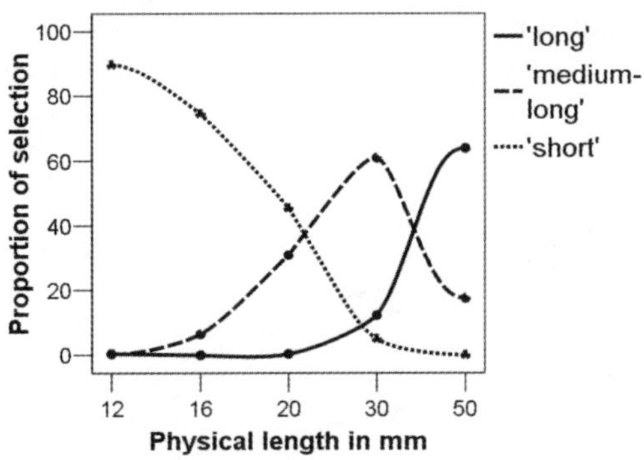

Figure 8. Proportion of selection of length attributes for the bolts of five different lengths, for the no-context condition (singly presented objects). The graph looks very similar for the context condition if pooled over all contexts.

For our distribution of bolt lengths, the central tendencies have the following values: median = 20.0 mm, geometric mean = 22.5 mm, arithmetic mean = 25.6 mm, midpoint = 31.0 mm (combination with frequency would shift this value farther to the left). The empirical data correspond best with the use of the midpoint (the mean of the extremes). If the median ("middle value") or the geometric mean was used, we would expect the 20 mm length to be judged *medium-long* most frequently. If the arithmetic mean was used, *medium-long* should be more equally distributed between 20 and 30 mm length. The clear frequency peak of *medium-long* for the 30 mm length is expected for the use of the midpoint, which in turn can be regarded as evidence for the use of extreme values. We conclude that psychophysical principles of category rating hold for assigning length attributes to a series of objects of a particular class, even if these are judged only once and singly (without simultaneous context). This is also compatible with the idea of an internal continuum of magnitudes for memory-based scaling (Petrov and Anderson 2005).

In contrast to size, the categorization of shape attributes is not based on a comparison with contextually given reference values (characteristics of an empirical distribution). Instead, the reference values are proposed to be given as idealtypic values (Vorwerg 2001a; see also Vorwerg and Rickheit 1999b).

For example, it was hypothesized that the categorization as *rectangular* would depend on an idealtypic ratio between length and width. As all slats in our material extend in a quite elongated way, their length-width ratio can be assumed to be unfavorable compared to the hypothesized ideal. This assumption corresponds with an inverse relation between length and proportion of categorization as *rectangular* in a given context (Fig. 9). This would mean that the shorter the slat, the more similar is its shape to the ideal length-width ratio.

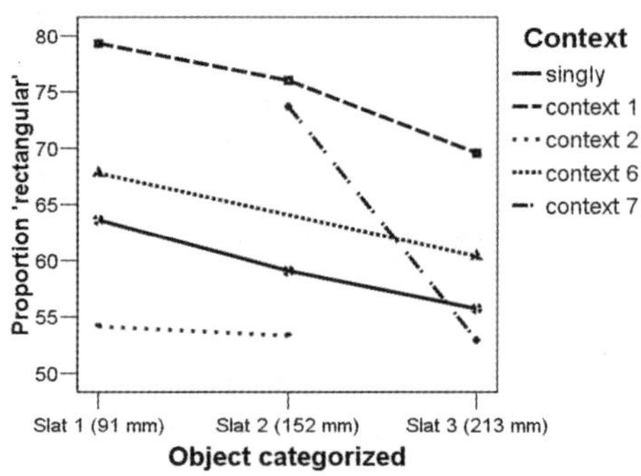

Figure 9. Proportion of categorization as *rectangular* in a different contexts. Contexts vary in what kinds of slats are included.

In a similar way, 'quadrangular' seems to depend on a certain ratio of sides. Therefore, quadrangular can not be regarded as a hyperonym in natural language – contrary to a logical point of view (see Vorwerg 2001b).

2.2.3. *What are the effects of context on size and shape dimensions?*

These results suggest that the categorization of shape is not ,absolute' in the literal sense of the word, but based on a comparison with (idealtypic) reference values. That is, the reference value is not determined by context; nevertheless a dimension level can more or less deviate from an ideal. If this is the case, one might expect context effects for shape attributes, too. Even though the reference values are not given by context, the presence of a ‚better example' of a category within the context might reduce the applicability of a shape adjective. This was found for the frequency of an object being categorized as 'round' for the cube (a cube with rounded-off corners), which is highest without the presence of the salient circular rim (27%), lower with the rim being far from the cube (13%) and zero with the rim being near the cube. These results are interpreted as evidence for the use of idealtypic reference values in the categorization of shape attributes. Therefore, shape adjectives are not 'absolute'; their applicability can vary depending on the similarity to the reference ideal and on the presence of other, more ideal-like objects in the context.

For size attributes, a dependency on context is generally assumed. We find that the effects of a simultaneous context are stronger for objects whose dimension level is within the middle area of the range. By and large, consistency effects (Haubensak 1992) set limits to the effects of simultaneous context as part of whole series of objects. Thus, the frequency of the selection of *kurz* (*short*) and *lang* (*long*) decreases or increases with the length of the slat as expected; this can be observed independent of the context. However, the isolated naming of the shortest slat yields a higher frequency of *mittellang* (*medium-long*) than that of a longer one (having the 'middle' length value of the three slats). In the context of all three slats simultaneously present, this ordering is switched. The mean length rating of the shortest slat is influenced by the number of longer slats and the object-context distance (see Vorwerg 2001b).

2.2.4. *How do different kinds of attribute dimensions relate to each other?*

There are a number of relationships between different kinds of attribute dimension. Some of these seem to inform us about the preferred interpretation of a shape adjective. Thus, there is a significant positive correlation between *länglich* (*elongated/longish*) and *mittellang* (*medium-long*) for both slats and bolts. However, *länglich* (*elongated/longish*) correlates negatively with *lang* (*long*) for slats, but positively with *lang* (*long*) for bolts and negatively with *kurz* (*short*) for bolts. This seems to indicate that *länglich* (*elongated/longish*), contrary to length attributes, is determined by a certain ratio between (physical) length and (physical) width.

The phenomenal width dimension can itself be determined relative to the extension along the main axis in space. If this is the case, a "proportion norm" is used instead of a "class norm" (Leisi 1953). Typically, the dimension of length is assigned to the maximum dimension of an object, the dimension of width to a secondary (usually perpendicular) dimension (see Lang 1987; for other factors determining the assignment of length/width, see Vandeloise 1988). However, a particular level on this secondary dimension could in principle be categorized from *narrow* to *wide* or from *thin* to *thick*. In our data, the categorization of thickness depends entirely on the ratio of secondary and primary dimension for the bolts (Fig. 10), as physically all bolts have the same diameter.

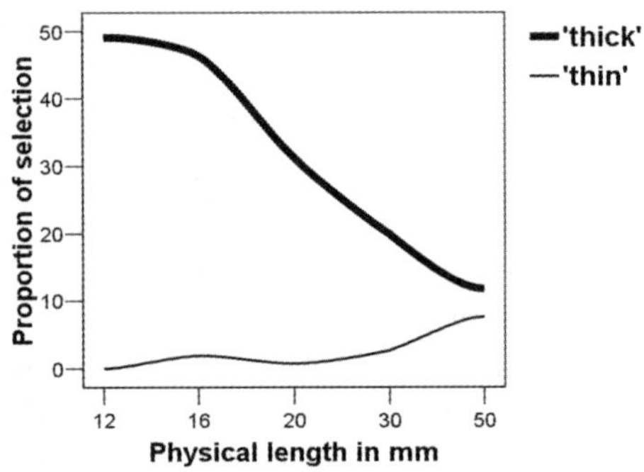

Figure 10. Proportion of selection of thickness attributes for the bolts of five different lengths, for the no-context condition (singly presented objects). All bolts have the same diameter. The categorization of thickness can entirely be put down to the ratio of length and diameter.

2.3. A model for object attributes based on experimental findings and data

As already discussed in the previous sections, a series of experiments was conducted in order to capture the language use of inexperienced human instructors (Brindöpke et al. 1995; Socher, Sagerer, and Perona 2000; Vorwerg 2001c). In the following, we describe how the experimental data and findings have been used to construct a computational model for mapping named object attributes to the visual object classes of a recognition component.

The shape and size adjectives considered in the computational model are those from the web-based study (Table 1). Additionally, frequently named color adjectives were included. For a complete list, see Table 2.

Table 2. Color, shape, and size adjectives included in the computational model.

Color	Shape	Size
gelb (yellow)	*rund (round)*	*lang (long)*
rot (red)	*sechseckig (hexagonal)*	*groß (big)*
blau (blue)	*flach (flat)*	*klein (small)*
weiß (white)	*rechteckig (rectangular)*	*kurz (short)*
grün (green)	*dünn (thin)*	*breit (large, wide)*
hell (light)	*länglich (elongated)*	*hoch (high)*
orange (orange)	*dick (thick)*	*mittellang (medium-long)*
lila (violet)	*schmal (narrow)*	*mittelgroß (medium-sized)*
holzfarben (wooden)	*rautenförmig (diamond-shaped)*	*eckig (angular)*

The evaluation of the web-based experimental study (see Sec. 2.2) provides frequencies of use for the different adjectives with regard to the object class and the object context. A qualitative evaluation has been discussed in the previous sections (see also Vorwerg 2001b; 2001d). The findings basically influence the structure of the proposed computational model. In particular, the following results are considered:

1. All attributes except *rund* (*round*) depend on context. But the context only partially determines the selection of it. There are three different types of slats with different lengths in the construction kit: a three-holed, a five-holed, and a seven-holed bar. In Sec. 2.2 a switch of the frequency ordering is reported for *mittellang* (*medium-long*). The isolated naming of a three-holed bar yields a higher frequency for *mittellang* than for a five-holed bar. In the context with all three types of bars present this ordering is switched.
2. The attribute selection in the corresponding dimensions, e.g. 'long' in the dimension 'size', is very specific to the object classes. Context objects have only a small influence. For example, the longest bolt is called 'long' although it is shorter in length than the shortest bar. This is not affected by whether or not there is a bar in the context set.
3. *Dick* (*thick*) correlates negatively with the length of an object. The bolts all have the same width, but the shortest bolt is called *thick* with much higher frequency.

4. *Eckig* (*angular*) is neither a super-concept of *rechteckig* (*rectangular*) nor of *viereckig* (*quadrangular*). It is partially used as an alternative naming.
5. *Rechteckig* (*rectangular*) correlates negatively with *lang* (*long*); *länglich* (*elongated*) correlates positively with it.

Altogether, it reveals that the meaning of shape and size attributes is difficult to capture. It is particularly difficult to directly extract the applicability of such attributes from image features. The solution that has been applied in the following is to use object class statistics (Socher, Sagerer, and Perona 2000; Wachsmuth and Sagerer 2002).

Bayesian networks (BNs) provide flexible means for modeling declarative knowledge in a statistical framework (Pearl 1988). Probabilistic conditional independencies are coded as a directed acyclic graph (DAG). In discrete BNs parameters are typically defined by conditional probability tables (CPTs). Each such parameter can be directly interpreted as conditional probability $p(A = a|B_1 = b_1,\ldots,B_n=b_n)$ where A is a child node and $B_1,\ldots,B_n$ are the parent nodes of A in the DAG. Figure 11 shows the DAG of the Bayesian network that has been deduced from the experimental findings. The *IntendedObjClass* node defines a random variable with 25 different states including one for each elementary object class, one for assembled objects, and one *undef*-state for inconsistent object descriptions. These can be described by different object nouns (*SType*-subnet), color (*SColor*-subnet), size, and shape adjectives. On the visual side, an object recognition component (Kummert et al. 1998) provides a type (*VType*) and a color (*VColor*) label. *VContext* distinguishes two different contexts as previously discussed in item (1.) of the experimental findings: all three different bars present or not present. We abstract from other context dependencies because this is the only one which qualitatively changes frequency orderings. The meanings of *angular* and *quadrangular* were split into a super-concept modeled by the variables *SAngular* and *SQuadrangular* and *other-angular* and *other-quadrangular* states in the variable *SShape*. Object names that are not known to denote an elementary object are instantiated in the variable *SObject*. It is an abstraction of the variable *SType* and denotes an assembled object with a higher probability than an elementary object type. The BN parameters are hand-crafted for the *SType*- and *SColor*-subnets. The parameters of the other parts of the network are estimated using the data collected in the WWW questionnaire. Evaluating the object class BN for the maximum *a posteriori* hypothesis of the variable *IntendedObjClass* provides a multi-modal object classification using visual and verbal features.

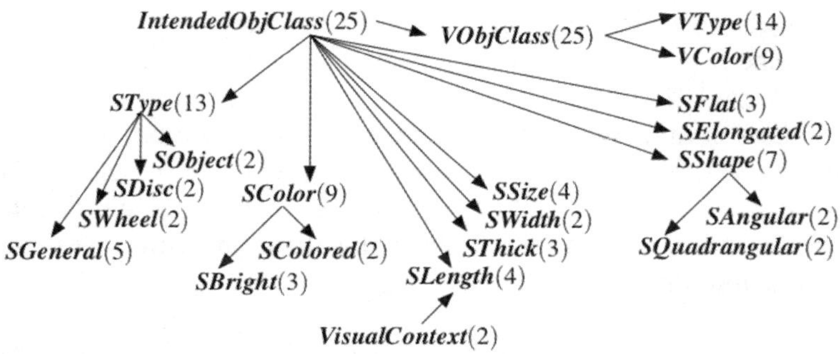

Figure 11. The Bayesian network for naming visual object classes: the numbers in brackets denote the dimension of each variable.

3. Verbal localization in visual space

3.1. Reference frame selection

Usually, one object's position is expressed in terms of another one's. That secondary object is used as a reference object or "relatum". Several factors are known to influence the choice of a reference object, as size, mobility, salience, knowledge of speaker and listener, and – in localization sequences – coherence strategies (Herrmann and Grabowski 1994; Herskovits 1986; Miller and Johnson-Laird 1976; Talmy 1983; Vandeloise 1991).

The visually perceived location is specified by perceived direction and distance (Loomis et al. 1996). Many spatial expressions denote either distance or direction relations. Both types may combine in natural language use (Schober 1993).

Direction differs from distance in that its determination requires a reference direction or orientation relative to which this spatial relation between intended object and reference object can be judged (Vorwerg 2003c). This is often called perspective or point of viewing (O'Keefe and Nadel 1978), as this type of spatial relation typically moves with the observer. For those viewpoint-related localizations, three elements are needed to establish a direction relation: the intended object, a relatum (or reference object), and a point of view (Herrmann 1990). Relatum and point of view may also coincide when the relatum has an intrinsic orientation; in this case the perspective or point of viewing of the relatum itself is used.

The main axes needed to determine the direction where an object is situated relative to the reference object constitute a spatial frame of reference. A number of classifications and different terminology have been used in the literature. The following classification schema based on Herrmann (1990) is proposed (Vorwerg 2003b; Vorwerg and Sudheimer 2006) because it combines the distinction between binary and ternary localizations and the kind of perspective used (Table 3). Moreover, it seems that the linguistic frames of reference distinguished here rely on different perceptual frames of reference; object-centered and body-centered binary localizations can be assumed to be computed differently.

Table 3. Taxonomy of frames of reference for direction specification based on Herrmann (1990). Assumed underlying perceptual frames of reference are given in brackets. Another point of view that may be adopted is the addressee's perspective.

Point of view	Binary localization	Ternary localization
Speaker (Observer)	egocentric (body-centered)	deictic (viewer-centered)
Other	intrinsic (object-centered)	extrinsic (environment-centered)

In many situations, multiple frames of reference are available and one of them has to be chosen for localization. Factors influencing the selection of a frame of reference for communicating spatial location include functional relations between intended object and relatum (Carlson 2000) and parameters of the communication situation (Clark and Wilkes-Gibbs 1986; Herrmann and Schweizer 1998; Schober 1993).

3.1.1. Perceptual saliency and initial reference-frame selection

Based on results from the research about spatial categorization, we tested the hypothesis that perceptual saliency may influence the choice of a spatial frame of reference (Vorwerg and Sudheimer 2006). Formal analyses (Herskovits 1986) as well as empirical results (Gapp 1995; Hayward and Tarr 1995; Vorwerg, Socher, and Rickheit 1996) support the conclusion that there are ideal or prototypical directions, which are named most easily and consistently. These idealtypic values seem to provide default values for the interpretation of directional terms. A perceived direction is processed in terms of (angular) deviation from such a salient reference direction (see Vorwerg

2001a). We expected that a location of an intended reference object at such a prototypical reference direction would enhance the probability of choosing the according frame of reference. This hypothesis was based on the idea that the main axes of spatial reference frames are constituted by (perceptually salient) cognitive reference directions, which function as prototypes for spatial categories.

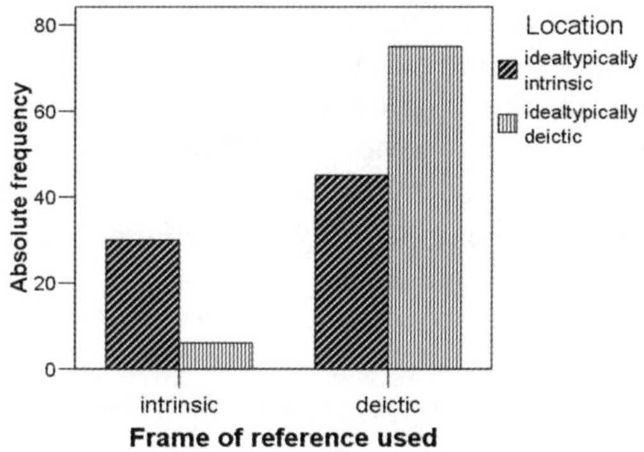

Figure 12. Location on a cognitive reference direction influences the choice of the frame of reference.

In order to find out whether a location at a reference direction would influence the choice of a reference frame, we asked participants to name the position of a small object relative to a toy plane serving as relatum. Participants were asked to use directional terms (such as *left* or *behind*) with respect to the reference object). The orientation of the plane was rotated by 45° relative to the line of sight of the speaker. This orientation enabled us to manipulate whether the intended object was located at an ideal intrinsic direction (defined by the axes of the plane) or at an ideal deictic direction (defined by the viewer). Results show that indeed locatedness on a cognitive reference direction influences which frame of reference is selected (Figure 12). A modifying factor is the avoidance of intrinsic lateral localizations (*left* and *right*) if these would require a mental rotation.

3.1.2. *Consistency effects*

In several types of discourse, object localizations are produced as part of a localization sequence. In some kinds of localization sequences the same relatum is involved in all of them. Some studies concerned with sequences of spatial specifications have found localization patterns or *strategies* (e.g. Ehrich and Koster 1983). Levelt (1982) discriminates between two kinds of 'orientation type' (deictic vs. intrinsic) for the way people describe two-dimensional spatial patterns. The rather consistent choice of reference frame within and between patterns (with about two thirds of the participants using a viewer-centered reference frame and one third using a movement-intrinsic reference frame) was explained by different cognitive styles. However, different starting conditions combined with a consistency principle (Haubensak 1992) could account for this kind of results as well. In order to explore this possibility, we investigated whether later utterances within a localization sequence would be influenced by preceding ones. In accordance with our hypothesis, we found that the probability of a reference frame to be chosen is a function of the initial items presented.

3.1.3. Verb semantics and interpretation of directional prepositions

In another study, the influence of verb meaning on the interpretation of direction terms (*in front of* vs. *behind*) was investigated in connection with the understanding of an instruction to place a car relative to another object (Vorwerg and Weiß 2006). Previous research had suggested that the interpretation of these directional prepositions might depend on the social situation (Grabowski, Herrmann, and Weiß 1993). However, language use varies with the social communication situation (for a review, see Rickheit and Vorwerg 2003). Therefore, different verbs had been used to invoke the intended social situation – *einparken* (*to park*) in the sense of 'to get into a parking space' vs. *rauslassen* (*to drop off*). We investigated whether the found effects of the social situation may be put down to the use of different verbs. This hypothesis was confirmed in a number of studies involving several verbs and combinations of verb and situation.

To sum up, besides other factors of reference-frame selection already known, perceptual saliency and verb meaning have been found to influence the choice of a frame of reference. Additionally, earlier localizations influence later ones within a localization sequence due to the general principle of consistency. The effectiveness of these factors shows that the applicability of a spatial term (specifically a term of direction) to a given spatial relation is, among other things, perceptually founded and also influenced by linguistic context.

3.2. Categorization of spatial relations

Both direction and distance can be regarded as attribute dimensions (Vorwerg and Rickheit 1998; 2000). An attribute can be localized by specifying direction or distance; and it can be identified on the basis of a localizing expression. Therefore, spatial terms are also used for object reference (see also 2.1). Similar to the size and shape dimensions considered in the previous section, direction and distance terms reflect perceived degrees or levels of an underlying physical dimension. Polar coordinates have been shown to be spontaneously used for encoding spatial location in visual perception (Mapp and Ono 1999), visual memory (Bryant and Subbiah 1993; Huttenlocher, Hedges, and Duncan 1991), and vision-related language (Franklin, Henkel, and Zangas 1995; Gapp 1995; Regier and Carlson 2001; Vorwerg 2001a). That is, the perceptual dimension of direction is based on directional angle, the perceptual dimension of distance is based on radial distance.

Similar to shape, phenomenal direction can be regarded as one of those dimensions whose categories differ qualitatively from each other, whereas phenomenal distance is one of those dimensions whose categories correspond with 'more' vs. 'less' of the particular dimension. Both kinds of attribute dimension differ in a number of aspects (see Vorwerg 2001a; 2004).

- *Distance.* The categorization of distance follows the same principles as the categorization of other quantitative attribute dimensions. The range of occurring distance values is subdivided to accommodate the number of categories allowed (Vorwerg and Rickheit 2000).
- *Direction.* The categorization of direction is based on a comparison with idealtypical reference directions. Linguistic, psychological, and computational results suggest that spatial domains are segmented into categories in a way akin to other categorical structures (e.g., Hayward and Tarr 1995; Regier 1995; Talmy 1983) and that direction relations are analog, overlapping, internally structured categories whose instances can be more or less typical for a direction category (see Vorwerg and Rickheit 1998, for a review). The typicality of a given direction for a direction category (referred to, e.g., as *to the left of* or *behind*) reflects the perceived degree of angular deviation from a reference axis, as revealed by a number of empirical studies. The typicality of a perceptual direction need not, but can be expressed linguistically by using qualifying degree terms or linguistic hedges (Franklin et al. 1995; Vorwerg and Rickheit 1999a; see also Table 4).

Table 4. Hedges used to qualify the degree of direction category membership in an unrestricted verbal localization studiy with German native speakers (from Vorwerg and Rickheit 1998).

German hedge	English translation
genau/exakt; direkt	*exactly; directly*
fast; fast genau; nicht ganz	*almost; almost exactly; not quite*
sehr leicht; (ein) bißchen; ein Stück	*very slightly; a little bit; a bit*
leicht; etwas	*slightly; somewhat*
versetzt	*shifted*
schräg	*oblique*

3.2.1. Cognitive reference directions for perception, memory and language

We have argued that the spatial frame of reference providing the main axes relative to which a direction can be specified (see previous section) serves as a reference frame for categorization at the same time (Vorwerg and Rickheit 1998). Accordingly, we argue that the notion of a frame of reference in spatial cognition is related to the more general concept of a reference-frame in categorization. And it can be assumed that – similar to shape – idealtypical values within the angular direction dimension serve as prototypes for categorization. Generally, any clearly directed axis of orientation (Klatzky 1998) can be used as a reference direction in relation to which other directions are judged. However, there seem to be preferred, perceptually salient orientations which often act as standard values in relation to which perceived object relations can be judged (Vorwerg and Rickheit 1999b; see also Vorwerg 2003c). These have been termed 'cognitive reference directions' in the sense of Rosch's (1975) 'cognitive reference points' within semantic domains (Vorwerg 2001a; Vorwerg and Rickheit 1998). Unless a given direction lies exactly at a cognitive reference direction, categorizing a direction as pertaining to a direction category (such as IN FRONT OF) means to tolerate a certain amount of angular deviation.

Distinguished orientations or directions suitable for relating other relations to them may be directions, "against which other visual directions or locations are reported with greatest acuity", Matin 1986: 20/17). It can be argued that those perceptually salient reference directions are used for memory encoding and verbal encoding as well (Vorwerg 2003c). Contrary to this position, Crawford, Regier, and Huttenlocher (2000) maintain that linguistic and non-linguistic direction categories do not coincide but have an inverse relation such that boundaries of non-linguistic categories form the prototypes of linguistic categories. This proposal is based on results which show that in reports from memory, judgments of spatial location are frequently biased away from the "ideal" vertical or horizontal and towards the diagonals (e.g. Huttenlocher, Hedges, and Duncan 1991). This finding has been interpreted as evidence for a compromise between the actual stimulus value and a central value representing a category. This consideration leads to the assumption that the prototypes of spatial categories should lie along the obliques, which in turn are known to lie approximately at the boundary between two linguistic direction categories. If this was the case, then we might expect the presence of real straight lines to have a similar effect as the imaginary straight lines and to act as category boundaries. However, it rather seems that any clear (physical) line or (perceptually salient) orientation can be used to localize other directions relative to it (Figure 13). With reference to the differentiation between two kinds of attribute dimensions (Vorwerg 2001a; see above), it can be argued that the encoding of direction (as a phenomenally 'qualitative' attribute dimension) is not based on a comparison with empirical mean values, but on a comparison with idealtypical reference values (Vorwerg 2003c). This kind of encoding may lead to contrast effects causing the bias observed.

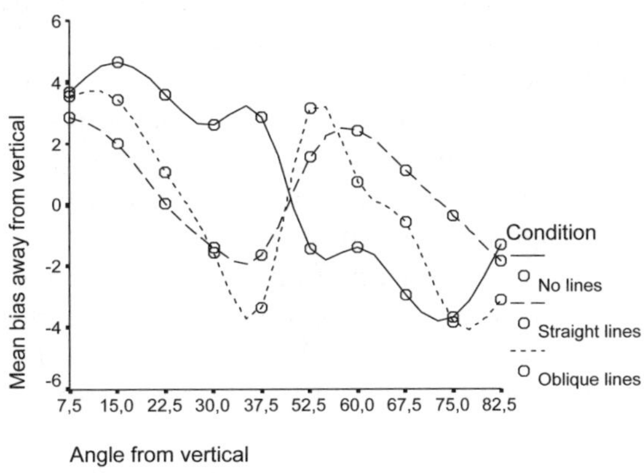

Figure 13. Bias effects for location reports from memory. In this experiment, the location of a dot in a circle has to be remembered and reproduced. Results show that remembered location is biased away from reference direction, may it be imaginary or physically given (from Vorwerg 2003c).

3.2.2. Principles of direction categorization

If we assume that a perceptually salient orientation is favored as an axis for a spatial frame of reference, the question arises how this orientation is related to the reference object. In order to be able to localize an intended object relative to a reference object, the view-point determined reference orientation has to be coordinated with the reference object; the axes constituting the frame of reference result from an interaction between point of view and reference object. A privileged point within the reference object for doing so could obviously be the center of mass. This would allow one single origo for all direction axes (Herskovits, 1986). On the other side, a relatum has a certain extension in space and cannot be reduced to a single point. Gapp's (1995) proposal was that the angular deviation underlying two-dimensional direction judgments might be computed from the nearest edge or corner of the (idealized) reference object. Experimental and computational work by Regier and Carlson (2001) has shown that both, the so-called proximal and center-of-mass orientations, influence the rated applicability of a vertical direction term (*above*) in 2D space. This finding corresponds well with a number of experimental results for 3D space received with rating, multiple-choice, and free-naming paradigms (see Vorwerg 2001a; Vorwerg and Rickheit 1999; Vorwerg et al. 1997). On the one hand, location near a central axis contributes to the frequency of "singular" direction naming (as opposed to combinations of two terms), and on the other hand, the spatial partitioning by the reference object (its extension) contributes as well. The empirical results provide evidence for the assumption that for modeling the spatial computations underlying direction categorization, the reference object's extension in space as well as its orientation must be taken into account. Another factor concerns the horizontal dimension involved (lateral vs. sagittal): The tolerance for assigning a given location to a singular (i.e. not a combined) direction category *within* a particular frame of reference is bigger for lateral direction terms (*left* or *right*) than for sagittal direction terms (*in-front* or *behind*) (e.g. Vorwerg 2001a). We have no evidence for an influence of radial distance on direction assignment (e.g., Vorwerg and Rickheit 1999).

3.2.3. A visual tilt effect for the sagittal reference direction

The necessity to incorporate the orientation of the reference object shows that a simple bounding box model (idealizing the reference object by a minimal box enclosing that object) does not come up to the complexity of direction categorization. However, the opposite idea, a completely object-based partitioning of space, which would rotate with different orientations of the relatum, does not conform to the psycholinguistic data, either (Vorwerg and Rickheit 1999; Vorwerg et al. 1997). For an elongated reference object that is rotated relative to the speaker's point of view, there is obviously a conflict between the object's axes and the viewer-centered reference frame as long as a deictic frame of reference is to used. Experimental data for the placement of a small object according to directional instructions referring to an elongated reference object (a kind of slat or bar) provide evidence that the positioning of an object *in front of* or *behind* a reference object with a pronounced main axis depends on the orientation of the relatum following a pattern similar to the Aubert effect (but reverse direction) or to the rod-and-frame effect for the perception of the vertical (Vorwerg 2001a). For small tilt or rotation levels there is an angular deviation from the sagittal in the same direction as the orientation of the relatum. For large rotation angles the placement is shifted in the opposite direction. However, the mean angular deviation is always smaller than the relatum's rotation angle (Fig. 14).

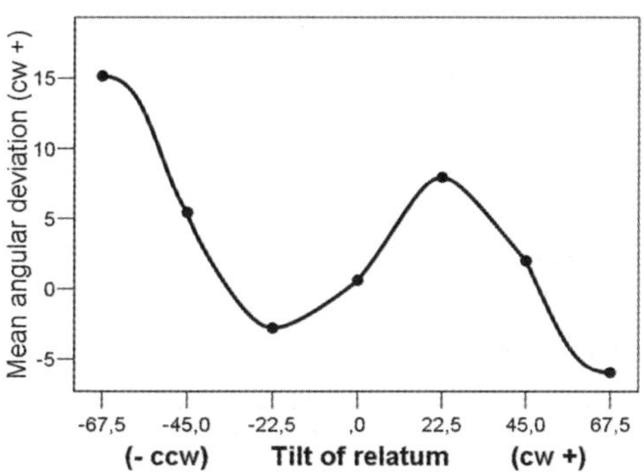

Figure 14. Tilt effect for the placement of a small object according to sagittal direction instruction: *vor/hinter* (*in front of/behind*). The tilt of the relatum (a bar of any of three lengths) is determined relative to the (deictic) sagittal. Both objects lie on a horizontal plane. After Vorwerg (2001a; the data have been reanalyzed on the basis of excluding only angular extremes – not Cartesian ones – from analysis).

The sagittal visual tilt effect in positioning according to direction instructions can be regarded as a basic effect of the structural organization of perception (comparable to the apparent vertical). The perceived orientation of the slat interacts with the visual sagittal, as it is determined by line of sight.

The results provide evidence for the use of the sagittal as a cognitive reference direction and the perceptual foundation of the categorization of directional relations, especially as the found effect is reflected in all language tasks used. We conclude that perceptually salient orientations are used as reference directions in perception, language, and memory. Altogether, the reported results on spatial categorization confirm that spatial language is to a large extent based on spatial perception.

Furthermore, the differentiation between two kinds of attribute dimensions has proven useful for direction and distance. Categorization is the link between visual perception and vision-based language. In order to understand what processes underlie the production and comprehension of object and spatial references with regard to intended and inferred word meaning, we need to look at the interface between vision and language taking into account context, flexibility, and relativity.

3.3. Region-based 2D modeling

A computational model that relates categories of spatial relations to geometric properties of the visually observed scene is needed to ground verbal localization in the visual space. Spatial expressions like *the cube in front of the bar* partition the space around the reference object (*the bar*) in a very loose fashion with a large degree of ambiguity. The meaning of a spatial relation depends on inherent properties of the objects involved, such as their relative distance, orientation, and shapes, but also on the specific context in which a relation will be named (Mukerjee 1997). In the following, we will concentrate on 'projective relations' that describe where objects are placed relative to each other (Clementini, Felice, and Hernández 1997). Various approaches have been proposed using acceptance areas (Hernández, 1994), fuzzy classes over the quantized space employing continuous membership functions (Fuhr et al. 1997), or potential fields (Gapp 1994; Olivier, Maeda, and Tsuji 1994). To date, there is no generally accepted domain-independent computational spatial model. Each model has its own restriction and limitations. The computational model presented in this section accounts for the following assumptions:

- *Dimensionality:* In this domain, the main spatial reasoning takes place on a table plane. Frequently, projective relations like *above* are used for the identification of objects lying behind a reference object on the table. Therefore, a 2D model is chosen.

- *Position and orientation:* The model is applied in a small scale environment on a table. Therefore, the scene topology and orientational relations are more relevant than geometric distance.
- *Shape:* Especially the shape of the reference object influences the applicability of a spatial relation. Simplifying the shape of an object by rectangular approximations does not account for objects localized in the near contact zone of complex assembled objects that can have arbitrary nonconvex shapes.
- *Robustness:* The computational model needs to be based on a visual representation that can be computed without much object knowledge, because we need to apply the computational model to objects that have been wrongly recognized, that have not been fully reconstructed, or that are out-of-domain objects. Thus, a blob representation has been selected.

In Figure 15, the 2D spatial model is illustrated. Acceptance areas are defined based on a space partitioning with regard to the shape of the reference object. Each area has an associated direction that points away from the blob area. The degree of containment weights the acceptance areas with regard to the localized object. A named spatial relation is interpreted as a specified 2D direction based on the current reference frame. The degree of applicability is computed by the scalar product of two vectors, the first specifying the degree of containment for each acceptance area and the second defining the degree of accordance between the named 2D direction and the directions associated with each acceptance area (Fuhr et al. 1997; Wachsmuth 2001).

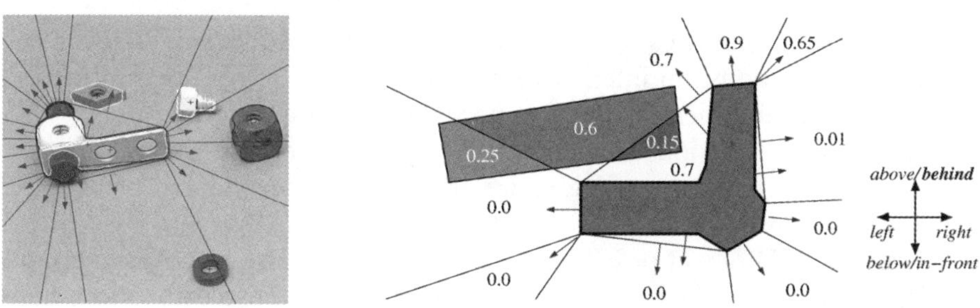

Figure 15. First-level representation of the 2D spatial model for *behind.* The space is partitioned into acceptance areas. The numbers in the acceptance areas specify the degree of accordance between the named direction *behind* and the directions associated with the areas. The numbers in the localized object specify the degree of containments of the object with regard to the acceptance areas. On the left side of this figure, we show space partitioning for an example image.

A second aspect of the 2D computational model is presented in Figure 16. The topological structure of the scene is taken into account by representing neighborhood relations in a scene graph. The model assumes that a speaker will select a reference object next to the localized object. The degree of applicability is down-weighted for object pairs that have no neighborhood relation.

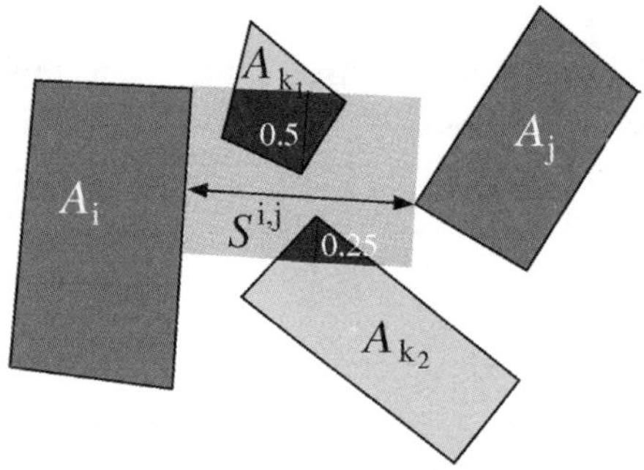

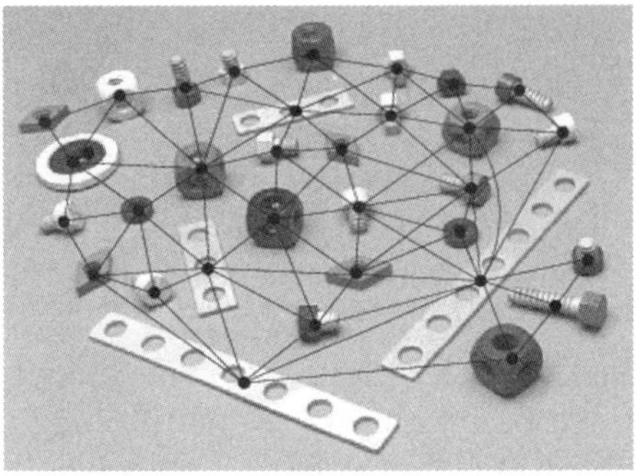

Figure 16. Neighborhood graph of the spatial model. Two objects have a neighborhood relation, if there is no object in between that separates them. On the left hand side, the two objects A_i and A_j are separated by the objects A_{k1} and A_{k2}. The right image shows the graph for an example image.

3.4. CAD-based 3D modeling

Although object identification and spatial reasoning can be solved using sets of 2D representations, an interactive assembly task requires 3D information. The location of an object in space is necessary for grasping purposes. While we can see in the previous section that 2D information is sufficient for creating a spatial scene representation, we have also experimented using a 3D scene representation (Fuhr et al. 1997).

We extract 3D object poses from stereo images based on CAD-like models. Single images are sufficient for model-based 3D pose estimation, however, it has been shown that the use of stereo images improves the accuracy significantly (Socher 1997). Object recognition is carried out by an Artificial Neural Network. For each object, image features, i.e. ellipses, edges, and vertices, are then fitted to CAD-like object models. The model-fitting minimizes the Mahalanobis distance between model and percept through the Levenberg-Marquardt algorithm. Object recognition as well as model-fitting

Figure 17. 3D reconstruction: input image of the left camera (left column), different views of the reconstructed scene (center and right column).

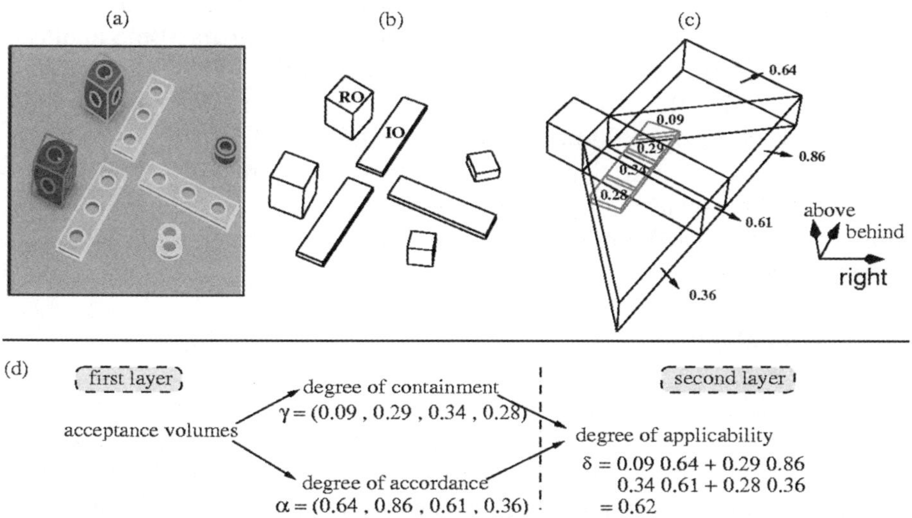

Figure 18. Extension of spatial model to 3D: (a) shows the 3D reconstruction; (b) depicts the 3D object boundaries; (c) visualizes the 3D partitioning of the visual space including the degree of containment and the degree of accordance with regard to the direction 'right,' (d) shows the computation steps for the calculation of the degree of applicability of the direction 'right' with regard to the intended object (IO) and the reference object (RO).

are incremental processes. They are done separately on each of the stereo images. The metric 3D reconstruction is then estimated applying the model-fitting procedure simultaneously to all objects available in the scene on both stereo frames (Socher, Merz, and Posch 1995). This also leads to a calibration of the stereo camera using only the objects in the scene. Figure 17 shows the 3D reconstruction of an example scene.

We abstract the object boundaries of the 3D scene (Fig. 18b) and use them to compute a 3D spatial model as described in Fuhr et al. (1997). The computation steps are similar to the 2D spatial model. The space partitioning is extended into the 3D space (Fig. 18c). Based on this, the degree of containment, the degree of accordance, and the degree of applicability are defined accordingly (Fig. 18d).

The cognitive validity of the spatial computational model was evaluated by a series of psycholinguistic experiments, in which participants either generated spatial terms for describing the directional relationship between a small intended object and a comparably large relatum, or rated the applicability of directional terms computed on the basis of the spatial model (Vorwerg et al. 1997). Results showed a general acceptance of the computed relations (mean rating = .90 on a rating scale from 0 to 1) and a significant correlation between participants' ratings and the degrees of applicability computed by the system. Further specific results found (e.g. dependency of rating on rotation of the relatum) can be explained by factors discussed in sections 3.1 and 3.2.

4. Cross-modal inference

Processing speech and corresponding visual scenes, the task for an inference engine is two-fold. First, object descriptions in language need to be linked to visual instances of the corresponding object in the scene. Secondly, language descriptions can be used in order to disambiguate or correct visual processing results.

A Bayesian Network model is built up for object reference (see Fig. 19) based on the object class and spatial models described in sections 2.3 and 3.3. This model can be used for both tasks. In the first step, the maximum *a posteriori* hypothesis (*map*) of the variable *IO* is computed. Secondly, given $IO^{(map)}$ the map hypothesis $IntendedObjClass_0^{map}$ is calculated considering visual and verbal evidences for object classification.

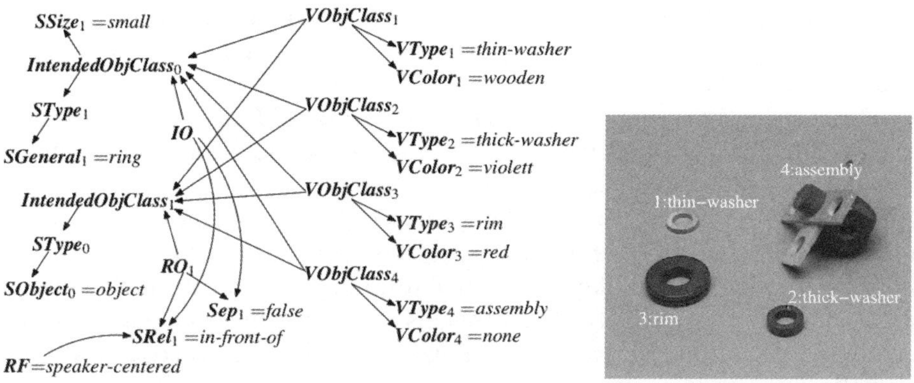

Figure 19. Generated Bayesian network for a scene with four objects (see image on the right) and the instruction *Take the small ring in front of the rotor.*

Two experiments have been conducted in order to generate test sets for evaluation purposes.

- Experiment 1 (Select-Obj): Ten participants verbally named objects in 11 different "baufix" scenes that were presented on a computer screen. The scenes contained between 5 and 30 elementary "baufix" objects. One object was marked by an arrow and the participant was supposed to give an instruction like *Take the yellow cube*. A total of 453 verbal object descriptions were thus collected (total number of words: 2394).
- Experiment 2 (Select-Rel): The experimental setting was equivalent to the experiment described before. This time, six participants were explicitly asked to name objects in six different scenes by using a spatial relation like *Take the red object behind the cube*. We collected a total of 174 verbal object descriptions (total number of words: 1396).

Given object recognition results on the "baufix" scenes and speech recognition results from the recorded instructions, the system is to compute the object that was marked by the arrow and should be localized by the speaker. A system answer is counted as correct if the system selects the marked object. The system is allowed to select additional objects of the same type and color as the marked one in case of similar probabilities.

In order to assess the influence of recognition error rates on identification results, we first measured the performance of the system on correctly labeled input data. In this case we got 95% correct system answers in both experiments. Failures in system answers were mostly due to speakers who gave instructions which were too unspecific, or who used an inappropriate or unusual wording (e.g., some participants occasionally used the term *nut* to refer to a bolt).

Considering noisy input, a speech error rate of 13% on words that were extracted by the system as verbal features decreased the identification rate by 3% and 5%, respectively; an object error rate (either wrong type or wrong color) of 20% (first experiment) and 36% (second experiment) decreased the identification rate by 5% in both experiments. If both inputs are noisy, their impacts are roughly additively combined resulting in an identification rate of 87% and 84%, respectively. These results show that the redundancy in the combined visual and verbal descriptions is exploited in order to deal with partially correct recognition results. The same kind of strategy also applies to the identification of aggregated objects which have no predefined semantic meaning for the system. Nevertheless, these can be identified by probabilistically ruling out other elementary objects and by exploiting spatial descriptions.

In the cases in which a unique object was selected – about 50% of all the cases – the object type can be inferred from visual as well as verbal descriptions (in most of these cases, additional objects were selected due to an underspecification of the speaker). Using the proposed probabilistic model, the object error rate could be reduced from 13% to 2% on the set of uniquely selected objects.

5. Conclusion

In order to produce and understand "visual" object references (i.e. verbal utterances referring to visually perceived objects), visual and linguistic information processing has to be integrated. At the outer level, the results need to be related to each other in order to solve the correspondence problem. This mapping in turn is partly based on underlying information coordination processes and, even more basic, on a perceptual foundation of dimensional and spatial language.

The coordination processes concern mainly the propagation of interim results of information processing to the other modality, which may be used for mutual recognition. Thus, the system's visual object error rate is being reduced by taking into account the language descriptions that result from speech recognition. Similar top-down influences are known for human perception as long as vision is ambiguous (perhaps due to reduced input or poor viewing conditions). Above and beyond recognition, the mutual integration from information from the other channel may also lead to a restriction or extension of categories – depending on typicality and context.

Typicality and context are also the most important factors in the perceptual foundation of linguistic categories of size, shape, color, and location. Words for size, shape, color, and location belong to those lexical items, the meanings of which are grounded in perceptual categories in a bottom-up way (Harnad 1990; 1996). Assuming that meanings are relations – relations between lexical units and conceptual representations – we propose that size, color, and shape adjectives as well as distance and direction terms are based primarily on perceptual representations that are both iconic and categorical. The categorization of visual object attributes can obviously not derive from invariant features. Instead, it is argued that they are formed according to similarity with reference values within an attribute dimension. These reference values constitute the core of the frame of reference in relation to which perceived values can be judged.

The kind of reference values used depends on the kind of attribute dimension (Vorwerg 2001a).

Characteristics of empirical distributions act as anchoring points for so-called linear or quantitative dimensions: The extremes (or endpoints) of a range form the poles for employing polar adjectives that are based on similarity to them; their midpoint is both the point of maximum dissimilarity from both poles and the starting point for building a third (a 'middle') category. These considerations are based on relational psychophysical research; they are confirmed by our psycholinguistic results. Our results further show that only simultaneously present objects are taken into account when judging a given object attribute. All values of a series conceptualized as belonging together and being of the same object category may contribute to a frame of reference, even when presented singly and successively – as long as a person is informed about the approximate range of values.

However, for so-called circular or qualitative dimensions, idealtypic values – mostly based on perceptual saliency – serve as cognitive reference points. Therefore, context dependency is limited for this kinds of attribute dimension. Nevertheless, all "non-idealtypic" values (e.g., *somehow round* or *relatively square*) may depend on context in their categorization. Values constituting a simultaneous context may have a specific impact on categorization for both kinds of attribute dimension (with the limitations described) as they are suited to anchor other values.

On top of this, attribute dimensions can also be categorized relative to another dimension. This seems to be a particularly important aspect for secondary, unidimensional size adjectives (such as width or thickness) which may be categorized relative to length as has been shown for the thickness of bolts. Categorizing those values according to their relation to another dimensional value puts them close to qualitative dimensions (this is reflected in cases of synonymy between *flat* and *low*, which may both be translated into German as *flach*). These considerations lead directly to a proposal made by Vorwerg (2001) for the general relativity principle underlying "qualitative" attribute dimensions: Their idealtypical values may be formed by certain relations between underlying subdimensions (see also Vorwerg and Rickheit 1998).

Regardless of what kind of comparison values are used – the principle of relativity seems to hold for all kinds of visual attribute dimension. It is the basis for object-category specificity and context dependency; and it is expressed in differing degrees of typicality, which provide the empirical basis for probabilistic modeling in psychophysics and psycholinguistics (cf. also Jurafsky 2002; Kuss, Jäkel, and Wichmann 2005).

In our research, we have sought to combine psychophysical and psycholinguistic methodology, and these in turn with computational methods. This approach is proposed as a way of closing the gap between analyzing simplified and idealized stimuli hand in psychophysical studies, and disregarding visual input or the specific situation of language use altogether in analyses of meaning. We propose that categorization mediates between perception and language and, in the case of object attributes, that it is the link between psychophysics and psycholinguistics.

In the specification of visual attributes for object reference, a number of – partly visually founded – processes are involved: (1) The utterance provides information to the listener about the object depending on the number of perceived alternatives (Olson 1970). (2) If there are several dimensions available for object naming, attribute selection may depend on perceptual saliency of a dimension or on the size or the number of perceived differences to context objects (Herrmann and Deutsch 1976). Prerequisites not dealt with here are the extraction of attribute dimensions from holistic object perception (Smith 1989) and the dimensional designation of spatial objects (Lang 1987). (3) In order to establish a reference frame for categorizing a given value on the dimension chosen, the object class has to be determined since reference frames are specific to object classes. (4) For quantitative attributes, extremes and midpoint of the series are determined in order to serve as reference points, relative to which a given value can be judged. This holds for objects presented in simultaneous context as well as for objects presented in isolation. At least for the latter, a representation in memory has to be assumed. (5) For specifying direction, a spatial frame of reference has to be chosen, whose half-axes determine the idealtypical values for direction categories (such as *in front of*), and which therefore can also serve as idealtypical cognitive reference directions for categorization. In order to be used for spatial reference, a reference direction has to be coordinated with the reference object (relatum) to determine origo and axes, taking into account the center and the edges of the relatum. For categorizing a visual direction relation (at least in the deictic reference frame), angular deviations from a primary axis are tolerated less than deviations from a secondary axis. The orientation of the reference object interacts with the orientation of the speaker in determining the apparent sagittal for deictic localization, producing a rod-and-frame-like tilt effect. (6) In all kinds of attribute dimensions, the actual categorization in a given situation depends on a comparison between the perceived value to be categorized and reference values for this visual dimension.

For successful communication concerning visual object attributes, the use of a similar frame of reference based on similar perceptual experience and providing a similar scaling of perceived dimension values seems a precondition. This is coupled with flexibility and cross-modal integration for ensuring understanding. Using probabilistic modeling, both kinds of processes can be simulated so as to account for communication between a human and an artificial communicator.

References

Arbeitsmaterialien B1

1994a *"Dies ist ein runder Gegenstand..." Sprachliche Objektspezifikationen.* Working paper. Collaborative Research Center 360. Bielefeld: University of Bielefeld.

1994b *"Wir bauen jetzt also ein Flugzeug ..." Konstruieren im Dialog.* Working paper. Collaborative Research Center 360. Bielefeld: University of Bielefeld.

Bierwisch, M.

1987 Semantik der Graduierung. In *Grammatische und konzeptuelle Aspekte von Dimensionsadjektiven,* M. Bierwisch, and E. Lang (eds.), 91–286. Berlin: Akademie-Verlag.

Brindöpke, C., M. Johanntokrax, A. Pahde, and B. Wrede

1995 *"Darf ich dich Marvin nennen?" Instruktionsdialoge in einem Wizard-of-Oz-Szenario.* Report 1995/7, Collaborative Research Center 360. Bielefeld: Universität Bielefeld.

Bryant, D. J., and I. Subbiah

1993 Strategic and perceptual factors producing tilt contrast in dot localization. *Memory and Cognition* 31: 773–784.

Budde, H.G.
1980 Partialsystembildungen innerhalb des musikalischen Differenzierungsbereichs. In *Wahrnehmen – Urteilen – Handeln,* A. Thomas, and R. Brackhane (eds.), 86–114. Bern: Huber.

Carlson, L. A.
2000 Object use and object location: The effect of function on spatial relations. In *Cognitive Interfaces: Constraints on Linking Cognitive Information,* E. van der Zee and U. Nikanne (eds.), 94–115. Oxford: Oxford University Press.

Christensen, H.
2003 Cognitive (vision) systems. *ERCIM News* 53: 17–18.

Clark, H. H., and D. Wilkes-Gibbs
1986 Referring as a collaborative process. *Cognition* 22: 1–39.

Clementini, E., P. D. Felice, and D. Hernàndez
1997 Qualitative representation of positional information. *Artificial Intelligence* 95: 317–356.

Crawford, E., T. Regier, and J. Huttenlocher
2000 Linguistic and non-linguistic spatial categorization. *Cognition* 75: 209–235.

Duygulu, P., K. Barnard, J. de Freitas, and D. Forsyth
2002 Object recognition as machine translation: Learning a lexicon for a fixed image vocabulary. In *Proceedings of the European Conference on Computer Vision*, Volume 4, 97–112.

Ehrich, V., and C. Koster
1983 Discourse organization and sentence form: The structure of room descriptions in Dutch. *Discourse Processes* 6: 169–195.

Eikmeyer, H.-J., U. Schade, M. Kupietz, and U. Laubenstein
1996 Connectionist syntax and planning in the production of object specifications. In *Conceptual and Semantic Knowledge in Language Production,* R. Meyer-Klabunde and C. v. Stutterheim (eds.), 18–30. Heidelberg: Universität Heidelberg.

Ford, W., and D. Olson
1975 The elaboration of the noun phrase in children's description of objects. *Journal of Experimental Child Psychology* 19: 371–382.

Franklin, N., L. A. Henkel, and T. Zangas
1995 Parsing surrounding space into regions. *Memory and Cognition* 23: 397–407.

Fuhr, T., G. Socher, C. Scheering, and G. Sagerer
1997 A three-dimensional spatial model for the interpretation of image data. In *Representation and Processing of Spatial Expressions,* P. Olivier, and K.-P. Gapp (eds.), 103–118. Hillsdale: Erlbaum.

Furnas, G., T. Landauer, L. Gomez, and S. Dumais
1987 The vocabulary problem in human-system communication. *Communications of the ACM* 30 (11): 964–971.

Gapp, K.-P.
1994 Basic meanings of spatial relations: Computation and evaluation in 3D space. In *Proceedings of AAAI-94*, 1393–1398. Seattle.
1995 An empirically validated model for computing spatial relations. In *KI-95: Advances in Artificial Intelligence,* I. Wachsmuth, C. Rollinger, and W. Brauer (eds.), 245–256. Berlin: Springer.
Grabowski, J., T. Herrmann, and P. Weiß
1993 Wenn "vor" gleich "hinter" ist – zur multiplen Determination des Verstehens von Richtungspräpositionen. *Kognitionswissenschaft* 3: 171–183.
Grosser, C., and R. Mangold-Allwinn
1990 "... und nochmal die grüne Uhr" – Zum Einfluß des Partners auf die Ausführlichkeit von wiederholten Benennungen. *Archiv für Psychologie* 142: 195–209.
Harnad, S.
1990 The symbol grounding problem. *Physica* D42: 335–346.
1996 The origins of words. A psychophysical hypothesis. In *Communicating Meaning. The Evolution and Development of Language,* B. M. Velichkovsky and D. M. Rumbaugh (eds.), 27–44. Mahwah: Erlbaum.
Haubensak, G.
1985 *Absolutes und vergleichendes Urteil. Eine Einführung in die Theorie psychischer Bezugssysteme*. Berlin: Springer.
1992 The consistency model: A process model for absolute judgments. *Journal of Experimental Psychology: Human Perception and Performance* 18: 303–309.
Hayward, W. G., and M. J. Tarr
1995 Spatial language and spatial representation. *Cognition* 55: 39–84.
Helson, H.
1948 Adaptation-level as a basis for a quantitative theory of frames of reference. *Psychological Review* 55: 297–313.
1964 *Adaptation-level Theory. An Experimental and Systematic Approach to Behavior*. New York: Harper & Row.
Hernández, D.
1994 *Qualitative Representation of Spatial Knowledge*. Berlin: Springer.
Herrmann, T.
1983 *Speech and Situation: A Psychological Conception of Situated Speaking*. Berlin: Springer.
1990 Vor, hinter, rechts und links: das 6H-Modell. *Zeitschrift für Literaturwissenschaft und Linguistik* 78: 117–140.
Herrmann, T., and W. Deutsch
1976 *Psychologie der Objektbenennung*. Bern: Huber.
Herrmann, T., and J. Grabowski
1994 *Sprechen. Psychologie der Sprachproduktion*. Heidelberg: Spektrum.

Herrmann, T., and M. Laucht
1976 On multiple codability of objects. *Psychological Research* 38: 355–368.

Herrmann, T., and K. Schweizer
1998 *Sprechen über Raum. Sprachliches Lokalisieren und seine kognitiven Grundlagen*. Bern: Huber.

Herskovits, A.
1986 *Language and Spatial Cognition: An Interdisciplinary Study of the Prepositions in English*. Cambridge, UK: Cambridge University Press.

Huttenlocher, J., L. Hedges, and S. Duncan
1991 Categories and particulars: Prototype effects in estimating spatial location. *Psychological Review* 98: 352–376.

Ide, I., R. Hamada, H. Tanaka, and S. Sakai
1998 News video classification based on semantic attributes of captions. In *Proceedings of the 6th ACM International Multimedia Conference,* 60–61.

Jackendoff, R.
1987 On beyond zebra: The relation of linguistic and visual information. *Cognition* 26: 89–114.

Jurasfsky, D.
2003 Probabilistic modeling in psycholinguistics: Linguistic comprehension and production. In *Probabilistic Linguistics,* R. Bod, J. Hay, and S. Jannedy (eds.), 39–95. Cambridge, MA: MIT Press.

Klatzky, R.
1998 Allocentric and egocentric spatial representations: Definitions, distinctions, and interconnections. In *Spatial Cognition. An Interdisciplinary Approach to Representing and Processing Spatial Knowledge,* C. Freksa, C. Habel, and K. F. Wender (eds.), 1–17. Berlin: Springer.

Krauss, R. M., and S. Glucksberg
1977 Social and nonsocial speech. *Scientific American* 236: 100–105.

Krauss, R. M., and S. Weinheimer
1964 Changes in reference phrases as a function of frequency of usage in interaction. *Psychonomic Science* 1: 113–114.

Kummert, F., G. A. Fink, G. Sagerer, and E. Braun
1998 Hybrid object recognition in image sequences. In *Procedings of the International Conference on Pattern Recognition, Volume 2,* 1165–1170.

Kuss, M., F. Jäkel, and F. A. Wichmann
2005 Bayesian inference for psychometric functions. *Journal of Vision* 5: 478–492.

Lang, E.
1987 Semantik der Dimensionsauszeichnung räumlicher Objekte. In *Grammatische und konzeptuelle Aspekte von Dimensionsadjektiven,* M. Bierwisch and E. Lang (eds.), 287–458. Berlin: Akademie-Verlag.

Lazarescu, M., S. Venkatesh, and G. West
1998 Combining NL processing and video data to query American Football. In *International Conference on Pattern Recognition,* 1238–1240.

Leisi, E.
1953 *Der Wortinhalt. Seine Struktur im Deutschen und Englischen.* Heidelberg: Winter.

Levelt, W. J. M.
1982 Cognitive styles in the use of spatial direction terms. In *Speech, place, and action,* R. J. Jarvella and W. Klein (eds.), 251–268). Chichester: Wiley.

Lockhead, G. R.
2004 Absolute judgments are relative: A reinterpretation of some psychophysical ideas. *Review of General Psychology* 8: 265–272.

Loomis, J. M., J. A. Da Silva, J. W. Philbeck, and S. S. Fukusima
1996 Visual perception of location and distance. *Current Directions in Psychological Science* 3: 72–7.

Mangold, R.
2003 Sprechen über Objekte. In *Psycholinguistik. Ein internationales Handbuch,* G. Rickheit, T. Herrmann, and W. Deutsch (eds.), 368–376. Berlin: de Gruyter.

Mangold, R., and R. Pobel
1988 Informativeness and instrumentality in referential communication. *Journal of Language and Social Psychology* 7: 181–191.

Mangold-Allwinn, R., S. Barattelli, M. Kiefer, and H. G. Koelbing
1995 *Wörter für Dinge. Von flexiblen Konzepten zu variablen Benennungen.* Opladen: Westdeutscher Verlag.

Mapp, A. P., and H. Ono
1999 Wondering about the wandering cyclopean eye. *Vision Research* 39: 2381–2386.

Martin, L., and G. Müller
1899 *Zur Analyse der Unterschiedsempfindlichkeit.* Leipzig: Barth.

Matin, L.
1986 Visual localization and eye movements. In *Handbook of Perception and Human Performance, Vol. 1: Sensory Processes and Perception,* K. R. Boff, L. Kaufman, and J. P. Thomas (eds.), 20/1–20/45. New York: Wiley.

Miller, G., and P. N. Johnson-Laird
1976 *Language and Perception.* Cambridge, UK: Cambridge University Press.

Mukerjee, A.
1997 Neat vs. scruffy: A survey of computational models for spatial expressions. In *Representation and Processing of Spatial Expressions,* P. Olivier and K.-P. Gapp (eds.). Hillsdale: Erlbaum.

Nagel, H.-H.
1999 From video to language – A detour via logic vs. jumping to conclusions. In *Integration of Speech and Image Understanding*, S. Wachsmuth and G. Sagerer (eds.), 79–100. IEEE Computer Society.

Naphade, M., T. Kristjansson, B. Frey, and T. Huang
1998 Probabilistic multimedia objects (Multijects): A novel approach to video indexing and retrieval in multimedia systems. In *International Conference on Image Processing,* 536–540.

Nothdurft, H. C.
1993 The role of features in preattentive vision: Comparison of orientation, motion and colour cues. *Vision Research* 33: 1937–1958.

O'Keefe, J., and L. Nadel
1978 *The Hippocampus as a Cognitive Map*. Oxford: Oxford University Press.

Olivier, P., T. Maeda, and J. Tsuji
1994 Automatic depiction of spatial description. In *AAAI-94,* 1405–1410.

Olson, D. R.
1970 Language and thought: Aspects of a cognitive theory of semantics. *Psychological Review* 77: 257–273.

Oviatt, S.
2002 Breaking the robustness barrier: Recent progress on the design of robust multimodal systems. In *Advances in Computers*, M. Zelkowitz (ed.), 305–341. San Diego: Academic Press.

Parducci, A.
1965 Category judgment: A range-frequency model. *Psychological Review* 72: 407–418.
1974 Contextual effects: A range-frequency analysis. In *Handbook of perception, Vol. 2,* E. C. Carterette and M. P. Friedman (eds.), 127–141. New York: Academic Press.

Parducci, A., R. C. Calfee, L. M. Marshall, and L. P. Davidson
1960 Context effects in judgment: Adaptation level as a function of the mean, midpoint, and median of the stimuli. *Journal of Experimental Psychology* 60: 64–77.

Pearl, J.
1988 *Probabilistic Reasoning in Intelligent Systems*. San Francisco: Morgan Kaufmann.

Pechmann, T.
1989 Incremental speech production and referential overspecification. *Linguistics*, *27*, 89–110.
1994 *Sprachproduktion. Zur Generierung komplexer Nominalphrasen*. Opladen: Westdeutscher Verlag.

Peeke, S. C., and G. C. Stone
1973 Focal and nonfocal processing of color and form. *Perception and Psychophysics* 14: 71–80.

Petrov, A., and J. R. Anderson
2005 The dynamics of scaling: A memory-based anchor model of category rating and absolute identification. *Psychological Review* 112: 383–416.

Regier, T.
1995 A model of the human capacity for categorizing spatial relations. *Cognitive Linguistics* 6: 63–88.

Regier, T., and L. A. Carlson
2001 Grounding spatial language in perception: An empirical and computational investigation. *Journal of Experimental Psychology: General* 130: 273–298.

Rickheit, G., and C. Vorwerg
2003 Situiertes Sprechen. In *Psycholinguistik. Ein internationales Handbuch,* G. Rickheit, T. Herrmann, and W. Deutsch (eds.), 279–294. Berlin: de Gruyter.

Rosch, E.
1973 On the internal structure of perceptual and semantic categories. In *Cognitive Development and the Acquisition of Language,* T. E. Moore (ed.), 111–144. New York: Academic Press.
1975 Cognitive reference points. *Cognitive Psychology* 7: 532–547.

Sarris, V.
1971 *Wahrnehmung und Urteil. Bezugssystemeffekte in der Psychophysik.* Göttingen: Hogrefe.
2000 Perception and judgment in psychophysics: An introduction into the frame-of-reference theories. In *Contributions to Acoustics: Results of the 8th Oldenburg Symposium on Psychological Acoustics,* A. Schick (ed.), 39–62. Oldenburg.

Schober, M. F.
1993 Spatial perspective taking in conversation. *Cognition* 47: 1–24.

Schultz, A. (ed.)
2004 *The intersection of cognitive science and robotics: From interfaces to intelligence.* Arlington: AAAI Press.

Smith, L. B.
1989 From global similarities to kinds of similarities: The construction of dimensions in the development. In *Similarity and analogical reasoning,* S. Vosniadou and A. Ortony (eds.), 146–175. New York: Cambridge University Press.

Socher, G.
1997 *Qualitative scene descriptions from images for integrated speech and image understanding.* Sankt Augustin: infix.

Socher, G., T. Merz, and S. Posch
1995 3D reconstruction and camera calibration from images with known objects. In *Proceedings of the British Machine Vision Conference, Vol. 1,* D. Pycock (ed.), 167–176). Birmingham.

Socher, G., G. Sagerer, and P. Perona
2000 Bayesian reasoning on qualitative descriptions from images and speech. *Image and Vision Computing* 18: 155–172.

Srihari, R. K.
1994 Computational models for integrating linguistic and visual information: A survey. *Artificial Intelligence Review* 8: 349–369.

Srihari, R., and D. Burhans
1994 Visual semantics: Extracting visual information from text accompanying pictures. In *Proceedings of the National Conference on Artificial Intelligence,* 793–798.

Stevens, S. S.
1975 *Psychophysics. Introduction to its perceptual, neural, and social prospects*. New York: Wiley.

Suhm, B., B. Myers, and A. Waibel
1996 Interactive recovery from speech recognition errors in speech user interfaces. In *International Conference on Spoken Language Processing,* 865–868.

Talmy, L.
1983 How language structures space. In *Spatial Orientation: Theory, Research and Application,* H. Pick and L. Acredolo (eds.), 225–282. Stanford: Stanford University Press.

Thomas, D. R., M. Lusky, and S. Morrison
1992 A comparison of generalization functions and frame of reference effects in different training paradigms. *Perception and Psychophysics* 51: 529–540.

Titchener, E. B.
1905 *Experimental Psychology. Vol. II. Part II. Instructor's Manual*. New York: MacMillan.

Treisman, A. M., and S. Gormican
1988 Feature analysis in early vision: Evidence from search asymmetries. *Psychological Review* 95: 15–48.

Vandeloise, C.
1988 Length, width, and potential passing. In *Topics in Cognitive Linguistics,* B. Rudzka-Ostyn (ed.), 403–427. Amsterdam: Benjamins.
1991 *Spatial propositions: A case study from French.* Chicago: Chicago University Press.

Vorwerg, C.
2001a *Raumrelationen in Wahrnehmung und Sprache. Kategorisierungsprozesse bei der Benennung visueller Richtungsrelationen.* Wiesbaden: Deutscher Universitäts-Verlag.
2001b Objektattribute: Bezugssysteme in Wahrnehmung und Sprache. In *Sprache, Sinn und Situation,* L. Sichelschmidt and H. Strohner (eds.), 59–74. Wiesbaden: Deutscher Universitäts-Verlag.

Vorwerg, C.
2001c Kategorisierung von Größen- und Formattributen. In *Experimentelle Psychologie. Abstracts der 43. Tagung experimentell arbeitender Psychologen*, A. Zimmer et al. (eds.). Lengerich: Pabst.
2001d Kategorisierung von Größen- und Formattributen. *Posterbeitrag, 43. Tagung experimentell arbeitender Psychologen*, Regensburg.
2003a Verstehen von Objektbenennungen. In *Psycholinguistik. Ein internationales Handbuch,* G. Rickheit, T. Herrmann and W. Deutsch (eds.), 609–622. Berlin: de Gruyter.
2003b Sprechen über Raum. In *Psycholinguistik. Ein internationales Handbuch,* G. Rickheit, T. Herrmann, and W. Deutsch (eds.), 376–399. Berlin: de Gruyter.
2003c Use of reference directions in spatial encoding. In *Spatial cognition III. Routes and navigation, human memory and learning, spatial representation and spatial reasoning,* C. Freksa, W. Brauer, C. Habel, and K. F. Wender (eds.), 321–347. Berlin: Springer.
2004 *Two kinds of attribute categorization.* Poster presented at the Annual Meeting of the American Psychological Society, Chicago, May 2004.
2006 *Selecting an attribute for object reference.* Manuscript in preparation.

Vorwerg, C., and G. Rickheit
1998 Typicality effects in the categorization of spatial relations. In *Spatial cognition. An interdisciplinary approach to representing and processing spatial knowledge,* C. Freksa, C. Habel, and K. F. Wender (eds.), 203–222. Berlin: Springer.
1999a Richtungsausdrücke und Heckenbildung beim sprachlichen Lokalisieren von Objekten im visuellen Raum. *Linguistische Berichte, 178,* 152–204.
1999b Kognitive Bezugspunkte bei der Kategorisierung von Richtungsrelationen. In *Richtungen im Raum,* G. Rickheit (ed.), 129–165. Wiesbaden: Westdeutscher Verlag.
2000 Repräsentation und sprachliche Enkodierung räumlicher Relationen. In *Räumliche Konzepte und sprachliche Strukturen,* C. Habel and C. von Stutterheim (eds.), 9–44. Tübingen: Niemeyer.

Vorwerg, C., and G. Socher
2006 *Sprachliche Spezifikation von Größen- und Formattributen. Bezugssysteme, Kontexteffekte und Interaktionen.* Manuscript in preparation.

Vorwerg, C., G. Socher, T. Fuhr, G. Sagerer, and G. Rickheit
1997 Projective relations for 3D space: Computational model, application, and psychological evaluation. In *Proceedings of AAAI-97,* 159–164. Cambridge, MA: MIT Press.

Vorwerg, C., G. Socher, and G. Rickheit
1996 Benennung von Richtungsrelationen. *Proceedings der zweiten Fachtagung der Gesellschaft für Kognitionswissenschaft*, 184–186. Hamburg: Universität Hamburg.

Vorwerg, C., and J. Sudheimer
2006 *Initial frame of reference selection and consistency in verbal localization.* Manuscript in preparation.
Vorwerg, C., and P. Weiß
2006 *How verb semantics affects the interpretation of spatial prepositions.* Manuscript in preparation.
Wachsmuth, S.
2001 *Multi-modal scene understanding using probabilistic models.* Dissertation. Bielefeld: Universität Bielefeld.
Wachsmuth, S., and G. Sagerer
2002 Bayesian Networks for Speech and Image Integration. In *Proceedings of the 18th National Conference on Artificial Intelligence*, 300–306. Edmonton.
Wachsmuth, S., S. Wrede, M. Hanheide, and C. Bauckhage
2005 An active memory model for cognitive computer vision systems. *KI – Künstliche Intelligenz* 2: 25–31.
Waibel, A., B. Suhm, M. T. Vo, and J. Yang
1997 Multimodal interfaces for multimedia information agents. In *Proceedings of the International Conference on Acoustics, Speech and Signal Processing*, 167–170.
Weiß, P., and S. Barattelli
2003 Das Benennen von Objekten. In *Sprachproduktion,* T. Herrmann and J. Grabowski (eds.), 587–621. Göttingen: Hogrefe.
Weiß, P., and R. Mangold
1997 Bunt gemeint, doch farblos gesagt: Wann wird die Farbe eines Objektes nicht benannt? *Sprache und Kognition* 16: 31–47.
Wever, E. G., and K. E. Zener
1928 The method of absolute judgment in psychophysics. *Psychological Review* 35: 466–493.
Witte, W.
1961 A mathematical model of reference systems and some implications for category scales. *Acta Psychologica* 19: 378–382.

Psycholinguistic experiments on spatial relations using stereoscopic presentation

Helmut Flitter, Thies Pfeiffer, and Gert Rickheit

Abstract. This contribution presents investigations of the usage of computer generated 3D stimuli for psycholinguistic experiments. In the first part, we introduce *VDesigner*. VDesigner is a visual programming environment that operates in two different modes, a design mode to implement the materials and the structure of an experiment, and a runtime mode to actually run the experiment. We have extended VDesigner to support interactive experimentation in 3D. In the second part, we describe a practical application of the programming environment. We have replicated a previous 2½D study of the production of spatial terms in a 3D setting, with the objective of investigating the effect of the presentation modes (2½D vs. 3D) on the choice of the referential system. In each trial, on being presented with a scene, the participants had to verbally specify the position of a target object in relation to a reference object. We recorded the answers of the participants as well as their reaction times. The results suggest that stereoscopic 3D presentations are a promising technology to elicit a more natural behavior of participants in computer-based experiments.

1. Introduction

1.1. Computer-based experiments raise the bar for empirical scientists

Modern empirical methods, such as eye gaze tracking or electroencephalography, provide the experimenter with high resolution data. However, to fully exploit their capabilities, the experimental setting has to be highly controlled and allow for exactly timed repetitions. Hence, the presentation of the multi-modal stimuli material is often controlled by computers. Conveniently, the presentation of auditory and visual stimuli is done directly using the multimedia hardware of today's standard computers.

This, however, increases the requirements for empirical scientists, who, in addition to their own profession, often have also to develop extensive skills in computer science to accomplish their daily work. Fortunately, there is a variety of tools available supporting the scientist's enterprise. Programming libraries, such as the free Python library Vision Egg for vision research, provide a powerful set of common routines to start with. Full featured packages, such as Neurobehavioral Systems' *Presentation* software or the *Experiment Builder* from SR Research, offer more guidance and also support for a broad range of hardware (e.g. fMRI scanners, EEG recording systems or response boxes). They often come with a programming language of their own. The eyetracking group at our Faculty of Technology (see Pomplun et al., this volume) have developed *VDesigner*, a visual programming environment for computer-based experiments (Koesling and Höner 2005; Koesling and Ritter 2001). VDesigner is as powerful and versatile as other, commercial experiment builder software; it has been in use for several years now and comes with an extensive set of components for stimuli presentation (audio, still pictures and movies) and recording. The developers of the VDesigner are driven by the motivation to make the implementation of an experiment design as easy as possible. VDesigner's high-level visual programming language is only one, but in our opinion a very effective way to achieve this. So fortunately, the bar seems to be lowering again.

1.2. 3D stimuli presentations for psycholinguistic experiments

In our natural surroundings, we perceive and organize our environment in a three-dimensional way (3D). We are, however, also familiar with two-dimensional (2D) representations – due to our experience with drawings or paintings, movies or television, to our exposure to advertising or to our work at the computer. This fact is exploited intensively in everyday life. In the context of computer assisted experimentation, the use of 2D materials, e.g. photographs, is particularly relevant as a convenient means to simulate 3D stimuli. Often, pictorial materials are presented in what has been termed 2½D mode (Marr 1982), i.e. 2D images of 3D scenes where only a restricted set of depth cues (Carr 1935) is available. In 2D images, linear perspective, relative or known size, coverage, shadows or texture gradients give at least a hint at depth (Hershenson 1999; Hochberg 1978). These monocular cues, however, then provide information different from those provided by binocular vision: Stereopsis, accommodation and convergence (Hershenson 1999) still tell us of the 2D nature of the picture we are looking at. Especially convergence and accommodation are relevant cues for computer-based experiments. They are used to discriminate depth information for distances between 0 m and 2 m (Cutting and Vishton 1995; Tresilian, Mon-Williams, and Kelly 1999), the typical distance between participant and screen. Yet when traditional monoscopic stimuli are presented, these cues cannot contribute to depth perception.

In a visual search experiment, Pomplun (1998) had participants view images using anaglyphic stereo (red-green). He showed that the presentation of 3D stimuli led to a variety of scanning strategies broader than when presenting the stimuli in 2D and suggested that even more natural conditions could be realized by means of 3D shutter glasses instead of the anaglyphic approach.

Gaggioli and Breining (2001) showed that the precision of depth estimation of single objects was significantly better when using stereoscopic instead of monoscopic presentations. According to their findings, this also holds for estimating depth differences of two objects. In their experiment on mental rotation – a stereoscopic version of Shepard and Metzler's (1971) classic that was originally run in monoscopic mode – they demonstrated that using stereoscopic presentation did not take a significant effect in terms of reaction times, but significantly increased the accuracy of the responses given by the participants.

Hence, it may be misleading to generalize the knowledge gained from psychological or psycholinguistic experiments using 2½D stimuli to the processing of visual information in natural environments without careful consideration. The restricted perception of depth could render such stimuli insufficient for the investigation of issues concerning 3D space, e.g. verbal localization or categorization.

1.3. Computer based 3D stimuli presentation – raising the bar even more?

Recent advances in 3D graphics hardware made Virtual Reality techniques available at reasonable prices. Using these for computer-based experimental research, we are able to overcome the restrictions of 2½D visual stimuli and allow a full stereoscopic presentation – something that Wheatstone (1838) certainly would have appreciated. Thus, we might increase external validity, i.e. get closer to natural experiences, while retaining internal validity, i.e. maintaining a high level of control.

While hardware is no longer an issue, the complexity of Virtual Reality software makes it difficult to apply Virtual Reality techniques to experimental research. The bar is rising again.

1.4. Lowering the bar – a visual programming approach

We believe that Virtual Reality technology probably is, but surely will be, a cornerstone to empirical research in cognitive sciences. This motivates us to put effort in the development of a high-level tool for experiment design. Our goal is provide scientists – novices to programming techniques – with the means to swiftly build robust Virtual Reality experiments. We start by extending our visual programming language for traditional computer-based experiment design to support a stereoscopic presentation of visual materials. In the interest of applicability and usability, the implementation will be based on a freely available 3D framework which will be encapsulated into a manageable set of active software components.

Figure 1. On the left, a stimulus from the original experiment in 2½D is shown. The stereoscopic stimulus is shown to the right. With shutter glasses, each eye sees its specific image. The picture printed here looks blurred as the images for the left and the right eye are shown simultaneously.

In the following section we will first describe the stereoscopic presentation technique and the hardware we used. The next section will then describe the VDesigner and a first implementation of basic components for the stereoscopic presentation of still images. After that, as a demonstration of the applicability of our approach, we will present a first experiment of a series comparing presentations using 2½D stimuli with presentations based on stereoscopic 3D (Figure 1). Besides testing the usability of our framework, the main objective of this study is to investigate whether or not the mode of presentation of stimuli has an effect on specific aspects of cognitive processing, in particular, on the choice of a frame of reference. The theoretical basis regarding the choice of a frame of reference for the verbal localization of objects has given rise to numerous pertinent experiments (see Vorwerg, 2001; Vorwerg, Wachsmuth, and Socher 2006). One of these experiments (Vorwerg and Sudheimer 2006) serves as the starting point for our empirical comparison.

We will conclude this chapter with the discussion of these first results, an overview of the experiments to follow, and an outline of the next steps regarding our 3D toolkit for experimental design.

2. Virtual Reality technology and hardware

2.1. Stereoscopic display

We choose a stereoscopic procedure for 3D stimulus presentation (Figure 1, right panel). Technically, the procedure is based on presenting perspectively correct pictures for the viewers' left and right eye respectively. A recent overview of the current state of the art regarding stereoscopic presentation technology can be found in McAllister (2002). For our study, we were interested in a low-cost solution, so we finally decided to use 3D shutter glasses (Figure 2). These are available for less than EUR 100.00 and are on the market for more than a decade. With 3D shutter glasses, the alternative perspectives are presented on a screen in rapid succession and the view of the "unstimulated" eye is obstructed through liquid crystal displays (LCDs).

Figure 2. A selection of the low-cost 3D shutter glasses tested in preparation of the experiments. The model on the right is a wired model from ELSA, the two others are infra-red wireless models from eDimensional (top) and H3D (left). The device at the left is a breakout box necessary for the software based solutions.

However, 3D shutter glasses are not the optimal solution, as they are obtrusive because the participants have to wear glasses. And the pictures are darker, as each eye only gets half the amount of light. Also, while the two perspectively shifted pictures allow the eyes to converge or diverge according to the intended depth, they still accommodate to the display screen (Holliman 2003) and thus not all binocular depth cues can be realized using this technique.

The glasses come in two kinds, wired or wireless using infra-red technology. The wireless models are slightly less obtrusive,but have been too prone to losing synchrony in our tests. For experiments we therefore recommend the wired models. They provide for an inexpensive solution for 3D presentation and, at the same time, for a naturalistic reproduction of colors, unlike anaglyphic (red-green) presentation techniques.

2.2. Computer hardware and graphic cards

The experiments were run on a 1.8 GHz Intel Celeron PC with 512 MB RAM running Windows XP with SP2. For the stereoscopic display we used a cathode ray tube display with 120 Hz in combination with 3D shutter glasses. The glasses (Figure 2) are low-cost models, which are sold for gaming purposes. In combination with standard 3D graphic adapters from NVIDIA and ATI, we first attempted to use an external breakout box in combination with a dedicated driver – a solution provided with most of the shutter glasses. As it turned out, these facilities did not prove as robust as required for scientific purposes. For one, they only allowed for full-screen stereoscopic display. Also, before switching to stereo mode, they needed a short initialization period during which the content was still presented monoscopically. And finally, we did not manage to switch back and forth between 3D and 2D content presentation during an experiment.

These problems were overcome by resorting to 3D graphics adapters that were capable of providing quad-buffer stereo facilities. These models provide the necessary output signal on board and no longer need the separate breakout box. Basic models with sufficient capabilities are available on the market at reasonable prices. We obtained a nVidia Quadro 4 980XGL AGP 128 from hp Compaq. In our tests, the graphics adapter-based solutions proved to be more stable, not exposing any of the restrictions of the breakout box solution: They did not require initialization and could even mix 2D and 3D content on one screen. Taken together, this provides substantially more freedom for experimental design. An additional advantage is that, with the graphics adapter-based solution, the debugging facilities of VDesigner can still be used when working with 3D components. Altogether, we can highly recommend the investment in this special purpose hardware – as it has saved us a lot of trouble..

3. Software

3.1. A visual programming environment for interactive experiments

For the implementation of our ideas of a stereoscopic presentation of stimuli, we cooperated with the eyetracking group at the Faculty of Technology. As a result, we were privileged to access the source code of VDesigner. Making use of its component based architecture we wrote a plug-in module, realizing our ideas. In the following, we will give a brief introduction to VDesigner and then go into detail about the extensions that we made to add support for stereoscopic 3D.

3.2. VDesigner basics

VDesigner is a visual programming environment for the design of computer-based experiments. It operates in two different modes, a design mode where the user can implement the experiment, and a runtime mode. Its graphic user interface (GUI) in design mode is divided into three major areas (Figure 3). The area in the center is a multilayer worksheet where an experiment can be programmed by selecting and joining high-level visual software components. The area on the left is a property page which shows the attributes of the visual component that is currently selected. The bar at the top provides menus for program control and a toolbar with a comprehensive repository of visual components.

Programming with VDesigner is done easily by selecting an appropriate component from the repository shown in the toolbar, placing the component on the workplace and connecting it to other components, thus specifying the program flow. The repository already contains a number of pre-defined components arranged by functional categories like 'Basics', 'System', 'Input', 'Graphics2D', 'FileIO', 'ScreenIO', and the like.

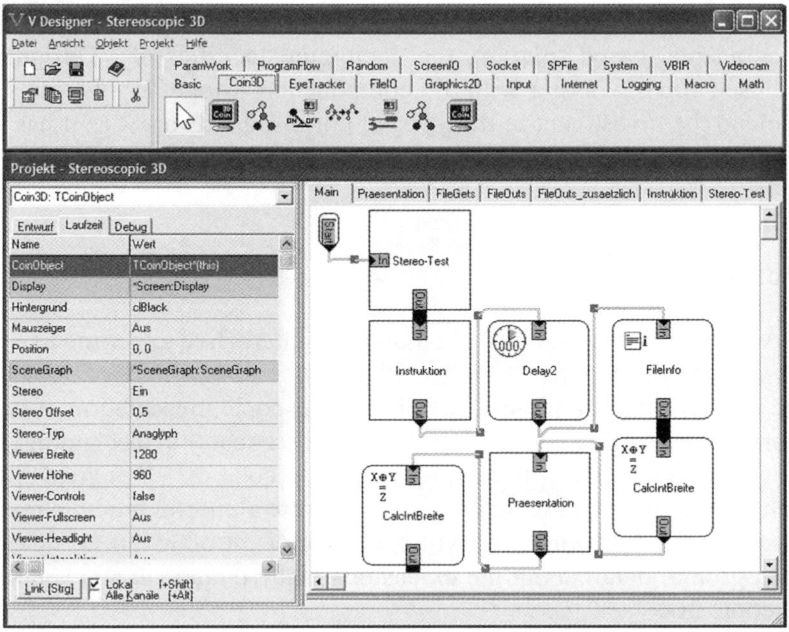

Figure 3. Design mode user interface of *VDesigner*. Major areas are: the worksheet (center), a property page (left), and a repository of visual components (top). The active property page shows a sample of the settings for the 3D presentation object.

The pre-defined components of VDesigner that provide functionality for

- stimulus presentation (audio, video, bitmap, or shapes),
- interaction handling (keyboard, mouse, or eye gaze),
- controlling the flow of the experiment,
- logging of events, and
- data recording.

Once an appropriate component, say an *ImageView* object for presenting a 2D picture, has been chosen from the repository and placed on the worksheet, it can further be configured using the property page. Here, all the attributes of the component (e.g. the location of the picture on the hard drive, or its position on the screen) can be modified. Finally, the components can be 'wired' to define the order of their execution. This way, a typical experiment comprising the presentation of pictures and the registration of keystrokes for reaction time measurement can be implemented with less than 20 components. More complex experiments like we did, involving the movement of objects by the participants accompanied by speech presentations, required up to one hundred or more components. Still it is easy to maintain an overview in such large projects, as special *Macro* components supply additional worksheet layers, allowing a high-level structuring of the experiment design. Thus, if required, researchers may define separate worksheets for introductory information, for training trails, and for different phases of the actual experiment (Figure 3).

3.3. Extending VDesigner to 3D

VDesigner provides a plug-in mechanism to allow for the integration of new components or collections of components. We decided to write our 3D extension as a collection of components which can be plugged into existing installations of VDesigner. This simplifies migration and ensures compatibility to existing projects. With an easy-to-use interface in mind, one of our design guidelines was to comply with the behavior of the existing components for presenting visual material. In our view, users should concentrate on what to present where and when, rather than having to bother about details of the presentation format. Switching between 2D and 3D modes should be as easy as exchanging a few components – this should also facilitate the upgrade of existing experiments to 3D. Still, while the design of 3D experiments within VDesigner has been kept as simple as possible, the creation of the 3D content may require additional skills. Fortunately, large collections of ready-to-go 3D objects are freely accessible via the internet. A good starting point could be the archive of stimulus material provided by Michael J. Tarr.

3.4. Components for 3D programming

For our implementation, we focused on the presentation of static 3D scenes, as we first wanted to be able to manage a robust 3D projection which is applicable for scientific research on visuospatial information processing in 3D. To date, the extension comprises four basic components:

- *Screen3D:* In VDesigner, the screen where 2D stimuli are to be shown is represented by a special *Screen* object. In line with this, we provided a *Screen3D* object for 3D stimuli. The difference is that the *Screen3D* object is again associated with the *Screen* object, so that 3D scenes can be shown either in a window against a 2D background or in full screen.

- *ConfigureScreen3D:* All the settings of the *Screen3D* object, such as its position and its size, its background color or the visibility of the mouse cursor, can be reconfigured during an experiment by means of the *ConfigureScreen3D* object.
- *SceneGraph:* While 2D content is defined in terms of bitmaps or videos, 3D content is defined in terms of a so-called scene graph. A scene graph provides all the information necessary to view 3D objects from any perspective. Each 3D scene presented during an experiment is represented by one special *SceneGraph* object. The presentation of the 3D scene is managed by *ChangeScene*.
- *ChangeScene:* This object is used to actually show the 3D content specified in a *SceneGraph* object on a *Screen3D*. This is different from the concept for presenting 2D content, as generally one and the same object is used to both specify the content and present it on the *Screen*. But since 3D scenes are more complex than 2D images, loading them from a file may take some time. While this may be a negligible factor for small scenes, the loading of larger scenes could impede the experiment. Therefore, we separated the functionality so that the scenes can be loaded at an uncritical point in time.

This surprisingly small number of components is all that is needed for ordinary experiments where static visual stimuli are presented to the participants for comprehension and reaction. We believe that the experiment presented below convincingly demonstrates this. There we use 3D stimuli in combination with reaction time measurement and speech recording. Beyond that, we are interested in the presentation of dynamic content and, in connection with that, the possibility to allow for an interaction of the user with the 3D scenery. This, however, is work yet to be done.

3.5. System integration

Technically, the implementation of the 3D extension is based on the open source *Coin3D* library (http://www.coin3d.org), a clone of the well-known *Open Inventor* framework. Coin3D is platform independent (it is available for Windows, Linux and MacOS), and it offers several advanced features of interest:

- *Monoscopic and stereoscopic projection:* Switching between monoscopic and stereoscopic display is as simple as pushing a button. Both software stereo and quad-buffer stereo are supported out of the box, and so is anaglyphic stereo.
- *File formats:* Coin3D supports popular file formats for 3D content: VRML, DXF and MultiGen Open Flight. VRML is also supported by free 3D editors, e.g. Blender 3D or WhiteDune, which can be used to create materials.
- *Animation:* It is possible to define dynamic content, e.g. moving objects or changing colors. This can be done in advance during the creation of the materials, or – in a more controlled manner – during the experiment.
- *Interaction:* All 3D objects are ready for interactive manipulation, for instance by means of a mouse or some special input devices.

Critical points in the software integration process were the embedding of the Coin3D window in VDesigner, the merger of the two different event systems for keyboard and mouse handling, and the synchronization of the different threads. Apart from these issues, the integration was straightforward.

4. The experiment

4.1. Participants

Ninety-six students from the University of Bielefeld participated in the 3D experiment in return for a payment of EUR 2.50 each. The mean age of the participants was 24.6 years. Of the 96 participants, 64 were females and 32 were males, 38 were enrolled in life sciences or technology, and 55 in social sciences or the humanities (3 answers missing). All participants had normal or corrected-to-normal vision; none were color blind.

4.2. Materials and procedure

Every participant viewed 32 pictorial stimuli in a fixed sequence. The stimuli were adapted from an earlier 2½D experiment (Vorwerg and Sudheimer 2005; see also Vorwerg, Wachsmuth, and Socher, this volume); they each showed a toy aircraft (as a reference object, or relatum) and a washer (as a target object). The participants' task was to verbally specify the location of the washer in relation to the aircraft. The actual position of the target was varied in 22.5° steps along a circle with the relatum at its center. In half of the trials, the relatum was rotated counterclockwise by 45° from the viewing axis (–45°; see Fig. 4a). In the other trials, it was rotated clockwise by 135° (+135°; see Fig. 4b). In Figures 4a and 4b, the arrowheads indicate the nose of the toy aircraft, and the numbered squares mark the positions of the washer. Participants were randomly assigned to one of two groups. One group viewed the 16 trials of the –45° condition first and then, without a break, the 16 trials of the +135° condition. For the other group of participants, the order of the trials was reversed.

In principle, it would have been possible to arrange the objects on different planes and at different levels (as indicated by the dotted lines in Figure 4c). However, in order to restrict to spatial layouts that lent themselves to interpretation, we did not exploit this possibility. We exclusively constructed 3D pictures in which the objects were located at the same level on a horizontal plane. The circle with the continuous line in Figure 4c marks this particular plane.

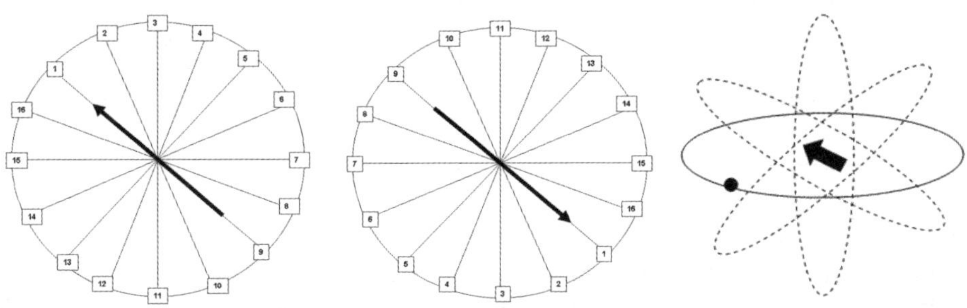

(a) target locations for the relatum rotated by –45°

(b) target locations for the relatum rotated by +135°

(c) plane and vertical angle of 3D presentation

Figure 4. The spatial arrangement of the stimuli (by courtesy from Vorwerg and Sudheimer 2006)

We were able to hold constant a number of factors by adopting the design of the previous 2½D experiment (orientation of the aircraft, positions of the washer) and by borrowing other materials from the previous study (e.g., the kind of objects used, the sequence of trials, and the instructions given to the participants).

Beyond that, it seemed reasonable to modify two details of the previous experiment. In their study, Vorwerg and Sudheimer (2006) used pictures which showed the aircraft and the washer lying on a wooden countertop. We are of the opinion that the (clearly visible) horizontal grain of the wooden countertop might take an effect on the verbal specifications of the relative positions of the objects. Therefore, we chose a uniform black background for the 3D displays.

The second modification was a limitation of the speech recording interval. We restricted this interval to 3000 ms in order to make the participants produce spontaneous utterances. This limitation also prevented any spillover from one trial to the next. With regard to data analysis, this modification called for robustification which will be discussed below.

4.3. Results

First, we computed the mean reaction times for all the trials in the 3D experiment ($M = 1533$ ms, $SD = 549$ ms). Trials with reaction times in excess of $M \pm 2$ SD were excluded from the analyses. For the sake of comparison of the 2½D experiment and the 3D experiment, we had to employ a standardized reaction time measure. So, the data from 2½D experiment were truncated in the same way as the data from the 3D experiment.

4.3.1. Answers

In the first step of the analysis, we compared the distributions of the answers given in the two experiments. For analysis, the answers were assigned to categories: Answers such as *somewhat below on the left*, *a little below on the left*, or *slightly below on the left* were pooled. Overall, there was a significant difference between the two experiments in the distributions of the answer categories (χ^2 (1, N = 5339) = 952.61, $p < .001$). Strikingly, the frequencies of the answers *above* and *below* (each with or without additional specifications such as *above on the right*) differed in that these answers hardly ever occurred in the 2½D experiment but were comparatively frequent in the 3D experiment (Fig. 5). In contrast, the answers *in front* and *in back* (again with or without additional specifications such as *in back on the left*) were given more frequently in the 2½D experiment than in the 3D experiment.

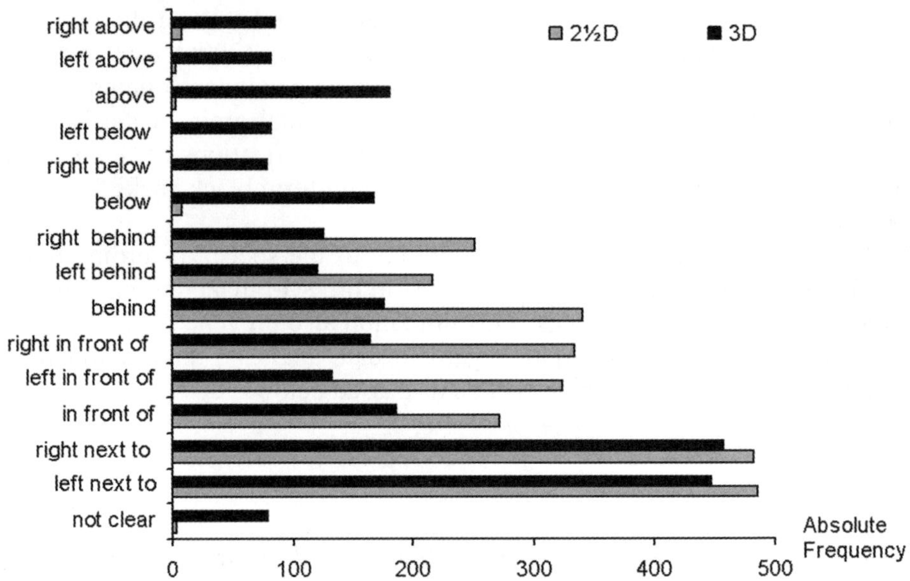

Figure 5. Answers (by categories) in the 2½D and the 3D experiment

Moreover, there was a comparatively high proportion of answers in the 3D experiment that had to be categorized as "other". Among these, there were contradictory answers (e.g. *below in front*, or *above in back*) or answers that contained self-corrections (*left; no, right in front*, or *left in front; oops, in back*).

4.3.2. Choice of referential system by mode of presentation

Each answer was categorized as to its occurrence under the various modes of presentation (2½D vs. 3D). Also, each answer was categorized as to its indicating the use of a particular referential system. At that, the categorization of an answer was done according to the factorial structure of the experiments: We had to take into consideration the combination of the orientation of the relatum (–45° vs. +135°) and the absolute position of the target object (16 levels). To give an example: If the washer were located at an (approximate) "10 o'clock" position (cf. Fig. 4a and 4b), the utterance *left in front* would indicate an intrinsic (i.e., relatum-based) referential system if the aircraft were rotated by –45° but a deictic (i.e., viewer-based) frame of reference if the aircraft were rotated by +135°.

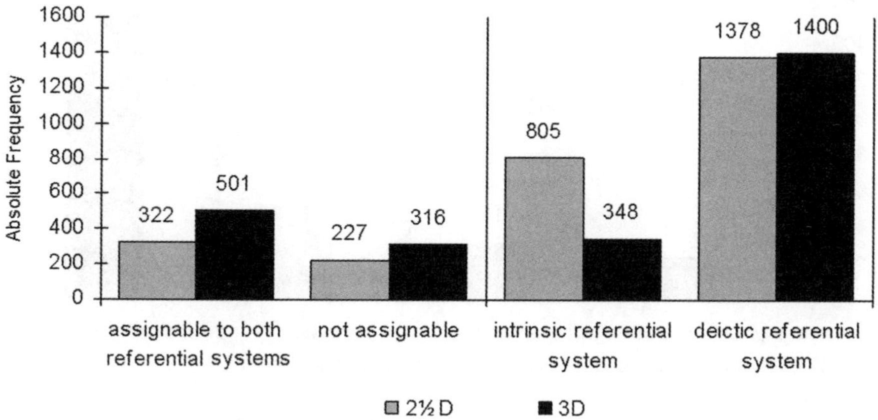

Figure 6. Choice of referential system by mode of presentation

The frequencies (Fig. 6) show significant differences between the two modes of presentation in the choice of an intrinsic or a deictic referential system (χ^2 (1, N = 5297) = 229.79, p < .001). More detailed analyses elucidate the origin of this difference. If we take into consideration only those answers that allow a clear-cut assignment to either an intrinsic or a deictic frame of reference (Fig. 6, right side), we find a statistically significant difference between distributions (χ^2 (1, N = 3931) = 134.82, p < .001): The deictic referential system is preferred (with almost the same frequency) in both presentation modes; in contrast, the non-preferred intrinsic system is even less likely to occur in 3D mode than in 2½D mode. No such effects were found for those answers (Fig. 6, left side) which could not be assigned unequivocally to one of the two referential systems (χ^2 (1, N = 1366) = 0.98, p = .323).

4.3.3. *Choice of referential system by orientation of the relatum*

In the further course of the analyses, we checked whether the orientation of the relatum takes an effect on the participants' choice of a referential system. When considering all valid answers (Fig. 7), it is obvious that the orientation of the relatum (–45° vs. +135°) indeed is a factor to be taken into account in the establishment of a frame of reference for the generation of a verbal object localization (χ^2 (3, N = 5297) = 192.07, p < .001).

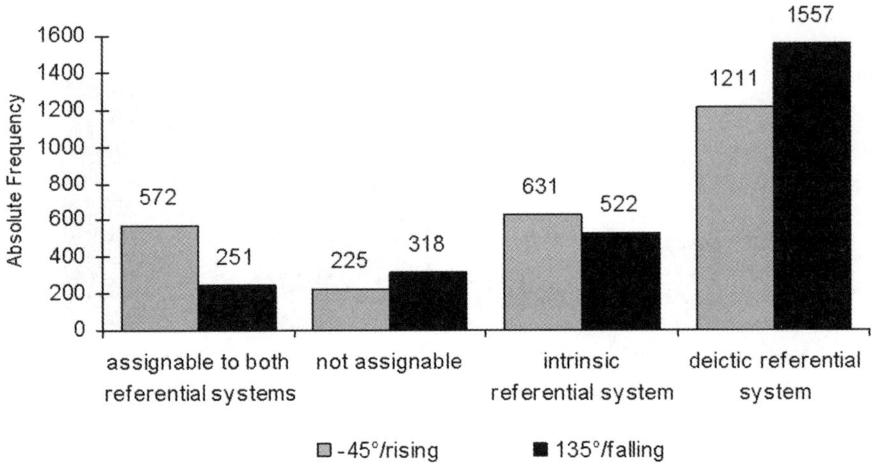

Figure 7. Choice of referential system by orientation of the relatum

On separating the two modes of presentation, and again taking into consideration only those answers that unequivocally can be assigned to either an intrinsic or a deictic frame of reference, analyses of the frequency distributions show that the effect can be traced back to the 2½D presentation mode (Fig. 8, left side: χ^2 (1, N = 2183) = 41.90, p < .001), while there is no such effect in the 3D mode (Fig. 8, right side: χ^2 (1, N = 1748) = 0.01, p = .935).

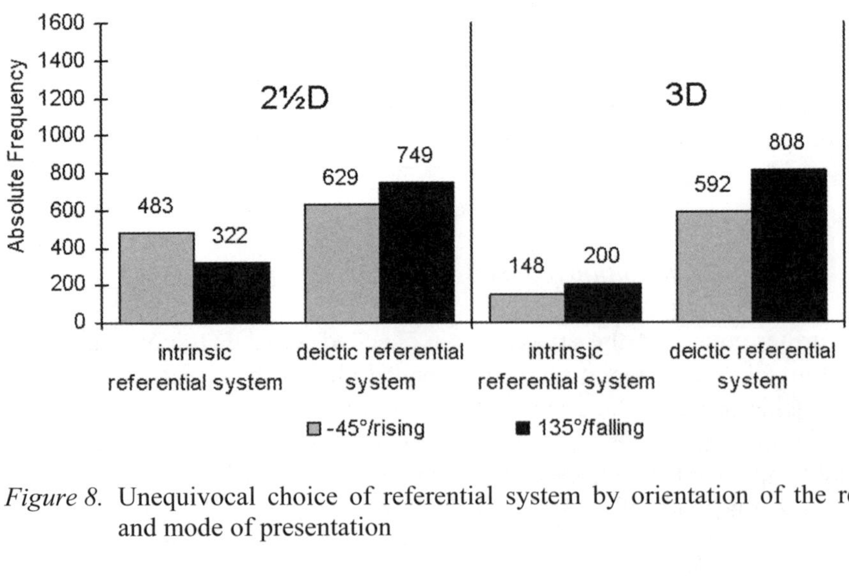

Figure 8. Unequivocal choice of referential system by orientation of the relatum and mode of presentation

4.3.4. Choice of referential system by target position

We also investigated if, and in which way, the choice of a referential system depends on the position of the washer in relation to the aircraft. In order to simplify the analysis, the trials were divided into 3 categories, according to the location of the target: Trials in which the target was located ideally in terms of a deictic referential system (25% of the trials), those with the target located ideally in terms of an intrinsic referential system (another 25% of the trials), and finally, those trials with the target located not ideally (the remaining 50%).

Overall analyses of the frequency distributions showed that the position of the target object did in fact influence the choice of referential system, both in 2½D presentation mode (χ^2 (6, N = 2732) = 432.85, p < .001) and in 3D presentation mode (χ^2 (6, N = 2565) = 174.02, p < .001). Figure 9 gives a summary overview of the empirical frequencies. On a closer look, however, the contingencies did not turn out as hypothesized: A deictic frame of reference was clearly chosen in 2778 trials (52.4% of the trials), and thus, clearly preferred over an intrinsic frame of reference which was chosen in 1153 trials (21.8%). A preference for the deictic reference frame even showed in those trials that lent themselves to structuring in terms of intrinsic reference. Likewise, the participants chose the deictic referential referential in 1287 (48.4%) of 2660 trials in which the target was not located ideally.

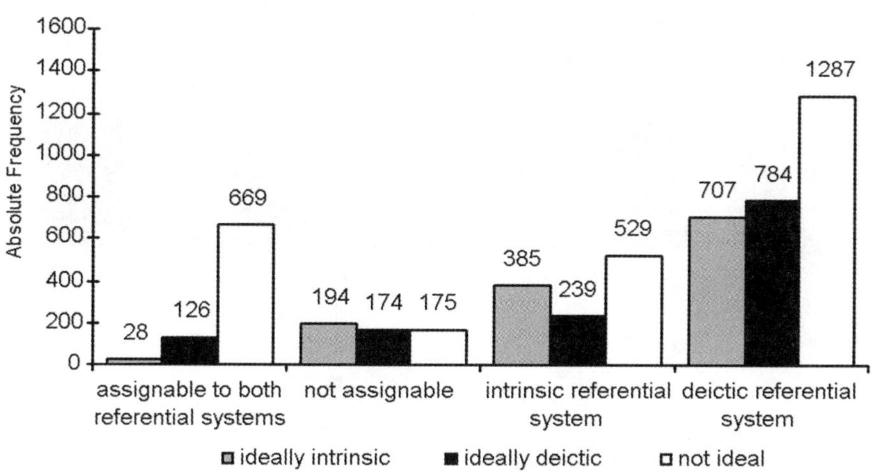

Figure 9. Choice of referential system by target position categories

4.3.5. Reaction times by mode of presentation

The difference between the onset of the 3D stimulus presentation and the onset of the speech in the wave recordings was taken to measure the reaction times of the participants. The wave files have been semi-automatically annotated for this. For analysis, we computed the means for both presentation modes separately. The mean reaction time in the 2½D experiment was 1439 ms (SD = 456.2); the mean reaction time in the 3D experiment was 1532 ms (SD = 445.9). The difference of approximately 100 ms proved to be statistically significant ($F(1, 5337) = 56.32$; $p < .001$).

4.3.6. Reaction times by referential system

The dependency of the reaction times on the referential system chosen is visualized in Figure 10 separately for the 2½D and the 3D experiment. The answers that were clearly given on the basis of a deictic reference frame took 1489 ms while those that were given on the basis of an intrinsic referential system took 1405 ms on average. Answers that were not assignable to any of the referential systems took 1632 ms, and indifferent answers took 1164 ms.

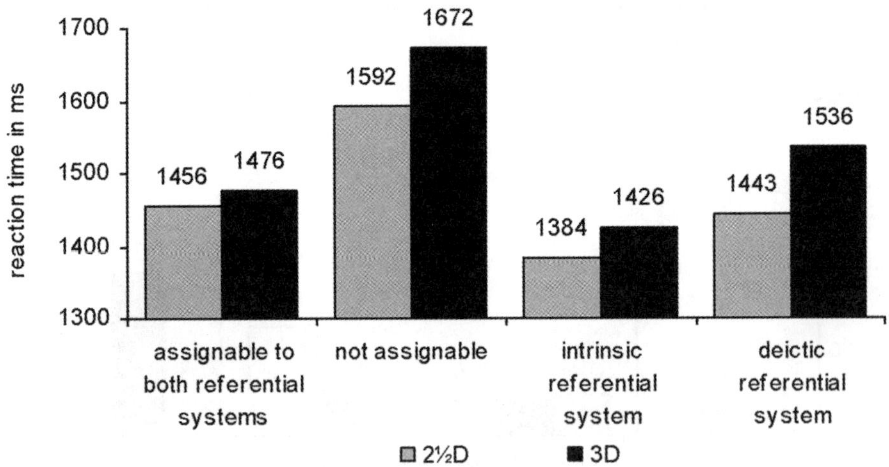

Figure 10. Reaction times by referential system

Separate one-way analyses of variance showed a significant effect of the choice of referential system on reaction times for the 2½D mode of presentation ($F(3, 2728) = 12.79$; $p < .001$) as well as for the 3D presentation mode ($F(3, 2561) = 20.16$; $p < .001$). Scheffé post hoc comparisons revealed the same pattern of results to hold for the two modes of presentation: The reaction times for the non-assignable answers were significantly longer than those for the other answer categories (all $p < .001$). Furthermore, the reaction times for answers given on the basis of a deictic frame of reference were longer than those given on the basis of an intrinsic frame of reference ($p = .034$ and $p = .001$, respectively). The remaining post hoc comparisons did not reach significance.

4.3.7. Reaction times by target positioning

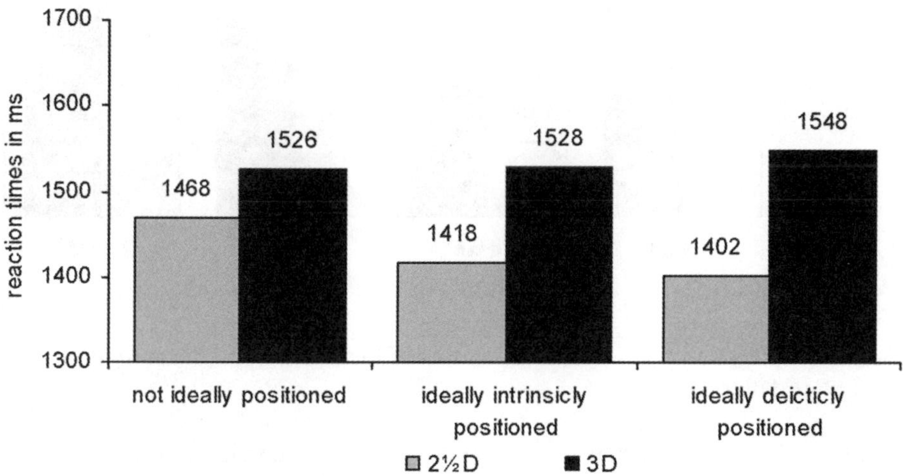

Figure 11. Reaction times by target position categories

Next, we investigated if and how reaction times were affected by the position of the target. As described above, target positions were encoded as a three-level factor comprising the categories 'location ideal for deictic reference', 'location ideal for intrinsic reference', and 'location not ideal'. Again, we conducted separate one-way analyses of variance of the 2½D and the 3D data. These data are visualized in summary in Figure 11. In the 2½D experiment, the position of the target had a significant effect on reaction time

(F (2, 2729) = 5.72; p = .003). Scheffé post hoc tests revealed a significant difference between the non-ideal location and the ideal-intrinsic location of the target (p = .009) on the one hand, and a marginally significant difference between the non-ideal and the ideal-deictic location of the target (p = .067) on the other hand. In contrast to this, in the 3D experiment no such effects were found (F (2, 2604) = 0.53; p = .589).

4.3.8. Reaction times by orientation of the relatum and presentation order

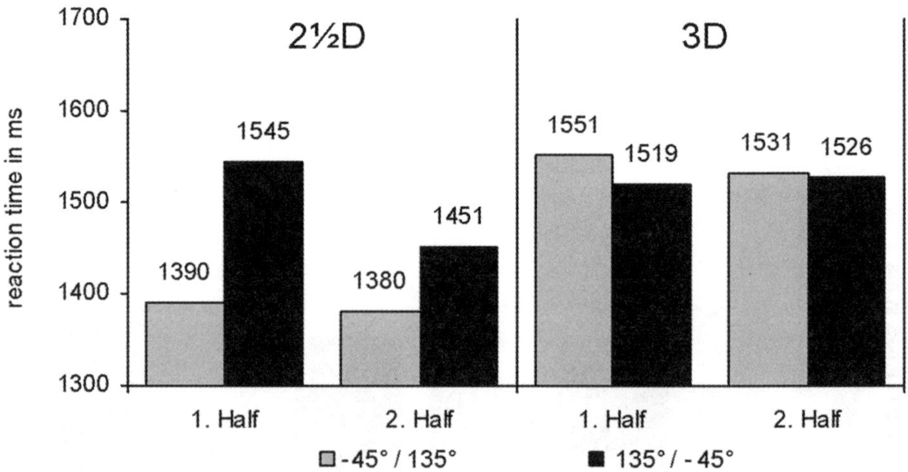

Figure 12. Reaction times by the orientation of the relatum and the order of presentation

Finally, we were interested in finding out how far the orientation of the relatum (–45° vs. +135°) and the change in orientation after the first half of the trials influenced reaction times. As described above, one group of participants completed the –45° trials before proceeding to the +135° trials in the second half of the experiment; in a second group, the order of presentation was reversed. We hypothesized that, in comparison, the +135° orientation of the relatum would be the more difficult one because, irrespective of the participant's choice of the referential system, it calls for a higher mental rotation effort in order to correctly name the position of the target. This higher cognitive effort should manifest in longer reaction times, and any effects of routinization should become apparent in a decrease in reaction latency over time.

Separate two-way analyses of variance were conducted for the 2½D and the 3D experiment. The factors entered in the analyses were the orientation of the relatum (–45° vs. +135°) and the order of presentation (–45°/+135° vs. +135°/–45°). Figure 12 gives the mean reaction times.

In the 2½D data, we found significant main effects of the orientation of the relatum ($F(1, 2728) = 5.85$; $p = .016$) and of the order of presentation of trials ($F(1, 2728) = 42.63$; $p < .001$) on reaction time. In addition, there was a significant interaction between the two factors, orientation and order ($F(1, 2731) = 8.84$; $p = .003$). In contrast, in the 3D data, neither the orientation ($F(1, 2603) = 0.59$; $p = .44$), nor the order ($F(1, 2603) = 1.17$; $p = .28$), nor their interaction ($F(1, 2606) = 0.14$; $p = .71$) took any effect.

4.4. Discussion

A previous 2½D experiment was the starting point for our study. We intended to investigate to what extent the findings from the 2½D experiment transfer to information processing in three-dimensional space. Therefore, we did a replication of the 2½D study in 3D, borrowing the design from the previous experiment but using stereoscopic presentation instead. In the experiment presented we removed the table from the stimuli, as its presence and especially its texture are controversial. The experiment was programmed and the stimuli were presented using an extended version of the VDesigner visual programming environment.

We found differences between the two modes of presentation in several of the analyses conducted. Generally, the processing of 3D materials took longer, and led to different answering strategies, than the processing of the 2½D materials. Hence, we assume that the processing of our three-dimensional pictorial stimuli takes more cognitive effort – and possibly, requires different cognitive processes – than the processing of the 2½D stimuli. As a consequence, this means that the results obtained in the 2½D scenario cannot be generalized to the 3D scenario without caution. This view is substantiated by two converging lines of evidence – one concerning the referential systems chosen in verbal object localization, i.e., qualitative aspects of processing, and one concerning the time required to accomplish this task, i.e., quantitative aspects.

Qualitatively, we found a wider variety of answers in 3D mode as compared to 2½D mode, although the instructions were identical in both experiments. The fact that the terms *above* and *below* were used frequently in the 3D experiment but hardly ever in the 2½D experiment, together with the fact that these terms often were accompanied by some further specification, suggest that simple answers are not sufficient to unequivocally describe the relative position of an object in three-dimensional space. The large proportion of answers that could not clearly be assigned to one particular frame of reference in the 3D experiment emphasizes the difficulties that are inherent in the verbal localization task.

Regarding referential systems, we were able to demonstrate that the deictic referential system which requires comparatively little cognitive effort was preferred, and used almost equally often, in both modes of presentation. In contrast, the intrinsic referential system which, in terms of cognitive effort, is rather demanding, was used much less frequently with 3D stimuli.

We were able to observe a comparable result for the choice of the referential system in dependence of the position of the relatum. We found that the effect of the simpler position of the relatum (–45°) was that the intrinsic referential system was chosen more often with the 2½D-presentation. The facilitating effect was not present for the 3D presentation; here the deictic system was always preferred. The preference of the simpler deictic referential system for the 3D mode of presentation was an observation we made with various independent variables (position of the relatum, ideal positioning of the target).

Further indication in favor of our assumption that the processing of the tasks in the three-dimensional mode of presentation shows a higher level of complexity is provided by the observations on the reaction times. On average, the reaction times for the 3D experiment were by 100 ms longer when looking at all measurements.

We found concordances between the experiments in regard to reaction times in connection with the chosen referential system. In both modes of presentation the fastest answers were given when an intrinsic referential system was chosen. At first sight, this finding is counterintuitive; one might have expected that the processing of the pictures on the basis of the intrinsic referential system increases the effort for the participants, thus leading to longer reaction times. Therefore, we assume that once the participant has mastered the task of "imagining oneself" to be in the scenario, he or she can name the target positions very quickly from the intrinsic point of view. This is even the case when the position of the relatum changes.

The increase in reaction times may be surprising and cannot be explained with this first experiment alone. A potential explanation is that the presence of the table surface with the structured texture in the 2½D stimuli induces a reduction of space to two degrees of freedom. Target and relatum are constantly perceived to be at the same level, the plane defined by the tabletop.

The increased freedom present in the 3D stimuli, which is documented by the diversification in the answer categories, consequentially made it harder to qualify the exact positions. This might be the case even though the participants have explicitly been told that both objects are positioned in the same plane. A more direct explanation could be that the stereoscopic display based on 3D glasses is more obtrusive and might have induced a feeling of uncertainty in untrained participants.

5. Conclusion

From a psycholinguistic perspective, the qualitative results of the experiments are promising. When perceiving 3D stimuli using a stereoscopic display, the participants used categories for the full range of 3D space. Thus research in e.g. spatial localization can benefit from this way of stimulus presentation.

5.1. Further experiments

The experiment presented is the first of a series of psycholinguistic experiments to investigate differences between 2½D and perspective or stereoscopic 3D presentations. In an upcoming experiment we will investigate how the presentation of the textured background influences both reaction times and categorization. This experiment and the experiment presented in this chapter will then be replicated using perspective 3D presentations only. The settings will be exactly the same, the participants will still have to wear the glasses, but there will be no difference between the images presented to both eyes and thus no stereoscopic effect. We hope that these conditions will shed more light on the questions raised in Section 4.4.

Another important question which remains to be investigated under a psycholinguist's perspective is, how close the computer-based experiments using stereoscopic 3D are to natural settings in "real (laboratory) life".

5.2. Remarks on the visual programming approach

The experiment presented was programmed with our extension for 3D stereoscopic presentations for the visual programming environment VDesigner. A student of computer linguistics, novice to the concepts of Virtual Reality graphics, was able to swiftly realize the implementation with only shallow training. As expected, the creation of the VRML files representing the 3D stimuli turned out to be the time consuming factor. Under the objective to achieve a similar visual appearance when rendered to screen, we had to carefully recreate the complex toy aircraft with our 3D models for the replication of the original experiment. We expect that the modeling time will be negligible, once a pool of appropriate generic 3D models for a research line has been built.

5.3. Future work

Having the possibility of producing static 3D stimuli on low-cost hardware greatly enhances the empirical methods available, especially for our own psycholinguistic research interests. Our research focuses on natural language instructions in construction task domains. In this scenario instructions are mostly about actions over objects. Investigating the processes involved in producing and understanding spatial references is therefore one of our special interests. Here the presentation of static 3D scenes already is sufficient. The next logical step is the development of components for manipulating these scenes dynamically during the experiment, either controlled programmatically or mediated through user interaction. This would further assist in the understanding of the part of the instruction describing the action.

The experiment presented in this chapter recorded speech and measured reaction-times. This allows us to get some idea of the general performance of the cognitive processes. To get closer to the processes involved especially when understanding spatial references, we are planning to combine the presentation of 3D stimuli with eye gaze tracking. While the VDesigner already provides components for eye gaze tracking, the following issues remain to be solved:

5.3.1. 3D calibration of eye tracker systems

Eye gaze tracking is an unobtrusive and highly informative measurement technique that has become increasingly popular in experimental research in cognitive science during the last years (e.g., Hyönä, Radach, and Deubel 2003). It is also a highly sensitive technique though, which requires careful calibration of the system prior to an experiment and frequent recalibrations (for drift correction) during an experiment. Standard eye tracking software provides extensive calibration facilities for both small-scale and large-scale presentation; however, these are tailored for 2D stimuli in that the software only returns the coordinates of fixations on the vertical plane that is used for stimulus presentation.

In order to enable eye movement tracking in 3D environments or in combination with 3D stimulus presentation, the software should ideally provide information on fixation coordinates in 3D space. As this is not supported yet by the standard software available from the manufacturers of eye tracking systems, we will have to develop our own calibration routines for the 3D setting. First experiments have already been carried out by Pomplun (1998), Essig, Pomplun, and Ritter (2004; 2005), and Pomplun et al. (2005) who used anaglyphic projections. Their solution is based on Parameterized Self-Organizing Maps (PSOMs), and we are confident that this solution will scale up when applied to our shutter glass approach.

5.3.2. Combining shutter glasses with eye tracker cameras

There is a conflict between the shutter-glasses needed to present the 3D content and the camera-based eye tracking technique being used. On the one hand the eye tracker wants to track the eyes and on the other hand we have to cover them with glasses. Looking through the glasses is not an option, as they always switch from a transparent to a blackened state, thus irritating the eye tracking software. We already managed to handle this problem by adjusting the cameras to look at the eyes from beneath the frame of the shutter-glasses, but we need to thoroughly test this approach before we can use it in an experiment. An alternative would be the usage of auto-stereoscopic displays which allow the presentation of stereoscopic images without the need for glasses.

Acknowledgements

We would like to thank Constanze Vorwerg and Janin Sudheimer for the data of the 2½D-experiment, Guido Heumer and Christian Zimmermann for the construction of the material and the programming of our experiment, and Bartosz Zielinski for his assistance in data analysis. – This research was conducted within the scope of the Collaborative Research Center 360 (projects A6, B4, C1, and C3) under a grant from the German Research Foundation (Deutsche Forschungsgemeinschaft).

References

Carr, H. A.
1935 *An Introduction to Space Perception.* New York: Longman's, Green.

Cutting, J. E., and P. M. Vishton
1995 Perceiving layout and knowing distances: The integration, relative potency, and contextual use of different information about depth. In *Handbook of Perception and Cognition: Perception of Space and Motion,* W. Epstein, and S. Rogers (eds.), 69–117. New York: Academic Press.

Essig, K., M. Pomplun, and H. Ritter
2004 Application of a Novel Neural Approach to 3D Gaze Tracking: Vergence Eye-Movements in Autostereograms, In *Proceedings of the 26th Annual Meeting of the Cognitive Science Society,* K. Forbus, D. Gentner, and T. Regier (eds.), 357–362. Mahwah: Erlbaum.
2005 A neural network for 3D gaze recording with binocular eye trackers. *International Journal of Parallel, Emergent, and Distributed Systems* (in press).

Gaggioli, A., and R. Breining
2001 Perception and cognition in immersive Virtual Reality. In *Communications Through Virtual Technology: Identity Community and Technology in the Internet Age,* G. Riva and F. Davide (eds.), 71–86, Amsterdam: IOS Press.

Hershenson, M.
1999 *Visual Space Perception.* Cambridge, MA: MIT Press.

Hochberg, J. E.
1978 *Perception (2nd ed.).* Englewood Cliffs: Prentice-Hall.

Hyönä, J., R. Radach, and H. Deubel (eds.)
2003 *The Mind's Eye. Cognitive and Applied Aspects of Eye Movement Research.* Amsterdam: Elsevier.

Koesling, H., and O. Höner
2002 VDesigner – eine visuelle Programmierumgebung für Eye-Tracking-Experimente in der sportspielspezifischen Expertiseforschung. In *Expertise im Sport: Lehren, Lernen, Leisten,* B. Strauss, M. Tietjens, N. Hagemann, and A. Stachelhaus (eds.), 211–222. Köln: BPS.

Koesling, H., and H. Ritter
2001 *VDesigner – A visual programming environment for eye tracking experiments.* Presented at 11th European Conference on Eye Movements, Turku, Finland.

Marr, D.
1982 *Vision: A Computational Investigation Into the Human Representation and Processing of Visual Information.* San Francisco: Freeman.

McAllister, D. F.
2002 Display Technology: Stereo and 3D Display Technologies. In *Wiley Encyclopedia of Imaging Science and Technology*, J. P. Hornack (ed.), 1327–1344. New York: Wiley.

Pomplun, M.
1998 *Analysis and Models of Eye Movements in Comparative Visual Search.* Göttingen: Cuvillier.

Pomplun, M., E. Carbone, H. Koesling, L. Sichelschmidt, and H. Ritter
2006 Computational models of visual tagging. In *Situated Communication,* G. Rickheit and I. Wachsmuth (eds.), 209–241. Berlin: de Gruyter (this volume).

Pomplun, M., E. Carbone, L. Sichelschmidt, B. M. Velichkovsky, and H. Ritter
2005 How to disregard irrelevant stimulus dimensions: Evidence from comparative visual search. In *Proceedings of ICCI 2005 – 4th IEEE International Conference on Cognitive Information,* W. Kinsner, D. Zhang, Y. Wang, and J. Tsai (eds.), 183–192. Piscataway: IEEE.

Shepard, R. N., and J. Metzler
1971 Mental rotation of three-dimensional objects. *Science* 171: 701–703.

Tresilian, J. R., M. Mon-Williams, and B. M. Kelly
1999 Increasing confidence in vergence as a cue to distance. *Proceedings of the Royal Society of London,* 266B: 39–44.

Vorwerg, C.
2001 *Raumrelationen in Wahrnehmung und Sprache. Kategorisierungsprozesse bei der Benennung visueller Richtungsrelationen.* Wiesbaden: Deutscher Universitäts-Verlag.
2003 *Cognitive reference directions in spatial categorization and reference frame selection*, Presented at 23rd Conference of the European Society for Cognitive Psychology, Granada, Spain.

Vorwerg, C., and J. Sudheimer
2006 *Initial frame of reference selection and consistency in verbal localization.* Manuscript in preparation.

Vorwerg, C., S. Wachsmuth, and G. Socher
2006 Visually Grounded Language Processing in Object Reference. In *Situated Communication,* G. Rickheit and I. Wachsmuth (eds.), 77–126. Berlin: de Gruyter (this volume).

Wheatstone, C.
1838 Contributions to the physiology of vision I: On some remarkable and hitherto unobserved phenomena of vision. *Philosophical Transactions of the Royal Society of London*, 128: 371–395.

Deictic object reference in task-oriented dialogue

Alfred Kranstedt, Andy Lücking, Thies Pfeiffer, Hannes Rieser, and Ipke Wachsmuth

Abstract. This chapter presents a collaborative approach towards a detailed understanding of the usage of pointing gestures accompanying referring expressions. This effort is undertaken in the context of human-machine interaction integrating empirical studies, theory of grammar and logics, and simulation techniques. In particular, we take steps to classify the role of pointing in deictic expressions and to model the focused area of pointing gestures, the so-called pointing cone. This pointing cone serves as a central concept in a formal account of multi-modal integration at the linguistic speech-gesture interface as well as in computational models of processing multi-modal deictic expressions.

1. Introduction

Deixis, especially deictic expressions referring to objects, play a prominent role in the research undertaken in the course of the Collaborative Research Center 360. This research focuses on scenarios in the construction task domain. A typical setting has two interlocutors communicating in face-to-face manner about the construction of mechanical objects and devices using a kit consisting of generic parts. In the investigated dialogues both participants typically use deictic expressions consisting of speech and gesture to specify tasks and select relevant objects.

This setting is also applied in the development of human computer interfaces for natural interaction in Virtual Reality (VR). Doing so, we employ an anthropomorphic virtual agent called "Max" who is able on the one hand to interpret simple multi-modal input by a human instructor, and on the other hand to produce synchronized output involving synthetic speech, facial display, and hand gestures (Kopp and Wachsmuth 2004). To improve the communicative abilities of Max, he needs to be equipped with the competence to understand and produce multi-modal deictic expressions in a natural manner.

This chapter describes (1) a genuine effort in collecting multi-resolutional empirical data on human pointing behavior, (2) formal considerations concerning the interrelation between pointing and referring expressions in dialogue, and (3) the application of the results in the course of reference resolution and utterance generation for the agent Max.

There is little doubt in the cognitive science literature that pointing is tied up with reference in various ways. Since Peirce at least, this has been the philosophers' concern when discussing reference and ostension. Its systematic investigation was considerably pushed ahead by McNeill's (1992; 2000) and Kendon's (1981; 2004) work on gesture. Especially McNeill's thesis that gesture and speech form an "idea unit" spread and has been reconstructed in cognitive psychology paradigms (de Ruijter 2000; Krauss, Chen, and Gottesman 2003). Moreover, the tight relation between motor skills and grasp of reference is investigated in developmental psychology. The index finger's prominent role for the evolution of species is a topic in anthropology and biology (Butterworth 2003). Concerning the ontogeny of pointing, there is a social and cultural-specific reinforcement of the infant coupling index-finger extension with the use of syllabic sounds (Masataka 2003). Clark's (1996) interactionist approach treats pointing as information on a concurrent dialogue track, and pointing and placing as attention getters in his recent article (Clark 2003).

The following quotation from Lyons (1977: 654), early as it is, subsumes much of the linguists' wisdom concerning the field of deixis and reference: "When we identify an object by pointing to it (and this notion, as we have seen, underlies the term 'deixis' and Peirce's term 'index' [...]), we do so by drawing the attention of the addressee to some spatiotemporal region in which the object is located. But the addressee must know that his attention is being drawn to some object rather than to the spatiotemporal region."

Pointing, then, is related to objects indicated and regions occupied. Lyons (1977: 657) also emphasizes that certain kinds of expressions are closely linked to pointing or demonstration: "Definite referring noun-phrases, as they have been analysed in this section, always contain a deictic element. It follows that reference by means of definite descriptions depends ultimately upon deixis, just as much as does reference by means of demonstratives and [...] personal pronouns."

However, it is not discussed in the literature how exactly pointing and verbal expressions are related compositionally. This is our main focus of interest here. Pursuing it, we follow a line of thought associated with Peirce, Wittgenstein and Quine, who favor the idea of gestures being part of more complex signs. Transferring this idea to deictic expressions we shall henceforth call complex signs composed of a pointing gesture and a referring expression *complex demonstration*. In other words, complex demonstrations are definite descriptions to which pointing adds content, either by specifying an object independently of the definite description (Lyons's 'attention being drawn to some object') or by narrowing down the description's restrictor (Lyons's 'spatiotemporal region'). In what follows, we refer to these two possibilities as the respective functions of demonstration, *object-pointing* and *region-pointing* (Rieser 2004).

If we take the stance that pointing provides a contribution to the semantic content of deictic expressions the question concerning the interface between the verbal and the gestural part of the expression arises. How can the interrelation between the two modalities be described and treated in computational models for speech-gesture processing? A central problem we are faced with in this context is the vagueness of demonstration, i.e. the question how to determine the focus of a pointing gesture. To deal with that, we establish the concept of *pointing cone* in the course of a parameterization of demonstration (Section 2). In Section 3 we investigate the role of pointing gestures and their timing relations to speech on the one hand and evaluate analytical data concerning the focus of pointing gestures (modeled as pointing cone) that were collected using tracking technology and VR simulations on the other hand. In Section 4 a multi-modal linguistic interface is conceived which integrates the content of the verbal expression with the content of the demonstration determined via the pointing cone. The application of the pointing cone concept to computational models for reference resolution and for the generation of multi-modal referring expressions is described in Section 5. Finally, in Section 6 we discuss the trade-offs of our approach.

2. The parameters of demonstration

In accordance with Kita (2002) we conceive of pointing as a communicative body movement that directs the attention of its addressee to a certain direction, location, or object. In the following we concentrate on hand pointing with extended index finger into concrete domains. In the context of multi-modal deictic expressions pointing or demonstration serves to indicate what the referent of the co-uttered verbal expression might be (Kendon 2004). If we want to consider the multiple dimensions of this kind of deixis more systematically, then we must account for various aspects:

1. Language is frequently tied to the gesture channel via deixis. Acts of demonstration have their own structural characteristics. Furthermore, co-occurrence of verbal expressions and demonstration is neatly organized, it harmonizes with grammatical features (McNeill 1992). Finally, since demonstration is tied to reference, it interacts with semantic and pragmatic information in an intricate way. Gestural and verbal information also differ in content. This results from different production procedures and the alignment of different sensory input channels. The interaction of

the differing information can only be described via a multi-modal syntax-semantic interface.

2. Besides the referential functions of pointing discussed in literature (e.g. Kita 2002; Kendon 2004), which draw on the relationship between gesture form and its function, we concentrate on two referential functions of pointing into concrete domains depending on the spatial relationship between demonstrating hand and referent. If an act of pointing uniquely singles out an object, it is said to have object-pointing function; if the gesture refers only with additional restricting material it is assigned region-pointing function. As we will see (Section 3.1), classifying referential functions needs clear-cut criteria for the function distinction.
3. Pointing gestures are inherently imprecise, varying with the distance between pointing agent and referent. Pointing singles out a spatial area, but not necessarily a single entity in the world. To determine the set of entities delimited by a pointing gesture we have to analyze which parameters influence the topology of the pointing area. As a first approximation we can model a cone representing the resolution of the pointing gesture. Empirical observations indicate that the concept of the pointing cone can be divided into two topologically different cones for object- and for region-pointing, with the former having a narrower angle than the latter. – It has to be stressed, however, that a cone is an idealization of the pointing area. First of all, we have to consider that depth recognition in vision is more difficult than recognition of width. Furthermore, the focus of a pointing gesture is influenced by additional parameters, which we can divide in perceivable parameters on the one hand (like spatial configuration of demonstrating agent, addressee, and referents, as well as the clustering of the entities under demonstration) and dialogue parameters on the other.
4. Pointing gestures and speech that constitute a multi-modal utterance are time-shared. One point of interest, then, is whether there is a constant relationship in time between the verbal and the gestural channel. Investigating temporal *intra*-move relations is motivated by the synchrony rules stated in McNeill (1992). Since the so-called *stroke* is the meaningful phase of a gesture, from a semantic point of view the synchronization of the pointing stroke and its affiliated speech matters most.
5. With respect to dialogue, a further point of interest is whether pointings affect discourse structure. To assess those *inter*-move relations, the coordination of the gesture phases of the dialogue participants in successive turns has to be analyzed. For instance, there is a tight coupling of the retraction phase of one agent and the subsequent preparation phase of the other suggesting that the retraction phases may contribute to a turn-taking signal.

To sum up, elaborating on a theory of demonstration means at least dealing with the following issues: (1) the multi-modal integration of expression content and demonstration content, (2) assigning referential functions to pointing, (3) the pointing region singled out by a demonstration ("pointing cone"), (4) intra-move synchronization, and (5) inter-move synchronization.

3. Empirical studies on pointing

As mentioned in the introduction, reference is one of the key concepts for every theory of meaning. Reference and denotation guarantee the *aboutness* of language – the property of being about something in the world. It is well explored how we refer with words (e.g. Chierchia and McConnell-Ginet 2000; Levelt 1989: 129–134; Lyons 1977). Similarly, there is a bulk of research on the usage of co-verbal gesture, such as the functions of gestures and their synchronization with speech in narrations (McNeill 1992).

However, there is only little work dedicated to demonstration as a device for referring to objects in multi-modal deixis. The empirical studies reported in Piwek and Beun (2001) and Piwek, Beun, and Cremers (1995) show that there is a different deictical treatment (high vs. low deixis) of objects distinguished by their degree of salience (givenness and noteworthiness) in Dutch cooperative dialogues. Beun and Cremers (2001) proved for task-oriented dialogue that focusing the attention by pointing reduces the effort needed to refer to objects as well as to identify them. Van der Sluis and Krahmer (2004) observe a dependence of the length of the verbal part of the expression on the distance between demonstrator and object demonstrated.

Although the above-mentioned studies support the assumption that pointing carries some part of the meaning of multi-modal deixis, a lot of questions concerning the details of the interface between the modalities in such expressions are still open. In 2001 we started our empirical work with explorative studies on these matters. The setting and the design of those studies were chosen to investigate temporal as well as spatial relations that tie together gesture and speech. On the one hand, we wanted to look whether the synchronization between the modalities as found in narratives (McNeill 1992) can be replicated in task-oriented dialogues. On the other hand, we wanted to get some insight into how the spatial properties of density and distance constrain the use of pointing gestures.

In the ongoing section we start with a brief sketch of the setting used for the studies and continue with a description of their results. Then we propose new methodologies to elucidate the pointing region as represented by the pointing cone and finally discuss current results.

3.1. Simple object identification games

We conduct our empirical studies in a setting where two participants are engaged in simple object identification games (Fig. 1), which restrict the *instructor-constructor* scenario investigated in the CRC 360 to the problem of referring. One of the participants (the instructor) has the role of the "description-giver". She has to choose freely among the parts of a toy airplane spread on a table, the pointing domain, and to refer to them. The other participant (the constructor), in the role of the "object-identifier", has to resolve the description-giver's reference act and to give feedback. Thus, reference has to be negotiated and established using a special kind of dialogue game (Mann 1988).

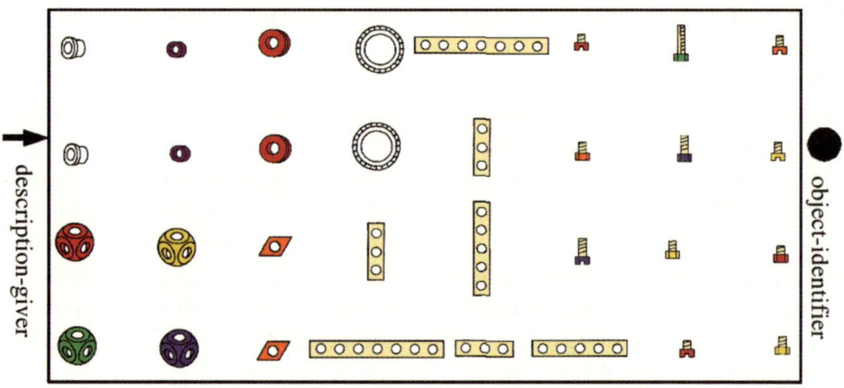

Figure 1. Simple object identification games in settings with objects arranged in a shape-cluster

3.2. Explorative studies on demonstration in dense domains

In the first explorative studies (Kühnlein and Stegmann 2003; Lücking, Rieser, and Stegmann 2004) the object identification games were recorded using two digital cameras, each capturing a different view of the scene. One camera recorded a total view seen from one side orthogonally to the table; the other took an approximate perspective of the description-giver.

The objects of the pointing domain were laid out equidistantly, that is, the distance between their centers was the same for all objects lying side by side. Their positions on the tabletop fit in a regular coordinate system and were not changed over the time of the study (Fig. 1). This move not only allowed us to determine the density holding among the objects but also provided us with a simple notion of distance, namely in terms of object rows, which can easily be converted into a linear measure.

Positioning of objects was clustered in two ways: according to color and according to shape (Fig. 1). The different distributions of objects should prevent the participants' pointing behavior from being influenced by certain prevalent traits. The two clusters together with a change of the participants' roles yielded four sub-settings for each single execution of the experiment.

The participants were not forced to use pointing gestures. Contrary to our assumption that this move assures natural referring behavior, a lot of participants avoided pointing. This problem has to be solved in future studies by giving more precise instructions.

From seven explorative studies conducted, only two involve the use of demonstration. Because of the role change, the results given below are based on four individuals acting as description-givers. They produced a total of 139 referring acts.

In order to get results concerning the relations between gesture and speech in dialogue, we applied descriptive and analytical statistical methods to the time-based annotation stamps of suitable dialogue data.

3.2.1. Annotation

The analysis of our corpus of digital video data is based on an annotation with the TASX-Annotator software package (Milde and Gut 2001). It allows an XML-based bottom up approach. Since the annotation data is stored in XML format, the extraction of the relevant information for purposes of statistical analysis can be realized via XSLT script processing straightforwardly. Details of the empirical setting and different annotation approaches are given in Kühnlein and Stegmann (2003).

As illustrated in Figure 2, the set of annotation tiers includes a transcription of the agent's speech at word level (`speech.transcription`) and a classification of the dialogue move pursued (`move.type`). The annotation of deictic gestures follows in essence the framework established in McNeill (1992). A gesture token has three phases: with respect to pointing gestures, the maximally extended and meaningful part of the gesture is called *stroke,* respectively *grasping* if an agent grasps an object. Stroke or grasping is preceded by the *preparation* phase, that is, the movement of the arm and (typically) the index finger out of the rest position into the stroke or grasping position. Finally, in the *retraction* phase the pointer's arm is moved back to rest position. The distinction between object- and region-pointing is captured on the `gesture.function` tier. The discriminating criterion was whether the annotator could resolve the description-givers pointing gesture to a single object.

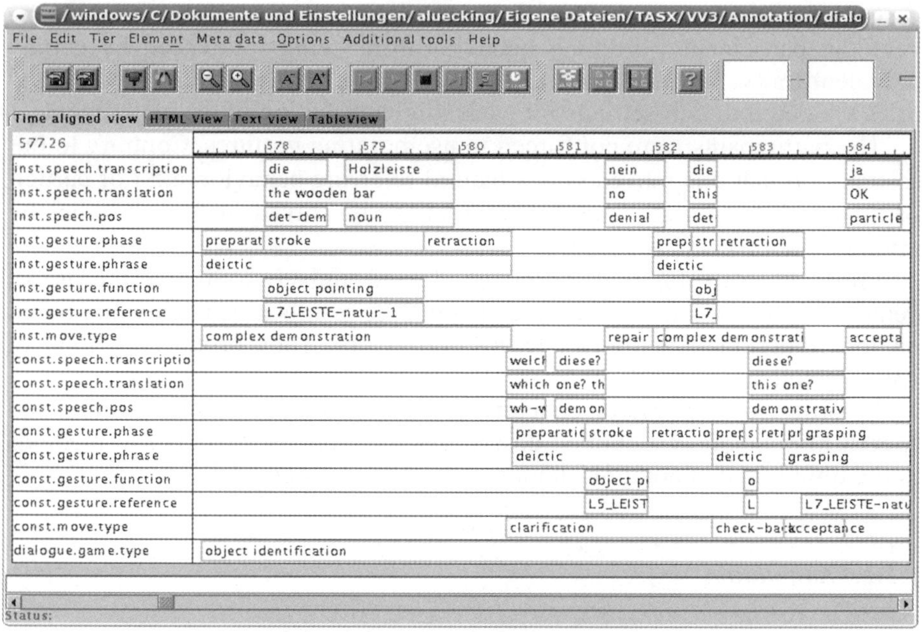

Figure 2. Annotation of a complex dialogue game. A screenshot from a TASX annotation session that exemplifies the annotation scheme applied in score format (see example for transcription of speech parts). From Lücking, Rieser, and Stegmann (2004)

All tiers are specified for the description-giver and the object-identifier; the respective tier names have an `inst.` or `const.` prefix (Fig. 2). So, for example, there is a tier labeled `inst.speech.translation` containing the utterance of the description-giver, and one labeled `const.speech.translation`, for recording the utterance of the object-identifier (the naming of the prefixes is due to the participants' roles in the standard scenario of the CRC 360).

To get a better grip on the kind of data we are concerned with, the speech portions of the sample dialogue from Figure 2 were extracted and are reproduced below.

(1) Inst: The wooden bar
[pointing to object1]

(2a)	Const:	Which one?
(2b)		This one? [pointing to object2]
(3a)	Inst:	No.
(3b)		This one. [pointing to object1]
(4)	Const:	This one? [pointing to object1 and grasping it]
(5)	Inst:	OK.

We have the dialogue move of a `complex demonstration` of the description-giver in (1) here, followed by a `clarification` move involving a pointing of the object-identifier (2a, 2b). The description-giver produces a `repair` (3a), followed by a new `complex demonstration` move (3b) to the object she had introduced. Then we have a new `check-back` from the object-identifier (4) coming with a pointing and a grasping gesture as well as an 'accept' move by the description-giver (5). The whole game is classified as an `object identification game`. The following events from different agents' turns overlap: (2b) and (3a) plus (3b); (3b) and (4).

3.2.2. Results

Rather than being mere emphasis markers, gestures contribute to the content of communicative acts. This can be substantiated by findings related to the semantic, the pragmatic, and the discourse level summarized in the following.

Finding 1: Gestures save words. The total amount of 139 referring acts adds up out of 65 referential NPs escorted by a pointing gesture (hereafter CDs, for 'complex demonstrations') and 74 NPs without pointing (DDs, short for 'definite descriptions'). Lücking, Rieser, and Stegmann (2004) found strong statistical evidence for the semantic contribution of pointings in comparing the number of words used in CDs with that in DDs (Fig. 3a) by means of a t-test that indicated a significant difference ($t = 6.22$, $p < .001$). This result can be couched into the slogan "Gestures save words". Thus, gestures contribute content that otherwise would have to be cast into clumsy verbal descriptions, making communicative acts more efficient.

Finding 2: Gestures as guiding devices. A related cognitive hypothesis was that the time the object-identifier needs to interpret the description-giver's reference (hereafter called "reaction time") is less after a CD than after a DD. The pointing gesture can be seen as guiding the object-identifier's eyes towards the intended object – or at least towards a narrow region where the object is located – and thus as shortening the object-identifier's search effort. To assess this point, we analyzed 39 CDs and 9 DDs from two description-givers as to the interval between the start time of the object-identifier's move and the end time of the description-giver's referring act (Fig. 3b). A comparison by means of a t-test did not yield a significant difference ($t = 1.4$, $p = .166$); however, measures of central tendency were in the hypothesized direction (Lücking, Rieser, and Stegmann 2004). A significant outcome might have been prevented by the fact that some objects are unique and therefore more salient (e.g., there is only one yellow cube as opposed to several yellow bolts), so that the object-identifier could quickly spot such objects when directed with appropriate DDs only. In addition, the object-identifier may have used the description-giver's gaze as a guiding device, especially with toy airplane parts that were located very close to the description-giver (Kühnlein and Stegmann 2003).

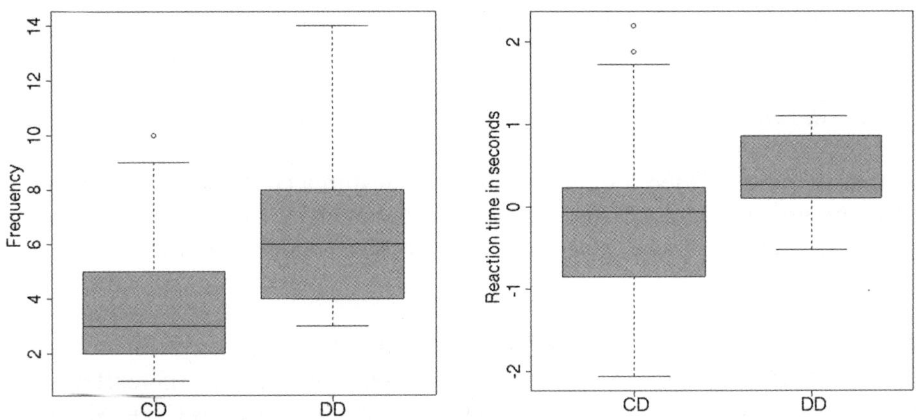

Figure 3. Box plots displaying (a) the number of words in CDs and in DDs, (b) object-identifiers' reaction times following instruction-givers' CDs or DDs. From Lücking, Rieser, and Stegmann (2004)

Finding 3: Intra-move temporal relations. At the beginning of this paper, a distinction was made between intra- and inter-move synchronization at the dialogue level. As regards intra-move synchronization, we accounted for the temporal relations holding between gesture phases and escorting utterances. Above all, we focused on two synchronization effects, namely *anticipation* and *semantic synchrony* (McNeill 1992: 25–26, 131). The semantic synchrony rule states that gesture and speech present one and the same meaning at the same time (McNeill's "idea unit"). Anticipation refers to the temporal location of the preparation phase in relation to the onset of the stroke's co-expressive portion of the utterance. This rule states that the preparation phase precedes the linguistic affiliate of the stroke. Table 1 summarizes the descriptive statistics (N = 25). The different rows represent synchronization valies; they were calculated as follows: (P) $preparation_{start} - speech_{start}$, (R) $speech_{end} - retraction_{start}$, and (S) $stroke_{start} - speech_{start}$. Note that we take the verbal affiliate to be the complete denoting linguistic expression, i.e. a possibly complex noun phrase.

Table 1. Temporal intra-move synchronization values: minimum (*Xmin*), 25% quantile (*Q25*), arithmetic mean (*M*), 75% quantile (*Q75*), maximum (*Xmax*), standard deviation (*SD*)

	Xmin	*Q25*	*M*	*Q75.*	*Xmax*	*SD*
P	–0.8	–0.2	0.3104	0.48	4.68	1.0692
R	–0.86	0.0	0.564	1.06	3.38	0.89
S	–0.02	0.48	1.033	1.24	5.54	1.128

Row P gives the values for the start of the preparation phase relative to the onset of the first word of the noun phrase. For each speech-gesture ensemble, the time stamp associated with the beginning of the first word of the utterance was subtracted from the time stamp for the start of the respective gesture's preparation phase. Hence, negative values in row P indicate that the start of the preparation phase precedes the verbal affiliate as is to be expected in the light of McNeill's anticipation rule. Contrary to McNeill (1992: 25, 131), we found that the utterance usually starts a little before the initiation of the gesture (compare the positive mean value in Table 1. This seems to contradict anticipation, given the way we operationalized McNeill's concept of the idea unit. – Similarly (compare the mean value in row R), the stroke ends (or the retraction starts) normally around 0.5 seconds before the end of the affiliate. Together with an average start of the stroke around 1 second after the onset of the utterance, this shows that the prototypical stroke does not cross utterance boundaries (Lücking, Rieser, and Stegmann 2004). This is to be expected in the light of McNeill's semantic synchrony rule. Note, however, that some extreme tokens (cf. *Xmin* and *Xmax* values) were observed that seem to contradict the McNeill regularities (Kühnlein and Stegmann 2003).

Finding 4: Inter-move temporal relation. Concerning inter-move synchronization, one point of interest was the alignment of the end of description-giver's preparation phase with object-identifier's retraction phase. A look into the dialogue video data reveals that two different cases have to be distinguished here. If the object referred to lies within object-identifier's reach, his initiation seems to regularly overlap with the description-giver's retraction. If the object referred to lies at the opposite side of the table, that is, out of his reach, the object-identifier first has to move around the table which delays initiation of his gesture. The temporal differences between the two gesture phases ($\text{preparation}_{\text{OI}}$ – $\text{retraction}_{\text{DG}}$, where the indices stand for the respective roles) were grouped accordingly into a within-reach case and an out-of-reach case. The outcomes are given in Table 2.

Table 2. Inter-move synchronization of preparation and retraction

	Xmin	*Q25*	*M*	*Q75*	*Xmax*	*SD*
within-reach	–2.06	–0.96	–0.4984	–0.06	2.2.6	0.89
out-of-reach	–1.36	0.4	1.54	1.7	8.76	2.19

If the object in question is within object-identifier's reach his initiation of grabbing it overlaps with the retraction of the description-giver by an average latency of half a second (Table 2; note also that the 75% quantile still yields a negative result!). This indicates that the description-giver's retraction phase might contribute to a turn-taking signal. Not surprisingly, there is no such overlap if the object is out of object-identifier's immediate reach (Lücking, Rieser, and Stegmann 2004).

Finding 5. Partitioning of the pointing domain. Moving from semantic and temporal to pragmatic issues, we also tried to find out whether there are contextual conditions constraining the use of gestures. This was defined in terms of frequencies of DDs vs. CDs utilized to refer to objects in different rows of the pointing domain – that is, basically, with respect to their distance as seen from the instructor. What is at stake here is whether the asymmetry that seems to exist in the raw data (cf. Table 3; Figure 4) is statistically sound. – Roughly three regions emerge (Kranstedt, Kühnlein, and Wachsmuth 2004; Kühnlein and Stegmann 2003): the first two rows constitute an area that is closest to the description-giver, called the *proximal* region. In opposition, rows seven and eight form the *distal* region, the area that is farthest away from the description-giver. The remaining four rows in the middle of the pointing domain are the *mid-range* region. Note that this partitioning corresponds to the ratings of gesture function (cf. Finding 6 below).

Table 3. Descriptive values for referring to objects in different rows of the domain

Row	1	2	3	4	5	6	7	8
CDs	3	6	10	10	10	11	7	8
DDs	10	11	7	9	6	6	7	18
Total	13	17	17	19	16	17	14	26

While the decrease of CDs and the increase of DDs in the distal region correspond with intuition, the results concerning the proximal reason are surprising. Maybe, one reason could be that some of the participants use gaze and head movements accompanied by a DD to guide the attention of the addressee to objects in the proximal region. Though, to capture this in the video data is difficult. This phenomenon of head or gaze pointing and possible other reasons for the observed decrease of CDs has to be addressed in further investigations.

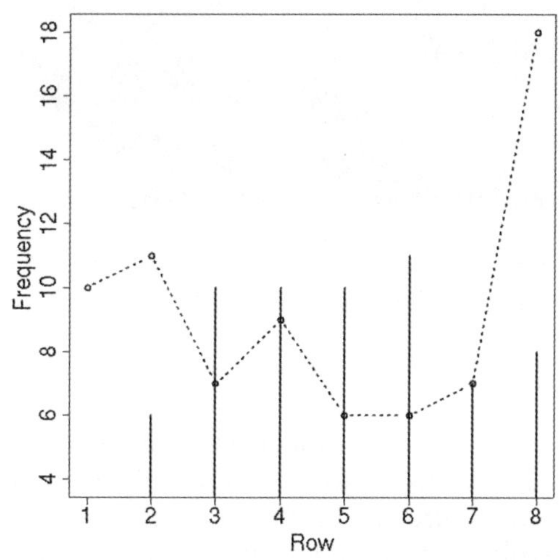

Figure 4. Plot for the modes of reference modeled by the eight rows of the reference domain; the bars depict the frequency distribution of CDs over the rows, the dashed line that of DDs. From Lücking, Rieser, and Stegmann (2004)

However, the relative distance of the object in question to the description-giver seems to be a contextual factor for the choice of the mode of reference to that object (Lücking, Rieser, and Stegmann 2004).

Finding 6: Object-pointing vs. region-pointing. As introduced in Section 2 (Parameter 2), we assume that pointing gestures serve one of two semantic functions: They uniquely pick out an object (object-pointing) or merely narrow down the region in which the intended object lies (region-pointing). In order to illustrate this distinction, an occurrence of each gesture function is shown in Figure 5. The extension of pointing gestures is modeled with a pointing cone. Figure 5 (left) depicts a case of region pointing, where several objects are located in the conic section of the pointing cone and the tabletop. There, the extension of the index finger does not meet the object in question. Against this, in object pointing the object is unequivocally singled out, i.e. it is the only object within the conic section (Fig. 5, right).

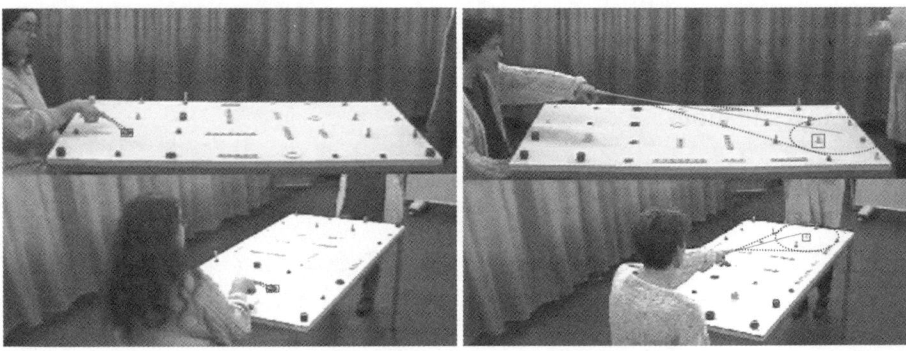

Figure 5. The two kinds of pointing found in the data. Left: Object-pointing. Right: Region-pointing. The prolongation of the index finger is indicated with a line, the pointing cone is indicated using dotted lines, and the box frames the intended object. From Lücking, Rieser, and Stegmann (2004)

From a semantic point of view, object pointings behave very much like referring expressions, whereas region-pointing tokens may be said to be predicative or relational in nature. The difference in meaning between those functions is formally explicated in the linguistic interface described in Section 4. – In the course of investigating whether the dialogue scheme used is reliable in terms of inter-rater agreement, the distinction between the two gesture functions turned out to be problematic in some ways: Although there is a strong consensus concerning the classification of pointings in regions very near and very far from the description-giver, there is a broad region in the middle where the raters differ in their estimation (Table 4). We see three kinds of reasons for the disagreement. Above all, the two-dimensional video-data lack the necessary depth of focus to admit the classification. Furthermore, the rating criterion is probably not well defined, so that the raters used varied interpretations (for example, one rater might be content with exactly one object lying in the projected pointing cone to vote for object pointing, while the other raise the bar in requiring the prolongated pointing finger (the "pointing beam") to meet the object). At last, it is feasible that the theoretically motivated function-distinction has no clear-cut realization in the empirical realm of the real world.

Table 4. Gesture function ratings. The region of disagreement is highlighted

Row		*1*	*2*	*3*	*4*	*5*	*6*	*7*	*8*
Rater 1	object-pointing	2	4	8	6	7	1	0	0
	region-pointing	0	1	2	1	3	9	7	5
Rater 2	object-pointing	2	4	6	2	2	0	0	1
	region-pointing	0	1	4	5	8	10	7	4

Finding 7: Distance-dependence of gesture vs. speech portions. The following two assumptions are corroborated: Firstly, there is a division of labor between gesture and speech in referring to objects; secondly, pointings loose resolution capacity in greater distances. Hence it follows that description-givers have to put the larger identifying burden into the verbal expression the farer away the intended object is in order to perform successful deictic acts. Indeed, in van der Sluis and Krahmer (2004) the dependence of the distance of the object in question on the informational share that has to be provided via each channel could be proved. To verify this dependence in our study, we can make use of the pre-structuring of the pointing domain into rows. The obvious statistical computation is to compare the number of words used in CDs to refer to objects in the different regions (distal, mid-range, and proximal). Therefore, an analysis of variance (ANOVA) was carried out on the number of words modeled by regions. Although there is a minor difference in the raw data (Fig. 6), the ANOVA did not yield a significant effect ($F = 0.53$, $p = .6$). This unexpected result can be explained by two facts: firstly, the sample is clearly too small to render such small differences in means significant. Secondly, a look at the videos reveals that the participants make use of overspecification: They provide more information than necessary to identify the object referred to, and thus – superficially – violate rules of parsimony and economy. This in turn might be an artifact of the setting. The simplicity and repetition of the identification task induced participants to use recurrent patterns of simple NPs, mostly composed of a determiner followed by an adjective and the head noun. On the other hand, the descrip-

tion-giver is anxious for securing object-identifier's comprehension, so that the latter is able to successfully and smoothly resolve the former's referential behavior.

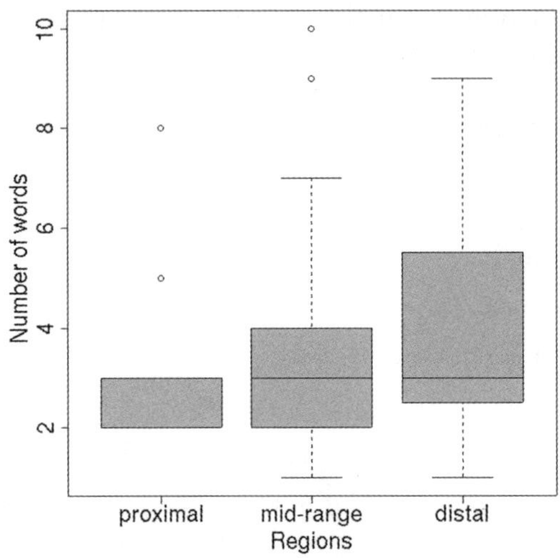

Figure 6. Box plot displaying the number of words used to refer to objects in the different regions. Regardless of differences in interquartile distance, the medians remain all about the same

3.2.3. Discussion

As has been shown above, our experimental setting provides us with rich empirical evidence to support our parameterization of demonstration presented in Section 2. Our findings that gestures save words and a tendency towards shorter reaction times after CDs further emphasize the need for a multi-modal linguistic interface (Parameter 1). This view is also empirically supported by the findings of Piwek and Beun (2001) and Beun and Cremers (2001).

The question of the temporal relations subsumed by the parameters (4) and (5) is captured by our third and fourth findings. It has to be noted that in our task-oriented setting we find higher temporal variability than in narrative dialogues (McNeill 1992). This imposes greater restrictions especially onto the speech-gesture resolution module, which has to be sufficiently general in order to process all occurrences of the relatively loose temporal relations of multi-modal deixis.

The partitioning of the pointing domain according to the distribution of CDs and DDs presented in the fifth finding – proximal vs. mid-range vs. distal – provided us with a useful spatial categorization, which is picked up in the description of our findings regarding the spatial constraints of demonstration. The distinction between the two referential functions object- and region-pointing, as proposed in Parameter 2, are backed by this partitioning (Finding 6). Together they provide the descriptive framework to describe our findings on the distance dependence of gesture and speech (Finding 7). Dealing with this interrelationship is necessary for both sides of speech-gesture processing, speech-gesture generation and speech-gesture recognition. The tendency we find in our experiments accords with the findings of van der Sluis and Krahmer (2004).

All issues touching upon the distance of referents are affected by the pointing cone, which is bound up with the vagueness of pointing. In this context, the cone also can be seen as a device to capture the focusing power of pointings in the sense of Piwek, Beun, and Cremers (1995) and Beun and Cremers (2001). Assessing the pointing cone (Parameter 3) and its three-dimensional topology is essential for our theoretical and computational models of the interface between gesture and speech in deictic expressions. However, the two-dimensional video data do not afford accurate statements about the spatial area singled out by a pointing gesture. Especially the position and orientation of the demonstrating hand and the outstretched index finger with respect to the objects on the tabletop, which are necessary for the computation of the size and form of the pointing cone, can only be estimated.

In sum, the empirical results in this study address the parameters 1, 2, 4, and 5. First approximations of the pointing cone (Parameter 3), give some clues but the empirical method used does not provide means to really grasp the pointing cone's topology. Hence, the pointing cone needs to be assessed with more precision, in particular, to account for possibly different cones associated with object-pointing and region-pointing.

3.3. Assessing the pointing cone

The results concerning the topology of the pointing cone are a consequence of the methods used for data collection and analysis. The two perspectives provided by the video recordings lead to too many ambiguities in the ratings, which have become evident in our inter-rater agreement tests. Therefore, methods are needed which grasp the topology of the pointing cone in its three-dimensionality and provide exact spatial data on pointing behavior. In addition, we search for methods to visualize pointing-beam, pointing cone, and their intersection with the pointing domain.

3.3.1. Tracker-based experiments

In our search for such methods we settled on a tracker-based solution (Kranstedt et al. 2006). It uses a marker-based optical tracking system to obtain adequate analytical data for the participant's body posture. Additional data for the fine-grained hand postures is collected using data gloves (Fig. 7a). The optical tracking system uses eight infrared cameras, arranged in a cube around the setting, to track optical markers each with a unique 3-dimensional configuration. A software module integrates the information gathered providing their absolute coordinates and orientations. We track head and back of the description-giver to serve as reference points. With two markers each, one for the elbow, and one for the back of the hand the arms are tracked. The hands are tracked using CyberGloves measuring flexion and abduction of the fingers directly. We do not specially track the object-identifier, as the relevant information, especially the identification of the demonstrated object, can easily be extracted from the recorded videos.

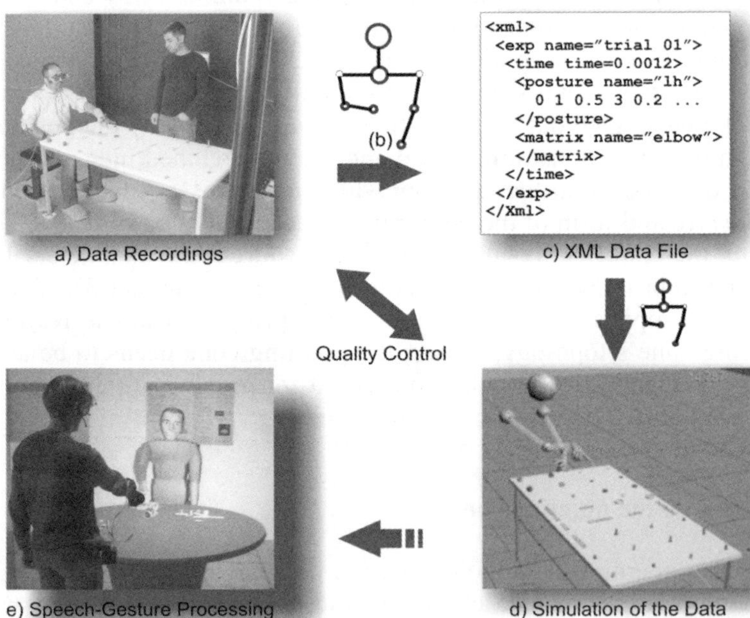

Figure 7. The description-giver is tracked using optical markers and data gloves (a). The data is integrated in a geometrical user model (b) and written to an XML file (c). For simulation the data is fed back into the model and visualized using VR techniques (d). The findings are transferred to enhance the speech-gesture processing models (e). From Kranstedt et al. (2006)

3.3.2. Representing the data

The information provided by the tracking systems (Fig. 7a) is fed into our VR application based on the VR framework Avango (Tramberend 2001), which extends the common scene-graph representation of the visual world.

A scene-graph consists of nodes connected by arcs defining an ownership relation. The nodes are separated into grouping nodes and leaf nodes. Every node is the target of an ownership relation, then called a "child", but only grouping nodes can also be a source or "parent". In addition to this basic distinction, the nodes in a scene-graph can have different types: geometry nodes, material nodes, etc., are used to define visual appearance. A single visual object may be the product of a combination of several such nodes interacting, separately defining one or more shapes, colors, or textures of the object. The position of an object in the world is determined by the multiplication of matrices defined in transformation nodes along a chain from the root node of the scene-graph to the object's geometry nodes. A special feature of the Avango VR framework is the data-graph, which is defined orthogonally to the scene-graph. It does not operate on the nodes in the scene-graph, but on subcomponents of them, the fields. Each node in the scene-graph can exhibit a set of fields defining its data interface. Examples of such fields are the matrices of the transforming nodes. The data-graph connects these fields with a dataflow relation, defining that the data from the parent field is propagated to the child field. Every time such propagation results in the change of a child field, a special trigger function is called in the scene-graph node owning the field. The node can then operate on the new data, change its state, and eventually provide results in some of its fields, which may induce the next propagation.

A group node acting as root of a subgraph represents the description-giver. This type of node does not have a graphical representation. It is a special kind of group node, a transformation group node, which is not only grouping its siblings but also defines a transformation to position them in space. The matrices of the transformation nodes in this subgraph are connected to *actuator* nodes representing the different tracking devices. These actuator nodes are defined in the PrOSA (Patterns On Sequences of Attributes) framework (Latoschik 2001a), a set of data processing nodes specialized for operating on timed sequences of values utilizing the data processing facilities of Avango. The subgraph representing the description-giver is updated according to the posture of the tracked user using field connections from the actuator nodes providing a coherent geometric user model (Fig. 7b). For recording the tracked data this user model is written to an XML file and can later be used for annotation or stochastic analysis (Fig. 7c).

3.3.3. Simulation-based data evaluation

To support data evaluation we developed tools to feed the gathered tracking data (Fig. 7c) back into the geometric user model, which is now the basis of a graphical simulation of the experiment in VR (Fig. 7d). This simulation is run in a CAVE-like environment, where the human rater is able to walk freely and inspect the gestures from every possible perspective. While doing so, the simulation can be run back and forth in time and thus, e.g., the exact time spans of the strokes can be collected. To further assist the rater, additional features can be visualized, e.g., the pointing beam or its intersection with the table. For the visualization of the person participating we use a simple graphical model (Fig. 7d) providing only relevant information. We preferred this in contrast to our anthropomorphic agent (Fig. 7e), as the visualization of information not backed by the recordings, such as the direction of the eye gaze, could mislead raters.

For a location independent annotation we created a desktop-based visualization system where the rater can move a virtual camera into every desired perspective and generate videos to facilitate the rating and annotation process when the graphic machines for the real-time rendering are not available. Using the annotation software, these videos can be shown side-a-side in sync with the real videos and provide additional perspectives, e.g., looking through the eyes of the description-giver.

3.3.4. Computation of pointing beam and pointing cone

The pointing beam is defined by its origin and its direction, the pointing cone in addition by its apex angle. To grasp the spatial constraints of pointing, one has to specify two things: For one, the anatomical anchoring of origin and direction in the demonstrating hand, and for another, the apex angle. We can calculate these parameters under the following assumptions:

- We know the exact position and orientation of the demonstrating hand and the extended index finger (provided by the tracking data).
- We know the intended referent (identified in the dialogue annotation).
- We have a statistically relevant amount of demonstrations to each object and each region in the pointing domain.

There are four different anatomical parts (the three phalanxes of the index finger and the back of the hand) at disposition for the anchoring. To discriminate between them, a hypothetical pointing beam is generated for each of them (see Fig. 8). We will choose the anchoring resulting in the least mean orthogonal distance over all successful demonstrations between the hypothetical pointing beam and the respective referent.

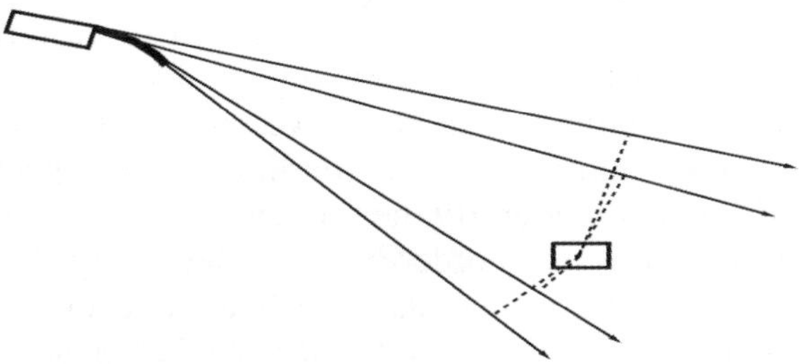

Figure 8. Four hypothetical pointing beams anchored in different anatomical parts of the hand. From Kranstedt et al. (2006)

Given the anchoring thus obtained, the calculation of the apex angle of the pointing cone can be done as follows: For each recorded demonstration the differing angle between the pointing beam and a beam with the same origin but directed to the nearest neighbor has to be computed. The computed angles decrease with the increasing distance between the demonstrating hand and the referent analogously to the perceived decreasing distance between the objects (Fig. 9).

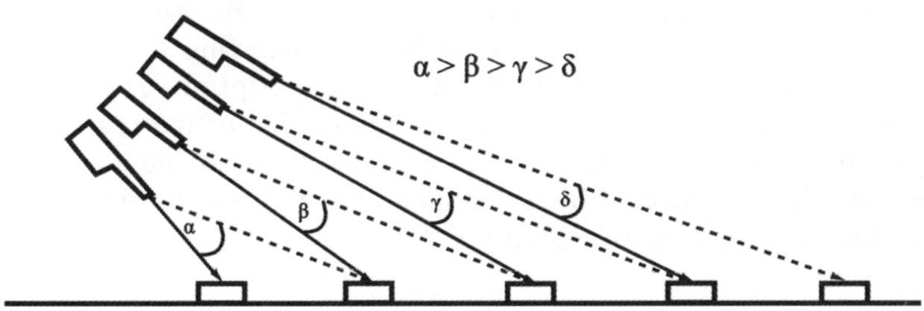

Figure 9. The angles between the beams to the referent and the next neighbor decrease with the distance to the referent (the dashed arrows represent the beams to the next neighbor). Despite similar distance to the referent, the beam to the object behind the referent results in a smaller angle than the beam to the object in front of the referent. This is because of the greater distance of the former one to the demonstrating hand. From Kranstedt et al. (2006)

We pursue two strategies for the calculation of the apex angle. In one experimental setting the description-givers are allowed to use both, speech and gesture to indicate the referent. Analyzing this data, we have to search for the differing angle correlating with the first substantial increase of the verbal expressions describing the referent. This angle indicates the borderline of the resolution of pointing the description-givers manifests. In the other experimental setting the description-givers are bounded to gestures only. In this data we have to search for the differing angle correlating with the distance where the number of failing references exceeds the number of successful references. This angle indicates the borderline in the object density where the object-identifier cannot identify the referent by pointing alone.

We assume that these two borderlines will be nearly the same, with the former being a little bit broader than the latter due to the demonstrating agent's intention to ensure that the addressee is able to resolve the referential act. The corresponding angles define the half apex angle of the pointing cone of object-pointing.

A first assessment of the apex angle of this pointing cone using a similar calculation based on the video data recorded in our first studies resulted in a half apex angle between 6 and 12 degrees (Kranstedt, Kühnlein, and Wachsmuth 2004; Kühnlein and Stegmann 2003). However, for this assessment a fixed hand position heuristically determined over all demonstrations was assumed and only a small number of annotated data was used. So, these results should be taken as a rough indication.

To establish the apex angle of the pointing cone of region-pointing we have to investigate the complex demonstrations including verbal expressions referring to objects in the distal region. The idea is to determine the contrast set from which the referent is distinguished by analyzing the attributes the description-giver uses to generate the definite description. The location of the objects in the contrast set gives a first impression of the region covered by region-pointing. The angle between the pointing beam and a beam touching the most distant object defines then in a first approximation the half apex angle of the pointing cone of region-pointing.

3.3.5. Discussion

The method proposed was tested in a first study in November 2004. There, our primary concerns were the question of data reliability and the development of methods for the analysis. The main study was conducted in September 2005. Video and tracking data from 60 participants consisting of 30 description-givers and 30 object-identifiers were collected. At the time of writing this text the analysis of the data is under preparation. The results seem promising, so that we will discuss our experience and highlight some interesting advantages of this approach.

The tracker-based recordings supplement the video recordings by providing 3D coordinates of the markers on the body of the description-giver specifying a full posture for every frame of the video. This data is more extensive and more precise than that gathered annotating the videos. Its collection can be automated to disencumber the manual annotation significantly speeding up the overall analysis. As the posture of the description-giver is known for every frame, extensive data for a statistical analysis is available, a precondition for gathering the anchoring of pointing beam and pointing cone and the topology of the cone.

The visual simulation of the gathered data provides us with a qualitative feedback of the tracker recordings. This proved to be useful, especially when running on-line. This way important preparations of the experimental setting, such as adjusting the illumination, avoiding occlusions or positioning and calibrating the trackers are easily done before the experiment, improving the quality of the data to be recorded. After the experiment, the simulation is used to review the data and identify problems, so that incomplete or defective recordings are recognized and separated as early as possible. This applicability renders the simulation a perfect tool for the quality assurance of the recorded tracking data. Furthermore, the simulation can be used to facilitate the annotation of the video recordings by providing a dynamic perspective on the setting. It is also possible to add a virtual pointing beam or pointing cone to the simulation. The intersection of the pointing beam and the table top can then be interpreted as an approximation of the location pointed to and the intersection of the cone with the table top as the area covered by the pointing gesture.

On the other hand the tracker-based recordings are a compromise where we preserve the natural dialogue setting only to some extent, e.g., as the participants are not used to wearing trackers which are physically attached to their bodies. In one trial this showed up in an extreme fashion when a participant used her hands with an outstretched index finger in a tool-like manner without relaxation. To compensate for such effects, an interactive preparation phase has to be introduced where people can familiarize themselves with the new environment. Still we believe this method to be less obtrusive than any modification concentrating on the index finger or the gesturing arm alone, as it involves the whole body of the description-giver without putting too much emphasis on a specific aspect, e.g., pointing gestures as such.
Overall, we are aware that the combination of optical markers and data gloves is more invasive than relying on video cameras alone. But at the time being they seem to be our most powerful empirical tool for a deeper investigation of the pointing cone's topology.

4. A multi-modal linguistic interface

In this section we introduce a formal attempt to integrate gestural deixis, in particular the pointing stroke, in linguistic descriptions, aiming at a theoretical model of deixis in reference that captures the object-/region-pointing distinction.

4.1. Complex demonstrations: object and restrictor demonstration

Objects originating from pointing plus definite descriptions are called complex demonstrations (CDs). The pointing stroke is represented as "↘", mimicking the index finger in stroke position. ↘ is concatenated with the verbal expression, indicating the start of the stroke in the signal and hence its functional role. In this respect, ↘ is treated like a normal linguistic constituent. Its insertion can be directly derived from the annotated data. Example (1) presents a well-formed CD "↘this/that yellow bolt" embedded into a directive as against (1') which we consider as being non-well-formed, the ↘ being absent in the CD.

(1) Grasp ↘this/that yellow bolt. (1') *Grasp this/that yellow bolt.

A unified account of CDs will opt for a compositional semantics to capture the information coming from the verbal and the visual channel. Abstracting from other less well understood uses such as abstract pointings, CDs are considered as definite descriptions to which demonstrations add content either by specifying an object independently of the definite description, thus acting as a definite description in itself, or by narrowing down the description's restrictor. We call the first use "object demonstration", pointing to an object, and the second one "restrictor demonstration", a semantic classification of pointing to a region. Graspings are the clearest cases of object demonstration.

Before we show how to represent demonstrations with descriptions in one logical form, we specify our main hypotheses concerning their integration. These are related to content under compositionality, i.e. their roles in building up referential content for the embedded proposition, and the scope of the gesture. Hypothetically then, demonstrations (a) act much like verbal elements in providing content, (b) interact with verbal elements in a compositional way, (c) may exhibit forward or backward dynamics depending on the position of ↘ (see examples (2) to (5) below), (d) involve, empirically speaking, a continuous impact over a time interval, comparable to intonation contours, and (e) can be described using discrete entities like the ↘.

4.2. Interpretation of complex demonstrations

The central problem is of course how to interpret demonstrations. This question is different from the one concerning the ↘'s function tied to its position in the string. We base our discussion of these matters on the following examples showing different empirically found ↘ positions and turn first to "object demonstration":

(2) Grasp ↘ this/that yellow bolt.
(3) Grasp this/that ↘yellow bolt.
(4) Grasp this/that yellow ↘bolt.
(5) Grasp this/that yellow bolt↘.

Our initial representation for the speech-act frame of the demonstration-free expression is

(6) $\lambda N\ \lambda u(N\ \lambda v\ F_{dir}\ (grasp(u,v)))$.

Here "F_{dir}" indicates directive illocutionary force; "N" abstracts over the semantics of the object-NP/definite description "this/that yellow bolt", i.e. "$\lambda Z.Z(\iota z(yellowbolt(z)))$", and "(grasp(u,v))" presents the proposition commanded. The ↘ provides additional information. If the ↘ is independent from the reference of the definite description the only way to express that is by somehow extending (6) with "v = y":

(7) $\lambda N\ \lambda u\ \lambda y(N\ \lambda v\ F_{dir}\ (grasp(u, v) \wedge (v = y)))$.

The idea tied to (7) is that the reference of *v* and the reference of *y* must be identical, regardless of the way in which it is given. Intuitively, the reference of *v* is given by the definite description "$\iota z(yellowbolt(z))$" and the reference of *y* by ↘. The values of both information contents are independent of each other. This property of independence will be reconstructed in the interface for multi-modal semantics.

Object demonstration and restrictor demonstration are similar insofar as information is added. In the object demonstration case, this is captured by a conjunct with identity statement; in the restrictor demonstration case the ↘ contributes a new property narrowing down the linguistically expressed one. The bracketing we assume for (3) in this case is roughly

(8) [[grasp] [this/that [↘yellow bolt]]].

Here, the demonstration contributes to the content of the N'-construction "yellow bolt". As a consequence, the format of the description must change. This job can be easily done with

(9) $\lambda R \lambda W \lambda K.K(\iota z(W(z) \wedge R(z)))$.

Here, K abstracts over the semantics of the directive, W is the predicative delivered by the noun, and R is the additional restrictor.

The demonstration ↘ in (3) will then be represented simply by

(10) $\lambda y(y \in D)$,

where *D* intuitively indicates the demonstrated subset of the domain as given by the pointing cone. We use the ∈-notation here in order to point to the information from the other channel. Under functional application this winds up to

(11) $\lambda K.K\ (\iota z(\text{yellowbolt}(z) \wedge z \in D))$.

Intuitively, (11), the completed description, then indicates "the demonstrated yellow bolt" or "the yellow-bolt-within-D".

4.3. Multi-modal meaning as an interface of verbal and gestural meaning

We started from the hypothesis that verbal descriptions and gestural demonstrations yield complex demonstrations, the demonstrations either independently identifying an object or contributing an area demonstrated, extending an underspecified definite description.

Even if we assume compositionality between gestural and verbal content, we must admit that the information integrated comes from different channels and that pointing is not verbal in itself, i.e. cannot be part of the linguistic grammar's lexicon. The deeper reason, however, is that integrating values for pointings-at would make the lexicon infinite, since infinitely many objects can be pointed at.

The representation problem for compositionality becomes clear, if we consider the formulas used for the imperative "grasp", i.e. the different forms (12), (13), and (14), stated below.

(12) $\lambda N\ \lambda u(N\ \lambda v\ F_{dir}\ (grasp(u, v)))$.
(13) $\lambda N\ \lambda u\ \lambda y(N\ \lambda v\ F_{dir}\ (grasp(u, v) \wedge (v = y)))$.
(14) $\lambda Q\lambda N\ \lambda u(N(Q(\lambda y\ \lambda vF_{dir}\ (grasp(u, v) \wedge (v = y)))))\ \lambda P.P(a)$ /*[grasp+↘]

Term (12) is the demonstration-free expression of the imperative form corresponding to the semantic information in a lexical entry for "grasp something". Term (13) already specifies an identity condition and says that one of the arguments to "grasp", *v*, has to be identical to some other, *y*, the latter being reserved for the pointing, but it does not yet contain a device which can guarantee compositionality of definite description and pointing information. In other words, there is no way of putting a value for *y* into the formula. This is achieved using (14). Evidently, and that's the important issue here, (14) does more than a transitive verb representation for "grasp" in the lexicon should do. It has an extra slot Q designed to absorb the additional object *a*, tied to the demonstration $\lambda P.P(a)$. Given the infinity argument above, we must regard (14) as a formula in the model-bound interface of speech and gesture, i.e. as belonging to a truly multi-modal domain, where, however, the channel-specific properties have been abstracted away from. That is, in the semantic information coded in the interface one does not see anymore where it originates from. This solution only makes sense, however, if we maintain that demonstration contributes to the semantics of the definite description used.

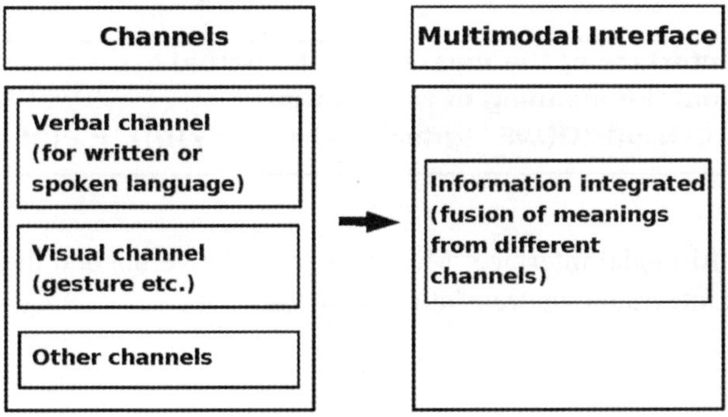

Figure 10. Information from different channels mapped onto the multi-modal interface

The general idea is shown in a rough picture in Figure 10 and illustrated in greater detail in Figure 11. The interface construction shown there for (12) to (14) presupposes two things: The lexicon for the interface contains expressions where meanings of demonstrations can be plugged into; demonstrations have to be represented in the interface as well. The number of demonstrations is determined by the intended model, see section 4.5.2.

Syntax and semantics have to be mapped onto one another in a systematic way. Now, the position of ↘ varies as examples (2) to (5) above show, in other words, the ↘ might go here or there. We can capture this feature in an underspecification model, which implies that we generally deal with descriptions instead of structures. The underspecification model coming nearest our descriptive interests is the *Logical Description Grammars* (LDGs) account of Muskens (2001), which has evolved from Lexicalized Tree Adjoining Grammar (LTAG), D-Tree Grammar, type logics and Dynamic Semantics. The intuitive idea behind LDGs is that, based on general axioms capturing the structure of trees, one works with a *logical description of the input*, capturing linear precedence phenomena, and *lexical descriptions for words* and *elementary trees*. A *parsing-as-deduction* method is applied yielding semantically interpreted structures.

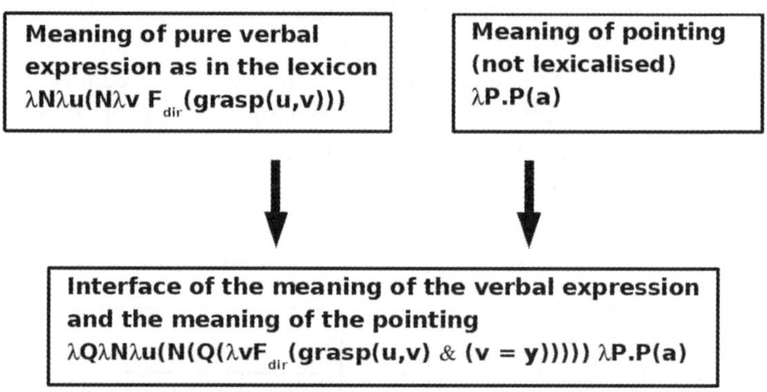

Figure 11. Multi-modal interface: Meanings from the verbal and the gestural channel integrated via translation of ↘

4.4. Underspecified syntax and semantics for expressions containing ↘

A simplified graphical representation of inputs (1) and (3) is given in Figure 12. '+' and '–' indicate components which can substitute ('+') or need to be substituted ('–'). Models for the descriptions in Figure 12 are derived pairing off '+' and '–'- nodes in a one-to-one fashion and identifying the nodes thus paired. Words can come with several lexicalizations as can ↘-s. Figure 12a specifies the elementary tree for the imperative construction. VP^{-} marks the place where a tree tagged VP^+ can be substituted. Figure 12b indicates how the demands of the multi-modal interface have to be fulfilled: V needs an NP⤓-sister whose tag ⤓ says that only stroke-information can be substituted resulting in a constituent V⤓ taking then a normal NP as an argument. Figure 12c introduces a referring stroke; (d) is the lexical entry for "bolt"; and (e) describes an NP-tree anchored with "the". The insertion of "yellow" is brought about using (f). Finally, (g) is used for ⤓-insertion before an AdjP. NP⤓$^+$ is needed to build up (14) and, similarly, AdjP⤓$^+$ for getting at (9).

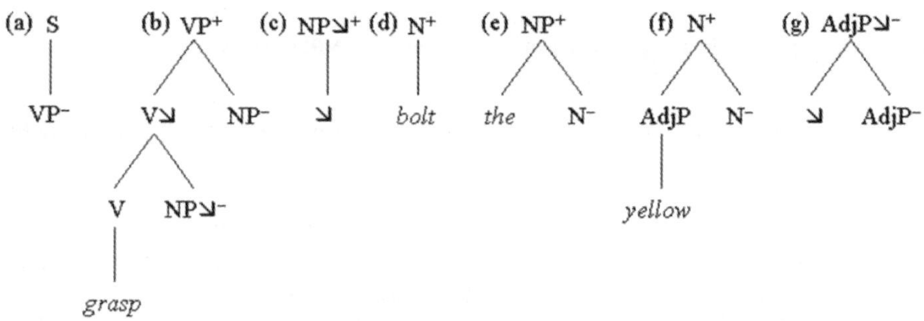

Figure 12. LTAG representation of the syntax interface for pointing and speech

The logical description of the input has to provide the linear precedence regularities for our example "Grasp this yellow bolt!" The *description of the input* must fix the underspecification range of the ⤓. It has to come after the imperative verb, but that is all we need to state; in other words, an underspecified description is at the heart of all the models depicted in (2) to (5). The *lexical descriptions for words* will also have to contain the type-logical formulas for compositional semantics as specified in (7) or (9). From the descriptions of the *elementary trees* we will get the basics for the "pairing-off" mechanism. Figure 13 shows the derived tree for the directive "Grasp ⤓ this yellow bolt!" with semantic tagging using the LTAG in Figure 12.

4.5. On the question of structures anchoring multi-modal meanings

We now want to seriously consider the problem of providing some meaning for formulas of the sort

(15) F_{dir} (grasp(you, ιz(yellowbolt(z))) ∧ ιz(yellowbolt(z)) = a),

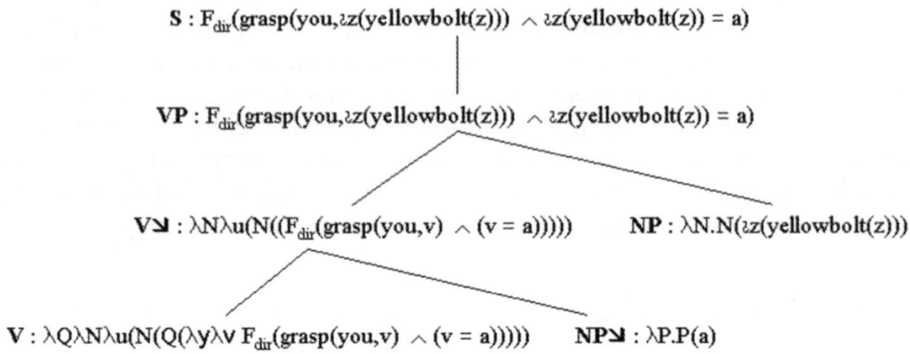

Figure 13. Derived tree for the directive "Grasp ↘ this yellow bolt!" with semantic tagging using the LTAG in Fig. 12

paraphrased as the directive speech act "Grasp the yellow bolt demonstrated!" Pursuing this we must discuss the following problems: First, which is the structure to be used for speech act interpretation? Second, which are the conditions of success for speech acts in general and (15) in particular? Third, which are the conditions of commitment and the satisfaction conditions for speech acts in general and (15) in particular? Fourth, what is the relation between empirical setting and model structure? To discuss these problems in a very preliminary way, we use the Illocutionary Logic (IL) approach (Searle and Vanderveken 1989), which allows us to touch upon some points of interest.

4.5.1. *The structure used for speech act interpretation*

Formula (15) describes an elementary illocutionary act with the directive illocutionary force as indicated by F_{dir}.

Hence, we will concentrate on how elementary (i.e. atomic in the strict sense) directives are treated in IL. In IL one uses the notion of context of utterance in order to specify the semantic and pragmatic conditions of illocutionary acts such as these. For building up contexts of utterance, we need four sets, I_1, I_2, I_3, I_4 for, respectively, possible speakers, hearers, times and places of utterance. In addition, we postulate a set W of possible worlds of utterance.

The set I of all possible contexts of utterance is a proper subset of the Cartesian product of the sets introduced individually: $I \subset I_1 \times I_2 \times I_3 \times I_4 \times W$.

As a consequence, every context of utterance $i \in I$ has five constituents, the so-called coordinates of the context: speaker a_i, hearer b_i, time t_i, location l_i and the world w_i. A context i is identified with the 5-tuple $< a_i, b_i, t_i, l_i, w_i>$. There is a linear ordering $\prec$ on I_3 (times). Possible worlds are taken to be primitive; as usual in modal logics, we need a designated world w_0, for the actual world. In addition, the set W comes with a binary relation R of accessibility, which we need in order to express different styles of possibility and necessity, mental states and future or past courses of events.

So far, we have provided an answer to our first question concerning the structure to be used for speech act interpretation. We now turn to the conditions of commitment and satisfaction for speech acts as mentioned in the second question.

What do success, commitment and satisfaction conditions, respectively, amount to for example (15)? First we investigate success, i.e. successful performance. To discuss this question, we need a couple of notions from general modal logics and from IL: The notion of possibility, $\Diamond$, is used as in normal systems of modal logics, *Des* is a modal operator indicating desire, and $\Pi_!$ serves as a modal operator for the directive illocutionary point used to model the semantics and pragmatics of requests. *U(w)* is the domain of objects associated with some world $w \in W$; in addition, domains for all possible worlds can be defined.

An elementary illocutionary act of the form F_{dir} (grasp(you, ιz(yb(z))) ∧ ιz(yb(z)) = a) is performed in the context of utterance i iff the speaker = description-giver a_i succeeds in the context of utterance i to

- express the illocutionary point $\Pi_!$ (request) on P = (grasp(you, ιz(yb(z))) ∧ ιz(yb(z)) = a),
- issue the commanded proposition P, i.e. issue the relevant locutionary act,
- presuppose that it is possible ($\Diamond$) for the addressee to grasp the yellow bolt demonstrated, i.e. $\Diamond$(grasp(you, ιz(yb(z))) ∧ ιz(yb(z)) = a), where you = addressee = object-identifier, and
- express a desire (*Des*) concerning the intended act, i.e. Des(grasp(object-identifier, ιz(yb(z))) ∧ ιz(yb(z)) = a).

These conditions provide only success requirements for the illocutionary act. We now turn to the description giver's commitments. Since the description-giver produces an utterance of (15) in w_i, we may assume that he is committed to the conditions of F_{dir} (grasp(you, ιz(yb(z))) ∧ ιz(yb(z)) = a), i.e., presuppositions, mental states and the like, for example, he must believe that the object to be grasped exists, that the addressee has not grasped it so far and he must sincerely intend that it should be grasped.

Finally, we turn to the notion of satisfaction for elementary speech acts of the form *F(P)*: An illocutionary act of the form *F(P)* is *satisfied* in a context of utterance *i* iff $P(w_i) = 1$ and is *not satisfied* otherwise in *i*. For F_{dir} (grasp(you, ιz(yb(z))) ∧ ιz(yb(z)) = a) this means that it is satisfied in *i*, iff (grasp(you, ιz(yb(z))) ∧ ιz(yb(z)) $(w_i) = 1$, i.e. iff the object-identifier grasps the demonstrated yellow bolt in w_i.

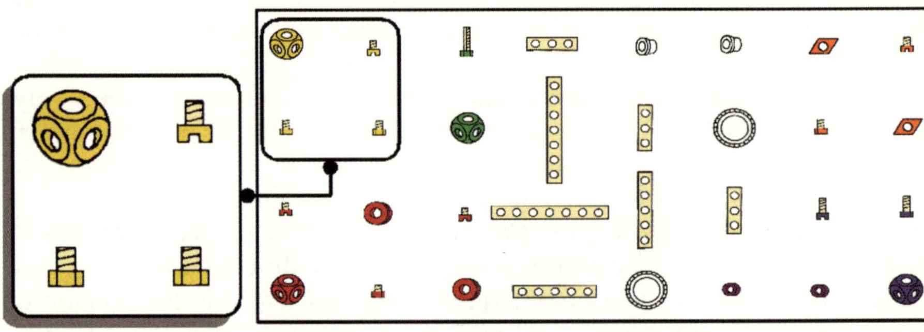

Figure 14. Experimental domain used as a sub-domain of the intended model for speech act interpretation

4.5.2. Logics and reality: experimental setting and model structure

Normally, if one has to set up models for speech act representations such as in (15) one is hard pressed for providing intuitive model descriptions, especially, if problems of reference are at stake and the models should in a way imitate natural referring conditions. We are better off in this respect: As the empirical data show, we have all the information necessary in order to add substance to the formal model described in the previous passages: Both agents in our object-identification dialogue are possible speakers and hearers, hence $I_1 = I_2 =$ {description-giver and object-identifier}, I_3 and I_4 get a natural interpretation as being related to the time and the place of the experiment, respectively. It is perhaps more difficult to decide on the *possible worlds of utterance*. The most suitable choice seems to be to map occurrences of speech act tokens onto contexts *i*. Our agents reside in the actual world, i.e. in the experimental setting. Hence, we have, paralleling speech act occurrences, contexts *i* of the following sort, distinguishable by the values of t_i: <*description-giver$_i$, object-identifier$_i$, t_i, l_i, w_0*>. We can exactly specify what the relevant part of $U(w_0)$, the set of objects that can be pointed at, is. It is shown in Figure 14 and is identical to one of the settings used in the experimental studies described in section 3 above. Using Figure 14 as depiction of our relevant sub-domain, we notice three yellow bolts in the left corner. This means that with respect to this model the satisfaction of (15) fails, since the definite description ιz(yb(z)) cannot be satisfied. As a consequence, the object-identifier might try to check-back saying "Which one do you mean?" Indeed, some such reaction is frequently found in our corpus. Notice that restrictor-demonstration has more chances of success, if D in ιz(yellowbolt(z) ∧ z ∈ D) can be instantiated to contain one of the yellow bolts, still, there are various options for a proper choice of D (Fig. 15).

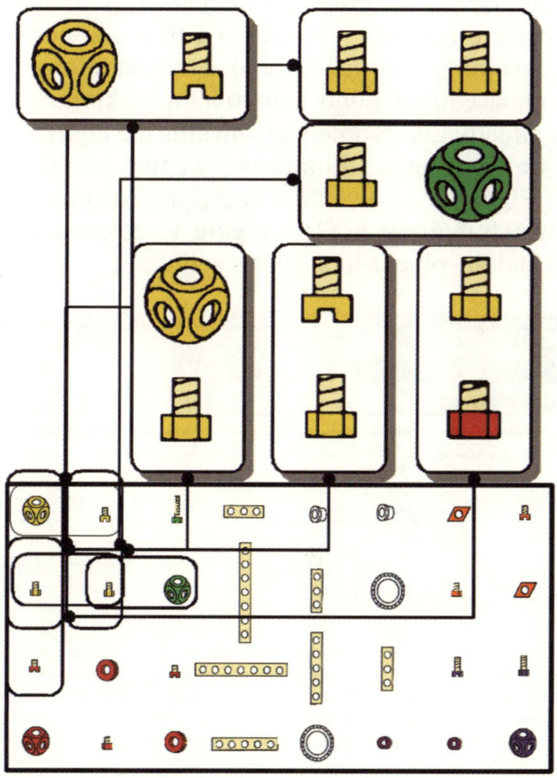

Figure 15. Some pair-subsets of the spotted sub-domain. Note that some pairs constitute models for successful CDs, while others do not

4.6. Modeling pointing effects in current theory of dialogue

So far, we have not developed a systematic description of the role of demonstration in natural dialogue. This will be the aim of this section, after a brief recapitulation of what we have got up to now. First, we showed how multimodal content, speech and gesture, can be integrated into a theory distinguishing between object-pointing and region-pointing. The theory maps multi-modal objects onto a speech act representation containing complex demonstrations, i.e. definite descriptions accompanied by demonstrations. This step is based on examples from an annotated corpus of object identification games. Second, we specified conditions of success, commitment and satisfaction for speech acts, using "Grasp ↘ this yellow bolt!" as an example. At that, we also discussed the relation between empirical setting and model structure, showing that the empirical setting can serve as an intended model. Third, using statistical methods, we extracted from our corpus data a potential regularity concerning turn-taking and demonstration: The description-giver's retraction phase might contribute to a turn-taking signal. Considering all that, we have already gone some way towards the description of dialogue.

In order to estimate what is still missing, we turn to a fairly easy example from the corpus: Figure 16 shows the transcript of a complete sub-dialogue, the wording of which is given in (16). Figure 17 offers snapshots of the description-giver's and the object-identifier's actions.

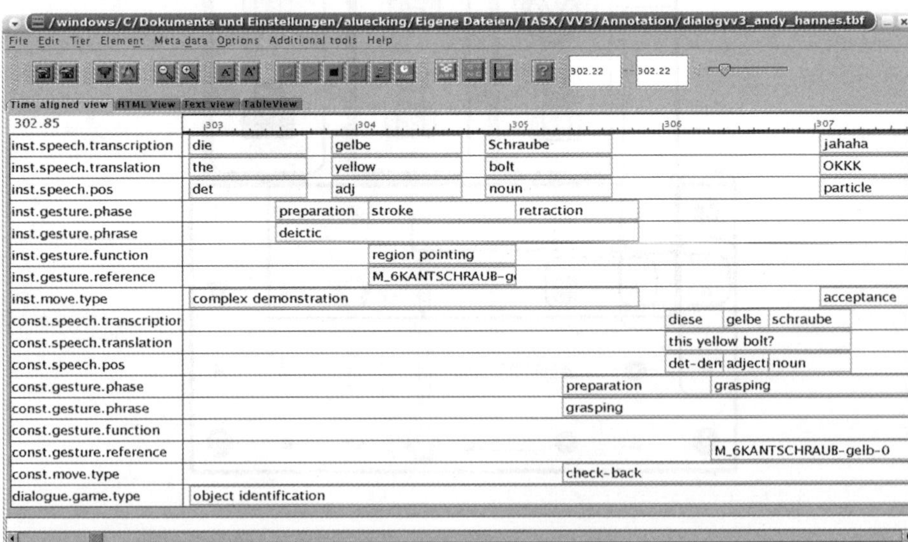

Figure 16. Complete sub-dialogue from the object-identification corpus

(16a) Description-giver: The yellow ↘bolt! [demonstrates yellow bolt]
(16b) Object-identifier: This ↘yellow bolt? [grasps indicated yellow bolt]
(16c) Description giver: OK OK OK.

We have a directive in (16a), a clarification question in (16b) and an 'accept' move in (16c). The directive and the clarification question are elliptical, lacking appropriate finite verbs. We can substitute 'grasp' and 'should I grasp' respectively. Taking the previous sections 4.1 to 4.5 as background, we are now able to develop the relevant intuitions: The description-giver issues a command. Its grammar and multi-modal semantics is as shown in Section 4.5 (15). The command is successfully performed but not satisfied. It would be satisfied, so we may assume, if the object-identifier simply took the yellow bolt with some sort of assertion or without a comment and the description-giver accepted the dialogue move. Why does the situation arise? Looking at the intended model for the satisfaction of the command, i.e. the table plus objects depicted in Figure 17, we see why it is not satisfied.

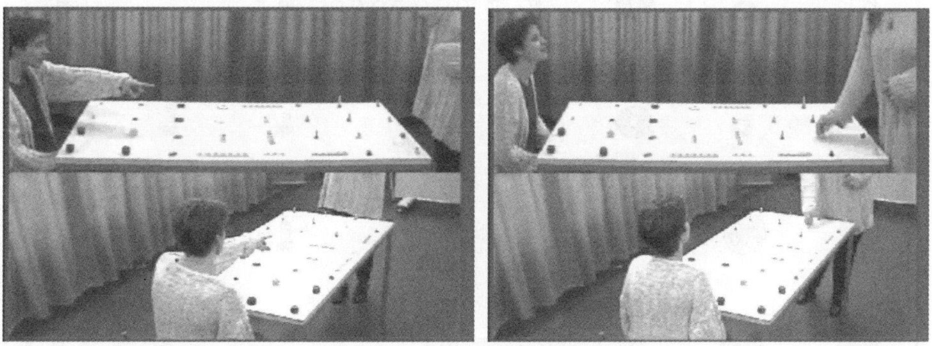

Figure 17 Description giver's and object-identifier's actions

As Figure 18 clearly indicates, neither conceptualizing the pointing as object-pointing nor as region-pointing will yield a uniquely referring definite description. We can even assume that the description-giver had the right intention to refer to the bolt which the object-identifier finally grasped, thus emphasizing that success and commitment conditions were indeed met, but the pointing resolution does not suffice for attaining satisfaction, since it is defined for $<description\text{-}giver_i, object\text{-}identifier_i, t_i, l_i, w_0>$, i.e. it also depends on the object-identifier. This explains why we have a clarification question of the object-identifier's ✋*This yellow bolt?* Observe that the reference of the grasping act provides no problem, since grasping can be conceived as borderline case of pointing. The clarification question thus functions as a means to achieve alignment between description-giver and object-identifier. In terms of the concept of pointing cone, the sequence of command and clarification question can be explained as follows: The semantics of the pointing cone taken as a "Platonic entity" may be OK, that is, it may single out a sub-domain which can be fused with the definite description in the multi-modal interface as discussed in Section 4.2, but its pragmatics is obviously not, the main problem being that the gauging of the pointing cone by the object-identifier does not yield an applicable description. More generally, in dialogues involving pointing the alignment of the pointing cone and its projection by the addressee of the pointing act have to be considered. In informal terms, the clarification question can be paraphrased as: Does the object grasped meet your referring intention? The description-giver's accept shows that it does.

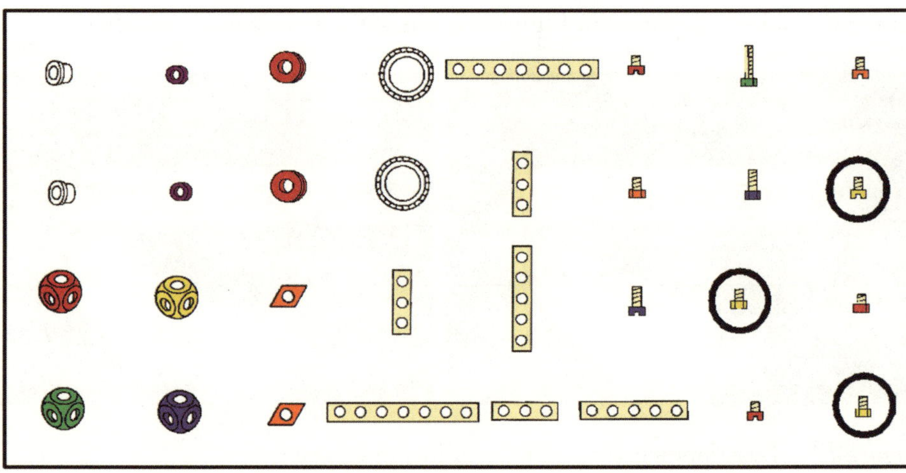

Figure 18. Intended model for satisfaction of the elliptical directive *The yellow↘bolt!* There are three yellow bolts at the right border, which explains that neither object-pointing nor region-pointing can be satisfied in conjunction with the definite description

A final observation coming from the transcript in Figure 16 is that description-giver's retraction phase and object-identifier's preparation phase overlap. If we want to use this trait in our theorizing, we have to introduce special annotation devices indicating the full structure of the demonstration. So, let us use ↓ for the preparation phase of a demonstration, ↘ for its stroke as before, usurping it now also for grasping, and ↑ for its retraction phase. In order to distinguish contributions of various agents, we decorate the arrows with agents' labels like $\downarrow_{\text{description-giver}}$, $\searrow_{\text{description-giver}}$, $\uparrow_{\text{description-giver}}$ etc. Using these means, we get the following annotation for the turns of (16):

(17a) $[_{NP}$ $[_{DET}$ The] $[_{N'}$ $\downarrow_{\text{description-giver}}$ $[_{ADJ}$ yellow] $\searrow_{\text{description-giver}}$ $[_{N'}$bolt]] $\uparrow_{\text{description-giver}}$].
(17b) $[_{NP}$ $\downarrow_{\text{object-identifier}}$ $[_{DEM}$ This] $[_{N'}$ $\searrow_{\text{object-identifier}}$ $[_{ADJ}$ yellow] $[_{N'}$bolt]]].
(17c) OK OK OK.

After these preliminaries, we look at the structure of the three-turn dialogue. Here we must integrate different traditions of dialogue description: The basic idea of agents cooperating and coordinating in dialogue comes from Clark (1996) and, more recently, from Pickering and Garrod (2004), the proposal that newly attached turns are bound to old content on the basis of discourse relations has been developed in dialogue game theory (Levin and Moore 1977), RST (Mann and Thompson 1987), and SDRT (Asher and Lascarides 2003); finally, surface orientation as a paradigm for dialogue description goes back to a proposal of Poesio and Traum (1997).

Now we determine the discourse relations involved. The expressions (16a) and (16b) are related by the fact that (16c) is a clarification question following a command. The command cannot be satisfied, since the object identifier is not able to spot the object indicated. The object-identifier's question is such that if it is answered by the description-giver, he or she knows whether the command is satisfied or not. We suggest a binary relation ICSP(α, β) (called 'indirect command satisfaction pair') to capture that α is a command and β a question. The answer to β will as a rule indicate whether the command is already satisfied by the addressee's action or whether he has to initiate a new action to finally carry out the description-giver's request. In other words, the question is closely tied to the satisfaction conditions of the command. More precisely, it is a question solely concerned with establishing the satisfaction of the command. As a consequence, it must be followed by an answer. Fulfilling this need, (16b) and (16c) compose a question answer pair (QAP), a relation as proposed by Asher and Lascarides (2003: 313). The description-giver's accept is also only concerned with the satisfaction problem.

We will refrain from specifying the formal details here, they are straightforward anyway. The structure of the whole dialogue is thus simply as depicted in Figure 19, in addition satisfying the constraint that $\uparrow_{\text{description-giver}} \circ \downarrow_{\text{object-identifier}}$, i.e. $\uparrow_{\text{description-giver}}$ and $\downarrow_{\text{object-identifier}}$ overlap.

α: The $\downarrow_{\text{description-giver}}$ yellow $\searrow_{\text{description-giver}}$ bolt! $\uparrow_{\text{description-giver}}$

ICSP

β: $\downarrow_{\text{object-identifier}}$ This $\downarrow_{\text{object-identifier}}$ yellow bolt?

QAP

γ: OKOKOK

Constraint: $\uparrow_{\text{description-giver}} \circ \downarrow_{\text{object-identifier}}$

Figure 19. Dialogue structure for example (16) according to SDRT

5. Processing deictic expressions

In this section we discuss the relevance of pointing in complex demonstrations from the perspective of human-computer interaction. The scenario under discussion consists of task-oriented dialogues, which pertain to the cooperative assembly of virtual aggregates, viz. toy airplanes. These dialogues take place in face-to-face manner in immersive virtual reality, realized in the three-side CAVE-like installation mentioned in Section 3. The system is represented by a human-sized virtual agent called "Max", who is able on the one hand to interpret simple multi-modal (speech and gesture) input by a human instructor, and on the other hand to produce synchronized output involving synthetic speech, facial display and gesture (Kopp and Wachsmuth 2004). As illustrated in Figure 20, Max and the human dialogue partner are located at a virtual table with toy parts and communicate about how to assembly them.

In this setting demonstration games can be realized to focus on the understanding and generation of complex demonstrations. In analogy to the empirical setting described in Section 3 these demonstration games follow the tradition of minimal dialogue games as proposed in, e.g., Mann (1988). However, we reduce the interaction to two turns. This enables us to directly compare the empirically recorded data with the results of speech-gesture processing, since our HCI interface already provides a framework for handling these basic interactions.

The narrow description of speech-gesture processing is split into two subsections. In the first one below the role of the pointing cone for speech-gesture understanding is highlighted. Special attention is given to its relevance for the computation of reference in the Reference Resolution Engine

(Pfeiffer and Latoschik 2004). The second subsection describes the algorithm for generating deictic expressions, especially how demonstrating by object- respectively region-pointing interacts with content selection for the verbal part of the expression.

Figure 20. Interacting with the human-sized agent Max in an immersive VR-scenario concerning the assembly of toy airplanes. From Kranstedt and Wachsmuth (2005)

5.1. A framework for speech-gesture understanding gesture recognition

In 3.3 we have seen how the information of the trackers is made accessible by the actuator nodes of the PrOSA framework to the VR application. For recognizing gestures, the fields exported by the actuators are connected to specialized detector nets, subgraphs of evaluation nodes designed to classify certain postures or trajectories. For instance, there are detector nets to detect an extended index finger called "`right-hand-index-posture`" or an extended arm called "`right-arm-extended`". Their results are provided in timed sequence fields, e.g., as collection of Boolean values identifying whether at a certain point in time the index finger was extended or not. High-level concepts such as "`right-is-pointing`" can then be identified combining the results of existing detector nets. Note that this is only a didactic example; the composition of detector nets used in the current system is far more complex. A more detailed description can be found in Latoschik 2001b).

5.1.1. The role of the pointing cone in early gesture processing

The dynamic environment of a VR setting imposes some difficulties for modeling the pragmatic effect of pointing gestures, that is, for identifying the intended objects or regions. At the time the system has finally reached the conclusion that the spatial area of the pointing gesture is important and the objects enclosed in the pointing cone are relevant, they might already have changed their positions or appearances. Their positions at the production time of the gesture are needed, but to gather tracking information about all objects in the environment during the full course of interaction is almost impossible. Instead we follow a proactive approach. After a gesture has been classified as a pointing gesture, additional nets take care of evaluating the corresponding pointing cones, collecting all enclosed objects in a special structure called space-map. These space-maps are then used by the following processes for the semantic interpretation of the pointing gesture. In this early processing steps, elaborated models of the pointing cones help to sustain a low memory profile while maintaining the descriptiveness of the gesture. This is accomplished taking a highly localized snapshot of the gesture's visual context.

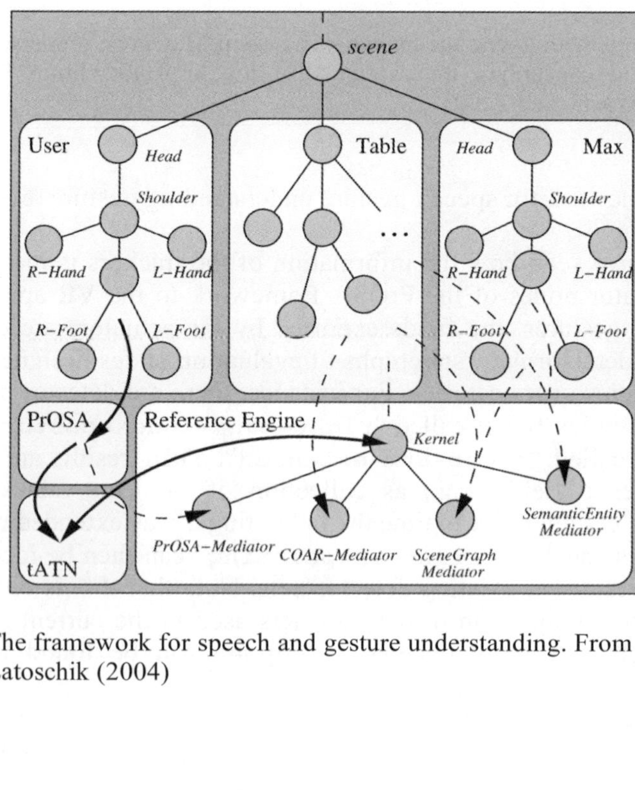

Figure 21. The framework for speech and gesture understanding. From Pfeiffer and Latoschik (2004)

5.1.2. Speech and gesture integration

For the understanding of multi-modal instructions and direct manipulative actions in the VR system, a tATN is used, an ATN specialized for synchronizing multi-modal inputs (Latoschik 2003). It operates on a set of states and defines conditions for state transitions. The actual state thereby represents the context of the utterance in which the conditions will be processed. In the extension, states are anchored in time by an additional timestamp `reach`. Possible conditions classify words, access PrOSA sequence fields for the gestural content or test the application's context. An important part of the context is the world model representing the visual objects. A module called reference-resolution engine (RRE) enables the tATN to verify the validity of the object descriptions specified so far, finding the matching objects in the world model. The set of possible interpretations of an object description delivered by the RRE will incrementally be restricted during the further processing of the utterance by the tATN. If the parsing process has been successful, these sets are used to finally fill in the action descriptions used for initiating the execution of the instruction. It is the RRE where the content of the pointing is finally integrated with content from other modalities and where the cone representations find their application.

5.1.3. The relevance of the pointing cone for the reference resolution

The task of the RRE is to interpret complex demonstrations (CDs) according to the current world model represented in heterogeneous knowledge bases (Fig. 21) for symbolic information such as type, color or function (*Semantic Entity Mediator*, *COAR Mediator*) and for geometrical information (*Scene-Graph Mediator*, *PrOSA Mediator*). This is done using a fuzzy logic-based constraint satisfaction approach.

When incrementally parsing a multi-modal utterance such as

(18) *Grasp ↘this/that yellow bolt*,

the tATN tries to find objects in the world satisfying the complex demonstration. For this the tATN communicates with the RRE using a constraint query language. A query corresponding to example (18) would be formulated like this:

```
(inst ?x)   (pointed-to instruction-giver ?x time-1)
            (has-color ?x YELLOW time-1)
            (has-type ?x BOLT time-2)
```

In order to process this query, the RRE has to gather the knowledge of several heterogeneous knowledge bases. The *PrOSA Mediator* is used to evaluate the `pointed-to` constraint. The `has-color` constraint requires the *SemanticEntity Mediator* and for the `has-type` constraint the knowledge of the *COAR Mediator* is used. The RRE integrates the responses from each mediator and tries to satisfy `(inst ?x)`. This could be a single object in the case of an object demonstration or in the case of a restrictor demonstration a set of possible objects, the subdomain of the world defined by the query (and initially by the CD). In both cases the RRE provides additional information about the saliency of the matches and the contributions of the single constraints to the overall saliency.

In our dynamic scenes the constraints can only be computed on demand, so fast evaluating constraints are necessary to meet the requirements of real-time interaction. Unfortunately, especially geometric constraints formulated verbally, e.g., by "to the left of the block" are computationally demanding: Even single constraints are highly ambiguous and fuzziness keeps adding up when several constraints are spanning over a set of variables. To improve performance the RRE uses therefore a hierarchical ordering of constraints to reduce the search space as soon as possible:

- Constraints on single variables are preferred on those over tuples of variables, e.g., (has-color ?x yellow t_1) is evaluated before (is-left-of ?x ?y t_2)
- Constraints on fast accessible properties are preferred, e.g., (has-color ?x yellow t_1) is evaluated before (has-size ?x big t_2) as the latter is context dependent.
- Hard constraints evaluating to `true` or `false` are preferred. Typical examples are constraints over names or types, which can be solved by looking them up in the symbolic KB. In contrast, constraints over geometric properties are generally soft and less restrictive.

The pointing cone is directly represented in the same KB as the geometrical aspects of the world model, so the variables can be resolved directly with optimized intersection algorithms. With an accurate direct representation of the pointing cone, the RRE bypasses the described problems with constraints extracted from speech. The geometrical context of a CD can be computed less costly and faster, while yielding more precise results. So to speak, pointing focuses attention.

5.1.4. Differentiating object-pointing and region-pointing

By default the `pointed-to` constraint discriminates between object-pointing and region-pointing based on the distances of the objects. This behavior can be overwritten by explicitly specifying the intended interpretation using the parameters `'object-cone` or `'region-cone` as in `(pointed-to instruction-giver ?x time-1 'object-cone)` where object-pointing, and therefore a more narrow cone, is forced.

5.2. Generation of deictic expressions

While much work concerning the generation of verbal referring expressions has been published in the last 15 years, work on the generation of multimodal referring expressions is rare. Most approaches use idealized pointing in addition to or instead of verbal referring expressions (e.g. Claassen 1992; Lester et al. 1999; Reithinger 1992). In contrast, only Krahmer and van der Sluis (2003) account for vague pointing, and distinguish the three types precise, imprecise, and very imprecise pointing.

We propose an approach (Kranstedt and Wachsmuth 2005) which integrates an evaluation of the discriminatory power of pointing with a content selection algorithm founded on the incremental algorithm published by Dale and Reiter (1995). Based on empirical observation and theoretical consideration, we use the pointing cone to model the discriminatory power of a planned pointing gesture and to distinguish its two referential functions, object-pointing and region-pointing discussed above. Figure 22 presents the algorithm; Figure 23 depicts an example which will be explained in detail further on in this section.

Using terminology proposed by Dale and Reiter (1995), we define the *context set* C to be the set of entities (physical objects in our scenario) that the hearer is currently assumed to be attending to. These can be seen as similar to the entities in the focus spaces of the discourse focus stack in the theory of discourse structure proposed by Grosz and Sidner (1986). We also define the set of *distractors* D to be the set of entities the *referent* r has to be distinguished from by a set of *restricting properties* R each composed of an attribute-value pair. At the beginning of the content selection process the distractor set D will be the context set C, at the end D will only contain r if content selection has been successful.

To achieve linear computation time, Dale and Reiter (1995) propose a determined sequence of property evaluation and dispense with backtracking. This leads to overspecification, but they can show that the generation results

```
contentSelectRE(referent r, properties P, context set C)
      restricting properties R ← {}
      distractors D ← C
      α ← objectPointingConeApexAngle
      β ← regionPointingConeApexAngle

1.    if     reachable?(r)
             then  R ← {(location,pointingAt)}
                   (h⃗,r⃗) ← generatePointingBeam(r)
                   if     getPointingMap((h⃗,r⃗),C,α) = {r}
                          then return R ∪ {type,getValue(r,type)}
                          else D ← getPointingMap((h⃗,r⃗),C,β)
2.    for each p ∈ P
            if     relationalProperty?(p)
                   then value v ← getRelationalValue(r,p,D)
                   else value v ← getValue(r,p)
            if     v ≠ null ∧ rulesOut(p,v,D) ≠ {}
                   then  R ← R ∪ {(p,v)}
                         D ← D \ rulesOut(p,v,D)
            if     D = {r}
                   if     (type,x) R for some x
                          then return R
                          else return R ∪ {type,getValue(r,type)}
      return failure
--------------------------------------------------------------------------
getPointingMap((h⃗,r⃗),C,α)
      pointing map M ← {}
      for each o ∈ C
             x⃗ ← getPosition(0,h⃗)
             β ← getAngle(x⃗,r⃗)
             if     β ≤ α
                    then insert(o,M,α)
      return M

rulesOut(p,v,D)
      return {x|x ∈ D ∧ getValue(x,p) ≠ v}

getRelationalValue(r,p,D)
      if     min{v|v=getValue(x,p) ∧ x ∈ D} = getValue(r,p)
             then return minValue(p)
      if     max{v|v=getValue(x,p) ∧ x ∈ D} = getValue(r,p)
             then return maxValue(p)
      return null
```

Figure 22. The content selection algorithm. It gets the referent, the set of properties holding true for this referent, and the set of objects in the domain under discussion and returns a list of property value pairs. The first part realizes the evaluation of pointing using the pointing cone. `generatePointingBeam` generates the pointing beam defined by two vectors, the origin and the direction. `getPointingMap` returns all objects inside the pointing cone defined by the beam and the apex angle. The second part is an adapted version of the incremental algorithm proposed by Dale and Reiter (1995)

fit well with the empirical findings if the sequence of properties is chosen accurately with respect to the specific domain. As described in Section 3, overspecification is also often found in our data. Therefore, the content selection algorithm gets a sorted list of properties in addition to the referent and the context set as input. Concerning the order of properties, in our corpus we typically observe the hierarchy type, color, size and relative location in the verbal part of the deictic utterances. In addition we consider absolute location to be expressed by pointing.

As a first step in the proposed algorithm for deictic expressions (see Figure 22, part 1), disambiguation of the referent by object-pointing is checked if the referent is visible to both participants. Using the PrOSA tools mentioned above, this is achieved generating a pointing cone with an apex angle of 20 degree anchored in an approximated hand-position and directed to the referent. If only the intended referent is found inside this cone referring is done by object-pointing. If object-pointing does not yield a referent, region-pointing is used to focus the attention of the addressee to a certain area making the set of objects in this area salient. The distractor set D is narrowed down to this set of objects. In both cases the property *location* with the value *pointingAt* indicating a pointing gesture is added to R.

For determining the other properties we use a simplified version of the incremental algorithm of Dale and Reiter (1995), which tests every property in P with respect to its discriminatory power (Fig. 22, part 2). Our algorithm is simplified in as much as in our current implementation the *findBestValue* function defined by Dale and Reiter is replaced by the simpler *getValue* function. The task of *findBestValue* is to search for the most specific value of an attribute that both, discriminates the referent r from more elements in D than the next general one does, and is known to the addressee. Only for the special case *type* we realize this search of the appropriate vaue on a specialization hierarchy ("screw" is used instead of "pan head slotted bolt"). We operate in a highly simplified domain with objects characterized by properties having only a few and well distinguished values. Thus, for the other properties like color we do not need such a sophisticated approach.

However, extending the basic algorithm by Dale and Reiter we also account for relationally expressed properties often found in our corpus. To evaluate these properties we use a function named *getRelationalValue*. This function needs a partial order for each property; in the current system this is only implemented for size and relative position. In the case of size we relate the property to the shape of the objects under discussion. Shape is a special property often used if the type of an object is unknown but is difficult to handle in generation. Therefore, we currently only account for it by evaluating size. The shape of some of the objects in our domain is characterized by one or two designated dimensions. For these objects size is substituted by, e.g., length respectively thickness ("long screw" is used instead of "big screw"). In the case of relative location we also use substitution. The relative location is evaluated along the axes defining the subjective coordinate systems of the dialogue participants (left-right, ahead-behind, and top-down). E.g., *getRelationalValue* returns "left" if the referent r is the left most located object in D.

The content selection for the example depicted in Figure 23 can be described as follows: The starting point is a query concerning the reference to a specific object named *five-hole-bar-0*, the intended referent r. As mentioned before, first the pointing cone for object-pointing is evaluated (Fig. 22, 1.). In this case, more than one object is inside the cone and region-pointing is evaluated next. The cone is visualized in Figure 23. As a result, the set of distractors D for property evaluation in part two of the algorithm is narrowed down to the two bars *five-hole-bar-*0 and *three-hole-bar-0* and some other objects. The property location with the value *pointingTo* indicating a pointing gesture is added to R. The second part starts with testing the property *type*. The type *five-hole-bar* is too specific, so the super-type *bar* is chosen. It rules out all objects except the two bars (now D = {*five-hole-bar-0, three-hole-bar-0*}), and *type* with the value *bar* is added to R. Next, the property *colour* is tested; it has no discriminatory power concerning the two bars. But the following relational property size discriminates the two objects. The shape of the bars is characterized by one designated dimension, length. For these objects *size* is substituted by *length*. In our case r has the maximum length of all objects in D, the property *length* with the value *long* is added to R. Now D contains only r, the algorithm finishes and returns R = {(*location, pointingAt*), (*type*, *bar*), (*length, long*)}.

The results of the content selection algorithm represented as a list of attribute-value-pairs are fed into a surface realization module generating a syntactically correct noun phrase. This noun phrase is combined with a gesture specification and both are inserted into a surface description template of a multi-modal utterance fetched from a database. The resulting description represents the locutionary act of one single communicative act (that is a multi-modal extension of speech act). As far as communicative acts are concerned, currently instances of the general types *query*, *request*, and *inform* can be expressed.

In the utterance descriptions cross-modal synchrony is established by appending the gesture stroke to the affiliated word or subphrase in the co-expressive speech. Based on these descriptions, an utterance generator synthesizes continuous speech and gesture in a synchronized manner (Kopp and Wachsmuth 2004). To replicate the empirical findings an offset of 0.2 seconds between the beginning of the gesture stroke and the affiliate is implicitly added during realization. In our example (Fig. 23), based on R = {(*location*, *pointingAt*), (*type*, *bar*), (*length*, *long*)} a pointing gesture directed to r is specified, the noun phrase “die lange Leiste” (the long bar) is built, and both are inserted into the utterance template. The complete utterance is synthesised and uttered by the agent Max.

“Meinst Du die lange Leiste?”
(Do you mean the long bar?)

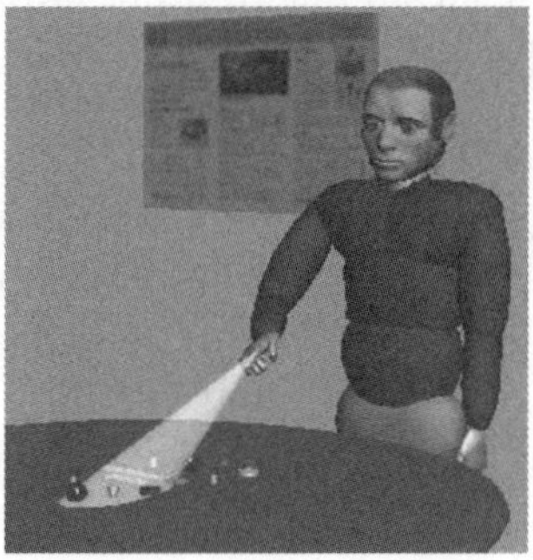

```
<definition>
   <parameter name="NP"/>
   <parameter name="Object"/>
   <utterance>
      <specification>
         Meinst Du <time id="t1"/>$NP? <time id="t2"/>
      </specification>
      <behaviorspec id="gesture_0">
         <gesture>
           <affiliate onset="t1" end="t2"/>
           <function name="refer_to_loc">
              <argument name="refloc" value="$Object"/>
           </function>
         </gesture>
      </behaviorspace>
   </utterance>
</definition>
```

Figure 23. A parameterized utterance specification expressed in MURML (Kranstedt, Kopp, and Wachsmuth 2002). The picture illustrates the resulting animation (German speech) including the visualized pointing cone

First evaluations of the generation results support the assumption that different apex angles for the pointing cones of region-pointing and object-pointing in settings with high object density are needed. In our VR setting, 40 degrees for region-pointing seems to be a good initial choice to get robust distinctions and natural expressions. However, this has to be studied in more detail empirically. The concept of the pointing cone based on a set of parameters guarantees that the cone’s form and size can be adjusted as further findings become available.

6. Conclusion

The collaborative research presented in this chapter raised the issue of pointing in complex demonstrations. We approached this issue from interlocked perspectives including empirical research, theoretical modeling and speech-gesture processing in human-computer interaction (Fig. 24).

Complex demonstrations comprise two fundamental kinds of referring to objects: Indicating via pointing, and describing using a definite description. The meaning of such utterances is seen as a composition of the meaning of the gesture and that of the verbal expression, with the gesture and the expression often being underspecified by their own. Therefore, we distinguish two referential functions of pointing: Object-pointing (referring successfully on its own) and region-pointing (referring successfully only in combination with a description). In order to model the distance-dependent decreasing precision of pointing, we introduced the concept of a pointing cone. The pointing cone captures the geometrical aspects of pointing and is used as an interface between the spatial context of pointing and its referential semantics.

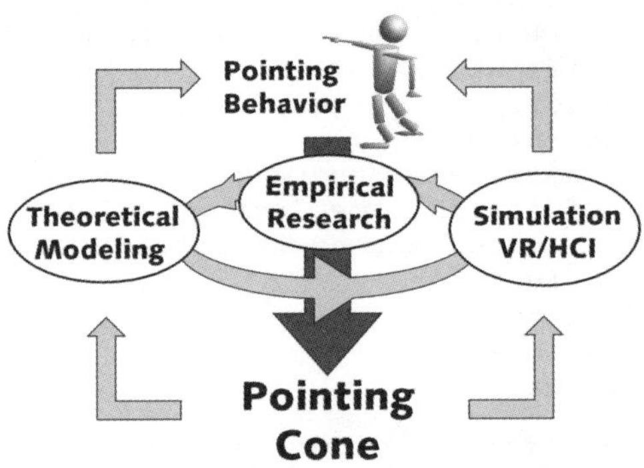

Figure 24. The pointing cone as the central concept is theoretically grounded and empirically measured with respect to the needs in speech-gesture processing. It constitutes a central building block in the formal construction of the meaning of complex demonstrations, and it is essential for setting up efficient methods of processing complex demonstrations in human-machine interaction

In our studies, a genuine effort was undertaken in collecting multi-resolutional empirical data on deictic reference ranging from the high levels of speech acts down to the delicate movements of the fingers. We worked out a detailed procedure to assess the geometrical properties of pointing using tracking technology for measuring the set of parameters relevant for computation of the pointing cone's size and form.

The results concerning the sub-domain determined by the base of the pointing cone serve as a basis for getting at the "pure semantics of pointing". According to the semiotics tradition, the pointing gesture itself can be conceived of as a sign with its own syntax, semantics and pragmatics. Following this lead, we may assume that the pointing gesture in itself is able to determine an extension, much like a proper name or relations as interpreted in logical semantics with respect to a model. As a consequence, the described experimental settings serve as a basis for the construction of realistic models lacking for example in the philosophical literature on demonstration.

Applying the concept of a pointing cone to human-computer interaction, it is shown that in reference resolution the cone not only accounts for expressing the extension of pointing. Its topology is also used for generating snapshots of the visual context associated with a gesture in early processing steps. These snapshots allow a low memory profile and help to unfold the restrictive power of pointing by narrowing down the search space and hence speed up the computation of reference.

In utterance generation, we use the empirically determined size of the pointing cone to estimate the borderline of the discriminative power of object-pointing in a planned utterance. If object-pointing does not yield a referent, region-pointing is used to draw the attention of the addressee to a spatial area. The objects inside this area constitute the contrast set for a content selection based on an adapted version of the incremental algorithm by Dale and Reiter (1995).

It has to be emphasized that the pointing cone as described in this contribution is an idealized concept. Observations from our empirical data indicate that several context dependent parameters influence the focus of a pointing gesture and therefore interact with the geometrical concept of a pointing cone. Especially the focus of region-pointing is influenced by additional spatial constraints on the one hand and the dialogue history on the other. For instance, it seems plausible that region-pointing singles out a whole object cluster even if the corresponding pointing cone does not cover the whole cluster. Or it may be clear to the interlocutors that a pointing gesture singles out a specific set of objects, even if the cone covers additional objects because they just talked about this set.

Extending our approach to incorporate dialogue semantics and pragmatics, a first step can be taken in the following way. Instead of using a model for success and satisfaction of directives along the lines of Searle and Vanderveken (1989) which now has contexts of utterance $i \in I$ with five constituents, speaker a_i, hearer b_i, time t_i, location l_i and the world w_i, we can also take account of the description giver's position at the table, positions of trunk, head, hand, index finger, the apex angle, and the like. We can then let the interpretation of the gesture depend on these fine-grained parameters and say that, relative to such and such parameters, the demonstration's extension will be such and such. This will be a refinement in comparison with the pure semantics approach moving the whole issue into the direction of 'classical' pragmatics but still relying on an objective ontology.

As far as we can tell from experiments it could well be that real object-identifiers lack the full interpretive power of both, pure semantics and classical pragmatics. A case in point is the little multi-modal dialogue analyzed, where we have a clarification question and the referent of the preceding multi-modal reference act is determined by agents' coordination. This moves us more into the direction of speaker's meaning, which relies on the speaker's individual possibilities given the situation at hand. Classical paradigms, situated in a Platonic realm, will not always do justice to speakers' worldly reactions.

References

Asher, N., and A. Lascarides
2003 *Logics of Conversation.* Cambridge, UK: Cambridge University Press.

Beun, R.-J., A. and Cremers
2001 Multimodal reference to objects: An empirical approach. In *Proceedings of Cooperative Multimodal Communication*, 64–86. Berlin: Springer.

Butterworth, G.
2003 Pointing is the royal road to language for babies. In *Pointing: Where Language, Culture and Cognition Meet,* S. Kita (ed.), 9–35. Mahwah: Erlbaum.

Chierchia, G., and S. McConnell-Ginet
2000 *Meaning and Grammar – An Introduction to Semantics.* 2nd edition. Cambridge, MA: MIT Press.

Claassen, W.
1992 Generating referring expressions in a multimodal environment. In *Aspects of Automated Natural Language Generation*, R. Dale, E. Hovy, D. Rosner, and O. Stock (eds.). Berlin: Springer.

Clark, H. H.
1996 *Using Language.* Cambridge, UK: Cambridge University Press.
2003 Pointing and placing. In *Pointing: Where Language, Culture and Cognition Meet,* S. Kita (ed.), 243–269. Mahwah: Erlbaum.

Dale, R., and E. Reiter
1995 Computational interpretations of the gricean maxims in the generation of referring expressions. *Cognitive Science* 18: 233–263.

de Ruijter, J. P.
2000 The production of gesture and speech. In *Language and Gesture,* D. McNeill (ed.), 284–312. New York: Cambridge University Press.

Grosz, B., and C. Sidner
1986 Attention, intention, and the structure of discourse. *Computational Linguistics* 12: 175–206.

Kendon, A.
1981 *Nonverbal Communication, Interaction, and Gesture*. The Hague: Mouton.
2004 *Gesture. Visible Action as Utterance*. Cambridge, UK: Cambridge University Press.

Kopp, S., and I. Wachsmuth
2004 Synthesizing multimodal utterances for conversational agents. *Comp. Anim. Virtual Worlds* 15: 39–52.

Krahmer, E., and I. van der Sluis
2003 A new model for the generation of multimodal referring expressions. In *Proceedings of the European Workshop on Natural Language Generation (ENLG 2003).*

Kranstedt, A., S. Kopp, and I. Wachsmuth
2002 MURML: A Multimodal Utterance Representation Markup Language for Conversational Agents. In *Proceedings of the AAMAS02 Workshop Embodied Conversational Agents – let's specify and evaluate them!*

Kranstedt, A., P. Kühnlein, and I. Wachsmuth
2004 Deixis in multimodal human computer interaction: An interdisciplinary approach. In *Gesture-based communication in human-computer interaction*, A. Camurri and G. Volpe (eds.), 112–123. Berlin: Springer.

Kranstedt, A., A. Lücking, T. Pfeiffer, H. Rieser, and I. Wachsmuth
2006 Deixis: How to determine demonstrated objects using a pointing cone. In *Proceedings of the 6th International Workshop on Gesture in Human-Computer Interaction and Simulation.* Berlin: Springer (in press).

Kranstedt, A., and I. Wachsmuth
2005 Incremental generation of multimodal deixis referring to objects. In *Proceedings of the European Workshop on Natural Language Generation (ENLG2005)*, 75–82.

Krauss, R. M., Y. Chen, and R. F. Gottesman
2000 Lexical gestures and lexical access: A process model. In *Language and Gesture*, D. McNeill (ed.), 261–284. Cambridge, UK: Cambridge University Press.

Kühnlein, P., and J. Stegmann
2003 *Empirical issues in deictic gesture: Referring to objects in simple identification tasks.* Technical report 2003/3, CRC 360. Bielefeld: University of Bielefeld.

Latoschik, M. E.
2001a A general framework for multimodal interaction in virtual reality systems: PrOSA. In *The Future of VR and AR Interfaces - Multimodal, Humanoid, Adaptive and Intelligent*, W. Broll and L. Schäfer (eds), 21–25. Chicago: IEEE Computer Society.
2001b *Multimodale Interaktion in Virtueller Realität am Beispiel der virtuellen Konstruktion.* Berlin: Akademische Verlagsgesellschaft Aka.
2003 Designing transition networks for multimodal VR-interactions using a markup language. In *Proceedings of the IEEE Fourth International Conference on Multimodal Interfaces, ICMI 2002,* 411–416. Pittsburgh: IEEE Computer Society.

Lester, J., J. Voerman, S. Towns, and C. Callaway
1999 Deictic believability: Coordinating gesture, locomotion, and speech in lifelike pedagogical agents. *Applied Artificial Intelligence* 13: 383–414.

Levelt, W. J. M.
1989 *Speaking: From Intention to Articulation.* Cambridge, MA: MIT Press.

Levin, J. A., and J. A. Moore
1977 Dialogue games: Meta-communication structures for natural language interaction. In *ISI/RR-77-53*. Information Sciences Institute (ed.), University of Southern California.

Lücking, A., H. Rieser, and J. Stegmann
2004 Statistical support for the study of structures in multimodal dialogue: Interrater agreement and synchronisation. In *Proceedings of the 8th Workshop on the Semantics and Pragmatics of Dialogue (Catalog '04)*, 56–64.

Lyons, J.
1977 *Semantics. Volume 2*. Cambridge, UK: Cambridge University Press.

Mann, B., and S. A. Thompson
1987 Rhetorical structure theory: A framework for the analysis of texts. *International Pragmatics Association Papers in Pragmatics* 1: 79–105.

Mann, W.C.
1988 Dialogue games: Conventions of human interaction. *Argumentation* 2: 512–532.

Masataka, N.
2003 From index-finger extension to index-finger pointing: Ontogenesis of pointing in preverbal infants. In *Pointing: Where Language, Culture and Cognition Meet,* S. Kita (ed.), 69–85.

McNeill, D.
1992 *Hand and Mind: What Gestures Reveal about Thought.* Chicago: University of Chicago Press.
2000 Catchments and contexts: Non-modular factors in speech and gesture production. In *Language and Gesture*, D. McNeill (ed.), 312–29. New York: Cambridge University Press.

McNeill, D.
2003 Pointing and morality in Chicago. In *Pointing: Where Language, Culture and Cognition Meet,* S. Kita (ed.), 293–306. Mahwah: Erlbaum.

Milde, J.-T., and U. Gut
2001 The TASX-environment: An XML-based corpus database for time aligned language data. In *Proceedings of the IRCS Workshop on Linguistic Databases*.
http:// medien.informatik.fh-fulda.de/tasxforce

Pfeiffer, T., and M. E. Latoschik
2004 Resolving object references in multimodal dialogues for immersive virtual environments. In *Proceedings of the IEEE Virtual Reality 2004,* Y. Ikei, M. Göbel, and J. Chen (eds.), 35–42. Chicago: IEEE Computer Society.

Pickering, M. J., and S. Garrod
2004 Towards a mechanistic psychology of dialogue. In *Behavioral and Brain Sciences* 27: 169–226.

Piwek, P., and R. J. Beun
2001 Multimodal referential acts in a dialogue game: From empirical investigations to algorithms. In *Proceedings of the International Workshop on Information Presentation and Natural Multimodal Dialogue (IPNMD-2001)*, 127–131.

Piwek, P., R. J. Beun, and A. Cremers
1995 *Demonstratives in dutch cooperative task dialogues*. IPO Manuscript 1134. Eindhoven: Eindhoven University of Technology.

Poesio, M., and D. Traum
1997 Conversational actions and discourse situations. In *Computational Intelligence* 13: 1–44.

Reithinger, N.
1992 The performance of an incremental generation component for multimodal dialog contributions. In *Aspects of Automated Natural Language Generation*, R. Dale, E. Hovy, D. Rosner, and O. Stock (eds.). Berlin: Springer.

Rieser, H.
2004 Pointing in dialogue. In *Proceedings of the 8th Workshop on the Semantics and Pragmatics of Dialogue (Catalog '04)*, 93–101.

Searle, J. R., and D. Vanderveken
1989 *Foundations of Illocutionary Logic*. Cambridge, UK: Cambridge University Press.

Tramberend, H.
2001 Avango: A distributed virtual reality framework. In *Proceedings of Afrigraph '01*.

van der Sluis, I., and E. Krahmer
2004 The influence of target size and distance on the production of speech and gesture in multimodal referring expressions. In *Proceedings of the 8th International Conference on Spoken Language Processing.*

Computational models of visual tagging

Marc Pomplun, Elena Carbone, Hendrik Koesling, Lorenz Sichelschmidt, and Helge Ritter

Abstract. The studies reported in this chapter exemplify the experimental-simulative approach of the interdisciplinary research initiative on "Situated Artificial Communicators". Two experiments on visual tagging strategies are described. In Experiment 1, participants were presented with random distributions of identical dots. The task was to look exactly once at each dot, with a starting dot specified. This setting allowed a quantitative analysis of scan path structures and hence made it possible to compare empirical scan paths to computer-generated ones. Five different scan path models were implemented as computer simulations, and the similarity of their scan paths to the empirical ones was measured. Experiment 2 was identical to Experiment 1 with the exception that it used items of varying color and form attributes instead of identical dots. Here, the influence of the distribution of colors and forms on empirical scan paths was investigated. The most plausible scan path models of Experiment 1 were adapted to the stimuli of Experiment 2. The results of both experiments indicate that a simple, scan path minimizing algorithm ("Traveling Salesman Strategy"; TSS) is most effective at reproducing human scan paths. We also found an influence of color information on empirical scan paths and successfully adapted the TSS-based model to this finding.

1. Introduction

One important aspect of situated communication is that it requires the interlocutors to generate comprehensive representations of their physical environment (Rickheit and Sichelschmidt 1999). This is the case not only in task-oriented dialogue, where interlocutors, being part of the environment, collaborate in solving physical problems (e.g., Rickheit 2005); this also applies to the production and comprehension of referential verbal expressions in general (e.g., Sichelschmidt 2005). Locatives, for instance, can hardly be used without recourse to a visuospatial frame of reference (see Vorwerg, Wachsmuth, and Socher, this volume). Successful reference to elements in the visual environment has as a prerequisite a detailed exploration of the surrounding scene (Henderson and Ferreira 2004). Visuolinguistic processing and scene exploration, in particular, the extraction of relevant information about what is located where in the scene, is mostly effortless. We are hardly aware of the fact that such scene perception is a serial process which involves adequate eye movements. The high efficiency of this process is not only based on the high speed of human eye movements, but also on our strategies to direct them (Findlay 2004). These strategies have been optimized during a long period of evolution. They are crucial for our understanding of the human visual system, visuolinguistic information processing, and the construction of technical vision systems (Najemnik and Geisler 2005). The studies reported here focus on a fundamental question: What factors determine the sequence in which we inspect a given set of items?

There are numerous approaches that have tried to provide at least partial answers to this question. Most experiments in the "classic" paradigm of visual search, but also studies that use sophisticated variants such as comparative visual search, use simple, abstract stimuli. In classic visual search (e.g., Treisman and Sato 1990; Wolfe, Cave, and Franzel 1989), participants are typically presented with a set of abstract items, such as letters or geometrical objects, and have to decide whether a designated target item is among them. In contrast, in comparative visual search (Pomplun 1998; Pomplun et al. 2001), participants have to detect the only difference between two almost identical sets of objects. While most studies rely on reaction times and error rates as the principal indicators for search performance, several researchers have also investigated the visual scan paths taken during visual search or comparison (e.g. Koesling 2003; Pomplun et al. 2001). Williams and Reingold (2001), for example, used a triple conjunction search task in which the presented items varied in the three dimensions color, form, and orientation. The authors analyzed the proportion of fixations on each distractor type. They found that the highest proportion of fixations was directed towards those distractors that were of the same color as the target. This finding suggests that it is well possible to use color information for choosing an efficient scan path: Only the subset of items with the appropriate color has to be searched.

Eye-movement patterns during visual search or comparison and viewing images have been used as a basis for modeling visual scanning strategies (e.g., Koesling, Carbone, and Ritter 2003; Pomplun et al. 2005). Several investigations were conducted by computer scientists intending to "teach" artificial vision systems to behave like the human visual system. Some models of human eye movements in realistic scenes use spatial filters in order to determine the most salient points in an image – the ones that are most likely to attract fixations (Parkhurst, Law, and Niebur 2002). These filters may be sensitive to contour features like sharp angles (Kattner 1994) or to local symmetries (Heidemann et al. 1996; Locher and Nodine 1987). Rao and Ballard (1995) proposed a model of parallel search employing time-dependent filters. The location of the first fixation in a search process is determined by a coarse analysis (low spatial frequencies) of the given scene, and the following fixations are based on analyses of increasingly higher spatial frequencies. Another approach (Rimey and Brown 1991) uses a Hidden Markov Model that is capable of learning efficient eye-movement behavior. It optimizes its scan paths iteratively towards highest efficiency of gathering information in a given scene. The Area Activation Model proposed by Pomplun, Reingold and Shen (2003) computes the informativeness and therefore the activation value of every point in the display, with more highly activated positions being more likely to be fixated than less activated positions. The scan path is determined by the method of local minimization of scan path length: The item fixated next corresponds to the activation peak closest to the current gaze position that has not been visited yet. Itti and Koch (2001) additionally emphasized the importance of the surrounding context for the saliency map and of top-down attentional processes. Recently, the saliency-based approach to visual attention has received some empirical support (Querhani et al. 2004).

To date, however, even the best attempts at computer vision are far from reaching the performance of the human visual system. One important reason for this fact might be that we do not yet completely understand the fundamental cognitive mechanisms which guide our attention so efficiently during the exploration of a scene. It seems that the scenes used in the modeling studies mentioned above are perceptionally too complex to yield insight into these mechanisms. In real-world scenes, a viewer's attention is guided by high-level factors, for instance, by the functional or conceptual relationships between items or the relevance of items to the viewer – factors that are responsible, among other things, for phenomena like change blindness (Henderson and Ferreira 2004; Henderson and Hollingworth 1999). It is almost impossible to parameterize such high-level factors and to obtain quantitative, clearly interpretable results from this kind of experiments.

Another problem is that neither the search or comparison tasks nor the viewing tasks described above are particularly well-suited to investigate scene inspection strategies. Gaze trajectories in these tasks yield only relatively coarse information about the exact structure of scan paths, i.e. the sequence of items that receive attention. This is because visual attention can be shifted without employing eye movements. During rapid processes of scanning, minute "covert" shifts of attention are likely to occur (for discussions, see Posner 1980; Salvucci 2001; Wright and Ward 1994). Therefore, gaze trajectories in search or viewing tasks do not indicate the whole sequence of attended items but – depending on task complexity and item density – only a small subset of it.

In order to obtain more comprehensive information about visual scan paths, we measured people's eye movements in a simplified scanning scenario which we refer to as "visual tagging" (see Klein 1988; Shore and Klein 2000). In the visual tagging scenario, the participants viewed a random distribution of dots that were identical except that one of them – the starting dot – was conspicuously brighter than the others. The task was to look exactly once at each dot in the display, starting with the specified dot. This task is similar to the one used by Beckwith and Restle (1966), who asked people to count large sets of objects. By analyzing reaction times for different types of object configurations, Beckwith and Restle found that the participants grouped the objects into subsets in order to count them efficiently and to avoid mistakes. In our experiments, however, we eliminated any possible interference of a concurrent counting task with the scanning process. Furthermore, we used eye tracking to measure the exact temporal sequence of dots attended to.

On the one hand, the visual tagging task is rather artificial. In everyday life we are not used to strictly avoiding repeated attention to the same object, because the "cost" of a redundant eye movement is small (see Ballard, Hayhoe, and Pelz 1995). Although there is ample empirical evidence for an attentional mechanism called inhibition of return (Klein 2000; Posner and Cohen 1984; Tipper et al. 1994), this mechanism alone is not sufficient to generate self-avoiding and complete scan paths as demanded by our task. Therefore, people's scan paths are likely to be influenced by cognitive processes operating at a higher level than those being usually involved in natural situations, e.g., free exploration of surroundings. In particular, path planning processes are expected to take place, because people have to hold in memory which dots they have already visited during task completion (Beckwith and Restle 1966; Melcher and Kowler 2001).

On the other hand, our task enabled us to investigate scan paths purely based on the stimulus geometry, i.e. on the locations of the dots. Neither item features nor relations between them (other than geometrical relations) biased the observed strategies. Moreover, the demand of attending exactly once to each item brought about an enhanced comparability of scan paths taken on the same stimulus. Restricting the analysis to those paths that met this demand made it easy to define a measure of similarity: The degree of similarity of a path A to another path B was calculated as the number of "jumps" (edges) between dots that appear in path A as well as in path B.

Experiment 1 investigated geometrical regularities of scan paths with the aim of identifying possible mechanisms that control human tagging strategies in scene inspection. Several models of such mechanisms were developed and implemented as computer simulations. The simulated scan paths were then compared to the empirical ones in order to evaluate the plausibility of the proposed mechanisms. Another important question was whether there are preferred directions of scan paths. In other words, does the rotation of the stimuli exert an influence on the scan paths?

Experiment 2 went one step further towards a more naturalistic setting: While the participants' task remained the same as in Experiment 1, the displayed items were given different color and form attributes. Beckwith and Restle (1966) showed that the distribution of color and form attributes influenced the time needed for counting a set of objects, with color having a substantially stronger effect than form. With the help of eye movement tracking, Experiment 2 directly investigated the influence of color and form on empirical scan paths. Moreover, the most successful models of Experiment 1 were refined in such a way as to account for this additional influence.

2. Experiment 1: Geometrical factors

2.1. Method

2.1.1. Participants

Twelve students from different faculties of the University of Bielefeld took part in Experiment 1 in return for payment. All of them had normal or corrected-to-normal vision; none of them was color-blind or had pupil anomalies.

2.1.2. Apparatus

Stimuli were presented on a 17" ViewSonic 7 monitor. The participants' eye movements were measured with the OMNITRACK 1 eye gaze recorder (see Stampe 1993). The system uses a headband with two miniature infrared video cameras as inputs of information about the position of the head relative to the environment and the position of the pupil relative to the head.

Thus, the position of the pupil relative to the environment can be calculated. This technique allows the participants to move their head from the straight-ahead position up to 15° in all directions, and therefore provides natural viewing conditions. Gaze positions are recorded at a frequency of 60 Hz. Fixations are calculated using a speed threshold in a 5-cycle time window, which means that only fixations with a duration of at least 83 ms are registered. The absolute spatial precision of the eye gaze position measurement ranges from 0.7° to 1°. By using a calibration interface based on artificial neural networks (Parametrized Self-Organizing Maps), we improved the precision of the system to approximately 0.5° (see Pomplun, Velichkovsky, and Ritter 1994).

2.1.3. Stimuli

Participants were presented with displays showing 30 dots (diameter of 0.5°) randomly distributed within a square area (18° per side) on a black background. The dots were of the same color (blue), with a designated starting dot being clearly brighter than the others (for a stimulus sample, see Figure 1, left). Five different dot configurations were randomly generated. In order to investigate directional effects on the scan paths, for instance top-to-bottom or left-to-right strategies corresponding to the viewers' direction of reading, each configuration was shown in four different orientations (rotated by 0°, 90°, 180°, and 270°). This resulted in a set of 20 stimuli to be used in Experiment 1.

2.1.4. Procedure

A written instruction informed the participants about their task. They had to look at each dot in the display once, beginning with the starting dot. Participants were told not to miss any dots or to look at any of them more than once. Furthermore, participants had to attend to each dot for at least half a second to make sure that they actually performed a saccade rather than a covert shift of attention towards the dot. After task completion the participants were to press a mouse button. The experiment started with two practice trials followed by the eye tracker calibration procedure and the 20 recording trials in random order. Each trial was preceded by a short calibration for drift correction, using a single target at the center of the screen.

2.2. Results

The recorded gaze trajectories were converted to item-based scan paths. In other words, the temporal order of attended dots had to be reconstructed, because our analysis was intended to refer to these rather than to fixation points. It turned out that this could not be done automatically. The occurrence of additional fixations (conceivably used by the participants to get their bearings), imprecise saccades as well as errors in measurement required human post-processing. Consequently, an assistant – who was naive as to the purpose of the study – did the allocation of fixations to dots manually, on the basis of the individual trajectories with sequentially numbered fixations superimposed on the stimuli. As a result of this semi-interpretative analysis, only 139 of the 240 converted paths (57.9%) were found to be consistent with the task, i.e., they visited each dot exactly once. The further analyses were restricted to these paths.

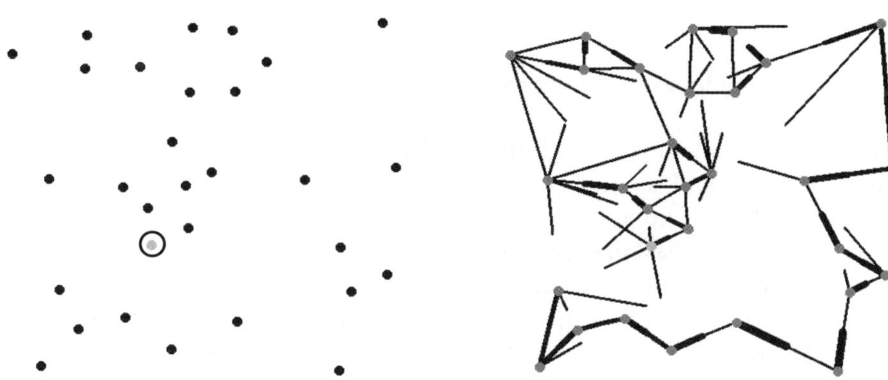

Figure 1. Sample stimulus (left; with starting point marked for purposes of illustration) and corresponding visualized results (right).

Figure 1 presents a visualization of accumulated data (right panel) for a sample stimulus (left panel). Thicker lines between dots indicate transitions (edges) used by a larger number of participants. The lines are bisected due to the two possible directions to move along these edges. Each half refers to those transitions that started at the dot next to it. Halves representing fewer than three transitions are not displayed for the sake of clarity. Figure 1 illustrates that in the absence of any conspicuous order (as in the upper left part of the sample stimulus) there is high variability of chosen edges across participants, whereas the linearly arranged dots (such as those on the right and at the bottom of the sample stimulus) were almost always scanned in the same order.

In addition, the quantitative analysis of the data allowed us to investigate the effect of rotating the stimuli: Were there directional influences on the scan paths, for example according to the viewer's reading direction? This was analyzed by comparing similarities (as defined above) between the scan paths of different participants. If the scan paths for the same stimuli shown in the same orientation were more similar to each other than the ones for different orientations of the same stimuli, this would indicate that the rotation exerted an effect. In fact, the average similarity value for the same orientation was 19.43 edges per path, while the value between different orientations was 19.42, constituting no significant difference, $t < 1$. Consequently, it was justified not to assume any directional influence. So we averaged the data for each of the five original stimuli over its four different orientations for all subsequent analyses.

2.3. Modeling tagging strategies

We developed and evaluated five different models of tagging behavior. Since the empirical data showed no significant dependence on the orientation of the stimuli, none of the models developed below include this factor. In order to obtain baseline data for the evaluation of the models, we calculated a composite path with maximal similarity to the observed paths ("optimum fit") for each stimulus. An iterative algorithm determined this path within the huge set of all possible acceptable paths, regardless of whether the path actually appeared in any one participant's data. The average similarity of optimum fit paths to empirical paths turned out to be 21.89, which exceeded the similarity of empirical ones to each other (19.43, cf. above). The calculation of optimum fit paths also shows that no simulation can produce paths of higher similarity to the empirical data than 21.89, which is considerably lower than the perfect similarity (identity) value 29 (all acceptable paths consist of 29 edges). This discrepancy demonstrates the high intrinsic variability of scan paths.

Serving as a second baseline, the similarity of completely randomly generated scan paths to the empirical paths was computed, yielding a value of as low as 1.75. A sample optimum fit path as well as sample paths computed by the models are given in Figure 2, referring to the sample stimulus in Figure 1. The five models that were evaluated are described below.

2.3.1. The "greedy" heuristic

One model that suggests itself for analysis is based on what can be termed the "greedy" heuristic. Among all dots that still need to be visited, the Greedy algorithm always jumps to the one that is geometrically nearest to the current "gaze" position. Although it produces plausible, locally optimized sections of scan paths, the Greedy strategy has one drawback: On its way through the stimulus, it leaves aside items of high eccentricity. As a consequence, these items have to be "collected" later on, which leads to unnaturally long saccades at the end of the scan path. The lack of memory constitutes a fundamental difference from empirically observed strategies. Nevertheless, even this simple model achieves a similarity value of 17.36, indicating that its strategy of always choosing the nearest item, that is, the local minimization of scan paths, is already tremendously better than a purely random strategy.

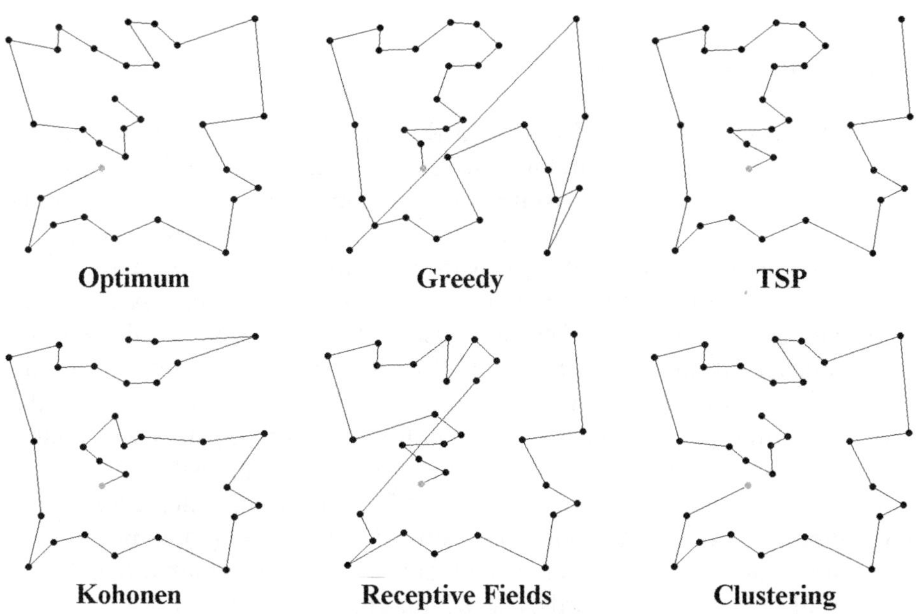

Figure 2. Scan paths generated by the five different models, plus the optimum-fit path, for the sample stimulus shown in Figure 1.

2.3.2. The "Traveling Salesman" approach

The shortcoming of the Greedy heuristic motivates the implementation of a "Traveling Salesman Strategy" (TSS) algorithm. The Traveling Salesman Problem is a basic paradigm in computer science: A salesman who has to successively visit a certain number of places wants to save time and energy, so his problem is to find the shortest path connecting all the places. In the present context, this means that the TSS Model algorithmically minimizes the overall length of its scan paths rather than just the length of the next jump. However, unlike standard TSS, the paths of this algorithm do not return to the starting dot. In the current formulation, only the choice of the first dot is constrained. The results show that this simulation gets much closer to the actual human strategies than the Greedy heuristic: The similarity value is 20.87, which is fairly close to the optimum fit value of 21.89. This finding suggests that not only the local optimization of scan paths – as operationalized in the Greedy algorithm – plays an important role in human scan path selection, but also their global optimization.

2.3.3. The "Clustering" model

The fact that the TSS Model has yielded the best result so far motivates the investigation of a refined variant of it. Consequently, we built a "Clustering Model" that is based on the assumption that human scan paths are generated by clusterwise processing of items (cf. Beckwith and Restle 1966). The model divides the process of scan path computation into two steps. In the first step, the configuration of items is divided into clusters. A clustering algorithm maximizes the between-cluster distances and minimizes the within-cluster distances with the help of a cost function. We set the parameters of this iterative procedure in such a way that it generates clusters that may have either compact or linear shape. Five to seven clusters with four to seven items each are calculated, which is perceptually plausible (see Atkinson, Campbell, and Francis 1976; Miller 1956). The second step consists in a TSS algorithm calculating local scan paths of minimal length connecting the dots within each cluster, as well as a global scan path of minimal length connecting all clusters. Afterwards, the within-cluster scan paths are linked together in the sequence specified by the between-cluster scan path. Thus, this model processes all dots within a cluster before proceeding to the next one, thereby operating like a hierarchical TSS algorithm. A similarity analysis showed that the Clustering Model selects paths slightly more similar to the empirically observed ones (21.12) than does the TSS Model. This may suggest that clustering is a component of human scanning strategies.

2.3.4. The "Self-Organizing Map" approach

When simulating cognitive processes, we should also consider neural network approaches, as their functional structure is biologically motivated. An appropriate neural paradigm is provided by Kohonen's self-organizing maps (SOMs), which are capable of projecting a high-dimensional data space onto a lower-dimensional one (see Kohonen 1990; Ritter, Martinetz, and Schulten 1992). SOMs are networks of simulated neurons, usually a one-dimensional chain or a two-dimensional layer. They learn in an unsupervised way to partition a given feature or input space into disjoint classes or areas and to represent their class by a typical feature vector. The feature space is a region of a classical vector space, where each vector $(v_1, v_2, \ldots, v_n)^T$ shows n different features or input signals. These vectors are presented to the network in random order, and a neuron fires if its stored feature, that is, its position vector, is the best approximation to the active input position to the network. Thus we create a map – the neural network – in which each mapped point – each neuron – represents a region of input patterns. If we also ensure that the topology of the input space is preserved, i.e., that neighboring feature vectors are mapped to neighboring neurons, or neighboring neurons stand for similar features, we get a low-dimensional structure representing a possibly high-dimensional input. This is done by iterating the following steps:

- Choose a random input vector $\mathbf{v}$ from feature space.
- Select a neuron j with $|\mathbf{v} - \mathbf{w}_j| \leq |\mathbf{v} - \mathbf{w}_i|, \forall\, i \neq j$, i.e., the neuron with the best representation $\mathbf{w}_j$ of $\mathbf{v}$; this is called the winner.
- Change all neuron weights $\mathbf{w}_i$ towards the input vector $\mathbf{v}$, with an adaptive step size h_{ij} that is a decay function of the network distance between neuron i and the winner j. Here, ε is an additional global adaptive step size parameter:

$$\mathbf{w}_i^{new} = \mathbf{w}_i^{old} + \varepsilon \cdot h_{ij} \cdot (\mathbf{v} - \mathbf{w}_j),\ \varepsilon \in [0, 1].$$

The change of neuron weights adjusts $\mathbf{w}_i^{old}$ towards a better representation vector and the smooth distribution of change around the winner produces the desired topology preservation. In our case, we are only interested in a mapping from discrete 2D points onto a linear chain representing fixation order.

Hence, the feature space is only the discrete set of dot positions in $\mathbf{R}^2$, one of them labeled as starting dot. Since the chain must begin at the starting dot, the first neuron is defined to be the winner if the starting dot is presented, irrespective of the actual feature-vector difference. In order to make sure that all dots are represented by neurons after the learning process, the network contains a number of additional nodes. Now, the probability to skip a dot is very low, but more than one neuron may become mapped to the same position. This must be resolved by a post-processing step to extract the simulated scan path from the chain of neurons. The paths generated by this model look quite natural at first sight. Their similarity to the human ones, however, is substantially lower (19.45) than the results obtained by the TSS-based models.

2.3.5. The "Receptive Field" simulation

Another biologically motivated approach in our set of models uses neurons with a particular type of receptive fields. In a neural network, natural or artificial, the term receptive field stands for the region of input space that affects a particular neuron (see, e.g., Hubel and Wiesel 1962; Lennie et al. 1990). Furthermore, the influence of stimuli in this region is not necessarily homogeneous, but dependent on variables such as the distance of the input vector from the center of the region. There may also be excitatory and inhibitory subregions, where a stimulus will respectively increase or decrease the activation of the neuron.

In our model, the receptive fields consist of an inhibitory axis and two laterally located, excitatory areas of circular shape (see Figure 3). We use 100,000 receptive fields that are randomly distributed across the input space. Their sizes vary randomly between 80% and 120% of the size of the relevant input space, i.e. the whole area in which dots are presented. There are eight possible orientations which are randomly assigned to the receptive fields. It is obvious from this description that the receptive fields are closely packed and overlap each other.

The activation of a neuron is highest if no dot is in the inhibitory region of the neuron's receptive field and as many dots as possible are in the lateral excitatory regions. The neuron with the highest activation (the winner neuron) thus indicates the most pronounced linear gap between two laterally located accumulations of dots. Therefore, the inhibitory axis of this neuron's receptive field can be considered to indicate the perceptually most plausible bisection of the stimulus.

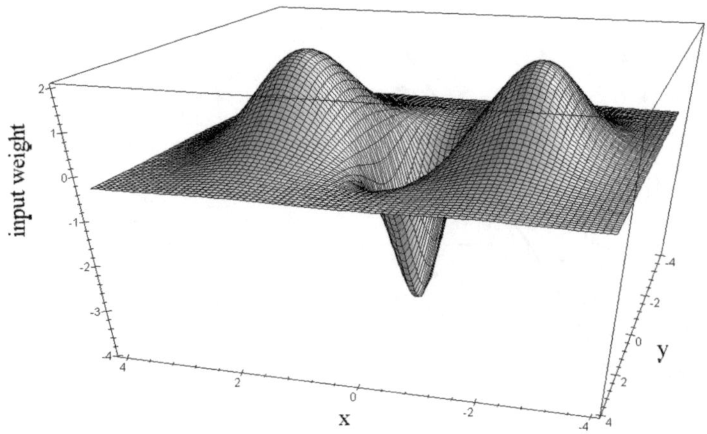

Figure 3. Illustration of the simulated receptive fields. The planar input space is represented by the dimensions x and y. Positive values of input weight signify excitatory connections, negative values signify inhibitory connections.

This first bisection separates the set of dots into two subsets. Each subset serves as the input to a new group of neurons with smaller receptive fields, calculating further bisections. This procedure is repeated until none of the sections contains more than four dots, since the number four is a plausible minimum estimate of the number of dots that can be perceived at the same time (see Atkinson, Campbell, and Francis 1976; Miller 1956). In Figure 4 (left), the model's hierarchical partitioning of the sample stimulus previously shown in Figures 1 and 2 is presented. The bisections are visualized by straight lines with numbers indicating their level in the hierarchy. The calculation of this structure – a binary tree – is our attempt to simulate a viewer's perceptual processing of the visual scene.

Finally, the scan path is derived by a TSS algorithm calculating the shortest scan path that begins at the starting dot. In the present context, however, it is not the geometrical distance that is minimized, but a linear combination of the geometrical distance and the tree distance between the dots. The tree distance between two dots *A* and *B* is the minimum number of edges in a path connecting the subsets A and B in the tree structure. If we choose the coefficients of the linear combination in such a way that the tree distance is more relevant than the geometrical distance, the model generates the scan path shown in Figure 4 (right panel). It strictly follows the hierarchical tree structure, which leads to geometrical deviations.

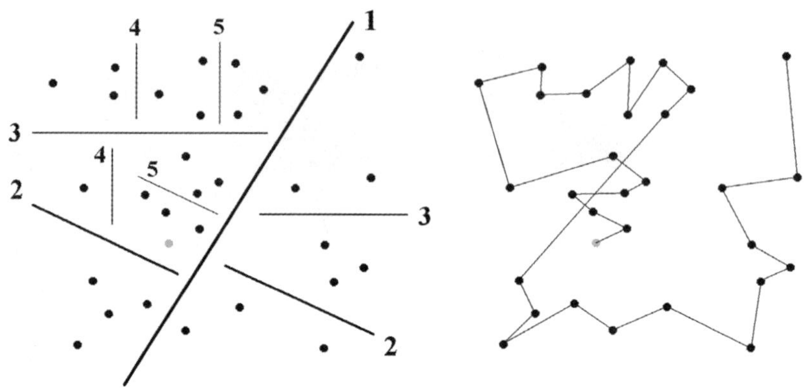

Figure 4. The model's hierarchical bisections (left) and the resulting scan path (right) for the sample stimulus shown in Figure 1.

As long as the model's linear coefficients are chosen such that the tree distance exerts a significant effect, neither the appearance of the simulated scan paths nor their calculated similarity to the empirical paths is convincing. When balancing the weights of the tree distances and the geometrical distances, we obtained scan paths with a similarity to the human paths of 18.73. The receptive field approach, at least in this rather simple form, does not seem to yield more plausible scan paths than does the TSS Model. This suggests that hierarchical partitioning does not seem to be an important perceptual mechanism underlying human visual tagging behavior.

2.3.6. Model comparison

Figure 5 displays a summary of the accuracies with which the various models simulate human scanning patterns, and it compares them to the optimum fit value. A one-way analysis of variance (ANOVA) was conducted on these data, excluding the optimum fit value, which was a global value that did not vary across individuals. The analysis revealed a main effect showing statistically significant differences between the similarity values, $F(4;44) = 32.34$, $p < 0.001$. Pairwise *t*-tests with Bonferroni-adjusted probability values were conducted to examine these differences more closely. All of the models reached significantly higher average similarity than the Greedy Heuristic; all $t(11) > 3.62$, $p < 0.005$. The Receptive Fields Model did not significantly differ in results from the SOM Model. These two models, in turn, were outperformed by both the TSS Model and the Clustering Model, all $t(11) > 4.84$, $p < 0.01$. Finally, the TSS Model did not significantly differ from the Clustering Model, $t(11) < 1$.

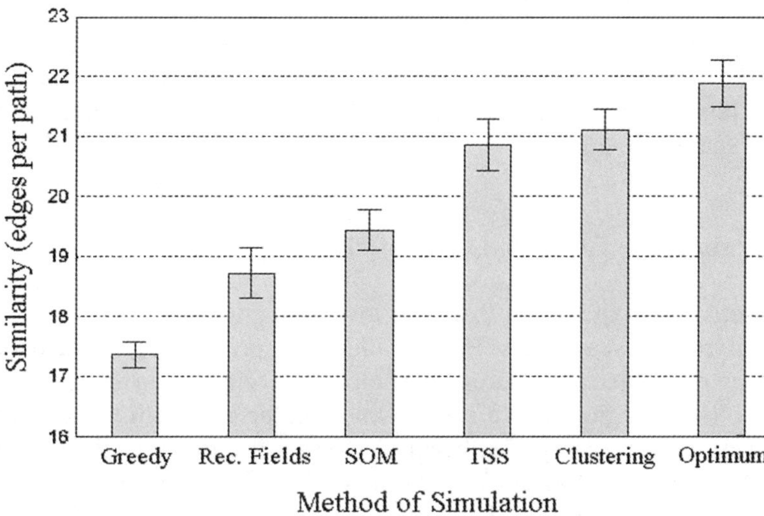

Figure 5. Similarity between the paths generated by the different models and the empirical scan paths, shown in ascending order, plus the optimum fit value.

2.4. Discussion

Basically, the results of Experiment 1 show that the simple TSS Model and Clustering Model yield better scan paths than the neural models, and that even the simple Greedy algorithm is not far behind. This finding should not be interpreted as evidence for a general incapability of neural models to explain scan path mechanisms. The neural models tested in Experiment 1 were of a very primitive nature. Multi-layered networks might be able to generate scan paths more similar to the empirically observed ones. Moreover, discretion is advisable in the interpretation of these data, since they are based on only five different dot configurations. Nevertheless, from the results above we can conclude that it is difficult to generate better simulations of human scan paths than those created by the simple TSS-based models. Thus the minimization of scan path length seems to be a basic principle in human scanning strategies.

Another important result of Experiment 1 is the independence of scan paths from rotations of the stimuli. In other words, the order in which a viewer scans a set of dots does not seem to change when the display is rotated by 90, 180, or 270 degrees. It is well-known from visual search experiments (e.g. Zelinsky 1996; Pomplun 1998) that viewers prefer to scan a display according to their reading direction, if they are allowed to freely choose the starting point. However, this was not observed in the present study. A possible reason is that the specified starting point induced rotation-invariant scanning strategies.

3. Experiment 2: Color and form attributes

The objective of Experiment 2 was to investigate the influence of color and form attributes on scan paths. Participants were presented with distributions of geometrical objects (squares, triangles, and circles) in different colors (yellow, blue, and green). We might expect color and form to influence the structure of chosen scan paths, because viewers are likely to take advantage of the additional structural information. As their main concern is to remember which of the items they have already visited, the introduction of color and form features might allow them to use perceptual groups of identical attributes as scan path units which need less effort to remember than do single items. This assumption is supported by the results of Beckwith and Restle's (1966) counting task. They found shorter reaction times when object colors were clustered, i.e. different colors were spatially segregated. They also found an analogous – but weaker – effect for clustering the objects by form. To examine potential corresponding effects on scan path structure, the stimuli in Experiment 2 had three different levels of color and form clustering.

If humans make use of the color or form information, these effects should be integrated into the models. It is plausible to assume that the attributes lead to a reduction in scan path variability, which could enable the models to yield better results than in Experiment 1. Here we took advantage of the findings of Experiment 1: Since the paths generated by the TSS and Clustering Models were most similar to the empirical data, we focused on the adaptation of these two approaches to the stimuli used in Experiment 2. In order to make the two experiments easier to compare, the design and procedure of Experiment 2 corresponded to Experiment 1. Based on the results of Experiment 1, however, we did not further investigate the effect of stimulus rotation. In addition, the introduction of color and form attributes required to change the way of indicating the starting item. In Experiment 2, we used a dynamic cue, namely a flashing red circle around the starting item, appearing for a short period after stimulus onset. This method of marking the starting item did not alter its color or form attributes. The participants' task was the same as in Experiment 1, namely to look once, and only once, at each item.

3.1. Method

3.1.1. Participants

Twenty new participants from different faculties of the University of Bielefeld took part in Experiment 2 in return for payment. They had normal or corrected-to-normal vision; none was color-blind or had pupil anomalies.

3.1.2. Stimuli

The stimuli consisted of 30 simple geometrical items (diameter of about 0.7°) of three different colors (fully saturated blue, green, and yellow) and three different forms (triangle, square, and circle) on a black background. Their spatial distribution was randomly generated within a display of 18° by 18° with a minimum distance of 1.5° between the centers of neighboring items in order to avoid item overlap or contiguity (see Figure 6). In each stimulus array, there were a balanced number of items with each color and form. The distribution of colors and forms was not always homogeneously random, as they were clustered to varying degrees in most trials. To explain the clustering algorithm, a formalized description of the stimulus patterns is necessary: A pattern is a set of N items (objects)

$$\mathbf{o}^{(n)} = \begin{pmatrix} o_x^{(n)} \\ o_y^{(n)} \\ o_c^{(n)} \\ o_f^{(n)} \end{pmatrix}, \quad n = 1,\ldots,N,$$

where $(o_x^{(n)}, o_y^{(n)})$ is the pixel position of the item's center in the display, $o_c^{(n)}$ is the item's color (1 = blue, 2 = green, 3 = yellow), and $o_f^{(n)}$ is the item's form (1 = square, 2 = triangle, 3 = circle).

Now the variable color clustering α_c is introduced. It is defined as the ratio between the mean distance $d_{c,dif}$ between all pairs of items with different colors and the mean distance $d_{c,id}$ between those with identical colors:

$$\alpha_c = \frac{d_{c,dif}}{d_{c,id}}$$

$$d_{c,dif} = \frac{\sum_{n_1=1}^{N} \sum_{n_2=n_1+1,\, o_c^{(n_1)} \neq o_c^{(n2)}}^{N} \Delta(n_1, n_2)}{\sum_{n_1=1}^{N} \sum_{n_2=n_1+1,\, o_c^{(n_1)} \neq o_c^{(n2)}}^{N} 1}$$

$$\Delta(n_1, n_2) = \sqrt{\left(o_x^{(n_1)} - o_x^{(n_2)}\right) + \left(o_y^{(n_1)} - o_y^{(n_2)}\right)}$$

For example, a value $\alpha_c = 2$ would mean that, on average, items of different colors are twice as distant from each other than items of the same color. In our setting of 30 items and three different colors this would correspond to a strongly segregated distribution containing large single-colored areas. $\alpha_c = 1$ would mean that there is no clustering at all. We define the parameter form clustering α_f analogously.

Figure 6 illustrates the correspondence between α_c, α_f, and the distribution of colors and forms in four different sample stimuli. While the panels (a) to (c) display stimuli with increasing color clustering and no form clustering, panel (d) shows a sample stimulus with high color clustering and high form clustering. These examples demonstrate an important feature of α_c and α_f for the present experiment: Color and form clustering can be varied independently from each other. Even in an array with both high color and form clustering, the separate concentrations of colors and forms usually do not correspond.

An iterative algorithm for generating color and form distributions with given parameters of color clustering α_c and form clustering α_c can easily be implemented. Starting with a random distribution, this algorithm randomly selects pairs of items and exchanges their color or form attributes, if this exchange shifts the distribution's clustering levels towards the given parameters. The algorithm terminates as soon as the difference between the actual and the desired α_c and α_f falls below a certain threshold, which was set to 0.05 in the present study.

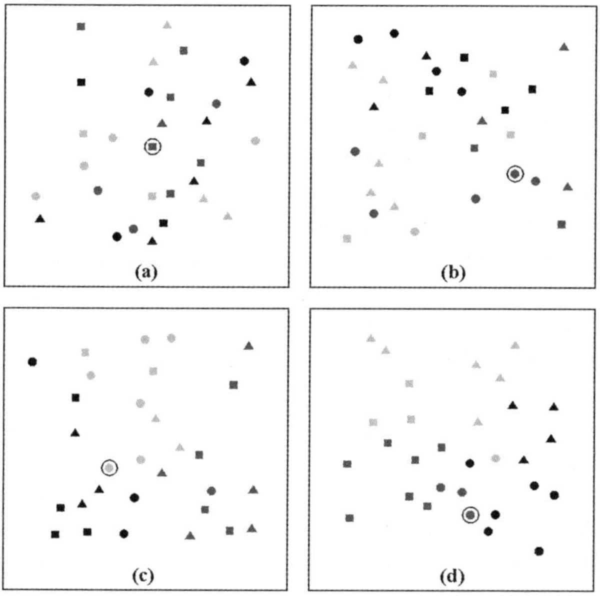

Figure 6. Examples of item distributions with different levels of color/form clustering: (a) no color and form clustering (1.0/1.0), (b) weak color and no form clustering (1.3/1.0), (c) strong color and no form clustering (1.7/1.0), and (d) strong color and form clustering (1.7/1.7). Circles indicate the starting items.

Three different levels of color and form clustering were used, namely "no clustering" (1.0), "weak clustering" (1.3), and "strong clustering" (1.7). Examples of stimuli at these levels can be seen in Figure 6. The nine possible combinations of different levels of color and form clustering constituted the stimulus categories of Experiment 2. Five stimuli of each category were used, leading to a total of 45 different stimuli. For two seconds after stimulus onset, a flashing red circle was shown around one of the items, signifying the starting item which was always the same across individuals for each given stimulus.

3.1.3. Apparatus and procedure

The apparatus was the same as in Experiment 1. Also, the procedure was the same as in Experiment 1, except that 45 trials were conducted in random order.

3.2. Results

As in Experiment 1, an assistant converted the recorded fixations into scan paths connecting the items in the display. The assistant was only shown the locations of the items, but not their color or form attributes. Just like in Experiment 1, the superimposed visualization of the participant's fixations and their temporal order allowed the assistant to mark the individual scan path item by item. The proportion of acceptable paths was 93.3%, which was substantially higher than in Experiment 1 (57.9%). Apparently, the additional color and form information helped the participants not to "get lost" during task completion. The individual features of the items seemed to facilitate reliable memorization and recognition. The incorrect paths were approximately equally distributed among the nine categories of stimuli, and so were excluded from the analysis.

For a qualitative analysis, we can inspect the calculated scan paths of maximal similarity to the empirical ones (optimum fit). The upper row of Figure 7 presents these paths for an unclustered, a strongly color-clustered, and a strongly form-clustered stimulus. There is no obvious evidence for the influence of color or form attributes on the viewers' strategy. Although there are some longer sections of scan paths exclusively visiting items of the same color or form, these items are always located closely together. This qualitative finding suggests that the location of items remains the most important factor to determine the structure of scan paths.

The quantitative investigation of the effects of color and form required a measure of color and form clustering within the empirically observed scan paths. An appropriate choice seemed to be the mean runlength with regard to these dimensions. In the present context, a run is defined as a sequence of items of the same color or form within a scan path. The runlengths ranged from one to ten, as there were always exactly ten items of each color and form in each stimulus array. In order to calculate a mean runlength across multiple paths, we employed a weighted mean to equally account for every single transition between items. Since longer runs comprise more transitions, we weighted each run with its runlength.

However, it is important to verify whether this measure indeed reflects the influence of item attributes rather than the geometrical structure of the stimulus. Even a participant who completely ignores color and form would generate longer runs with increasing strength of clustering in the stimulus. This is due to the fact that, according to the results of Experiment 1, viewers seem to prefer short scan paths, so neighboring items are disproportionately likely to be scanned successively. Clustering moves items with the same features closer together and thus increases the average color and form runlengths in empirical scan paths.

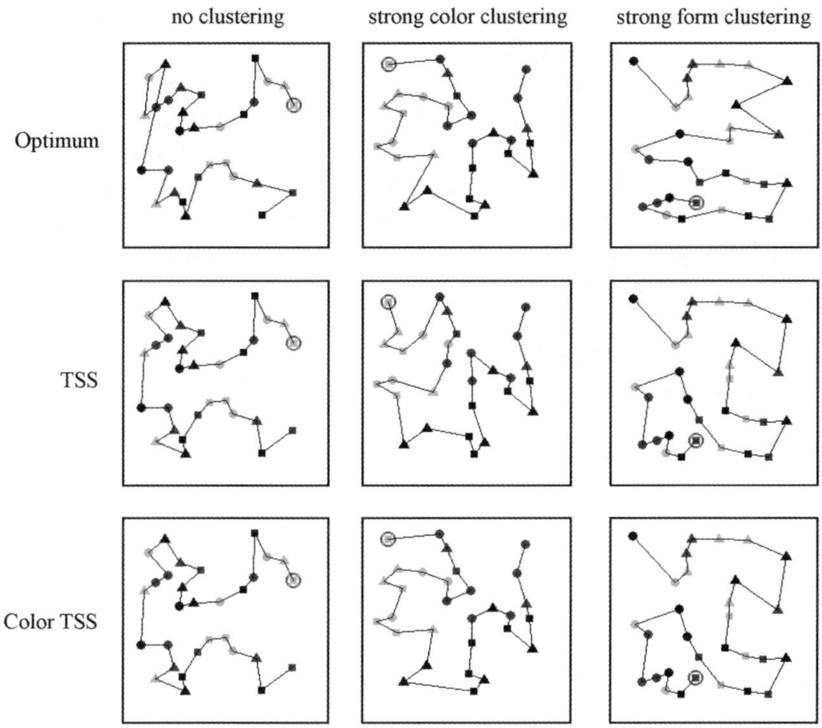

Figure 7. Scan paths generated by the participants (optimum-fit paths), the TSS Model, and the Color TSS Model. Circles indicate the starting items.

Fortunately, there is a "color and form blind" model, which yields paths of high similarity to the empirical ones, namely the TSS Model. We applied the TSS Model to each stimulus used in Experiment 2 to generate baseline predictions about the color and form runlengths in that stimulus. In a comparative analysis of observed scan paths, we then divided all color and form runlengths by the TSS-predicted runlengths, thereby obtaining relative runlengths. Rather than absolute runlengths, relative runlengths reveal the influence of item attributes on an individual's scan path. Relative color runlength 1, for instance, would indicate no difference to the TSS Model and thus no influence of color attributes on empirical scan paths. Longer relative runlengths would indicate increasing influence.

Figure 8 shows the participants' relative color and form runlengths at the three levels of color and form clustering respectively. A two-way ANOVA revealed statistically significant main effects of the two factors "dimension" (color vs. form), $F(1; 19) = 9.97$, $p < 0.01$, and "strength of clustering" (no vs. weak vs. strong clustering), $F(2; 38) = 4.77$, $p < 0.05$. There was also a significant interaction between the two factors, $F(2; 38) = 5.81$, $p < 0.01$, which was due to the fact that clustering had a significant effect on relative color runlength, $F(2; 38) = 5.56$, $p < 0.01$, but not on relative form runlength, $F(2; 38) = 2.36$, $p > 0.1$. For the color dimension, pairwise *t*-tests with Bonferroni-adjusted probabilities revealed a significant difference between no clustering (1.092) and strong clustering (1.213), $t(19) = 3.94$, $p < 0.005$. The differences to the weak clustering condition (1.131), however, were not significant, both $t(19) < 1.67$, $p > 0.3$. Finally, the overall relative color runlength (1.145) differed reliably from the value 1, $t(19) = 3.41$, $p < 0.005$, whereas overall relative form runlength (0.999) did not, $t < 1$.

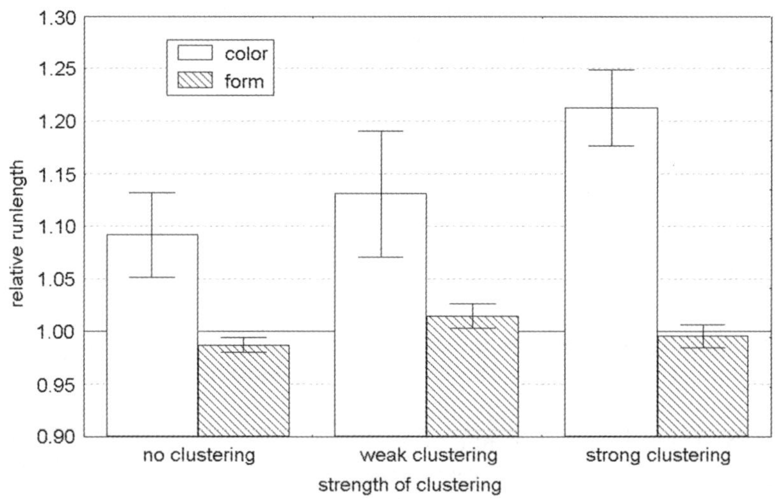

Figure 8. Mean relative color and form runlengths as functions of the strength of color and form clustering respectively.

Taken together, these findings suggest that viewers use color information to guide their scan paths, because the color runlength in their scan paths is longer than predicted by the TSS Model. This effect of color guidance increases with the strength of color clustering in the stimuli. The participants' form runlengths, however, do not exceed the predicted ones and do not depend on form clustering in the stimuli. Hence, we assume that viewers do not use form information when performing the task.

3.3. Refinement of scan path models

The results of Experiment 1 motivated the adaptation of both the TSS Model and the Clustering Model to stimuli containing items with color and form attributes. Since the Clustering Model can be viewed as a refinement of the TSS Model, we started with adjusting the TSS Model. The first question was how we could bias the TSS algorithm to react to color in the same way as the average viewer does. Basically, the model should still calculate scan paths of minimal length, but in doing so, it should weight the purely geometrical distances by the color (in)congruence (color distance) between the neighboring items. Such a weighting is achieved by multiplying the distance between two items of different colors by a constant factor – the color weight – and leaving the distance between items of the same color identical to their geometrical distance.

Obviously, the algorithm's behavior will then strongly depend on the color weight. A color weight of 1 would lead to a standard TSS algorithm which would not be influenced by color information at all. In contrast, a color weight of, say, 1,000 would make the algorithm use a minimum of transitions between different colors. Regardless of the arrangement of items, the algorithm would first visit all items of the starting item's color *A*, then inspect all items of color *B*, and finally those of color *C*. Within the color groups it would behave like a conventional traveling salesman algorithm, taking the shortest passages possible. By adjusting the color weight it is possible to control the influence of colors and hence the average color runlength produced by the TSS algorithm. Since the goal is to adapt the TSS Model to the empirical data, i.e. to produce the same runlengths as generated by the participants, the color weight needs to be adjusted for the best match.

What is the response of the TSS algorithm to increasing the color weight? As might be expected, it reveals a tendency towards the avoidance of transitions between items of different colors, because these transitions increase the overall length of the scan path above proportion. Figure 9 shows color runlength as a function of the color weight ranging from 1.0 to 1.5. The mean runlengths are displayed separately for each of the three levels of color clustering in the stimuli. Additionally, the empirically obtained runlengths for these levels are shown as horizontal lines.

We find the TSS runlengths to increase approximately linearly with increasing color weight. Higher levels of clustering lead to steeper runlength slopes. Interestingly, there is no single value of the color weight to yield the best-matching runlengths for all levels of clustering. For each level, the intersection between the runlength curve of the TSS Model and the participants' runlength occurs at a different color weight. These are the values:1.11 for the no clustering condition, 1.23 for weak clustering, and 1.33 for strong clustering. Loosely speaking, the viewers seem to apply higher color weights with increasing color clustering in the display.

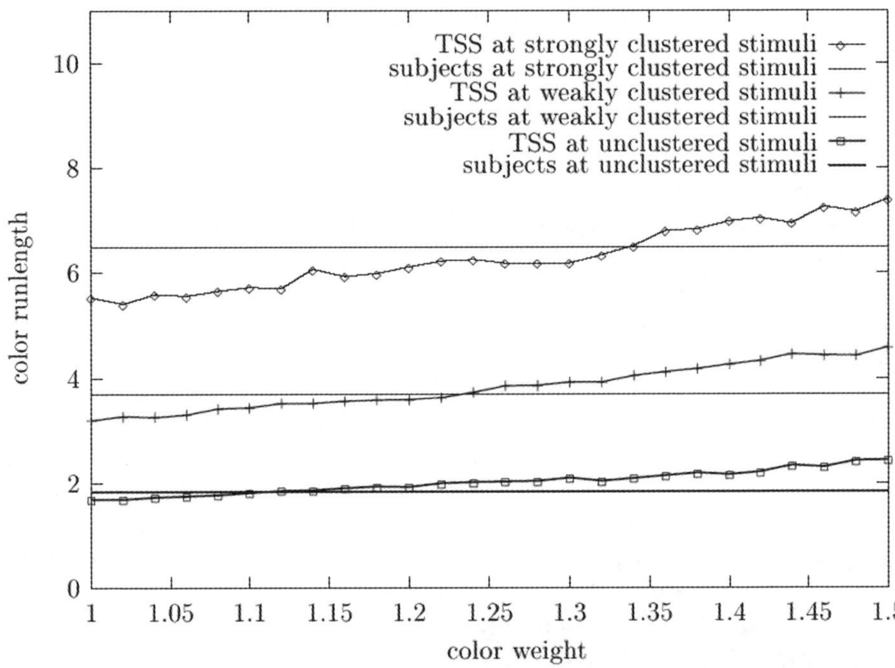

Figure 9. Color runlength generated by the TSS Model as a function of the strength of color clustering and the introduced color weight. Horizontal lines indicate empirical runlengths.

In light of these data, we must consider if the introduction of color weights, as described above, is an adequate method of modeling the observed color effects. Since the model needs different color weights depending on the strength of color clustering, we have to pose the question whether this approach is really plausible. An alternative idea would be to assign color weights for sequences of transitions rather than for single transitions. Starting with the value 1.0, the color weight for a whole group of successive transitions within the same color would decrease linearly with the number of items in that group. This arrangement would make the choice of longer color runs increasingly attractive to the TSS algorithm. However, testing this approach yielded a result that was in some respects inverse to the previous one: For increasing levels of color clustering, the alternative method needed decreasing weights for long color runs in order to produce scan paths of good similarity to the empirical ones.

To solve this problem, we could try to combine the two approaches or to use more complex functions to determine the relevant distances between items. A basic rule of modeling is, however, to use as few freely adjustable parameters as possible. The more of these parameters are integrated into a model, the easier it is for the model to fit any data, which weakens the reliability of conclusions drawn from the model's performance. Therefore, we kept our desired model, which we named the Color TSS Model, as simple as possible by extending our initial approach. Figure 9 suggests a linear dependence of the required color weight on the strength of color clustering. Recall that the three levels of color clustering correspond respectively to the values 1.0, 1.3, and 1.7 on the cluster measure α_c, with a maximum deviation of 0.05. We determined the parameters of the linear function to yield runlengths most similar to the empirical ones:

$$\text{color weight} = 0.264\, \alpha_c + 0.799$$

Three sample paths generated by the resulting Color TSS Model are shown in the lower row of Figure 7. In fact, some subtle differences to the TSS paths (middle row) can be found indicating that the new model better corresponds to the empirically observed strategies (upper row). A similarity analysis showed that the scan paths generated by the Color TSS Model were indeed more similar to the observed patterns (similarity value 19.51) than those produced by the unadjusted TSS Model (19.18).

Finally, we adapted the Clustering Model of Experiment 1 to the stimuli of Experiment 2. This was achieved analogously to the adaptation of the TSS Model. We implemented the stimulus-dependent color weight for both the first step (calculation of clusters) and the second step (cluster-based TSS) performed by the Clustering Model. The same functional relationship between color weight and color clustering in the stimulus which was calculated for the Color TSS Model led to optimal runlength values for the Clustering

Model as well. The improvement of the Clustering Model achieved by its adjustment to color attributes turned out to be considerably smaller than for the TSS Model. We measured the similarity to the empirical scan paths in Experiment 2 for both the unadjusted Clustering Model and the new Color Clustering Model. While the Color Clustering Model produced results slightly more similar to the empirical paths (19.03) than those generated by the original Clustering Model (18.95), it could neither compete with the TSS Model nor with the Color TSS Model.

Figure 10 shows a survey of similarities between the models' paths and the empirical ones, in ascending order. In addition, the values for the Greedy Model (17.25) and the optimum fit (20.65) are presented. A one-way analysis of variance showed a statistically significant main effect, i.e. differences between the five models, $F(4; 76) = 65.74$, $p < 0.001$. Pairwise t-tests with Bonferroni-adjusted probabilities revealed that, as in Experiment 1, the Greedy heuristic yielded a significantly lower value than all other models, all $t(19) > 9.43$, $p < 0.001$. While there were no reliable differences between the Clustering Model, the Color Clustering Model, and the TSS Model, the Color TSS Model produced a significantly higher value than all its competitors, all $t(19) > 3.50$, $p < 0.024$.

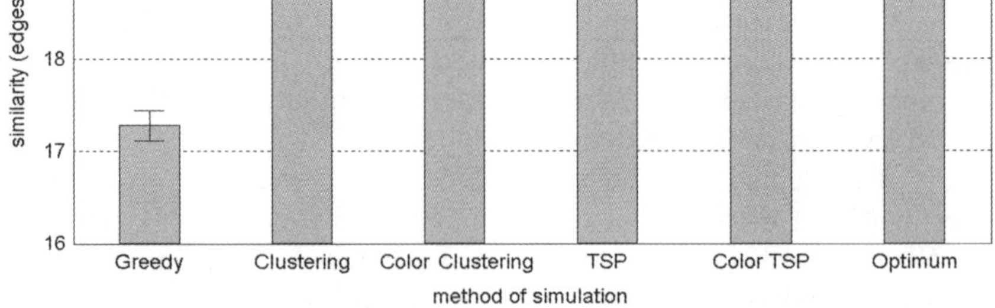

Figure 10. Similarity between the empirical scan paths of Experiment 2 and those yielded by the different models, plus the optimum-fit path.

4. General discussion

Experiment 1 provided us with some fundamental insights into visual scanning strategies. First, the results suggest that the present scanning task does not induce any preferred direction for scanning, e.g. top to bottom or left to right. The reason might be that using a random distribution of items and a specified starting point makes this kind of schematic strategy rather inefficient. Second, the five scan path models differ substantially in their abilities to reproduce empirical scan paths. The TSS Model and the closely related Clustering Model yield clearly better results than their competitors, showing that the minimization of overall scan path length might be an important determinant of human gaze trajectories. This does not imply that artificial neural networks are unable to generate human-like scan paths. Further research is necessary to determine adequate structures of neural networks for modeling human scanning behavior.

Experiment 2 confirmed the results of Experiment 1. Moreover, it yielded information about the influence of color and form attributes on empirical scan paths. While participants seem to ignore the items' forms, they use the items' colors in the scanning process, as demonstrated by disproportionately long color runs in their scan paths. The influence of color grows with increasing strength of color clustering in the stimulus. This color guidance is possibly employed to reduce memory load for generating self-avoiding scan paths. It requires less effort to keep in memory the clusters already visited and the items visited within the current cluster than to keep in memory the visited area of the display on the basis of single items, especially if suitably large clusters are available. The perceptual grouping by form, however, does not seem to be strong enough to significantly influence the participants' scanning strategies.

These results are in line with those obtained by Beckwith and Restle (1966), who found that clustering items by color or form reduced the time needed to count them, with color having a substantially stronger effect than form. Our findings are also compatible with eye-movement studies investigating saccadic selectivity in visual search tasks (e.g. Williams and Reingold 2001). Distractor items that are identical to the target in any dimension attract more fixations than others. Again, this effect is disproportionately large for the color dimension.

Conclusions concerning differences across dimensions, however, may not generalize beyond the set of items used in the experiment. In Experiment 2, other item sets, e.g. bars in different orientations, might have led to form-biased scan paths. Reducing the discriminability between colors would at some point have eliminated the influence of color on the scan paths. From the present data we can only confidently conclude that fully saturated colors affect scanning strategies, whereas regular geometrical forms do not.

Disproving our assumption, the effect of color on scan paths did not reduce their variability. The optimum-fit value was actually lower in Experiment 2 (20.65) than in Experiment 1 (21.89), indicating higher differences between individual paths in Experiment 2 than in Experiment 1. This is probably due to the fact that, in Experiment 2, the effect of color varies considerably between individuals, which increases the range of applied strategies. The large standard error for relative color runlengths (see Figure 8) illustrates these individual differences.

Based on the empirically obtained color effect, the TSS and Clustering Models have been adapted to colored items. When using a weight for transitions between items of different colors to achieve this adaptation, this weight has to increase linearly with the strength of color clustering in the stimuli. Loosely speaking, the effect of color attributes on empirical scan paths seems to vary linearly with the amount of color clustering in the stimulus. We found the adaptation of the TSS Model – the Color TSS Model – to be a small but clear improvement over the standard TSS Model. The Color TSS Model is also superior to the Clustering Model and its refined variant, the Color Clustering Model, and hence can be considered the "winner" of our competition.

Neither Experiment 1 nor Experiment 2 showed a significant difference in performance between the "color-blind" TSS and Clustering Models. Only the adaptation to colored items was achieved more effectively for the TSS Model. This does not mean that human viewers do not apply clustering strategies. In fact, the winning Color TSS Model performs clustering itself, since it fits its scan paths to the color clusters given in the stimulus. While this method of clustering could to some extent be adapted to human strategies, this could not be done with the more complex and less flexible algorithm used by the Clustering Model.

Altogether, the difficulties encountered in surpassing the plain TSS Model indicate that the geometrical optimization of scan paths, i.e., the minimization of their length, is the main common principle of human scanning strategies under the given task, even when additional color and form information is provided. Further research is needed to verify the applicability of the findings to real-world situations. For this purpose, stimuli could be photographs of real-world scenes – such as the breakfast scenes used by Rao and Ballard (1995) – and the task could be be to memorize the scene, to detect a certain item, or to give a comprehensive verbal description (Clark and

Krych 2004; de Ruijter et al. 2003). Will scan path minimization still be the dominant factor? Will the scanning strategies be influenced by the distribution of color and form attributes, by figural or functional interpretation, or by pragmatic considerations?

Answering these questions will be an important step towards understanding the principles our visual system employs when creating gaze trajectories. More generally, it will contribute to our understanding of human cognition in situated communication, where higher-level factors, visuolinguistic processes, and communicative goals, strategies, and routines are to be taken into account (Garrod, Pickering and McElree 2005; Rickheit 2005). In this context, the present work can be viewed both as an intermediate step of import in the ongoing investigation of human cognition, and as a starting point for a promising line of research.

Acknowledgements

We are grateful to Thomas Clermont, Peter Munsche and Karl-Hermann Wieners for their assistance in conducting the experiments. Moreover, we would like to thank Kai Essig, Sonja Folker, Alex Gunz, Jiye Shen and Boris M. Velichkovsky for their helpful comments on earlier drafts of this paper. The research reported here was funded by the Deutsche Forschungsgemeinschaft (Collaborative Research Center 360, project B4).

References

Atkinson, J., F. W. Campbell, and M. R. Francis
1976 The magical number 4±0: A new look at visual numerosity judgements. *Perception* 5: 327–334.

Ballard, D. H., M. M. Hayhoe, and J. B. Pelz
1995 Memory representations in natural tasks. *Journal of Cognitive Neuroscience* 7: 66–80.

Beckwith, M., and F. Restle
1966 Process of enumeration. *Psychological Review* 73: 437–444.

Clark, H. H., and M. A. Krych
2004 Speaking while monitoring addressees for understanding. *Journal of Memory and Language* 50: 62-81.

de Ruijter, J. P., S. Rossignol, L. Voorpijl, D. W. Cunningham, and W. J. M. Levelt
2003 SLOT: A research platform for investigating multimodal communication. *Behavior Research, Methods, Instruments, and Computers* 35: 408–419.

Findlay, J. M.
2004 Eye Scanning and Visual Search. In *The interface of language, vision, and action: Eye movements and the visual world,* J. M. Henderson and F. Ferreira (eds.), 134–159. New York: Psychology Press.

Garrod, S. C., M. J. Pickering, and B. McElree
2005 *Interactions of language and vision restrict 'visual world' interpretations.* Presented at the 13th European Conference on Eye Movements, Berne, Switzerland, 14-18 August.

Heidemann, G., T. Nattkemper, G. Menkhaus, and H. Ritter
1996 Blicksteuerung durch präattentive Fokussierungspunkte. In *Proceedings in Artificial Intelligence*, B. Mertsching (ed.), 109–116. Sankt Augustin: Infix.

Henderson, J. M. and F. Ferreira
2004 Scene perception for psycholinguists. In *The interface of language, vision, and action: Eye movements and the visual world,* J. M. Henderson and F. Ferreira (eds.), 1–58. New York: Psychology Press.

Henderson, J. M., and A. Hollingworth
1999 High-level scene perception. *Annual Review of Psychology* 50: 243–271.

Hubel, D. H., and T. N. Wiesel
1962 Receptive fields, binocular interaction and functional architecture in the cat's visual cortex. *Journal of Physiology (London)* 160: 106–154.

Itti, L., and C. Koch
2001 Computational modeling of visual attention. *Nature Reviews Neuroscience* 2: 194–203.

Kattner, H.
1994 Using attention as a link between low-level and high-level vision. *Technical report*, Department of Mathematics and Computer Science, Technical University of Munich, Germany [http:// www.informatik.tu-muenchen.de/people/stud/Kattner/TUMI9439/contents.html].

Klein, R. M.
1988 Inhibitory tagging system facilitates visual search. *Nature* 334: 430–431.
2000 Inhibition of return. *Trends in Cognitive Sciences* 4: 138–147.

Koesling, H.
2003 *Visual Perception of Location, Orientation and Length: An Eye-Movement Approach.* ScD Thesis, University of Bielefeld, Germany. PDF file [http://bieson.ub.uni-bielefeld.de/volltexte/2003/244/].

Koesling, H., E. Carbone, and H. Ritter
2003 *Modelling visual processing strategies in perceptual comparison tasks*. Paper presented at the 12th European Conference on Eye Movements, Dundee, Scotland, 20-24 August.

Kohonen, T.
1990 The Self-Organizing Map. *Proceedings of IEEE* 78: 1464–1480.

Lennie, P., C. Trevarthen, D. van Essen, and H. Wässle
1990 Parallel processing of visual information. In *Visual Perception: The Neurophysiological Foundations,* L. Spillmann and J. S. Werner (eds.), 103–128. San Diego: Academic Press.

Locher, P., and C. F. Nodine
1987 Symmetry catches the eye. In *Eye Movements: From Physiology to Cognition*, A. Levy-Schoen and J. K. O'Regan (eds.), 353–361. Amsterdam: North Holland.

Melcher, D., and E. Kowler
2001 Visual scene memory and the guidance of saccadic eye movements. *Vision Research* 41: 3597–3611.

Miller, G. A.
1956 The magical number seven, plus or minus two: Some limits on our capacity for processing information. *Psychological Review* 63: 81–97.

Najemnik, J., and W. S. Geisler
2005 Optimal eye movement strategies in visual search. *Nature 434*: 387–391.

Parkhurst, D., K. Law, and E. Niebur
2002 Modeling the role of salience in the allocation of overt visual attention. *Vision Research* 42: 107–123.

Pomplun, M.
1998 *Analysis and Models of Eye Movements in Comparative Visual Search.* Göttingen: Cuvillier.

Pomplun, M., E. Carbone, L. Sichelschmidt, B. M. Velichkovsky, and H. Ritter
2005 How to disregard irrelevant stimulus dimensions: Evidence from comparative visual search. In *Proceedings of ICCI 2005 – 4th IEEE International Conference on Cognitive Information*, W. Kinsner, D. Zhang, Y. Wang, and J. Tsai (eds.), 183–192. Piscataway: IEEE.

Pomplun, M., E. M. Reingold, and J. Shen
2003 Area activation: A computational model of saccadic selectivity in visual search. *Cognitive Science* 27: 299–312.

Pomplun, M., L. Sichelschmidt, K. Wagner, T. Clermont, G. Rickheit, and H. Ritter
2001 Comparative visual search: A difference that makes a difference. *Cognitive Science* 25: 3–36.

Pomplun, M., B. M. Velichkovsky, and H. Ritter
1994 An artificial neural network for high precision eye movement tracking. In *Lecture notes in artificial intelligence: Proceedings KI-94,* B. Nebel and L. Dreschler-Fischer (eds.), 63–69. Berlin: Springer.

Posner, M. I.
1980 Orienting of attention. *Quarterly Journal of Experimental Psychology* 32: 3–25.

Posner, M. I., and Y. A. Cohen
1984 Components of visual orienting. In *Attention and Performance 10*, H. Bouma and D. G. Bouwhuis (eds.), 531–554. Hillsdale: Erlbaum.

Querhani, N., R. von Wartburg, H. Hügli, and R. Müri
2004 Emprirical validation of the saliency-based model of visual attention. *Electronic Letters on Computer Vision and Image Analysis* 3: 13–24.
Rao, R. P. N., and D. H. Ballard
1995 Learning saccadic eye movements using multiscale spatial filters. In *Advances in Neural Information Processing Systems,* G. Tesauro, D. Touretzky, and T. Leen (eds.), 893–900. Cambridge, MA: MIT Press.
Rickheit, G.
2005 Alignment und Aushandlung im Dialog. *Zeitschrift für Psychologie* 213: 159–166.
Rickheit, G., and L. Sichelschmidt
1999 Mental models – some answers, some questions, some suggestions. In *Mental Models in Discourse Processing and Reasoning*, G. Rickheit and C. Habel (eds.), 9–40. Amsterdam: North-Holland.
Rimey, R. D., and C. M. Brown
1991 Controlling eye movements with Hidden Markov Models. *International Journal of Computer Vision* 7: 47–65.
Ritter, H., T. Martinetz, and K. Schulten
1992 *Neural Computation and Self-Organizing Maps*. Reading, MA: Addison-Wesley.
Salvucci, D. D.
2001 An integrated model of eye movements and visual encoding. *Cognitive Systems Research* 1: 201–220.
Shen, J., E. M. Reingold, M. Pomplun, and D. E. Williams
2003 Saccadic selectivity during visual search: The influence of central processing difficulty. In *The Mind's Eye. Cognitive and Applied Aspects of Eye Movement Research,* J. Hyönä, R. Radach, and H. Deubel (eds.), 65–88. Amsterdam: Elsevier.
Shore, D. I., and R. M. Klein
2000 On the manifestations of memory in visual search. *Spatial Vision* 14: 59—75.
Sichelschmidt, L.
2005 More than just style: An oculomotor approach to semantic interpretation. In *Proceedings of 2005 Symposium on Culture, Arts, and Education*, J. C.-H. Chen, and K.-C. Liang (eds.), 118–130. Taipei: NTNU Press.
Stampe, D. M.
1993 Heuristic filtering and reliable calibration methods for video-based pupil-tracking systems. *Behavior Research Methods, Instruments, and Computers* 25: 137–142.
Tipper, S. P., B. Weaver, L. M. Jerreat, and A. L. Burak
1994 Object-based and environment-based inhibition of return of visual attention. *Journal of Experimental Psychology: Human Perception and Performance* 20: 478–499.

Treisman, A., and S. Sato
1990 Conjunction search revisited. *Journal of Experimental Psychology: Human Perception and Performance* 16: 459–478.

Vorwerg, C., I. Wachsmuth, and G. Socher
2006 Visually grounded language processing in object reference. In *Situated Communication*, G. Rickheit and I. Wachsmuth (eds.), 77–126. Berlin: de Gruyter (this volume).

Williams, D. E., and E. M. Reingold
2001 Preattentive guidance of eye movements during triple conjunction search tasks. *Psychonomic Bulletin and Review* 8: 476–488.

Wolfe, J. M., K. R. Cave, and S. L. Franzel
1989 Guided search: An alternative to the feature integration model for visual search. *Journal of Experimental Psychology: Human Perception and Performance* 15: 419–433.

Wright, R. D., and L. M. Ward
1994 Shifts of visual attention: An historical and methodological overview. *Canadian Journal of Experimental Psychology* 48: 151–166.

Zelinsky, G. J.
1996 Using eye saccades to assess the selectivity of search movements. *Vision Research* 36: 2177–2187.

Neurobiological aspects of meaning constitution during language processing

Horst M. Müller

Abstract. Certain aspects of meaning constitution such as its time course or modularity are described from a biological point of view based on neuroanatomical and neurophysiological facts. In addition, the multimodality of verbal communication (e.g., mimic, gestures) is pointed out and discussed as one reason for the robustness, efficiency and speed of language processing. After a short introduction into the functional neuroanatomy of hearing and language processing, both the most common neurolinguistic techniques for investigating language and examples of neurolinguistic findings are reported.

1. Introduction

The human ability to speak has its origins in processes, functions, and features of the human nervous system because in principle all cognitive phenomena can be traced back to a neural substrate. From a biological point of view the phenomenon "language" merely is an especially powerful developmental step of communication within a species and within the evolution of cognition (Müller 1990).

When we look at a conversation between humans from a biological point of view it can be classified as a form of human expressiveness behavior. Therefore, a spoken dialog merely is communicative behavior. If this communicative behavior takes place in a natural communication setting 'face-to-face' (ecological validity), the adequate stimulus of verbal communication does not only include articulated language but also non-verbal signals, contextual and situational information and actualities. This means that spoken language communication is a highly multimodal process. During the understanding of language we do not only have to conduct phonological, morphosyntactical, and semantic analyses but we also have to analyze and interpret expectations, situational references of the action, and contextual references of the immediately preceding auditory as well as non-verbal communicative signals (e.g. Rickheit 2001). In this totality only, language communication can be natural and efficient. Facial expression is the most important source for signals in non-verbal communication. This is the reason why the faces of non-human primates became hairless during evolutionary development. Of the about 640 muscles in the human body in total, as much as 43 muscles are responsible for frowning the forehead and 15 for laughing. The movement of the lips when speaking, for example, adds greatly to the robustness of language communication. This is due to the articulatory features and the correlation between lip and tongue position and the articulated sound. This way about 20% of the information is taken in by the interlocutor. Lip reading is assigned a very important role not only in professional lip reading but also in everyday dialogs (Campbell, Dodd, and Burnham 1998).

This means that several sensory systems are involved in the analysis of the interlocutor's language behavior: The auditory system, the visual system, and to a small degree the olfactorial system (possible tactile parts in communication will not be considered here). For the production of language behavior this means that aside from the cognitive processes of language planning and motor articulation there are processes involved consciously or unconsciously, such as motor processes for the facial gestures, gesture in general, and the overall body posture. During language comprehension the listener has to perceive, analyze, and integrate a great amount of multimodal information. The amount of phonological information from auditory utterances can reach very high level because in conversation we articulate approximately two to six syllables per second. Supported by an expectational background, the listener is able to process morphosyntactic, prosodic, and semantic analyses of the auditory system, a visual analysis of facial expression, gestures, etc., as well as the multimodal integration of these individual pieces of information within a time frame of about 100 to 1000 ms after the speaker has produced the utterances. The listener seldom needs several seconds for the said to be understood unlike for example in an ambiguous or alluding situation. This extraordinary speed of language comprehension is understandable, if – as is usually the case in cognitive models – massive parallel neural processes in the central nervous system are assumed (e.g. Müller 2003).

The capacity of language processing clearly shows the so-called sentence shadowing: when hearing the own mother tongue trained people are able to repeat the heard utterance with a delay of a mere 200 to 250 ms (Marslen-Wilson 1985). During this time the perceptual, analytical, and production processes can be completed by the person shadowing the speaker. Above and beyond that, only little more time is needed during shadowing to do simple repairs of mistakes in the given utterances. This amazing capacity is possible only because there are processes on each neural level of language processing which heighten the efficiency. These include, for example, efficient neural filters which strip the enormous amount of incoming language information from parts which are not needed for the following neural analysis system. This is a process of data reduction, which already begins with the filtering features of each sensory organ and continues on each neural step. Here, only certain features are detected and processed by feature detectors on each level. This leads to a multistage "slenderized" and simplified amount of information to be processed. Aside from this data reduction the already saved mental concepts are activated and used by higher processing levels of the central nervous system. This means that the mental concepts are assigned to neural information as soon as possible and processed further from there on. The exact shaping of these concepts was acquired during the course of phylogeny or ontogeny (individual experience) and is changeable (plasticity) all through life. Language comprehension is possible within a time frame of a few tenths of a second due to this shaping and simplification. Contrary to what had often been assumed in earlier cybernetic models of communication in the 60s, no definable chunks of information are really transported between the interlocutors using verbal and non-verbal channels. It would be inefficient and much too time-consuming to transport and especially to analyze all information of a conversation between interlocutors audio-visually. Language behavior is simply released by information already present in the listener's brain. The linguistic utterance, therefore, does not transport a meaning but functions as a trigger for the activation of already present meaningful elements. The speaker can never be completely certain about which meaning exactly he releases in the listener. This vagueness of language can even be found with simple concepts of objects (e.g. *chair* or *closet*) and even more so with feelings or colors. It can be said that a linguistic message is only the outwardly perceivable 'tip of the iceberg' of cognition. A very substantial part of the assignment of meaning is not perceivable from the outside but is generated by the listener. The perceivable language utterance functions as a trigger for already established attitudes, meanings, and components of the knowledge about the world of the listener (Müller 2003). On each level of the linguistic utterance the listener creates results of the analysis and assigns meaning. Step-by-step these are simply touched and guided by the speaker.

Three different explanatory attempts from the area of evolutionary/theoretical biology, anatomy, and neurolinguistics are presented in the following in order to give indications and proof for the high efficiency and speed of language processing:

- Categorization according to evolutionary epistemology.
- Functional anatomical facts about language processing in the brain.
- Neurolinguistic findings on the time course of the constitution of meaning.

2. Categorization according to evolutionary epistemology

The stripping of unwanted information and the limitation of perceiving feature complexes, which in phylogeny so far have been sufficient, can often be found in nature. Cognitive processes also underlie basic evolutionary conditions. Cognition, according to Konrad Lorenz, is a negative print of the environmental characteristics of living beings because certain properties of this environment are mirrored in the characteristics of the sensory organs and process of thinking. The adaptation of cognition to the respective environment can be found on all levels, the anatomy and function of the sensory organs and neural processing as well as the function of the processes of thinking. From the viewpoint of evolutionary epistemology founded by Lorenz, there has not only been an ongoing adaptation of the bodily features of organisms but also an adaptation of cognitive processes and the neural connections lying underneath (e.g. Vollmer 1987). In terms of understanding language behavior this means that incoming information is categorized in the brain as efficiently and fast as possible on every step of the processing hierarchy – from the assignment of phonemes/segments to the pragmatic level.

The categorization can be seen as one of the universal principles of organismic cognition. Therefore, in regard to the complex behavioral performance of human language, a multilevel, emergent, and hierarchical structure of categorization levels is called for: From very basic levels of phonological analysis using feature detecting neurons in the auditory pathway, over complex pattern detection processes by associations of neurons in the cortex to language specific partial performances in the syntactic analysis or the activation of semantic concepts. Even though this categorization hierarchy is still only assumed and there is no physiological proof for it yet, it seems likely on the basis of many pieces of circumstantial evidence. This means that the existence of linguistic categories can be assumed from a neurophysiological viewpoint (Müller and Weiss 2000). In light of this view prejudices often found in human-human interaction (often unwanted) are seen as efficiency heightening and time saving effects. Riedl (1980), for example, sees them as "pre-judices" about the world which allow meaningful actions under a lot of time pressure in the first place.

3. Functional anatomy of language perception and comprehension

There are many anatomical indications in the auditory pathway which speak for the assumption that massive parallel processing is taking place. The incoming information is not processed linearly but divided early on and processed separately. The individual building blocks of information come together again in the respective main areas after only a few neural changeovers and form the basis for new chunks of information, which in turn are processed independently of location and time. This parallelism becomes evident from the course of the fibers.

The information coming from each ear is sent to the medulla oblongata in the brain stem through the approximately 30,000 to 50,000 fibers of the eighth cranial nerve (Nervus vestibulocochlearis). The information is connected to the primary auditory cortex using several processing nuclei. The auditory pathway runs through several nuclei in the rhombencephalon, the mesencephalon, and the diencephalon to the primary auditory cortex in the telencephalon. Most of the fibers run contralaterally, which means that they run into the opposite brain hemisphere and only a small part does not cross over and stays on the side of the respective sensory cells, i.e. they work ipsilaterally (see Figure 1). The auditory pathway is a very complex network because there are several crossings into the other brain hemisphere and above and beyond that, there are certain fiber parts which skip the next processing step up or else run back to processing nuclei deeper down in form of so-called downward fibers.

First, the information is sent from the auditory hair cells in the organ of Corti in the inner ear to bipolar nerve cells in the spiral ganglion in the cochlea. The final branches of each bipolar neurite reach about 75 to 100 neurons of the nucleus cochlearis which is made up of about 88,000 neurons (Dunker et al. 1972; Trincker 1977). At this point the primary afferent fibers divide up into two branches which project onto two complexly built nuclei. One branch goes to the nucleus cochlearis ventralis and the other to the nucleus cochlearis dorsalis in the medulla oblongata. From the nucleus cochlearis ventralis there are fibers which run to the upper olive on the same side (ipsilateral) and to the contralateral upper olive via the trapezoidal body. The upper olive is made up of about 34,000 neurons. A first calculation and processing from both sides already takes place on this level of connection because both olives receive sensory input from both ears. One branch of fibers runs from the nucleus cochlearis dorsalis to the nucleus lemnisci lateralis on the contralateral side as do the fibers from the ipsilateral olive. At the same time fibers run from there to the contralateral side which results in a second crossing to other side. A third changeover to the contralateral side takes place when the fibers perform a crossing to the ipsilateral and contralateral colliculus inferior. Some of the fibers go to the colliculus superior. The majority, however, runs to the corpus geniculatum mediale in the metathalamus. The pars prinicipalis, which is assumed especially important for hearing, has about 360,000 neurons. The pars magnocellularis consists of about 58,000 neurons. Widely branched fibers, so-called auditory radiation, run from the corpus geniculatum mediale to the primary auditory cortex (cf. Dunker et al. 1972; Trincker 1974; 1977). Together the colliculi inferiores and superiores form the quadrigeminal plate which makes up the tectum in the mesencephalon. Approximately 360,000 neurons are assumed to make up the lower quadrigeminal (colliculi inferior). The colliculi inferior plays an important part in the acoustically induced reactions concerning orientation: together with spinal cord efferences there are certain afferences which lead to a movement of the head towards the source of the sound (Trepel 1999).

Above and beyond the above described main path of the projections going upward to the auditory cortex, there is a parallel projectional system to the cortex of the cerebellum. This is a fiber connection which has only one to two synaptic crossings between the nuclei in the cochlea and the middle part of the cerebellum (vermis cerebelli) (Trincker 1977).

The primary auditory cortex lies in the area of the first Heschl's gyrus on the dorsal plane of the gyrus temporalis superior corresponding to Brodman's area 41. The are an estimated 10.2 million neurons in the auditory cortex (Duncker et al. 1972). The first synaptic crossing of the auditory path takes place directly in the sensory cells. This means that the course of the auditory projection consists of merely five to six neural steps.

However, the projection becomes more complex due to crossings, divergences, and the existence of paths leading the information back. During the immediate process this leads to longer feedback chains. The primary auditory cortex in each hemisphere receives information coming from the cochleas of both ears because of the multiply crossed paths. A unilateral central lesion therefore does not lead to the complete failure of one ear but only to a more or less severely reduced performance. On the other hand, experiments with dichotic listening (cf. for example Hugdahl 1988), in which each ear, separate from the other, gets the same or different stimuli, were able to show a preference for one side. Syllables such as *ma* and *pa* are heard and repeated correctly irrespective of whether they are presented to the right or the left ear. The information from the right ear does, however, get to left language dominant hemisphere to a greater extent because of the anatomical crossing of the fibers. If the syllable is presented only to the left ear the information has to be crossed over using the corpus callosum to the left language dominant hemisphere after the right-hemisphere's primary acoustic analysis. This is the reason for a processing advantage for certain types of language information which are perceived by the right ear (Kimura 1967). If both syllables *ma* and *pa* are presented competitively and at the same time to only one ear, only the syllable presented to the right ear is perceived consciously. This right-ear-advantage is sustainable, however, only for certain consonants, e.g. /b/, /d/, /t/, but not for vowels (Schwartz and Tallal 1980).

To some extent, special feature detectors work in parallel on the level of sensory language perception, i.e. from the sensory cells in the ear to the auditory cortex. In a first step these feature detectors extract special phonological features of the utterance. This means that there are neurons, for example, which react with electrical activity only to plosives but not fricatives. Other neurons show activity only if they perceive features which typically occur in vowels (Keidel 1992). Neurons which work as feature detectors and "consider" only certain features of a vocal utterance and react with electrical activity to this do not only occur in human beings. This type of stimulus filtering and consideration of certain features is – from a phylogenetic point of view – a very old characteristic of the acoustic system. This property is also present in other mammals. Aside from electrophysiological experiments there are behavioral experiments which show, for example, that chinchillas are able to decide between syllables such as *da* and *ta* in a two-choice experiment (Kuhl and Miller 1978). Some of the physiological fundamentals of phoneme perception in humans are already present in lower mammals, who use this ability in their acoustic communication (Müller 1997).

As results from different areas of experimental neurophysiology have shown there are higher processing centers in the central nervous system (CNS) which are characterized by neurons which answer only to highly specific stimuli of the respective modality (Kandel, Schwartz, and Jessel 1991). It seems to be a fairly widespread principle of central nervous processing to capture the information coming from one sensory organ in the periphery first and only in a second step to filter it in the following processing steps according to features which continually become more complex. Neural feature detectors of this kind, which react to certain complex parts of a stimulus pattern, have been described for many sensory systems in animals. These feature detectors for example react directional or frequency specific. A toad, for example, has visual neurons which answer to a bar moving horizontally (worm schema) but not to one moving vertically (Laming and Ewert 1984).

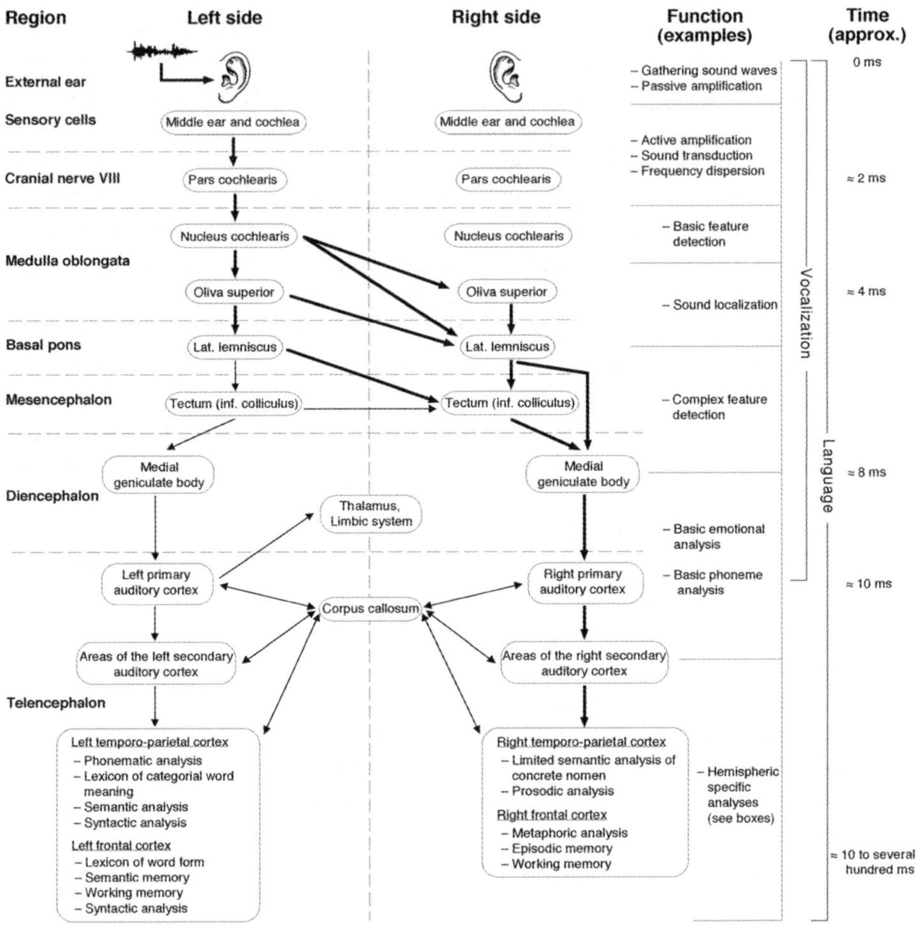

Figure 1. Simplified schema of the perception and processing of animal vocalization and human language in the auditory pathway. Presented are the most important stages in the brain stem (medulla, pons, mesencephalon), diencephalon, and in the neocortex. With the exception of the thalamus, none of the backtracking paths are indicated. The values concerning the temporal processing are only approximates because the parallelism of the stages of analysis does not show up in the picture. Even though the auditory nerve contains only about 30,000 fibers, the actual crossings in the auditory path are much more complicated due to the backtracking paths than those of the visual system (approximately 1 million fibers). The auditory path, on the other hand, has only five or six levels of neurons switched one after the other on the way to the primary auditory cortex (taken from Müller 2003).

Feature detectors have also been proven in fish whose side line organ, reacting to movements of the water, is similar to an acoustic system (Müller 1996). Aside from simple feature detectors there are complex detectors such as neurons for facial recognition which exclusively answer to abstract facial features (Gross and Sergent 1992). The same is true for the acoustic system. There are already acoustic neurons in the mesencephalon of fish which function as feature detectors and exclusively react to simple sine tones or exclusively to complex frequency and amplitude modulated signals (Müller 1996). In the frame of the hierarchical analysis of complex pattern detectors processed in the central nervous system there is acoustic information which for example only reacts to certain stimulus frequencies or sequences of stimuli and pays attention only to communication signals sent by the own species (Buchfellner et al. 1989). The higher the processing step in the CNS the more natural, special, and behaviorally relevant the sensory stimuli have to be in order to trigger neural activation. This means that only some features from a multitude of theoretical features will be paid attention to. And this is what in end explains the existence of categorization and prototypicality in cognition.

Above and beyond that, it is assumed from a neurobiological viewpoint that the first use of such complexes of stimuli make the processes of language communication become optimally observable. Up to now mostly partial processes of language communication were investigated. This includes, for example, word reading, sentence reading, context free listening to words and sentences and so forth. It is further assumed that the maximal robustness and speed of language processing, which are normal in every day life, as well as the actually present extent of brain physiological processes become obvious only once all partial performances of language communication interact (Müller 2004). A critical mass is reached through these building blocks of communication. This critical mass allows to measure and capture the resulting brain physiological processes in their entirety.

A schematic presentation of the individual processing stages and the temporal course during language processing is illustrated in Figure 1 using the auditory pathway.

It can be seen in Figure 1 – according to the vertical division (on the right side) – that human language processing is based on the phylogenetically older anatomical and physiological conditions of animal vocalization. Thus, many partial performances of the analysis of vocalization are used in central nervous language processing. This is also the reason why mammals and birds are successful pattern recognizers of language stimuli; a dog, for example, can be conditioned with the dog owner's spoken language commands.

The sensory cells in the cochlea transform the language signal into electrical signals in dependency of the frequency. The first analysis in form of a simple pattern recognition is already performed in the medulla. Here, neurons react to certain acoustic patterns of complex stimuli with a typical answer behavior for each respective stimulus. The localization of the source of the sound, which from a phylogenetical point of view is very important, is performed at the level of the olive-complex. The exact position of the source of the sound is determined according to the different latencies which are a result of the varying distance between the source and the outer ear (auricle). Neurons in the olive, which each have one dendrite running to the left and to the right side, are capable of determining these latencies within a millionth part of a second and thereby contribute to the localization of the position of the source. Parts of the information coming from the early processing of the sound signal in the brain stem are crossed over to the other side at least three times. The recognition of complex acoustic features by neurons, working as feature detectors, starts on the level of the colliculus inferior. These neurons are crucial contributors to the detection of sounds which belong to the own species as well as to the detection of speech units on a sub-phonematic level. This analysis continues on the next level, which is the corpus geniculatum mediale. It remains uncertain whether the detection of phonemes is conducted by neurons of the geniculatum or by neurons of the primary auditory cortex. The essential information from the sound evaluation is present on the level of the primary auditory cortex, if not earlier, in order to conduct a phoneme recognition. The primary emotional evaluation has begun in the thalamus even before this level is reached. The information for the thalamus for the primary emotional evaluation is sent there via returning paths. The perceived signals (vocalization sounds or language) are analyzed according to emotional feelings in the thalamus. All returning paths which contribute to the complexity of the auditory path are not shown here, only the onc to the thalamus is.

If we summarize the results from the neurobiology of language processing so far, we have to draw an incomplete first picture of the central processes in the cortex. This picture has to be understood as an extremely simplified schema. Following this, it seems likely that the phonemic analysis is conducted in the temporo-parietal cortex (Wernicke's area) of the dominant hemisphere. It remains unclear, however, which units (e.g. phonemes, segments, syllables) the analysis favors. It can still be assumed that a semantic analysis is carried out in this area, whereas at least parts of the word form lexicon seem to be represented in the temporal lobe. First results indicate that there is a representation of lemmas according to categories – e.g. "tools" or "fruit" (Damasio et al. 1996). The syntactical analysis probably takes place in the frontal lobe of the dominant hemisphere (Broca's area). The representation of morphological and phonological information of words is assumed here in a word form lexicon. The semantic memory and parts of the working memory are set in the anterior area of the frontal lobe (Andreasen et al. 1995; Petersen et al. 1988; Tulving 1994).

In comparison to the dominant hemisphere the subdominant hemisphere has few but also important functions (Seldon 1985). There is, for example, a very reduced linguistic analysis in the subdominant (right) temporo-parietal area (analogous to Wernicke's area). With the help of fMRI-studies it has been able to show that the activity is heightened slightly when the demand for sentence analysis goes up (Just et al. 1996). The frontal lobe in the subdominant hemisphere mainly conducts the prosodic analysis, i.e. the analysis of the sentence melody. Above and beyond that, the frontal lobe is ascribed some importance in the analysis of metaphors (Bottini et al. 1994). Also the recognition of faces (Tempini et al. 1998) and the processing of proper names (Müller, Weiss, and Rappelsberger 1999; Van Lancker and Ohnesorge 2002; Yen et al., submitted) are conducted with the contribution of right hemispheric activity.

4. The time course of meaning constitution

The first assignment of meaning in natural language utterances (tested for spoken English and German) already takes place 100 to 120 ms after the articulation process has begun (Müller and Kutas 1996; Schuth, Werner, and Müller 2001). Friederici, Hahne, and Mecklinger (1996) found a latency of 100 to 120 ms (ELAN) for early ERP-effects connected with the syntactical analysis of natural German utterances. A comparably early analysis was found for the visual system as well (Schendan, Ganis, and Kutas 1998), which, however, is predestined for faster processing of information due to physical factors. Skrandies (2004) was able to show meaning dependent differences in an EEG after a mere 80 ms when presenting words visually. However, visual stimuli have different basic conditions: They are captured holistically and are available to the cognitive system also after the presentation. This is based on the fact that visual stimuli are kept in the visual-spatial scratch pad of the working memory for a short period of time. With auditory stimuli this is very different: the processing time is longer because of the linear sequence of the units in time carrying the information (phonemes/segments, morphemes, words, phrases, sentences). The cognitive processing time actually necessary for the comprehension of natural sentences is a lot shorter than the time needed for the motor articulation of the physical utterance of a sentence. Therefore, visual perception is superior to auditory processing in regard to the durational efficiency. However, during the visual presentation of sentences, further important carriers of information for the process of understanding during language communication are deleted altogether: Information on prosody and intonation, non-verbal signals and so forth. The findings on the processing of visual language stimuli in experiments on reading, however, are able to contribute proof on the enormous speed of language processing processes, because, apart from eye movements, there are other language processes taking place during reading, namely, for example, the grapheme-phoneme conversion in clusters. Further information on the individual processes of this morphological analysis is presented by Schriefers (1999), for word recognition by Frauenfelder and Floccia (1999), for contextual aspects by Zwitserlood (1999), and for prosodic analysis by Cutler (1999).

The analysis of natural language utterances in situated contexts has to be done by a processing system which can act in a frame of tenths of seconds. If we look at the time course for the attribution of meaning of language processes, we can formulate the following statements and constraints concerning spoken language:

Time constraints of phoneme recognition
First of all, the speech signal is processed like any other auditory stimulus (e.g. noise). There are no hemisphere specific differences up the level of the central nervous system of the primary auditory cortex. The primary acoustic analysis of the speech signal needs at least 6–10 ms because the auditory path from the sensory hair cells to the primary auditory cortex includes five to six synaptic connections. Each takes about 1 ms, whereby we do not take the acceleration through more direct and delay of the processing through recursive fibers into account here. Phoneme recognition can start here at the earliest, which means that the processing time for phoneme recognition lies somewhere between 10 and 15 ms (cf. Figure 1).

Time constraints of word recognition
Word recognition can, at the earliest, start after about 100 ms. Word recognition already includes language specific analysis steps in addition to the mere acoustic analysis and shows hemisphere specific differences: Although the linguistic information reaches both ears and the information is projected into the contralateral hemisphere, the analysis steps after the auditory cortex are

completed hemisphere specifically. The higher language specific analysis steps are divided up between the hemispheres. The dominant hemisphere, however, takes over the greater amount of processing steps. The left hemisphere is the dominant one in 96% of all clearly right-handed people, 85% of all ambidextrous individuals, and in 73% of all strong left-handed people (Knecht et al. 2000).

Time constraints of morpho-syntactic analysis
The syntactic analysis necessary for the attribution of meaning in the case of complex utterances can be detected in an EEG after about 180 ms (Hahne and Friederici 2002; Neville et al. 1991).

Time constraints of semantic-pragmatic analysis
The primary semantic analysis is completed after about 400 ms at the latest. This can be achieved due to the so-called N400-component which can be captured gradually in its extent and show the different degrees of violation against the rules of semantic well-formedness (Kutas 1997). The actual semantic analysis has got to be completed sooner than after 400 ms because otherwise there would not be, for example, speech shadowing below 400 ms, which can even contain repairs. – This comparably high processing speed in language processing seems to require the assumption of an efficient categorical system. Therefore, the primary attribution of meaning takes place by way of a default (but plastic) "minimal recognition". For the final attribution of meaning a more time consuming continuing analysis is necessary. A complete and exhaustive interpretation can be done deliberately by the listener. This means that several parallel processes of analysis can be assumed which, at different times, provide the consciousness with attributions of meaning with different degrees of depth and accuracy. In everyday life the more imprecise but faster processes of analysis together with context information and the listener's expectations surely suffice in order to analyze what was heard. However, in the case of more complex or unexpected utterances, the more time consuming, more extensive, and deeper levels of analysis are necessary.

5. Neurolinguistic experiments

Those brain physiological processes which underlie language communication can be used in experiments in order to draw conclusions about the structure and function of language processes. Two conjectural parts of language functioning, for example, can be seen as two distinct entities if they can be separated using a physiological measurement. Such a dissociation is possible if two partial language performances can be separated from each other using, for example, the following cues:

- different time courses of processing within a time frame of milliseconds,
- separate processing area in the brain,
- differences in large-scale synchronization between cooperating brain areas,
- frequency specific activity differences within one brain area.

Different aspects of the constitution of language meaning can be examined in neurolinguistics using such differences in processing, for example, the time course of the constitution of meaning. Furthermore, correction and reparsing processes within the analysis can be captured, as well as language alignment processes during the course of a dialogue and language processes in working memory.

In linguistic discussions it can very often be found that several – individually well-founded and comprehensible – hypotheses dealing with specific aspects of language processes compete with each other. In such a case, it makes sense to support some hypotheses using empirical findings and to classify other hypotheses as less likely. This does not mean, however, that a well-founded hypothesis has to be rejected because of a single empirical counter finding. These empirical findings are very important, however, especially when they have been brought about using different methods and experimental settings. Useful theories have to be compatible with empirical findings.

New types of facts, which have been made possible through the insight we have presently in the working brain, can be used for the forming of models and theories in linguistics (and cognitive science in general). There are a number of invasive and non-invasive electrophysiological methods (e.g. EEG, intracranial recordings), optical methods (e.g. Near Infrared Brain Imaging), magnetoelectrical methods (MEG, TMS), and other methods of brain imaging (e.g. fMRI, PET), which are useful for the examination of language processing. The project *Cortical Representation and Processing of Language* of the Bielefeld Collaborative Research Center 360 (*Situated Artificial Communicators*) used not only psycholinguistic methods (e.g. reaction time measurement, electro dermal activity) but also the following neurolinguistic methods:

Analysis of event-related potentials
Using electroencephalographic measurements (ERP-analysis), we are able to predict the temporal course of language processing with a resolution of a few milliseconds. Here, we measure the electrical activity of big neuron populations in sum using a non-invasive method (scalp electrodes). The morphosyntactic analysis during the processing of sentences can be captured as well as semantic analysis processes or even the load of the working memory during sentence comprehension (e.g. Müller, King, and Kutas 1997).

Functional magnetic resonance imaging
Using examinations with functional magnetic resonance imaging (fMRI-analysis), we can locate language processes with a high spatial resolution within a range of millimeters in different regions of the brain. Aside from the separation using the temporal criteria of the ERP-analysis, the fMRI also supplies a second criterion for the dissociation of individual components of cognitive processes using topographical data (e.g. Yen et al. 2005; Yen et al., submitted; Weiss et al., submitted).

EEG coherence analysis
The third criterion, which is especially important in language processing for the dissociation of individual components and subprocesses of language, comes from spectral-analytical examinations of the electroencephalogram (EEG-coherence analysis). This method allows the separation of distinct cognitive processes which run in parallel and are performed at the same time in the same location. In ERP-analyses and fMRI examinations such parallel processes would only lead to a sum of the activity. The measuring of frequency selective synchronization processes allows the separation of parallel activities. Spectral-analytical methods allow the separate examination of primary-sensoric processes of acoustic analysis, memory processes, processes of syntactical analysis, and semantic analysis using frequency band specific activities. Former EEG-coherence analyses only had a temporal resolution of about one to two seconds (e.g. Weiss, Müller, and Rappelsberger 2000; Weiss and Rappelsberger 1996), while coherence analyses based on the ARMA-model allow a resolution of up to several ms (Schack et al. 1995). This high temporal resolution allows the first exact examination of the temporal course of processing steps during sentence processing. The parallel processing of information as well as the oscillating processes of big neuron compounds are typical features of the central nervous system, which means that especially cognitive processes can be analyzed using coherence analysis (e.g. Weiss and Müller 2003).

For the processing of varyingly complex relative clauses using EEG-coherence analysis, Weiss et al. (2005), for example, were able to show that the ERPs previously determined by Müller, King, and Kutas (1997) can be broken down even further. Müller, King, and Kutas (1997) had shown for relative clauses in spoken language at which point in time there is a heightened load on the working memory. The frontal negativation shown in the ERP-analysis, which goes back to the summed and simultaneous activity of several ten thousand neurons, is primarily due to the disruption of the parsing of the main clause and the parsing of the embedded clause (cf. Fig. 2).

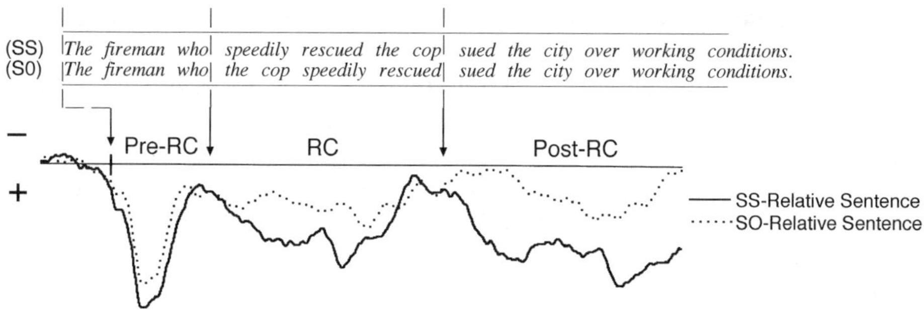

Figure 2. The mean course of the ERP for relative clauses (RC) of the so-called SS-type (subject-subject; solid line) and of the SO-type (subject-object; dotted line). Sentences of the more difficult SS-type demand more of listener's working memory. This heightened working memory load can be seen most clearly for the sentence parts RC and post-RC when looking at the increased negativation in the SO-sentences. A more detailed breakdown of the neural activity cannot be conducted because ERPs show summed activity only (from Müller, King, and Kutas 1998, modified).

What remains unclear, however, is the observed temporal course of the negativation which could be seen in the ERP at a point in time at which – according to linguistic theory – the load on the working memory could not have been that high. Using the new spectral-analytical methods of the EEG-coherence analysis, Weiss et al. (2005) were able to determine parallel processing taking place during this phase of the sentence analysis separately in the course of time in the EEG. The following partial processes can be presented due to their frequency selectivity: (1) the processes of the working memory seen in the theta-band activity, (2) the morpho-syntactic analyses seen in the beta 1-band activity, and (3) the garden-path-effect of the object-subject-sentences seen in the processes of the gamma-band (Fig. 3).

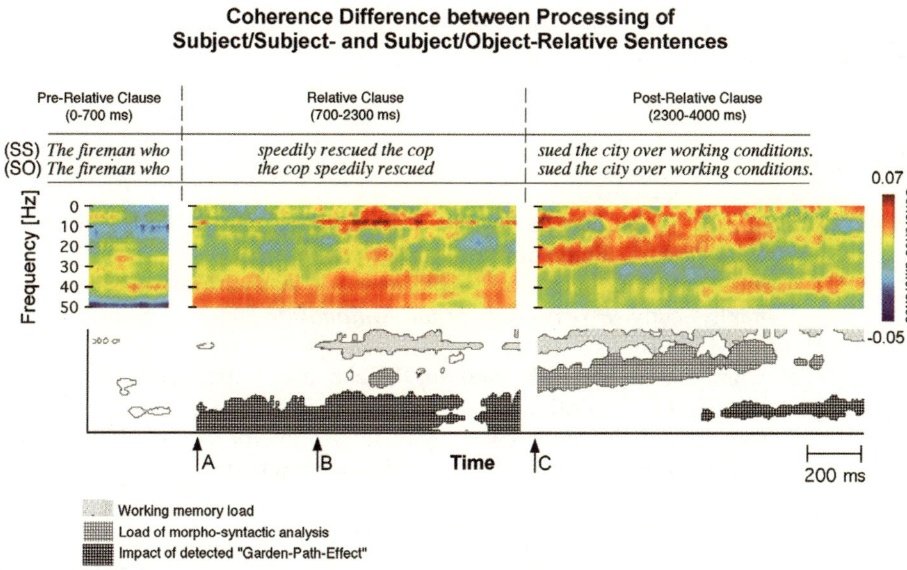

Figure 3. EEG coherence differences between two types of relative clauses – the less difficult subject-subject (SS) and the difficult subject-object relative clauses (SO). This figure shows a time-frequency matrix for the three sentences parts "pre-relative clause", "relative clause", and "post-relative clause" for the frequencies from 0 to 50 Hz. These three sentence parts show clearly separable frequency specific activities. The lower part of the figure shows these three distinguishable parts using different hues of shading. The beginning of the three different activities (arrows) come together exactly at the theoretically expected point in time of the detected garden path effects (A), of the working memory load (B), and of the heightened demand of the morpho-syntactic analysis (C) (taken from Weiss et al. 2005, modified).

Over the course of the last years, insight has been gained in regard to the modularity and time course for the level of word recognition and processes as well as for the analysis of varyingly complex sentences. On the whole, it can be said that language allocation processes take place with an extremely high speed of only a few tenths of a second. Aside from functional-anatomical preconditions which allow such a high processing speed on the level of the sensory primary analysis, neurolinguistic findings show that for higher level processing we can assume a massive parallelism of processing. This parallelism of processing steps has been demanded for a long time from the linguistic and computer science point of view (Marslen-Wilson 1975) because this is the only way that the high processing speed observed in psycholinguistic research can be accounted for.

References

Andreasen, N. C., D. S. O'Leary, S. Arndt, T. Cizadlo, R. Hurtig, K. Rezai, G. L. Watkins, L. L. Ponto, and R. D. Hichwa
1995 Short-term and long-term verbal memory: A positron emission tomography study. *Proceedings of the National Academy of Sciences USA* 92: 5111–5115.

Bottini, G., R. Corcoran, R. Sterzi, E. Paulesu, P. Schenone, P. Scarpa, R. S. Frackowiak, and C. D. Frith
1994 The role of the right hemisphere in the interpretation of figurative aspects of language. A positron emission tomography activation study. *Brain* 117: 1241–1253.

Buchfellner, E., H.-J. Leppelsack, G. M. Klump, and U. Häusler
1989 Gap detection in the starling *(Sturnus vulgaris)*. II. Coding for gaps by forebrain neurons. *Journal of Comparative Physiology* 164A: 539–549.

Campbell, R., B. J. Dodd, and D. Burnham (eds.)
1998 *Hearing by eye II: Advances in the psychology of speechreading and auditory-visual speech*. Hove: Psychology Press.

Cutler, A.
1999 Prosodische Struktur und Worterkennung bei gesprochener Sprache. In *Sprachrezeption,* A. D. Friederici (ed.), 49–83. Göttingen: Hogrefe.

Damasio, H., T. J. Grabowski, D. Tranel, R. D. Hichwa, and A. R. Damasio
1996 A neural basis for lexical retrieval. *Nature* 380: 499–505.

Dunker, E., J. Groen, R. Klinke, H. Lullies, and K. P. Schaefer
1972 *Hören, Stimme, Gleichgewicht: Sinnesphysiologie II.* München: Urban & Schwarzenberg.

Frauenfelder, U. H., and C. Floccia
1999 Das Erkennen gesprochener Wörter. In *Sprachrezeption,* A. D. Friederici (ed.), 1–48. Göttingen: Hogrefe.

Friederici, A. D., A. Hahne, and A. Mecklinger
1996 Temporal structure of syntactic parsing: Early and late event-related brain potential effects. *Journal of Experimental Psychology: Learning, Memory and Cognition* 22: 1219–1248.

Gross, C. G., and J. Sergent
1992 Face recognition. *Current Opinion in Neurobiology* 2: 156–161.

Hahne, A., and A. D. Friederici
2002 Differential task effects on semantic and syntactic processes as revealed by ERPs. *Cognitive Brain Research* 13: 339–356.

Hugdahl, K. (ed.)
1988 *Handbook of dichotic listening: Theory, methods, and research.* Chichester: Wiley.
Just, M. A., P. A. Carpenter, T. A. Keller, and W. F. Eddy
1996 Brain activation modulated by sentence comprehension. *Science* 274: 114–116.
Kandel, E. R., J. H. Schwartz, and T. M. Jessell
1991 *Principles of Neural Science.* 3. Ed. New York: Elsevier.
Keidel, W. D.
1992 Das Phänomen des Hörens: Ein interdisziplinärer Diskurs, Teil 1 und 2. *Naturwissenschaften* 79: 300–357.
Kimura, D.
1967 Functional asymmetry of the brain in dichotic listening. *Cortex* 3: 163–178.
Knecht, S., B. Dräger, M. Deppe, L. Bobe, H. Lohmann, A. Flöel, E.-B. Ringelstein, and H. Henningsen
2000 Handedness and hemispheric language dominance in healthy humans. *Brain* 123: 2512–2518.
Kuhl, P. K., and J. D. Miller
1978 Speech perception by the chinchilla: identification functions for synthetic VOT stimuli. *Journal of the Acoustical Society of America* 63: 905–917.
Kutas, M.
1997 Views on how the electrical activity that the brain generates reflects the functions of different language structures. *Psychophysiology* 34: 383–398.
Laming, P. R., and J.P. Ewert
1984 Visual unit, EEG and sustained potential shift responses to biological significant stimuli in the brain of toads *(Bufo bufo)*. *Journal of Comparative Physiology* 154A: 89–101.
Marslen-Wilson, W. D.
1975 Sentence perception as an interactive parallel process. *Science* 189: 22–228.
1985 Speech shadowing and speech comprehension. *Speech Communication* 4: 55–73.
Müller, H. M.
1990 *Sprache und Evolution: Grundlagen der Evolution und Ansätze einer evolutionstheoretischen Sprachwissenschaft.* Berlin: de Gruyter.
1996 Indications for feature detection with the lateral line organ in fish. *Comparative Biochemistry and Physiology* 114: 257–263.
1997 *Neurolinguistische und kognitive Aspekte der Sprachverarbeitung.* Habilitationsschrift. Bielefeld: Universität Bielefeld.

Müller, H. M.
2003 Neurobiologische Grundlagen der Sprache. In *Psycholinguistik: Ein internationales Handbuch*, G. Rickheit, T. Herrmann, and W. Deutsch (eds.), 57–80. Berlin: de Gruyter.
2005 Speech Processing. In *Encyclopedia of Linguistics, Vol. 2*, P. Strazny, (ed.), 1023–1024. New York: Fitzroy Dearborn.

Müller, H. M., J. W. King, and M. Kutas
1997 Event related potentials elicited by spoken relative clauses. *Cognitive Brain Research* 5: 193–203.
1998 Elektrophysiologische Analyse der Verarbeitung natürlichsprachlicher Sätze mit unterschiedlicher Belastung des Arbeitsgedächtnisses. *Klinische Neurophysiologie* 29: 321–330.

Müller, H. M., and M. Kutas
1996 What's in a name? Electrophysiological differences between spoken nouns, proper names, and one's own name. *NeuroReport* 8: 221–225.

Müller, H. M., and S. Weiss
2000 Prototypen und Kategorisierung aus neurobiologischer Sicht. In *Prototypentheorie in der Linguistik: Anwendungsbeispiele, Methodenreflexion, Perspektiven*, M. Mangasser-Wahl (ed.), 55–71. Tübingen: Stauffenburg.

Müller, H. M., S. Weiss, and P. Rappelsberger
1999 Differences in neuronal synchronization during spoken word processing. In *From Molecular Neurobiology to Clinical Neuroscience*, N. Elsner, and U. Eysel (eds.), 107. Stuttgart: Thieme.

Neville, H., J. L. Nicol, A. Barss, K. I. Forster, and M. F. Garrett
1991 Syntactically based sentence processing classes: evidence from event-related brain potentials. *Journal of Cognitive Neuroscience* 3: 151–165.

Petersen, S. P., P. T. Fox, M. I. Posner, M. Mintun, and M. E. Raichle
1988 Positron emission tomographic studies of the cortical anatomy of single-word processing. *Nature* 331: 585–589.

Rickheit, G.
2001 Situierte Kommunikation. In *Spektren der Linguistik,* S. Anschütz, S. Kanngießer, and G. Rickheit (eds.), 95–118. Wiesbaden: Deutscher Universitäts-Verlag.

Riedl, R.
1980 *Biologie der Erkenntnis: Die stammesgeschichtlichen Grundlagen der Vernunft*, 2. Ed. Berlin: Parey.
1987 *Begriff und Welt: Biologische Grundlagen des Erkennens und Begreifens*. Berlin: Parey.

Schack, B., G. Grieszbach, M. Arnold, and J. Bolten
1995 Dynamic cross-spectral analysis of biological signals by means of bivariate ARMA processes with time-dependent coefficients. *Medical & Biological Engineering & Computing* 33: 605–610.

Schendan, H. E., G. Ganis, and M. Kutas
1998 Neurophysiological evidence for visual perceptual categorization of words and faces within 150 ms. *Psychophysiology* 35: 240–251.

Schriefers, H.
1999 Morphologie und Worterkennung. In *Sprachrezeption*, A. D. Friederici (ed.), 117–153. Göttingen: Hogrefe.

Schuth, A., R. Werner, and H. M. Müller
2001 Die Benennung von Personen und Objekten aus Sicht der Kognitiven Linguistik. *Abstracts der 1. Jahrestagung der Gesellschaft für Aphasiebehandlung*, 66.

Schwartz, J., and P. Tallal
1980 Rate of acoustic change may underlie hemispheric specialization for speech perception. *Science* 207: 1380–1381.

Seldon, H. L.
1985 The anatomy of speech perception: Human auditory cortex. In *Cerebral cortex. Vol. 4: Association and auditory cortices,* A. Peters & E. G. Jones (eds.), 273–327. New York: Plenum Press.

Skrandies, W.
2004 Die Bedeutung von Wörtern und elektrische Hirnaktivität des Menschen. In *Neurokognition der Sprache*, H. M. Müller, and G. Rickheit (eds.), 91–106. Tübingen: Stauffenburg.

Tempini, M. L. G., C. J. Price, O. Josephs, R. Vandenberghe, S. F. Cappa, N. Kapur, and R. S. J. Frackowiak
1998 The neural systems sustraining face and proper-name processing. *Brain* 121: 2103–2118.

Trepel, M.
1999 *Neuroanatomie: Struktur und Funktion.* 2. Ed. München: Urban & Fischer.

Trincker, D.
1974 *Taschenbuch der Physiologie, Bd. III/1: Animalische Physiologie III, Zentralnervensysteme I, Sensomotorik.* Stuttgart: Fischer.
1977 *Taschenbuch der Physiologie, Bd. III/2: Animalische Physiologie III, Zentralnervensysteme II und Sinnesorgane.* Stuttgart: Fischer.

Tulving, E., S. Kapur, F. I. Craik, M. Moscovitch, and S. Houle
1994 Hemispheric encoding/retrieval asymmetry in episodic memory: Positron emission tomography findings. *Proceedings of the National Academy of Sciences USA* 91: 2016–2020.

Van Lancker, D., and C. Ohnesorge
2002 Personally Familiar Proper Names Are Relatively Sucessfully Processed in the Human Right Hemisphere; or, the Missing Link. *Brain and Language* 80: 121–129.

Vollmer, G.
1987 *Evolutionäre Erkenntnistheorie: Angeborene Erkenntnisstrukturen im Kontext von Biologie, Psychologie, Linguistik, Philosophie und Wissenschaftstheorie*. 4. Ed. Stuttgart: Hirzel.

Weiss, S., and H. M. Müller
2003 The contribution of EEG coherence to the investigation of language. *Brain and Language* 85: 325–343.

Weiss, S., H. M. Müller, M. Mertens, and F. Wöhrmann
"Tooth and Truth": An fMRI study on the comprehension of concrete and abstract lexical items (submitted).

Weiss, S., H. M. Müller, and P. Rappelsberger
2000 Theta synchronization predicts efficient memory encoding of concrete and abstract nouns. *NeuroReport* 11: 2357–2361.

Weiss, S., and P. Rappelsberger
1996 EEG coherences within the 13-18 Hz band as correlates of a distinct lexical organization of concrete and abstract nouns in humans. *Neuroscience Letters* 209: 17–20.

Weiss, S., H. M. Müller, B. Schack, J. W. King, M. Kutas, and P. Rappelsberger
2005 Increased neuronal synchronization accompanying sentence comprehension. *International Journal of Psychophysiology* 57: 129-141.

Yen, H. L., H. L. Liu, C. Y. Lee, Y.-B. Ng, and H. M. Müller
2005 Are proper names really different from common nouns? A view of brain processing. *Proceedings of the 11th Annual Meeting of the Organization for of Human Brain Mapping*, #708, Toronto.

Yen, H. L., H. L. Liu, C. Y. Lee, Y.-B. Ng, and H. M. Müller
Functional anatomy of proper name processing in Mandarin Chinese: An fMRI study (submitted).

Zwitserlood, P.
1999 Gesprochene Wörter im Satzkontext. In *Sprachrezeption,* A. D. Friederici (ed.), 85–116. Göttingen: Hogrefe.

Neuroinformatic techniques in cognitive neuroscience of language

Matthias Kaper, Peter Meinicke, Horst M. Müller, Sabine Weiss, Holger Bekel, Thomas Hermann, Axel Saalbach, and Helge Ritter

Abstract. Processes of language comprehension can successfully be investigated by non-invasive electrophysiological techniques like electroencephalography (EEG). This article presents innovative applications of neuroinformatic techniques to EEG data analysis in the context of Cognitive Neuroscience of Language to gain deeper insights in the processes of the human brain. A variety of techniques ranging from principal component analysis (PCA), independent component analysis (ICA), coherence analysis, self-organizing maps (SOM), and sonification were employed to overcome the restrictions of traditional EEG data analysis, which only yield comparably rough ideas about brain processes. Our findings, for example, allow to provide insights in the variety within EEG data sets, perform single trial classification with high accuracy, and investigate communication processes between cell assemblies during language processing.

1. Motivation

In cognitive science non-invasive methods of analyzing language processes in a working brain allow for completely new insights about language functions. Results about functional neuroanatomy, the time course in milliseconds, and the separate observation of parallel language processes supply the empirical data which are necessary for building a well-founded linguistic theory. Some of these non-invasive methods in cognitive neuroscience have a long tradition (e.g. electroencephalography, EEG), others were developed more recently (e.g. near infrared spectroscopy, NIRS). These methods all have in common that their adequate use was made possible only by the great advances of computer assisted data processing in the area of cognitive neuroscience. Electroencephalography and functional magnetic resonance imaging (fMRI) produce data which became usable for the analysis of cognitive processes only through the rapid advances in the development of hardware and software during the last twenty years. The present success of these methods in the area of cognitive neuroscience needs a simplified handling of huge amounts of data (e.g. about 250 million number values pile up during an one-hour EEG experiment with 64 electrodes) and the development of new algorithms for analyses which allow a different non-linear access to the graphs measured. Therefore, it is apparent that the Fourier transforms or frequency band specific cross correlations necessary for coherence analyses (e.g. Weiss and Müller 2003) and applied to these numbers can only be conducted with high computing power. The EEG of patients examined in the 70ies was inspected visually by experienced neurologists in order to get a rough indication of brain areas which are disturbed. Today computer assisted methods of analysis are able to detect event related potentials (ERPs) with a magnitude of 1-2 μV in the noise of an EEG-signal the size of approximately 100 μV (ERP-analysis). Especially for cognitive processes very often not those ERP-components are important which are based on simultaneous activity of many thousand neurons in sum, but the transient processes of cell assemblies which take part at the same time and location. These processes can be captured using spectral analysis (e.g. coherence analysis). Above and beyond that, there are especially the non-linear methods of analysis which so far allow unusual insight into the functioning of the brain. The further development of analysis algorithms plays a decisive role after the signal recording hardware has been optimized technically and in respect to the apparatuses. The advances that are to be expected for the next decades will essentially be based on improved and newly developed methods of analysis. The present contribution will use electroencephalography as an example and explain several of these methods of analysis using data from experiments with language processing.

2. Analyzing electroencephalographic data

The most common analysis technique of the EEG is the analysis of the event-related potential (ERP), which relies on many repetitions of trials. The resulting wave form is a very general measure, since it averages out any individual details and retains only the average information among up to several hundred trials. Furthermore, only processes in the brain which occur at a fixed time after an event, in other words which expose a constant latency, are visible in the ERP.

In recent years, several efforts have been started to develop more subtle methods which allow for a differentiated analysis and therefore a deeper understanding of the underlying cognitive processes. The rapid development of new computation methods together with more powerful hardware, made it possible to analyze these huge databases with new, sophisticated methods from neuroinformatics, for example.

Furthermore, it became possible to base analyses on only very few trials, which enabled researchers to perform on-line analyses of brain signals, opening up exciting new possibilities for Brain-Computer Interfaces (BCI) in order to control technical devices by brain signals. While intracortical electrodes were successfully employed to control e.g. robotic arms in animal studies (Chapin 1999; Nicolelis 2001), it is desirable to apply non-invasive techniques like EEG for human Brain-Computer Interfaces (Wolpaw et al., 2002; Birbaumer et al. 1999). Neuroinformatic techniques are capable of increasing the speed and accuracy of such devices: For instance, we have developed a BCI for communicating letter sequences that improves upon reported communication bandwidths by employing recent machine learning techniques in conjunction with a P300-ERP based classification scheme (Kaper et al. 2004; Meinicke et al. 2003a). In this article we will describe how very similar methods can be employed to analyze brain activity with regard to neurolinguistic questions.

In the following, we present several techniques, which we applied to EEG data in order to gain deeper insight into processing. Each method is briefly introduced before our results on EEG data, recorded in two experiments, are presented.

As a first (rather 'classic') method, we briefly will describe principal component analysis (PCA) and demonstrate its use for the visualization of activity relationships between different scalp sites as a function of task conditions. Next, we will discuss the related technique of independent component analysis (ICA), reporting results from a study in which we applied a variant of ICA to identify EEG features that allow to discriminate different task contexts during a listening task. We will then describe the important technique of coherence analysis, which has become increasingly popular during the last decade for identifying functional interactions between well-reported brain locations. We will argue that the combination of coherence analysis with self-organizing maps can lead to a very powerful visualization technique for the rapid 'browsing' of transient coherence patterns, which can be analyzed in both the spatial and the frequency domain.

While the combination of coherence analysis and self-organizing maps offers a likely and promising approach for large scale exploratory data analysis on EEG signals, a complementary method is to employ machine learning techniques in order to construct 'black-box'-classifiers from training data that can identify different task contexts from raw EEG signals. As a major example of this approach – which in spirit comes closest to the BCI work stated earlier – we will report on results achieved with a support vector machine (SVM) and the lately developed maximum contrast classifiers (MCC) operating on the data that were also used in the previous experiments.

Finally, we will argue that the technique of sonification, i.e. the use of sound to render data structure, offers a very promising alternative method that can complement vision-oriented approaches in interesting ways.

2. Principal component analysis

2.1. Algorithm

Principal component analysis (PCA) finds a data representation by projecting the signal along principal directions constructed in such a way that they capture most of the data variance. From a given data set, PCA computes a linear transformation **W** in order to find its representation for each single data vector **x**

$$s = \mathbf{W}x$$

in the space spanned by the principal axes of variances (or 'components'). The direction $\mathbf{w}_1$ of the first principal component explains most of the variance. It obeys

$$\mathbf{w}_1 = \arg\max_{\|\mathbf{w}\|=1} E\{(\mathbf{w}^T\mathbf{x})^2\}$$

with E{ } denoting the expectation value of its argument. A convenient way to calculate w is to use the covariance matrix $E\{\mathrm{xx}^T\} = C$. Sorting the eigenvectors of C according to their eigenvalues yields the PCA directions $\mathbf{w}_i$. Any subsequent direction $\mathbf{w}_k$ *(k>1)* can recursively be defined by

$$\mathbf{w}_k = \arg\max_{\|\mathbf{w}\|=1} E\{[\mathbf{w}^T(\mathbf{x} - \sum_{i=1}^{k-1} \mathbf{w}_i \mathbf{w}_i^T \mathbf{x})]^2\}$$

All resulting components are mutually uncorrelated and offer a new basis for representing the data. A common way to represent a large number of high dimensional data vectors is to plot them as data points in a 2-dimensional scatter plot in which the axes are chosen along the first two principal directions $\mathbf{w}_1$ and $\mathbf{w}_2$.

By retaining only a subset of PCA components that constitute the directions of largest variance, the original data can be approximated by lower-dimensional vectors (dimensionality reduction by Karhunen-Loeve-expansion (Karhunen 1947)). PCA has been widely used, for example, to obtain prototypes of spatial activation patterns or components for representing the variance of a dataset (Coles et al. 1986). Here, by using PCA, we wish to visualize the proximity of scalp sites in terms of EEG activation pattern belonging to specific task conditions.

2.2. Application

Within a neurolinguistic experiment we applied PCA in order to visualize similarities of EEG patterns at different scalp sites on a 2-dimensional plane. Participants were listening to either naturally spoken sentences, pseudo-speech signals, or silence. EEG was recorded from 19 channels according to the international 10-20-system. Data were band pass filtered (0.5-35 Hz) and artifacts were eliminated using a median-based artifact elimination technique.

The resulting feature vectors were projected onto the first two PCA components. The proximities of the different scalp sites in this map can then indicate similarities between the associated EEG signals. Figure 1 depicts three such maps, each of them pertaining to a different experimental condition (silence vs. pseudo-speech vs. normal speech).

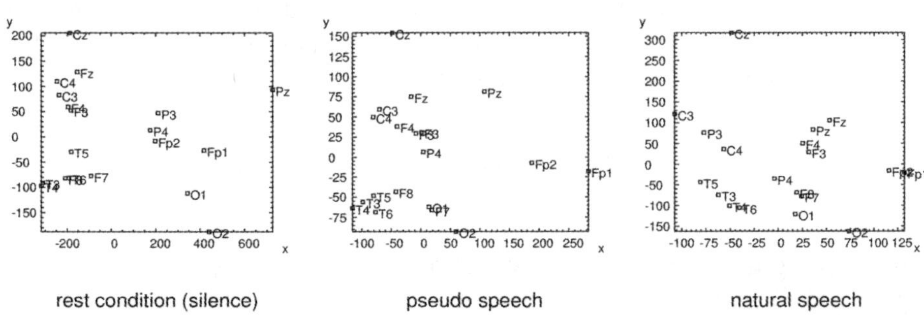

Figure 1. Projections of scalp site EEG time series onto the first two PCA components for silence, pseudo-speech, and natural speech stimuli. Similarities in activity at different electrode positions are reflected by the proximities of the depicted electrode sites. While frontal sites are widely scattered in the first condition, they become more densely clustered (i.e. similar) for the latter two conditions (Bekel 2002).

As can be observed in Figure 1, frontal sites become more similar from the 'silence' to the 'pseudo' to the 'speech condition'. Furthermore, their distance to the other scalp sites increases, which could be a hint at an increase in memory demands (Bekel 2002).

3. Independent component analysis

3.1. Algorithm

While PCA always finds orthogonal principal directions, independent component analysis (ICA) is not restricted to this constraint. Unlike PCA, it does not try to find directions of maximal variance, but instead tries to find axes of maximal statistical independence (Hyvärinen, 1999). This can be formulated as

$$E\{g_1(x_i)g_2(x_j)\} - E\{g_1(x_i)\}E\{g_2(x_j)\} = 0, \text{ for } i \neq j$$

Since this equation is required for any functions g_1 and g_2, ICA goes beyond a search for mere uncorrelatedness. However, uncorrelatedness is equivalent to statistical independence whenever $x_1 \ldots x_m$ follow a joint Gaussian distribution. Thus, ICA becomes equivalent to PCA in this case and, therefore, is not interesting in the case of Gaussian variables (Hyvärinen 1999).

Similar to PCA, ICA can be regarded as finding a linear transform $\mathbf{s} = \mathbf{Wx}$ in such a way that the variables s_i are statistically as independent as possible. Minimizing the loss function

$$L = -n \log |\det \mathbf{W}| - \sum_{i=1}^{N} \sum_{j=1}^{d} \log f_j(s_{ij})$$

with N being the number of samples and d being the dimensionality of $\mathbf{s}$, is equivalent to maximizing independence. Previous work employed ICA for example for artifact elimination and separation of independent processes (Jung et al. 2000; Makeig et al. 2004), using methods that implicitly assume an unimodal signal distribution. Introducing the concept of quantizing density estimation (QDE) with f being a density estimator (Meinicke and Ritter 2002), we were able to perform ICA with the advantageous property of being flexible in adapting to multimodal signal distributions.

3.2. Application

Using the same data as in the previous section, we applied ICA in order to find discriminative features in the EEG data, providing a measure for the degree of how specific features contribute to a differentiation between the conditions (Kwak, Choi, and Choi 2001). We augmented the data by one channel containing the binary class information of the data. ICA calculates a demixing matrix, showing how the remaining channels contribute to the binary channel. Hence, this way we can investigate which scalp sites contribute to the differentiation between conditions. This procedure was performed for the six frequency bands delta (0.5-4 Hz), theta (4-8 Hz), alpha-1 (8-10 Hz), alpha-2 (10-12 Hz), beta-1 (12-18 Hz), and beta-2 (18-30 Hz), respectively. For the twenty ICA directions with the highest discriminative power, Figure 2 depicts the features with the highest contributions to a direction within a specific frequency band and scalp site. While most of the information responsible for the distinction between 'speech' and 'silence' stems from frontal and central sites, mainly in the alpha-1 band, 'pseudo' and 'silence' discrimination emphasizes the influence from parietal sites, which also seem to be the most responsible sites for 'speech vs. pseudo'. Note that apparently only little frontal information is employed for the differentiation between the two latter conditions. These results are congruent with previous coherence-based findings (Weiss and Rappelsberger 1996; Müller and Weiss 2002). However, the present ICA-based maps allow some additional clues, for instance, Figure 2 indicates that the delta band plays an important role in discriminating between the experimental conditions. This is in good agreement with findings which suggest that the delta band plays an important role in decision making and in attentional processes (Harmony 1999).

4. EEG coherence

Electroencephalographic (EEG) data is highly polluted by noise and artifacts such as influences from muscle activity and electromagnetic radiation. A common way to enhance the low signal-to-noise ratio is to build so-called Event-Related Potentials (ERP) by averaging a large number of trials belonging to a condition. Thus, only pattern in the EEG which are systematically related to this event remain in the ERP. This kind of analysis shows the sum of all synchronously active neurons within a few cm^2 and relies on many repetitions of trials. During ERP analysis the resulting curve is a very rough measure, since it only represents the average information up to several hundred trials. Furthermore, only those processes in the brain which occur at a fixed time after an event – in other words, which expose a constant latency – are visible in the ERP.

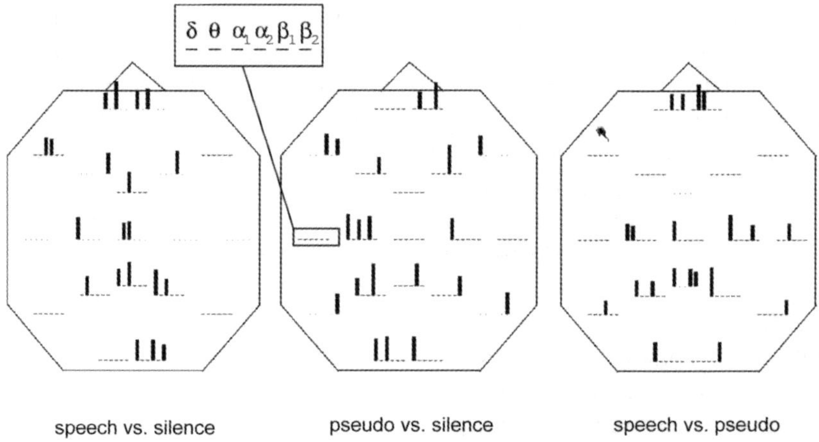

Figure 2. ICA-based discriminative features for the frequency bands delta, theta, alpha-1, alpha-2, beta-1, and beta-2 differentiating between the conditions speech, silence, and pseudo. While the distinction between 'speech vs. pseudo' mainly relies on information from posterior sites, 'pseudo vs. silence' exposes widely distributed patterns from both hemispheres. The 'speech vs. silence' distinction is based on more central processes. A psychophysiological explanation for the 'speech vs. pseudo' finding could be that one of the major differences between these conditions are processes relying on e.g. the imagination of the meaning of the stimuli in the speech condition resulting in more occipital activation (Meinicke et al. 2004).

A completely different method for EEG analysis, which quantitatively measures the linear dependency between two distant brain regions as expressed by their EEG activity, is the calculation of the signal coherence between electrodes. Scalp recorded EEG coherence is a large-scale measure, which depicts dynamic functional interactions between electrode signals separated by longer distances. High coherence between EEG signals recorded at different sites of the scalp hint at an increased functional interplay between the neuronal networks underlying the generation of these signals within a certain frequency band. Coherence values lie within a range of 0 to 1, whereby 0 means that corresponding frequency components of both signals are not correlated; 1 means that frequency components of the signals are fully correlated with constant phase shifts, but may show differences in amplitude. Therefore, coherence may also be interpreted as a measure for stability of phase between the same frequency components of two simultaneously recorded EEG signals.

4.1. Algorithms

There are several methods of investigating coherence, among which there are adaptive autoregressive moving average (ARMA) models (Schack et al. 1995) and power spectra correlations employing either Fourier transform (Rappelsberger 1998; Rappelsberger and Petsche 1988) or wavelet analysis (e.g. Varela et al., 2001).

ARMA models try to predict a data point x_n of a channel **x** by a linear combination using the autocorrelation coefficients a_i of a certain number of p predecessors:

$$\mathbf{x}_n = a_1\mathbf{x}_{n-1} + a_2\mathbf{x}_{n-2} + \ldots + a_p\mathbf{x}_{n-p}$$

If we introduce another channel **y**, we can predict the data point x_n by previous data from the same channel (autocorrelation), but on the other hand, we could also try to employ data from channel **y** for this purpose, and vice versa (cross-correlation). The cross-correlation indicates to which degree both channels are statistically dependent within a specific time span. Thus, we obtain a possibility of also extracting frequency information. By augmenting the previous equation to multidimensional channels and autocorrelation matrices ***X*** and ***A*** and further considering the noise ***Z***, we obtain

$$\mathbf{x}_n - \sum_{k=1}^{p} \mathbf{A}_k \mathbf{X}_{n-k} = \mathbf{Z}_n - \sum_{j=1}^{q} \mathbf{B}_j \mathbf{Z}_{n-j}$$

Here, the parameters ***A*** and ***B*** are fitted in such a way that the residual noise is minimized to the EEG data. The resulting values can provide information about coherence by, for example, calculating the normalized degree of dependence

$$D(n) = \frac{\sum_{k=1}^{p}[(a_{12}^{k})^2(a_{21}^{k})^2] + \sum_{j=1}^{q}[(b_{12}^{k})^2(b_{21}^{k})^2]}{\sum_{k=1}^{p}\sum_{j=1}^{q}\sum_{l,m=1}^{2}[(a_{lm}^{k})^2(b_{lm}^{j})^2]}$$

The alternative approach of *power spectra correlations* relies on calculating the normalized cross-power spectra $Wco(t,f)$ for a time window centered at time t and a frequency f:

$$WCo(t,f) = \frac{|SW_{xy}(t,f)|}{\sqrt{|SW_{xx}(t,f) \cdot SW_{yy}(t,f)|}}$$

While $SW_{xx}(t,f)$ and $SW_{yy}(t,f)$ denote the auto-spectra of the two EEG channels **x** and **y**, $SW_{xy}(t,f)$ is the cross-spectrum of these channels. When employing wavelets for power spectra calculation, they can be determined by

$$SW_{xy}(t,f) = \int_{\delta/2}^{t+\delta/2} W_x(\tau,f) \cdot W_y^*(\tau,f) d\tau$$

Since the Fourier transform is not very well-suited for non-stationary signals like EEG data, we prefer to employ wavelets for the calculation of the power spectra. Furthermore, continuous wavelet analysis provides an adjustable frequency resolution. $\boldsymbol{W_x}$ describes the convolution between the signal and the scaled and translated wavelet Ψ (e.g. the standard Morlet-wavelet):

$$W_x(\tau,f) = \int_{-\infty}^{-\infty} x(t) \cdot \Psi_{\tau,f}^*(t) dt$$

4.2. Application

Studies on coherence range from intracortical recordings in animals via subdural, subcortical, and scalp EEG/MEG to recordings in humans under normal and pathological conditions. Most of the studies were performed with patients (mainly psychiatric populations) and only a few dealt with the relation between coherence and cognitive information processing in healthy human adults. A general acceptance and increasing interest in EEG coherence analysis as a method of monitoring frequency dependent large-scale synchronization during intact and disturbed human information processing was not established before the 1990s. Since then, however, the number of studies linking EEG coherence to cognitive information processing in healthy humans has been increasing steadily and strongly. In general, brain regions activated by cognitive operations show increased coherence (= neuronal cooperation or synchronization) within certain frequency bands, depending on the nature and difficulty of the task. Each task seems to reflect characteristic patterns of coherence changes. In particular, the application of coherence analysis to EEG data during language processing and language related tasks (see Figure 3) proved as a promising tool in order to investigate rhythmic, large-scale properties of EEG signals accompanying linguistic function (Haarmann et al. 2002; Petsche, Etlinger, and Filz 1993; Schack et al. 2003; Stein et al. 1999; Volf and Razumnikova 1999; Weiss et al. 2005; Weiss and Müller 2003).

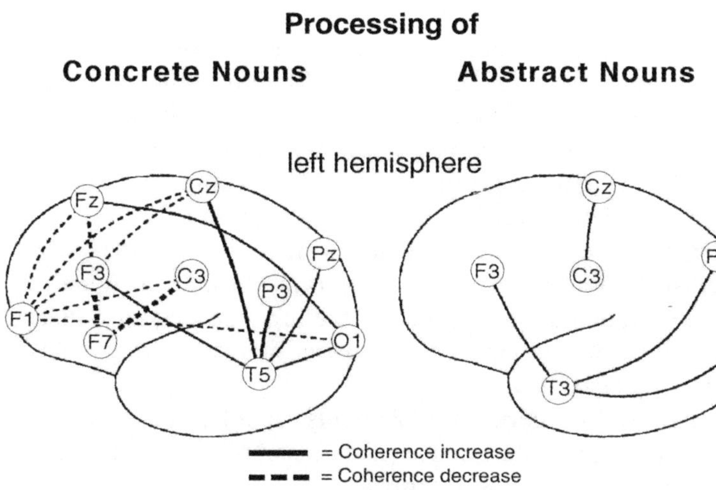

Figure 3. Coherence differences between processing of concrete and abstract nouns compared to a resting condition. For the evaluation of significant increases or decreases of coherence, Wilcoxon matched-pairs tests were applied. The rank sums obtained were converted to error probabilities and presented topographically in schematic models of the brain's hemispheres. Significant intrahemispheric coherence decreases and increases were presented in a side view of the brain's left hemisphere and are symbolized by broken and full lines, respectively ($p \leq 0.05$). More brain regions act synchronously during the processing of concrete nouns than during the processing of abstract nouns from (Weiss and Rappelsberger 1996, modified).

5. Self-organizing maps

5.1. Algorithm

The self-organizing map (SOM) is a non-linear method of creating low-dimensional 'maps' from high-dimensional data in such a way that (metric) similarity among data items in the original, high-dimensional input space becomes translated into spatial proximity in the resulting map (Kohonen, Schroeder, and Huang 2001; Ritter 1995). From the viewpoint of data analysis, the SOM provides a non-linear generalization of PCA, allowing to capture more variance in a two-dimensional map than PCA as a linear method would.

SOMs can be constructed from a data set either by a batch algorithm or in an iterative fashion. In both cases the map is created on a lattice of nodes identified by their discrete lattice positions *r*. Each node *r* carries a feature vector $\mathbf{w}_r$ from the input data space. The SOM algorithm implements a data-driven, competitive learning scheme among these prototypes in such a way that the whole set of prototype vectors develops into a discrete approximation of the input data distribution with the additional constraint that neighboring nodes carry (metrically) similar prototypes.

This way, the discrete lattice of nodes maps the original, high-dimensional data distribution in a topology-preserving fashion: neighboring nodes get identified with neighbor locations in the input space (for a discussion of topological defects in the case of dimension mismatches, cf. Bauer, Herrmann, and Villmann 1999).

The iterative SOM algorithm implements the adaptive competition process by selecting a random sequence of data samples *x*, performing the following two steps for each chosen sample:

(1) Determination of 'best-match' node *s* by

$$s = \arg\min_r \| x - w_r \|$$

(2) Adaptation step

$$w_r(t+1) = w_r(t) + \alpha h_{rs}(t)(x - w_r(t))$$

where h_{rs} ensures that the adaptation step is confined to a local neighborhood of the best-matching unit *s*. To this end, h_{rs} is usually chosen as

$$h_{bi} = \exp -\left(\frac{\|\mathbf{r}_b - \mathbf{r}_i\|^2}{2\sigma^2(t)} \right)$$

This procedure will either be repeated as long as the adjustment to the weight vectors $\mathbf{w}_i$ are above a specific threshold or for a predefined number of iterations.

5.2. Application

We ran a neurolinguistic experiment in which the participants had to listen to auditorily presented word lists of either abstract or concrete nouns that were to be memorized. For each single trial we calculated wavelet coherence for 39 different time steps in the frequency bands theta and beta-1. Pairwise coherences between the 19 electrodes yield a 171-dimensional vector of wavelet coherences. Feature vectors were the differences *WCo(t,f)-WCo(t',f)* representing the change of coherence between the time *t* and *t'* for a specific frequency *f*. Thus, decrease and increase of coherence within trials were calculated. The SOM was visualized in a browseable three-dimensional map providing user interactions like rotation, zoom and translation. Distances between neighboring prototypes were visualized as the height of the blocks.

As is illustrated by Figure 4, the SOM conveniently allows to 'browse' the extremely high-dimensional space of coherence patterns, offering a rapid overview of the data collected in the experiment. Beside two large groups of patterns of enhanced and depressed coherence involving many sites (opposite map corners), the more central map areas show patterns in which coherences of electrode subsets are sparser. Neighboring prototypes tend to represent similar coherence patterns. Thus, left and right hemispheric interactions are located in different regions of the map.

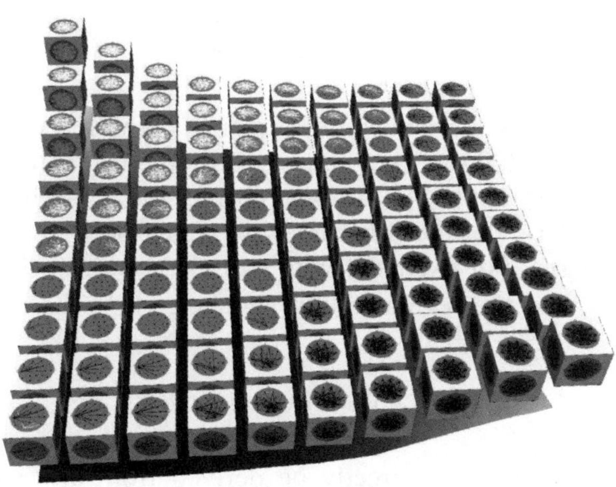

Figure 4. A 10x10 grid of EEG coherence prototypes as calculated by the SOM algorithm. Here, the distribution of the coherence patterns changes within the beta-1 band are depicted. White connections represent decrease and black connections increase in coherence (Kaper et al. 2005).

6. Machine-learning classification

6.1. Algorithms

In machine-learning classification, a classifier learns from a dataset to separate different classes of this set in order to generalize to new, unseen data. A classical example for this approach is the recognition of handwritten digits: A classifier is trained on a set of handwritten digits and should afterwards be able to correctly assign (new) handwritten digits to a specific class., e.g. '8' (Liu, Sako, and Fujisawa 2002).

In recent years, support vector machines (SVM) became a very popular method for classification tasks since they exhibit good classification and generalization abilities (Vapnik 1995). The general geometrically inspired idea behind SVMs is that they try to find a separating hyperplane in the data space with as much distance as possible ('large margin') to the data of the different classes. Usually, it can not be avoided that a small number of data points always lies on the 'wrong' side of the hyperplane as described by the normal vector **w**, giving rise to 'penalties' ξ which have to be minimized. Omitting mathematical detail which can be gleaned from e.g. Schölkopf and Smola (2004), the demands can be integrated in a target function, which has to be minimized. This function can be described by

$$\frac{\|\mathbf{w}\|^2}{2} + C\sum \xi$$

An alternative approach are maximum contrast classifiers (MCC), developed in (Meinicke et al. 2003c). They are based on the estimation of discriminative densities according to the different classes and try to maximize a measure of 'contrast' C, i.e. the differences of class-specific densities between any pair of classes. For example, with two classes c_1, c_2, the discriminative densities $\hat{p}(\cdot)$, and the regularization parameter γ_{max}, the contrast is calculated as

$$C_{c_1}(\mathbf{x}, c_2) = \min\{\hat{p}(\mathbf{x} \mid c_2) - \hat{p}(\mathbf{x} \mid c_1), \gamma_{max}\}$$

Unlike SVMs, MCCs can directly be derived from any valid probability density function for the data at hand. Furthermore, MCCs are defined within a general multiclass setup and therefore directly are able to differentiate between more than two classes.

6.2. Application

We also applied MCC and SVM on a dataset of the neurolinguistic EEG data previously described in the PCA section. Data were transformed into the frequency domain using short time Fourier transformation (STFT). Afterwards, for each frequency band, a median-based artifact elimination was applied. After some outlier elimination we took about 1000 spectral vectors (1 s windows) from each condition for classifier training.

Both classifiers were quite successful in classifying the test data. As can be seen in Table 1, MCC reached almost the same classification rates as the SVM (Meinicke et al. 2003b). Note that the classifiers employ *single* trials in order to learn and perform the classification task. Thus, no aggregated information in terms of e.g. ERPs is employed. Thus, using such a classifier, it is possible to assign EEG data to a certain class from just one single trial. It is harder to differentiate between 'speech' and 'pseudo' than between 'pseudo' and 'silence,' showing that on the single trial basis more similar processes are at work within the latter two conditions. For theoretical reasons (Müller, Weiss, and Rappelsberger 1997), 'speech' and 'pseudo' should be hardest, and 'speech' vs. 'silence' easiest to discriminate. Our results are in agreement with the first hypothesis, while they contradict the latter one.

Table 1. Classification accuracy in separating two classes, based on single trials. Support vector machines (SVM) and maximum contrast classifiers (MCC) expose similar classification accuracies. Classification of single trials can be performed with an accuracy of 68.5% up to 78.7%, depending on the condition and classifier.

Method	Speech vs. Silence	Pseudo vs. Silence	Speech vs. Pseudo
SVM	74.2%	78.7%	68.5%
MCC	72.8%	78.3%	69%

7. Sonification

Human listening skills have so far only rarely been exploited for the analysis of high-dimensional data or multi-channel time series like EEG. *Sonification* transforms the data under analysis into data-driven sound in order to enable the listener to increase understanding, to get 'insight', or to detect previously unknown structures in the data. EEG is a particularly attractive data domain, since here the data possess structure in the temporal, the spectral, and the spatial dimension, and auditory analysis is the technique of choice to discover changes in rhythmical and spectral structuring. The simplest sonification technique is audification, where the data series are more or less directly scaled, time-stretched, and used as a sound signal. Audifications allow us to gain a qualitative overview of long-term measurements. However, temporal and spectral properties are highly coupled in audification. We developed different techniques for the exploratory analysis of EEG data, among them spectral mapping sonification, which allows control over compression and spectrum of the acoustic representation, distance matrix sonification (explained below), and differential sonification, which allows the quick comparison of two datasets (e.g. one participant exposed to different experimental conditions) according to their spatial and spectral differences (Hermann et al. 2002).

7.1. Algorithm

Distance Matrix Sonification (DMS) focuses on the synchronization of different brain areas as a function of time. For analysis the time-dependent distance matrix

$$D_{ij}[m] = \| \mathbf{s}_i[m] - \hat{\mathbf{s}}_j[m] \|$$

containing the Euclidian distance between the normalized spectral vectors $\hat{\mathbf{s}}$ of channels *(i, j)* in the *m*-th window which begins at sample $C \cdot m$, with C being the offset between successive windows, is used. Figure 5 depicts some distance matrices for successive time frames.

Small entries (dark) in the distance matrix indicate similar spectral activation in the corresponding channels. High similarity is certainly expected for nearby electrodes on the scalp, for example for matrix elements close to the diagonal. Interesting events are long-range couplings, corresponding to small matrix elements while the topological distance of the channels is high. DMS implements a transformation to sound which lets such events stand out in the display: The sonification is rendered by superimposing short pitched sound grains whose amplitude is scaled with the similarity $exp(-D_{ij}(m))$ while their pitch increases with spatial distance. Thus, loud and high-pitched sound contributions indicate interesting couplings. Furthermore, the sound grains are localized in a stereo auditory display, which means that couplings within the left/right hemisphere are audible on the left/right audio channel. By the mapping used, interesting events are automatically more salient. In addition, the listener's skills in recognizing rhythms is addressed since the sonification maintains the temporal structure of the EEG data.

Figure 5. 19x19-distance matrix for spectral vectors for three succeeding frames. The channels are ordered as depicted from left to right. Small values are represented by dark colors and indicate similar activity between respective channels.

7.2. Application

Since sonification is a qualitative information display, aiming to support the detection of new features, it is difficult to assess its value numerically. However, we provide some sonification examples for data from the first psycholinguistic experiments of this article as described in the PCA section in order to illustrate the method. The sound examples are sequences of data for two different conditions (pseudo speech/speech), separated by a noise burst. Qualitative properties like the overall coupling and lateralization may be inferred. So far we have not yet detected interesting rhythmical structure differences, although it might be promising to continue research in this direction.

8. General discussion

Advances in computational methods in the area of neuroinformatics, statistical data analysis, and machine learning have opened up new avenues for analyzing brain signals and to correlate them with cognitive processes. This has created new 'windows' to the brain. Classical methods, such as ERP-analysis, can now be complemented by approaches that permit the extraction of significant patterns and correlations of brain activity from rather short data segments, bringing real-time (or close-to-real-time) signal analysis and applications, such as Brain-Computer Interfaces, within reach.

Focusing on experimental settings from the domain of neurolinguistics, we have illustrated some of these approaches from research carried out in the context of the Collaborative Research Center 360, addressing the issue of situated communication.

One major tier of our research has been along the direction of novel visualization techniques in order to support interactive, exploratory data analysis of brain signals. We have shown how classical techniques, such as PCA and coherence analysis, in particular when combined with powerful non-linear postprocessing techniques, such as self-organizing maps, can lead to novel visualizations of brain activity patterns that facilitate the 'browsing' of huge amounts of EEG data for significant, task-related correlations in brain activity. We are of the opinion that extending this 'data mining approach' can significantly contribute to finding increasingly better ways to 'translate' low-level brain activity into representations reflecting the underlying information processing operations so that we can better 'watch' some of the cognitive processes in the brain.

This work has been complemented by a second major research line aiming at a data-driven identification of significant features for distinguishing between task settings, and for constructing classifiers that can perform such discrimination in an automated 'black-box' fashion even on short data segments. Here, we have developed special variants of ICA which are particularly flexible with regard to the underlying statistical data distribution, and we have developed the technique of *maximum contrast classifiers* (MCC) in order to enable a multi-class discrimination of EEG signals with high generalization. We have shown that this technique is very competitive with support vector machines, but with the benefit of a clear statistical interpretation together with a straightforward and natural extension to multi-class problems.

Thirdly, we have presented some results from sonification, suggesting a novel direction to build 'perceptual interfaces' to brain activity that augment visualization with special techniques for rendering EEG data as sound in order to tap our highly developed auditory capabilities for detecting significant activity patterns. We have shown how this novel approach can be combined with preprocessing techniques borrowed from data mining in order to selectively enhance potentially interesting events and to facilitate the comparison of different data sets.

While the results achieved so far already may appear very encouraging, we think that by far the greater part of the potential of these novel techniques has not been realized yet. Extrapolating progress over the last decade, we are of the opinion that the development of intelligent data processing algorithms combining methods from neuroinformatics, statistics and machine learning has a bright future and can be a major contributor to our quest to translate brain activity into representations from which we can discern (some of) the cognitive processes that happen in our brains.

References

Bauer, H. U., M. Herrmann, and T. Villmann
1999 Neural maps and topographic vector quantization. *Neural Networks* 12: 659–676.

Bekel, H.
2002 *Datamining auf EEG-Signalen zur Untersuchung kognitiver Sprachverarbeitung*. Diploma thesis, Faculty.of Technology. Bielefeld: University of Bielefeld.

Birbaumer, N., N. Ghanayim, T. Hinterberger, I. Iversen, B. Kotchoubey, A. Kübler, J. Perelmouter, E. Taub, and H. Flor
1999 A spelling device for the paralysed. *Nature* 398: 297–298.

Chapin, J. K., R. A. Markowitz, K. A. Moxon, and M. A. L.Nicolelis
1999 Direct real time control of a robot arm using signals derived from neuronal population recordings in motor cortex. *Nature Neuroscience* 2: 664–670.

Coles, M. G. H., G. Gratton, A. F. Kramer, and G. A. Miller
1986 Principles of signal acquisition and analysis. In *Psychophysiology – Systems, Processes, and Applications*, M. G. H. Coles, E. Donchin, and S. W. Porges (eds.), 183–221. New York: Guilford Press.

Haarmann, H.J., K. A. Cameron, D. S. Ruchkin
2002 Neural synchronization mediates on-line sentence processing: EEG coherence evidence from filler-gap constructions. *Psychophysiology*, 39, 820–825.

Harmony, T.
1999 Do specific EEG frequencies indicate different processes during mental calculation? *Neuroscience Letters* 266: 25–28.

Hermann, T., P. Meinicke, H. Bekel, H. Ritter, H. M. Müller, and S. Weiss
2002 Sonifications for EEG data analysis. *Proceedings of the International Conference on Auditory Display*, www.icad.org, 37–41.

Hyvärinen, A.
1999 Survey on Independent Component Analysis. *Neural Computing Surveys* 2: 94–128.

Jung T.-P., S. Makeig, W. Westerfield, J. Townsend, E. Courchesne, and T. J. Sejnowski
2000 Removal of eye activity artifacts from visual event-related potentials in normal and clinical subjects. *Clinical Neurophysiology* 111: 1745–1758.

Kaper, M., P. Meinicke, U. Grossekathoefer, T. Lingner, and H. Ritter
2004 BCI competition 2003, dataset IIb: Support vector machines for the P300 speller paradigm. *IEEE Transaction on Biomedical Engineering*: 1073–1076.

Kaper, M., A. Saalbach, A. Finke, H. M. Müller, S. Weiss, and H. Ritter
2005 Exploratory data analysis of EEG coherence using Self-Organizing Maps. *Proceedings of the International Conference on Neural Information Processing, ICONIP* (accepted).

Karhunen, K.
1947 Über Lineare Methoden in der Wahrscheinlichkeitsrechnung. *Annales Academiae Scientiarum Fennicae, Series A1: Mathematica-Physica* 37: 3–79.

Kohonen, T. and M. R. Schroeder, and T. S. Huang
2001 *Self-Organizing Maps*. New York: Springer.

Kwak, N., C.-H. Choi, and J. Y. Choi
2001 Feature extraction using ICA. In *Proceedings of ICANN 2001,* LNCS 2130, 568–573. Berlin: Springer.

Liu, C.-L., H. Sako, and H. Fujisawa
2002 Performance evaluation of pattern classifiers for handwritten character recognition. *International Journal on Document Analysis and Recognition* 4: 191–204.

Makeig, S., A. Delorme, M. Westerfield, J. Townsend, E. Courchesne, and T. J. Sejnowski
2004 Electroencephalographic brain dynamics following visual targets requiring manual responses. *Public Library of Science – Biology* 2: 747–762.

Meinicke, P., T. Hermann, H. Bekel, H. M. Müller, S. Weiss, and H. Ritter
2004 Identification of discriminative features in EEG. *Journal for Intelligent Data Analysis* 8: 97–107.

Meinicke, P., M. Kaper, F. Hoppe, M. Heumann, and H. Ritter
2003a Improving transfer rates in brain computer interfacing: A case study. In *Advances in Neural Information Processing Systems 15,* S. Becker, S. Thrun, and K. Obermayer (eds.), 1131–1138. Cambridge, MA: MIT Press.
Meinicke, P., M. Kaper, S. Weiss, H. M. Müller, and H. Ritter
2003b Using maximum contrast classifiers for EEG data analysis. In *Proceedings of the European Cognitive Science Conference 2003,* F. Schmalhofer, R.M. Young, and G. Katz (eds.), 417. Mahwah: Erlbaum.
Meinicke, P., and H. Ritter
2002 Independent Component Analysis with quantizing density estimators. In *Proceedings of the Third International Conference on Independent Component Analysis and Signal Separation,* T.-W. Lee, T.-P. Young, S. Makeig, T. J. Sejnowski (eds.), 224–229. San Diego: Academic Press.
Meinicke, P., T. Twellmann, and H. Ritter
2003c Discriminative densities from maximum contrast estimation. In *Advances in Neural Information Processing Systems 15*, S. Becker, S. Thrun, and K. Obermayer (eds.), 1009–1016. Cambridge, MA: MIT Press.
Müller, H. M., and S. Weiss
2002 Neurobiologie der Sprache: Experimentelle Neurolinguistik. In *Arbeitsbuch Linguistik,* H. M. Müller (ed.), 406–422. Paderborn: Schöningh.
Müller, H. M., S. Weiss, and P. Rappelsberger
1997 EEG coherence analysis of auditory sentence preocessing. In *Quantitative and Topological EEG and MEG Analysis,* H. Witte, and U. Zwiender (eds.), 429–431. Jena: Universitätsverlag.
Nicolelis, M. A. L.
2001 Actions from thoughts. *Nature* 409: 403–406.
Petsche, H., S. C. Etlinger, and O. Filz
1993 Brain electrical mechanisms of bilingual speech management: An initial investigation. *Electroencephalography and Clinical Neurophysiology* 86: 385–394.
Rappelsberger, P.
1998 Probability mapping of amplitude and coherence: Technical aspects. In *EEG and thinking*, H. Petsche, and S. Etlinger (eds.), 63–78. Wien: Österreichische Akademie der Wissenschaften.
Rappelsberger, P., and H. Petsche
1988 Probability Mapping: Power and Coherence Analysis of Cognitive Processes. *Brain Topography* 1: 46-54.

Ritter, H.
1995 Self-organizing feature maps: Kohonen maps. In *The Handbook of Brain Theory and Neural Networks*, M. A. Arbib (ed.), 846–851. Cambridge, MA: MIT Press.

Schack, B., G. Grieszbach, M. Arnold, and J. Bolten
1995 Dynamic cross-spectral analysis of biological signals by means of bivariate ARMA processes with time-dependent coefficients. M*edical & Biological Engineering & Computing* 33: 605–610.

Schack, B., S. Weiss, and P. Rappelsberger
2003 Cerebral information transfer during word processing: Where and when does it occur and how fast is it? *Human Brain Mapping* 19: 18–36.

Schölkopf, B., and A. J. Smola
2002 *Learning with Kernels*. Cambridge, MA: MIT Press.

Stein, A.v., P. Rappelsberger, J. Sarnthein, and H. Petsche
1999 Synchronization between temporal and parietal cortex during multimodal object processing in man. *Cerebral Cortex* 9: 137–150.

Vapnik, V.
1995 *The Nature of Statistical Learning Theory*. New York: Springer.

Varela, F., J.-P. Lachaux, E. Rodriguez, and J. Martinerie
2001 The Brainweb: Phase and synchronisation and large-scale integration. *Nature Neuroscience* 2: 229–239.

Volf, N. V., and O. M. Razumnikova
1999 Sex differences in EEG coherence during a verbal memory task in normal adults. *International Journal of Psychophysiology* 34: 113–122.

Weiss, S., and H. M. Müller
2003 The contribution of EEG coherence to the investigation of language. *Brain and Language* 85: 325–343.

Weiss, S., H. M. Müller, B. Schack, J. W. King, M. Kutas, and P. Rappelsberger
2005 Increased neuronal synchronization accompanying sentence comprehension. *International Journal of Psychophysiology* 57: 129–141.

Weiss, S., and P. Rappelsberger
1996 EEG coherence within the 13-18 Hz band as a correlate of a distinct lexical organization of concrete and abstract nouns in humans. *Neuroscience Letters* 209: 17–20.

Wolpaw, J., N. Birbaumer, D. McFarland, G. Pfurtscheller, and T. Vaughan
2002 Brain computer interfaces for communication and control. *Clinical Neurophysiology* 113: 767–791.

Situated interaction with a virtual human – perception, action, and cognition

Nadine Leßmann, Stefan Kopp, and Ipke Wachsmuth

Abstract. In Virtual Reality environments, real humans can meet virtual humans to collaborate on tasks. The agent *Max* is such a virtual human, providing the human interactant with a face-to-face collaboration partner in the CRC 360 construction tasks. This paper describes how *Max* can assist by combining manipulative capabilities for assembly actions with conversational capabilities for mixed-initiative dialogue. During the interaction, *Max* employs speech, gaze, facial expression, and gesture and is able to initiate assembly actions. We present the underlying model of *Max*'s competences for managing situated interactions, and we show how the required faculties of perception, action, and cognition are realized and connected in his architecture.

1. Introduction

Virtual humanoid agents offer an exciting potential for interactive applications in Virtual Reality (VR). Cohabiting a virtual environment with the humans, virtual agents appear as equal partners that share the very situation with the human interactant and can collaborate on or assist in any task to be carried out. The way they are conceived (Gratch et al. 2002), they can engage with the human partner in face-to-face conversation and demonstrate many of the same communicative behaviors as displayed by humans. Thus, they allow for the exanimation of multimodal conversational behavior in various situational contexts. During the last years, the Collaborative Research Center 360 has introduced one such virtual human as an instance of a situated artificial communicator, the anthropomorphic agent *Max* (Kopp et al. 2003). *Max* is visualized in human-size in a CAVE-like VR environment where he assists the human interlocutor in assembling complex aggregates with virtual "baufix" parts (Fig. 1). In this setting, the two interactants meet in a familiar face-to-face fashion and become collaboration partners in a situated interaction. The human interactant – who is equipped with stereo glasses, data gloves, optical position trackers, and a microphone – can issue natural language commands along with coverbal gestures, or can directly grasp and manipulate the 3D "baufix" models to carry out assembly actions. Likewise, she can employ natural language and gesture when addressing *Max*. The agent has the same capabilities, being able to initiate assembly actions or to engage in multimodal dialogue using prosodic speech, gesture, eye gaze, and emotional facial expressions.

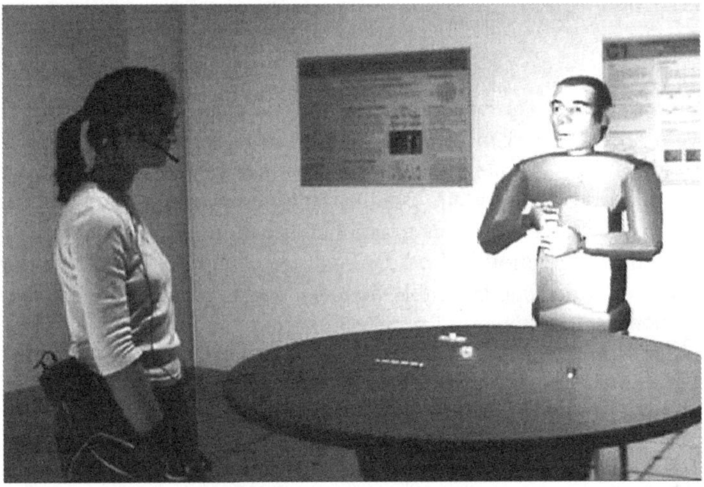

Figure 1. In a CAVE-like Virtual Reality environment, *Max* guides the human partner through interactive construction procedures.

The rationale for our research is to use an embodied conversational agent in order to investigate aspects of situated communication and collaborative, mixed-initiative dialogue in a dynamic environment. The scenario is an extension of the original CRC 360 setting, in which the human has the fixed role of an instructor and the artificial communicator the role of an executive constructor. Our scenario is more symmetric. While the overall interaction is guided by the human's wish to build a certain assembly, roles may flexibly switch between the interaction partners according to their competences. That is, either the human or *Max* may carry out an action or may instruct the partner to perform an action. Section 2 explains this setting in detail and points out the characteristics of the interactions that taking place. This analysis will lead the focus to the capabilities of goal-directed, interactive behavior in face-to-face conversations that are required from the agent.

To date, research on interactive systems has mostly concentrated either on dialogue, seen as spoken exchange of information, or on planning and executing goal-directed actions to follow instructions. Little work has aimed at integrating both realms. Such an interaction, however, demands both since the agent shall be able to collaborate by taking actions in the world and by conversing about them, possibly in an intertwined manner. Section 3 presents an interaction model that forms a basis for attaining these capabilities. It extends existing models to an account of both communicative and manipulative intentional actions, as well as of nonverbal, unwitting communication occurring in situated dialogues. It lends itself to realization through nested rational behaviors, which can be regarded as different kinds of intentional actions originating from shared processes. Building on this model, we have developed an underlying cognitive architecture that allows *Max* to communicate and cooperate with a human partner in a scenario of interleaving actions and perceptions. Section 4 describes our architectural approach and the interplay of the agent's capabilities of perception, action, and cognition. Section 5 takes an in-depth view at these issues and demonstrates how this architectural framework is applied to accomplish the capabilities of situated interaction we are targeting for *Max*.

2. Interaction scenario

Max's overall task is to assist the human in VR-based construction procedures of "baufix" assemblies. Both collaboration partners stand across a virtual table that has a number of "baufix" parts lying on it. The human can perform assembly actions in the aforementioned manners. *Max* is able to provide support whenever his partner does not know how to continue constructing an aggregate. Figure 2 shows a typical interaction in which both partners cooperatively solve a construction problem.

Looking at this interaction example, we can identify several challenges the agent has to meet:

- *Interplay of communication and manipulation:* Communicative actions and assembly actions are, each in their own right, equal, intertwined parts of the goal-directed interaction. That is, both participants contribute by either communicating something or by directly manipulating objects, with different types of actions being more appropriate in different contexts.
- *Dynamic environment*: The environment, in which the interaction takes place, is constantly changing. Both interactants can freely move and manipulate objects or carry out assembly actions at any time. *Max* thus

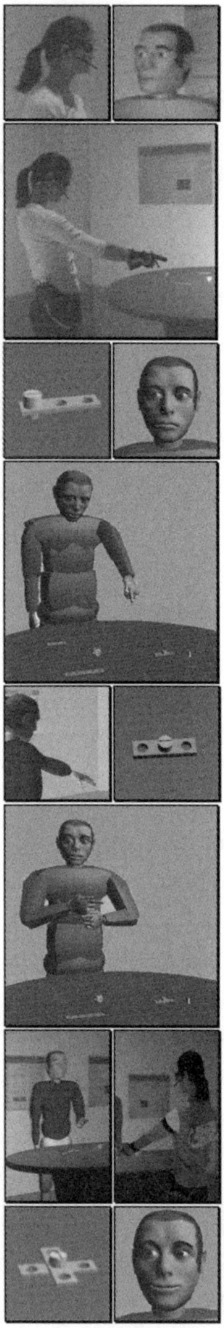

1 Human: *Let us build a propeller.*
2 Max: *Okay.*
3 Max: *First, insert a bolt…*
4 Human: *Which bolt?*
5 Max: *…in the middle of a bar.*
6 Max: *Any bolt.*
7 Human [puts the yellow bolt into the first hole of a three-hole bar]

8 Max: *No, that was the wrong hole.* [Max undoes the action]

9 Max: *Again, a bolt needs to be inserted in the middle hole of a bar.*
10 Human [puts the yellow bolt into the middle hole of a three-hole-bar]
11 Max: *Alright. Now, insert this* <pointing gesture> *bolt into another three-hole-bar.*
12 Human: *Do it yourself.*
13 Max: *Okay, I will do it.*
14 Max [connects the objects as instructed]

15 Max: *And now the bar needs to be turned* <iconic gesture> *crosswise to the other bar.*

[A long pause occurs as the human does not react]
16 Max: *Well, then I will perform the construction step.*
17 [The objects are rotated as instructed]
18 Max: *Great. We have just completed the assembly of a propeller.*

Figure 2. *Max* assists the human partner in assembling a propeller. Panels on the left depict the artificial communicator, the human communicator, and the object at various points in time during the interction. Sample dialogue on the right is translated from German.

monitors the scene, including his partner, and keeps track of the current state of the assembly procedure.

- *Mixed initiative*: Initiative in the interaction switches between the interlocutors, without one participant being permanently the master and the other one following slavishly. Initiative can be seen as the license to induce an intention with the interaction partner. While the human has the initiative in the beginning (1) when he poses a goal to achieve, *Max* assumes initiative in 3 by bringing up a new sub-goal. The human interactant takes the initiative back in 12 by performing a request. When having the initiative, *Max* recognizes that his interaction partner refuses (as in 11) or hesitates to conduct an action (as in between 15 and 16), and he performs the action himself.
- *Goal concretization*: Originally, the human interactant asks in 1 for a propeller to be built, defining the overall goal of the assembly procedure. Since there are several possibilities to construct a propeller out of "baufix" parts, however, this goal needs to be concretized further. This is done implicitly by the human who employs specific parts in his construction actions 7 and 10. *Max* recognizes and keeps track of these implicit situational commitments, and he refines his subsequent explanations accordingly in 11 (now mentioning a three-hole-bar).
- *Failure detection, feedback & retrace*: The agent detects wrong assembly actions performed by his partner (as in 7) and informs the human about the occurrence and the specific kind of the failure (8). Furthermore, *Max* undoes the action and retraces his assembly explanations. He then re-explains the wrongly performed manipulation in a more elaborated way, now emphasizing that the bolt must be put in the middle *hole* of the bar (9).
- *Turn-taking:* Throughout the dialogue, both interactants manage the exchange of turns. In 4, the human interlocutor interrupts *Max* and rigorously takes the turn to pose a clarification question. *Max* grants the floor at the next possible point (after 5) and answers the question (6). Turn-taking generally occurs more smoothly employing specific, mostly non-verbal behaviors to coordinate the flow of conversation.
- *Engagement and emotional display*: Both agents establish and maintain a connection while jointly undertaking the construction, i.e. they show engagement in their collaboration (Sidner, Lee, and Kidd 2005). *Max* demonstrates this by committing himself and contributing to the task, and by displaying on his face that even his mood is affected by the outcome of actions.

In summary, we note that the collaborative construction procedures we are looking at here are characterized by a high degree of interactivity, with frequent switches of initiative and roles of the interactants. The participants reconcile their contributions to the interaction with the need for regulating it by performing multiple activities simultaneously, asynchronously, and in multiple modalities. In consequence, though being goal-directed, the interaction runs in nested threads and appears fairly unpredictable. Contributions are either communicative or manipulative, and the effects of the latter can only be taken in from the situational context.

3. Aspects of interaction – modeling dialogue behavior

Participating in situated interactions like the ones explained in the previous section requires the agent to cope with numerous aspects of dialogue and more generally collaborative action. The basis for this is a sufficiently comprehensive model of what is going on in the interaction, along with powerful capabilities of managing it. Adopting the information state approach to dialogue (Traum and Larsson 2003), we frame in this section an *interaction model* to define the aspects along which the interaction evolves from the agent's point of view, and we lay down a formal notion of *interaction move* to explicate what actions can bring about. We thus stipulate what facets of interaction *Max* must take into account, but we do not make any provisions as to how these aspects can be fully represented or reasoned about. In fact, one of our main tenets is that only by means of situated interaction management, i.e. by closely coupling these processes to external and discourse context, the agent is able to meet the abovementioned demands.

3.1. Interaction model

Traditional approaches to dialogue modeling can roughly be distinguished as state-based/frame-based approaches or agent-based approaches (McTear 2002). The state-based approaches rest upon explicitly represented dialogue states, and define how a dialogue move leads from one state to another, frequently employing some form of dialogue grammar. Agent-based approaches adopt notions of dialogue as collaboration between two or more agents with mental states. To model their dialogue behavior, speakers are assigned mental attitudes like beliefs, goals or plans, as well as social attitudes like commitments or obligations (Traum 1997). The recent information state approach provides a framework for formalizing both dialogue models in a unified manner (Traum and Larsson 2003). It assumes that each agent maintains information states (ISs) that are employed in deciding on next actions and are updated in effect of dialogue acts performed by either interactant. A particular dialogue manager, then, consists in a formal representation of the contents of the ISs plus update processes that map from IS to IS given certain dialogue moves.

Several systems have been based on this theoretical framework, concentrating on different aspects of dialogue, e.g., the GODIS system (Larsson et al. 2000), or the WITAS project (Lemon et al. 2001). On the same basis, Traum and Rickel (2002) have proposed a model of multimodal dialogues in immersive virtual worlds that comprises layers for *contact, attention, conversation, obligations*, and *negotiation*. The conversation layer further defines separate dialogue episodes in terms of *participants*, *turn*, *initiative*, *grounding*, *topic*, and *rhetorical connections* to other episodes. Rules state how communicative signals can be recognized and selected to cause well-defined changes to a layer. Building on this previous work, we also define a model that frames interaction along a set of layers. An interaction state is then defined as a combination of states across these layers.

However, most existing models have focused either on dialogues where the agents are only planning (e.g. Chu-Carroll and Carberry 2000) – with the plan to be executed at a later time – or on dialogues where the agents are only executing some previously created plan (e.g. Ardissono and Cohen 1996). As Blaylock, Allen, and Ferguson (2003) point out, this does not allow for modeling dialogues where mixed-initiative collaboration and interleaving acting and planning take place, as in our setting. In addition, we posit that not only spoken communicative acts contribute to an interaction and count as conversational acts, but also manipulative actions must be characterized as such. We therefore introduce a model that includes a layer accounting for the formation, maintenance, overlap, and rejection of the goals of interactants. Goals cover the rational behind any kind of intentional action and abstract away from their situational realization.

The interaction model consists of the following layers:

- *Initiative*: Who has brought up the goal that the interactants are pursuing in the current discourse segment.
- *Turn*: Who has the turn. We distinguish between four states: *my-turn*, *others-turn* (or a unique name for a specific interaction partner, respectively), *gap*, *overlap*.

- *Goals*: The goals that have been pursued so far as well as the, possibly nested, goals that are still on the agent's agenda for the remainder of the interaction. Each goal may either have arisen from the agent's own desires, or was induced due to obligations following social norms or a power relation *Max* is committed to Traum and Allen (1994).
- *Content*: The propositional content that has been or will be subject of the discourse, defined in a logic-based notation.
- *Grounding:* The discourse state of content facts, denoting whether the agent assumes a fact to be new to the conversant or part of the common ground (Clark and Brennan 1991).
- *Discourse structure:* The organization of the discourse in segments that can relate to goals and refer to or group the entries in the content and goal layers. Each discourse segment has a purpose (DSP; Grosz and Sidner 1986), and they are related based on the relationships among their DSPs, all of which are part of one intentional structure.
- *Partner model*: What is known about the dialogue partner(s), also covering aspects of negotiation and obligations. It is the basis of retrospective analysis and thus plays a central role for the agent being situated in an evolving interaction.

3.2. Interaction moves

Any action by an interactant may alter the agent's internal representation of the state of interaction. In general, actions can be two-fold. On the one hand, there are subtle signals that are immediately displayed in reaction to a change of internal states of an agent, for example, facial display of emotion. Though not being communicatively intended, these actions may alter an agent's interaction model, e.g., by allowing an accretion of new information to the *partner model*. We focus here on intentional actions, either communicative or manipulative, which make up for the progress of interaction. They are selected and performed in order to achieve a desired state of the world. In mental attitudes terms, we think of them as being produced following specific kinds of nested intentions, which in turn are resultant of some goal-directed planning process. For example, when touching a bolt or saying "move the bolt closer to the bar", one might have the intention not just of manipulating the object but of mating it with a bar, building a propeller, and assisting the partner.

Modeling such behaviors requires having an account of their functional aspects, in addition to their mere overt actions. For manipulative acts, these aspects can easily be defined as the direct consequences (or post-conditions) of the manipulation in the world, which in turn need to be related to the current intention structure. For communicative acts, the functional aspects are not so easy to pinpoint in the first place. However, there is a long tradition of viewing speaking as acting. Austin (1962) pointed out multiple acts (or 'forces') of making a single utterance: the locutionary act of uttering words, and the perlocutionary act of having some effects on the listeners, possibly even effecting some change in the world. To its perlocutionary end, an utterance always performs a certain kind of action, the illocutionary act. Adopting this notion, Searle (1969) coined the term *speech act* which is supposed to include an attitude and a propositional content. Other researchers have used terms like communicative acts (Allwood 1976; Poggi and Pelachaud 2000), conversational moves, or dialogue moves.

The notion of functional aspects of communicative actions is particularly beneficial to multimodal systems, for it allows abstracting away from a signal's overt form to core aspects that only got realized in certain ways (e.g., Traum and Rickel 2002). The basic idea, as pointed out by Cassell et al. (2000), is that every verbal and nonverbal behavior (e.g. an eyebrow raise) fulfills a function, and that it may serve several communicative goals. That is, a single behavior can be employed in various circumstances to fulfill different conversational functions and the same function may be realized through different sets of behaviors. The function a behavior fulfills is either propositional (meaning-bearing) or interactional (regulative), and several behaviors are frequently employed at once in order to pursue both facets of discourse in parallel. Poggi and Pelachaud (2000) define a communicate act, the minimal unit of communication, as a pair of a signal and a meaning. The meaning includes the propositional content conveyed, along with a performative that represents the action the act performs (e.g. request, inform, etc.). By defining large lexicons, worked out in detail for gaze behavior and facial expression, the authors map performatives onto appropriate nonverbal signals.

Having formulated the main aspects of a communicative act and a manipulative action, we can now define the basic units of interaction in our setting. Such a unit can be either communicative or manipulative, for both actions contribute to the collaborative assembly procedure. We thus subsume them under the concept of an *interaction move* that is defined in terms of the following slots:

- *Action*: The illocutionary act the move performs. The act can either be purely manipulative ('connect', 'disconnect', 'take', or 'rotate') or communicative. In the latter case, a performative encodes the kind of action as described below.

- *Goal*: The perlocutionary force of the move, i.e., what the move is meant to accomplish. This can be either a desired state of the world ('achieve' something), or it can be the mere performance of an action ('perform' something).
- *Content*: Propositional facts that are conveyed by the move and that are needed to further specify the action and the goal.
- *Surface form*: The entirety of the move's overt verbal and nonverbal behaviors, employed to convey all of the aspects represented here.
- *Turn-taking*: The function of the move with respect to turn-taking, either 'take-turn', 'want-turn', 'yield-turn', 'give-turn', or 'keep-turn'.
- *Discourse function*: The function of the move with respect to the segmental discourse structure, either 'start-segment', 'contribute', or 'close-segment' (cf. Lochbaum, Grosz, and Sidner 2000).
- *Agent*: The agent that performs the move.
- *Addressee*: The addressee(s) of the move.

These slots together capture all informational aspects that are relevant about an action in our model of interaction. They are not independent from each other, nor are they self-sufficient. Instead, the slots are supposed to mark the specific signification of particular informational aspects. In general, they provide a frame structure that can be incrementally filled when interpreting or generating an action. At that, some of the slots may remain empty, e.g., for smallish moves like raising a hand, which may solely fulfill a turn-taking function.

3.3. Semantics – expectations – obligations

The meaning of an interaction move is defined by what it realizes, i.e. by the effects it brings about in terms of the aspects captured by the interaction model. These effects can often not be defined in a clear-cut way as they can depend on multiple aspects of the interaction move and the context in which it is performed. For example, even a simple move that fulfils the turn-taking function want-turn will result in a new turn-taking state self only when executed in the state gap (no one has the turn). For this reason, information state based systems typically employ a large number of update rules to model the context-sensitive effects of particular moves.

For a manipulative move, the effects are directly implied by the action and can be extracted via perception of the environment. Given sufficiently powerful perceptive capabilities, the current scene thus serves as an external part of the representation of the interaction state for the agent. Communicative moves can generally bear a multitude of different actions, and we explicitly encode the action of each move by its performative. One can differentiate between general types of performatives, e.g., Poggi and Pelachaud (2000) distinguish the three types inform, query, request. Extending these, we add a fourth type, namely, propose – an action playing a central role in collaborative situations where the course of action is frequently being negotiated:

1. *inform-performatives:* provide informational facts, i.e., characterized by the desire to change the addressee's beliefs
2. *query-performatives:* procure informational content in order to establish a new belief or to verify an existing one
3. *request-performatives:* request a manipulative action
4. *propose-performatives:* propose propositional content or an action

The first two performatives mainly concern the propagation of information carried out by communicative acts. *Request acts* aim at manipulative actions, whereas *propose* applies to both kinds of action but is characterized by a high degree of tentativeness. Originating in one of these general types, a performative can often be narrowed down through subsequent specification during interpretation or generation (Poggi and Pelachaud 2000). The final performative will be tailored to the content on which it operates (e.g., whether it asserts or requests a propositional fact, an action, or an opinion) as well as to contextual factors like the actual situation, the addressee, the type of encounter, or the degree of certainty. This can even happen retrospectively, when the performative of a previous move is fully disclosed at a later point in the conversation. We represent these refinements using a compositional notation, e.g. *inform.agree*, and we start out with a, yet extensible, set of performatives as shown in Table 1.

The agent-based approach allows us to utilize – in addition to mental categories like beliefs, goals, and plans – social attitudes like the expectations a sender connects to a move or the obligations it imposes on the recipient. Traum (1996) argues that obligations guide the agent's behavior, without the need for recognizing a goal behind an incoming move, and enable the use of shared plans at the discourse level. That is, obligations form a direct source of intentions besides the individual goals of the agent, both of which

Table 1. Performatives with corresponding type of content (second column) and short explanations

Inform		
inform.assert	proposition	assert a fact
inform.reassert	proposition	assert a fact again
inform.confirm inform.disconfirm	proposition	confirm/disconfirm the truth value of a fact
inform.ref	referential expression	describe a reference
inform.understood inform.not_understood	proposition/ action expression, proposition	signals (no) understanding, optionally a reason can be given
inform.compliment inform.criticize	proposition/ action expression	signals affective state towards action or attribute
inform.commit inform.refuse	action expression, proposition	signals disposition to perform an action, optionally a condition/ reason can be given
inform.agree inform.disagree	action expression, proposition	signals agreement with proposal, action, or proposition; optionally a condition or reason can be given
Query		
query.if	action expression / proposition	question that can be answered by yes/no
query.ref	referential expression	question about a reference
query.how	action description / proposition	question about an action / proposition
Request		
request.order	action expression	own interest, dominant
request.advice	action expression	other's interest
request.beg	action expression	own interest, polite/subordinate
request.indirect	action expression	indirect form of a request
Propose		
propose.proposition	proposition, uncertain	expressing an opinion
propose.action	action expression, uncertain	proposing an action
propose.action.offer	action expression, uncertain	offer to perform an action
propose.ref	referential expression	uncertain, reference

may even be contrary to each other. Still, the agent has the choice whether to adopt an obligation or not and this decision can be influenced by social conventions or the social relationship between the interlocutors.

In our case, *Max* is supposed to be cooperative and to help his human interlocutor whenever possible. Therefore, obligations are modeled such that an incoming interaction move will lead to the instantiation of a *perform*-goal to handle it. If this move was a *query* or *request, Max* will thus be conducting the action asked for according to his capabilities. In case of a *proposal*, he is only obliged to address the request, and his further deliberation decides upon how to react.

The core semantics of an *inform-performative* is to provide information to the interlocutor. When performing such an action, *Max* does not expect an answer and, if no response is given, the agent assumes the addressee to understood the information and to agree with it; the agent believes his goal to be achieved just by performing the communicative act in absence of a complaint. In contrast to *inform*, the agent will expect some reaction when having used a *query-performative*. The addressee can inform the agent that he does not know the answer or does not want to answer, but he is obliged to react in some form. If the interlocutor does not respond at all, the agent's goal will not be satisfied and he may try to encourage the interlocutor to respond. The same holds for a *request-performative*, which, however, differs with respect to the sender's expectations. Here only the performed action will satisfy the agent's goal. The agent will therefore wait for the addressee either to act or to refuse. The *propose-performative* lies in between the other performatives since the agent also expects a reaction, but it may range from performing the proposed action to agreeing or disagreeing to the proposal in question.

With respect to *initiative*, the performative along with the discourse function of the move are needed to state rules for identifying the holder of the initiative. The idea is that initiative is subordinate to the intentional hierarchy of discourse structure (Strayer and Heeman 2001). As Lochbaum, Grosz, and Sidner (2000) point out, the initiative is held by the segment initiator while the non-initiator contributes to the purpose of the current segment, e.g. answering a question in a sub-dialogue. If the general performative is an *inform-performative,* the speaker has the initiative when a new discourse segment is started. In case of a *query-performative,* the speaker has the initiative, except when following up on a question or command or if the question is a clarification question and contributes to the discourse segment. The *request-performative* always leaves the initiative with the speaker as longs as the interlocutor obeys. For *propose-performatives*, it is not clear from the beginning whether they lead to an initiative shift or not, for this depends on the interlocutor's reaction. If the speaker tries to start a new discourse segment and the interlocutor accepts the proposal, the initiative gets transferred to the speaker; if the proposal is not acknowledged, initiative does not switch.

To illustrate our model, in Table 2 we analyze the first seven interaction moves of the example dialogue given in Figure 2 (printed in italics). In doing so, we use a formal, logic-like notation that is explained in more detail below. Terms printed in bold indicate the various analysis slots.

Table 2. Example showing components of interaction moves

IM	**Interaction Move**	*Let us build a propeller.*	*Ok.*	*First, insert a bolt in the middle of a bar.*
AC	**Action**	propose.action	inform.agree	inform.request
GO	**Goal**	(Achieve (Exists prop))	(Perform (Inform.agree))	(Achieve (Connected $s $b $p1 $p2))
CO	**Content**	(Build prop we)	(Build prop we)	(Connect $s $b $p1 $p2) (Inst $s bolt) (Inst $b bar) (Center_hole $b $p2))
SF	**Surface form**	<words>$_t$	<words>$_t$	<words>$_t$
TT	**Turn-taking**	take | give	take | keep	| give
DF	**Discourse function**	start-segment (DSP=prop)	contribute	start-segment (DSP=prop-s1)
AG	**Agent**	Human	Max	Max
AD	**Addressee**	Max	Human	Human

IM	*Which bolt?*	*Any bolt.*	*[puts bolt into first hole of bar]*	*No, that was the wrong hole.*
AC	query.ref	inform.ref	connect	inform.disagree
GO	(Perform (Query.ref $s))	(Perform (Inform.ref $s))	(Achieve (Connected bolt-2 bar-1 port-1 port-3))	(Perform (Inform.disagree (Connect ...)))
CO	(Inst $s bolt)	(Inst $s bolt)	(Connect bolt-2 bar-1 port-1 port-3)	(Not (Center-hole bar-1 port-3))
SF	<words>$_t$	<words>$_t$	<manipulation>	<words>$_t$
TT	take | give	take | yield	take | yield	take | yield
DF	contribute	contribute	contribute	contribute
AG	Human	Max	Human	Max
AD	Max	Human	Max	Human

To represent propositional facts in the *goal* and *content* slots, predicates or relations are indicated by a capital letter. Unbound variables are prefixed with a $ symbol. For example, "(Inform.ref $s)" represents that a reference will be communicated, with the unbound variable $s being the referent. An unbound variable indicates underspecification inherent to the content of the move (in this example, there is no particular entity being referred to, yielding an indefinite article). Note further that the *content* and the *goal* slot together specify the informational aspects of the move, with some of these aspects marked as being the goal.

4. Architectural approach

The previous section laid down a formal basis for modeling dialogue behavior, building on an agent-based approach. To employ this model for situated discourse in a dynamic environment, *Max* needs to rest upon an architecture that realizes and tightly integrates all the faculties of perception, action, and cognition required. This architecture is outlined in Figure 3. While at first sight it seems to employ the classical perceive-reason-act triad, it was conceived such that all processes of perception, reasoning, and action are running concurrently. Perception and action are directly connected through a *reactive* component, affording reflexes and immediate responses to situation events or user actions. Perceptions are also fed into *deliberative* processes taking place in the reason section. These processes are responsible for interaction management by interpreting user input or environmental manipulations into *interaction moves*, deciding which action to take next, and composing interaction moves to realize it. To this end, they draw upon different kinds of knowledge from different types of memories and employ an extensible set of self-contained planners. As symbolized by the cognitive, inner loop, they further draw upon internal feedback information, e.g., originating from the body model of the agent. Both the reactive and the deliberative component act through instantiating *behaviors* in the act section of the architecture. Finally, an integrated emotion system (Becker, Kopp, and Wachsmuth 2004) defines an explicit emotional state of the agent and how it changes over time, being influenced by and influencing all parts of the architecture.

This architecture complies with design criteria that have been successfully employed in other dialogue systems and embodied conversational agents (e.g. the *STEVE* system (Rickel and Johnson 1999) or the *FXPAL* architecture employed in the *REA* agent (Cassel et al. 2002)). In contrast to these systems, however, *Max*'s architecture is based on more cognitively motivated tenets. Additionally, it is specifically geared towards situated interaction, embedding deliberation into a hybrid architecture to account for fast reactive responses and the agent's embodiment. This enables *Max* to deliberate and reason even when he is not holding the turn – a capability indispensable for dealing with a dynamic environment or being able to intervene, e.g., when the human partner is performing a wrong manipulative action.

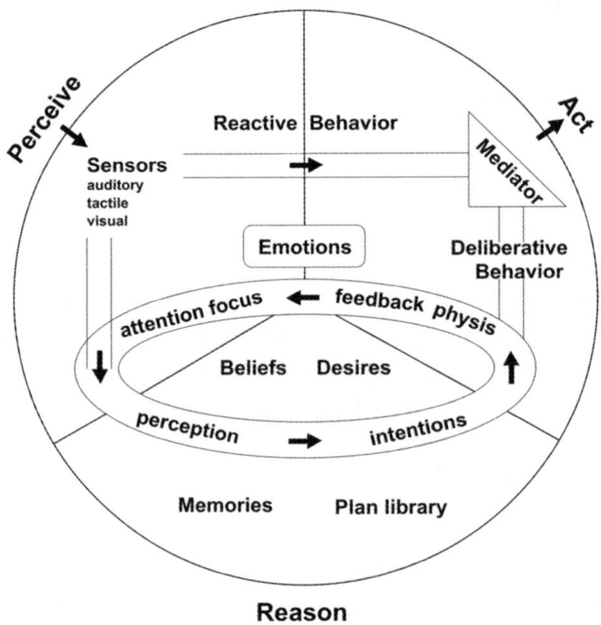

Figure 3. Outline of the architectural framework of *Max*

4.1. Perception

Situatedness refers to the ability to exploit the current situation as a source of knowledge. Being situated in a dynamic environment and engaging in highly situated interactions thus requires *Max* to pay close attention to the dynamic environment as well as to his human interaction partner. Visual perception of the virtual environment is emulated by virtual sensors attached to *Max's* eyes, simulating his point of view and computing the virtual objects sighted in a view frustum (Fig. 4, left). In addition, the agent relies on information about the success or failure of construction actions, emanating from an underlying assembly simulation system (Jung, Latoschik, and Wachsmuth 1998a). Perception of the human partner in the real world is achieved by an infrared tracking system that detects the positions and orientations of the human's head and hands, as well as information about hand posture by data gloves gathering (Latoschik 2001). Verbal input from the human interactant is fed into this framework through an auditory sensor. This sensor encapsulates a speech recognizer developed in CRC 360 (Fink et al. 1998), operating on a vocabulary appropriate for the "baufix" construction scenario.

Building on these input devices, perception is led by context-sensitive foci and, in addition, directly triggers reactive responses. Inspired by the ACT-R approach to connect perceptual with cognitive processing (Anderson and Lebiere 1998), percepts that have been acquired and interpreted are encapsulated in dedicated modules that assert the most relevant information as beliefs in a central working memory. This either happens when new data is recognized, or when the focus of attention is shifted. Note that new data may also arise from internal reasoning. For example, when a known aggregation of "baufix" parts is recognized, i.e. it is conceptualized, this information immediately pops up as a new belief.

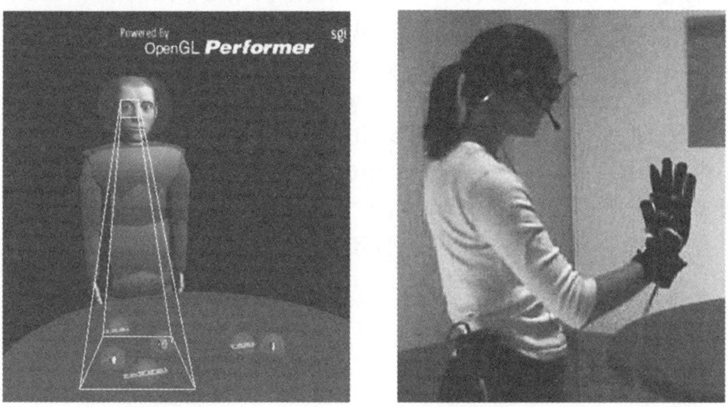

Figure 4. Virtual and real-world perception of *Max*

4.2. Memories and knowledge bases

The central working memory of the architecture contains all current beliefs the agent's reasoning and deliberation is operating on. These beliefs may concern different kinds of knowledge, and they may originate from perceptions of the agent, be entries of specialized knowledge bases that got activated, or relate to individual plan-contexts of the pursued intentions. Beliefs are represented as relations with attribute lists, augmented with information about its origin (perception, interaction move, etc.), the time of assertion, and the frequency of its retrieval. The link to the information source of a relation eases the retrieval of additional information on demand. If the agent seeks information not present in his working memory, associations can lead to the activation of related background knowledge. An example for this is an incorporated *COAR* knowledge bases (Jung 1998b), which provides the agent with taxonomic knowledge about "baufix" parts and their possible functional roles in the construction of an aircraft. The tags indicating assertion time and number of retrievals are used to simulate characteristics of natural cognitive memory, namely limited capacity and decay of information due to forgetting. If a belief has been asserted for a long time and only retrieved rarely, it is removed from the working memory. Thus, the agent's world model is situated in that it is restricted to only those beliefs that are relevant for processing the current state of interaction. This helps keeping the amount of facts in a bearable range and allows for faster reasoning.

Still, being situated does not only pertain to drawing upon the external context, but also refers to having an account of the actions in the immediate past that have led to the current situation. The working memory therefore also maintains a close connection to a discourse memory, which serves to keep track of the temporal order of events and the history of interaction in terms of different, possibly nested contexts. It is modeled as a stack of limited size in which the last elements are removed after a period of time. Its entries are composed of *interaction moves* (Sect. 3.2) along with fields for representing their discourse-level interrelations as inferred from the agent's intention structure.

4.3. Reasoning and deliberation

The deliberative processes of the agent are carried out based upon a general, widely respected model of rational reasoning, the Belief-Desire-Intention approach (Bratman 1987; Rao and Georgeff 1991). BDI provides good facilities for modeling intentional actions, performing complex tasks under specific context conditions, and recovering from failure or interruption. The basic idea of BDI is to describe the internal state of an agent by means of a set of mental categories, and to define a control architecture by which the agent rationally selects actions based on their representation. The mental categories are (1) *beliefs* comprising the agent's knowledge about the world, (2) *desires* representing the states of the world the agent wants to achieve or actions the agent seeks to perform, and (3) *intentions*, consisting of a current goal combined with a plan chosen to achieve it. Plans represent intended courses of action. They are augmented with pre-conditions and context conditions constraining their applicability, as well as with a utility function that helps assessing their priority for achieving a goal in a certain situation. We distinguish between *perform*- and *achieve*-plans, which differ with respect to the goals they can be used for. While perform-plans are used for merely executing a plan, achieve-plans are used to reach a certain state of the world and are only executed as long as this goal has not been achieved. The BDI-interpreter continually pursues the plan with the highest utility value as an intention. We use JAM/UM-PRS (Huber 1999; Lee et at. 1994) for our BDI interpreter, suitably extended for our purpose as follows.

4.3.1. Plans as mental attitudes

One key aspect of the architecture is that plans are employed to abstractly guide the agent's behavior, as well as to uniquely determine the exact actions to be executed. Plans can either directly trigger specific behaviors to act, but may also invoke dynamic, self-contained planners that construct context-dependent actions or, again, plans. That way, complex plans can be hierarchically expanded on demand by the instantiation of lower-level plans. For example, an integrated *assembly planner* derives construction plans of aggregates on the fly from assembly group representations being specified in the frame-based representation language COAR (Jung 1998b). These plans consist of abstract construction steps that state which kinds of objects need to be assembled in which ways to build e.g. a propeller or an aircraft's tail rudder.

A judicious use of plans thus allows the agent to reduce the complexity of controlling dynamic behavior and to constrain itself to work towards goals, while still keeping options to adapt to the run-time situation (Winikoff et al. 2002). Plans are therefore kept as general as possible and are refined to situated context not until necessary. That is, we regard plans as *mental attitudes*, as opposed to recipes that just consist of the knowledge by which actions a goal might be achieved (cf. Pollack 1990, 1992). Our architecture comprises a plan library (see Fig. 3) that can, at first, be seen as a collection of recipes representing possible courses of actions. Once the agent rationally selects a plan and binds or constrains its arguments, however, it becomes an intention on an intention stack, encompassing information about the context and the goals responsible for it to come into existence. In result, the plan has become more than just a recipe since it is characterized by the agent's attitudes towards the realization of his goal.

Commitments can concern e.g. individual variables in specific plan contexts – which frequently occurs in underspecified instructions (cf. Sect. 2). For example, the type of an object used in a certain action is restricted, whereas its identity need not be fully stipulated (use a bar, regardless which one). We thus extended the BDI interpreter to the use of constraints. A variable can thereby be confined by constraints possibly arising in the ongoing discourse interaction. As a variable is used in a specific plan context, and as variable bindings are passed on to sub-goals and sub-plans, constraining a variable affects its value in the complete context. Abstract concepts as well as situated specified propositions and actions become thus readily manageable in the BDI framework.

4.3.2. Implicit learning of variants

To supplement conversational aspects of memory, *Max* must be able to deal with user initiated variants of well-known structural aggregates, e.g. the human partner starts to build a propeller out of five-hole bars as opposed to the known three-hole-bar propeller. That is, *Max* must be able to dynamically conceptualize what the human interaction partner is assembling and to constrain and adapt its plans accordingly. Exploiting information from the underlying assembly simulation system (Jung, Latoschik, and Wachsmuth 1998), this dynamic conceptualisation is done in an *episodic short-term memory* capable of grouping recent construction steps into an episode, based on the aggregate that has been assembled (Voss 2003). When the human interactant demands a variant of an aggregate built in a recently completed episode, *Max* extends his long-term memory to this new aggregate concept in accordance with his recent episodic experiences (Voss and Wachsmuth 2003). After augmenting his long-term knowledge through this unsupervised and concurrent implicit learning mechanism, *Max* can then conceptualize a learnt variant as such in the following situations. Moreover, this capability is one way for him to get to know different variants of an assembly goal, which in turn allows him to perform goal concretization during interaction (see Sect. 2).

4.4. Acting and reacting

The act section of the architecture is in charge of processing all behaviors triggered by the reactive and deliberative components, e.g., to perform manipulative or communicative actions. Once instantiated there, behaviors can activate themselves dynamically when certain preconditions set in and, then, compete for control over the required effectors (certain joints of *Max's* skeleton, muscles of his face model, or speech). A *mediator* manages access to the effectors and resolves conflicts in favor of the behavior with the highest utility value. Reactive behaviors include gaze tracking and focusing the human interactant in response to prompting signals (calling "Max" or touching his shoulder). In addition, incessant secondary behaviors reside in this component. They can be triggered or modulated by deliberative processes as well as the emotional state of the agent. These behaviors make the agent appear more lifelike and include eye blink, breathing, and sway. With regard to deliberatively triggered, intentional actions – above all interaction moves – the act section must comprise of modules that turn them into executable behaviors. This includes generating and synthesizing tightly synchronized speech and graphics animation for multimodal utterances as explained in Section 5.4.

5. Situated interaction management

Based on the basic architectural principles described in the previous section, situated interactive behavior of *Max* is realized by the interplay of several modules. Figure 5 shows a zoom-in on some of the individual modules the agent's architecture comprises of. *Interaction moves* are the main data structure for interfacing between these modules. On the input side, they are used to specify and structure the incoming information, possibly relating the information to external objects or previous interaction moves; on the output side, they serve as a container which gets filled during the generation process of an agent's response. Every move by both *Max* and his human partner gets memorized in the *discourse memory* which serves as a dialogue history.

5.1. Input processing

In the perception module (top left section of Fig. 5), components that are responsible for the processing of sensory input data are displayed. The per-

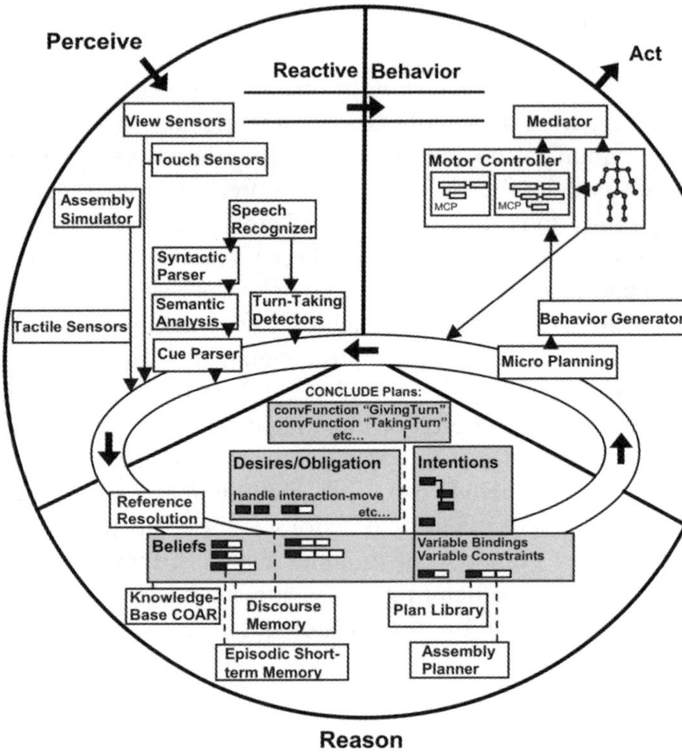

Figure 5. A zoom-in on some of the individual modules of the architecture and the data structures being processed during reasoning

ception module is responsible for providing the agent with a permanent flow of situational changes. Information is gathered by view and touch sensors as well as from the assembly system underlying the VR simulation. Additionally, input data is processed by speech parsing, via applying detectors for gesture recognition, and by multimodal integration. The detectors are realized using compute nodes that are combined in hierarchically organized networks (using the *PrOSA* framework; see Biermann and Wachsmuth 2003; Latoschik 2001). Special detectors are set up for turn-taking signals, e.g., responding to the human partner holding up a hand with fingers stretched (Fig. 4, right) or starting to speak. These turn-taking detectors are activated according to the conversational state serving as a situated attention focus. Whenever the detectors are activated and observe a certain combination of signals, this information is fed into the cognitive loop for being processed by appropriate reactive plans.

As for the analysis of speech input, several processing steps take place leading from perception to the reasoning layer where longer-term mental states are taken into account (Fig. 6). A keyword-spotter linked to the parser is used to calculate a first guess for the general performative of the utterance by analyzing its syntactical structure. This helps, for example, to distinguish between *queries* and *informs*. A semantic analysis and reference resolution are evoked to differentiate between the external objects and actions involved. Additionally, the utterance is scanned by the parser for cue words that may indicate a general performative (e.g. "I propose" clearly signals a *propose-performative*). The evolving data is filled into an *interaction-move* frame that is passed on to reasoning processes. Here, it is matched against the context of the agent's current mental state as well as against the discourse history to determine candidate interpretations (see Sect. 5.2). Figure 6 illustrates how data originates from processes on different levels of the cognitive architecture during handling an incoming interaction move.

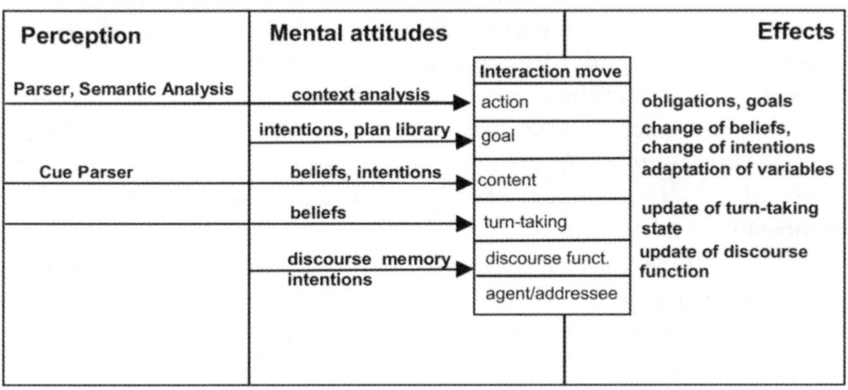

Figure 6. Handling an interaction move

5.2. Plan-based interaction management

How the agent behaves in the interaction is determined by the BDI control architecture. It draws upon specific plans for analyzing input moves as well as selecting and generating responses in a context dependent manner, leading to either communicative or manipulative moves.

5.2.1. Dealing with incoming interaction moves

A variety of plans are used for handling incoming *interaction moves*. These plans differ with regard to what informational aspects they focus on, how they are executed, and if they constitute a single step in a longer processing pipeline or if the plan triggers a direct reaction of the agent.

Turn-taking functions are processed in a direct manner. Yet, to decide whether to allow an immediate interruption, the corresponding plan must take into account the mental state of the agent, the goals he pursues, and the dominance relationship between the interlocutors. For example, depending on the performative *Max* is using, he will allow an immediate interruption in some cases even before he has analyzed the content of the interlocutors interaction move. To handle such situations, a turn-taking model is used (Leßmann, Kranstedt, and Wachsmuth 2004) that combines concepts of the FMTB architecture (Cassell et al. 2000), i.e. to distinguish a behavior from its conversational function, with ideas of the turn-taking layer of the dialogue model of Traum and Rickel (2002). Our model consists of two steps: First, a rule-based, context-free evaluation of the possible turn-taking reactions takes into account the current conversational state and the action of the interactant's utterance. These rules are incessantly applied and integrated using data-driven *conclude* plans to ensure cooperative dialogue behavior. The second step is a context-dependent decision upon different response plans, possibly leading to new intentions.

The propositional content of an incoming *interaction move*, if present, is processed by plans for determining the context it belongs to (e.g. to resolve anaphora). To this end, it is checked whether the move relates to the current goals, or to an interaction move performed before. This is done by calculating a correlation value between the content facts carried by the interaction move and the goal context. For example, finding the correct context for the human's clarifying question in Figure 2 (4) is a prerequisite to respond properly. As the content of the question is a reference to an object which is constrained to the type bolt, and this fits perfectly with the context of the agent's current goal to connect a bolt and a bar, the agent's current goal can serve as a valid context. In addition, the agent needs also to be able to resolve references to external objects in the virtual world, which is done using a constraint satisfaction-based algorithm (Pfeiffer and Latoschik 2004).

If the agent succeeds in searching a candidate context, it adds an *obligation*-goal to handle the interaction move as a sub-goal to the goal to which the move contributes. Otherwise, a new *obligation*-goal is added as a top-level goal. By associating the interaction move with one of his goals, the agent is able to deal with multiple threads at the same time and keep apart their individual contexts. In result, incoming information is structured according to its content, but also depending on the context – an important aspect of being situated in the ongoing interaction.

Finally, the action of the incoming move, i.e., its performative as determined during interpretation, is essential for drawing the right conclusions and taking the proper reactions. Different plans are thus used to handle moves with different performatives. For example, these plans may include verifying a proposition, answering a question, or constraining a parameter involved in a plan as explained in the following section.

5.2.2. Situated refinement of underspecified task representations

Being situated in ongoing assembly tasks, the agent has to adapt his planned courses of action to events occurring during plan execution e.g. the usage of specific objects or proposals made by the interlocutor. In our example interaction (Fig. 2), the original goal of the assembly procedure was to build a propeller (1), which, then, gets refined to a three-hole-bar propeller. The agent has to keep track of these commitments, and then to refine further explanations accordingly. Constraint specifications are used to represent goals in an abstract, underspecified manner which can then be concretized implicitly and dynamically in the ongoing interaction.

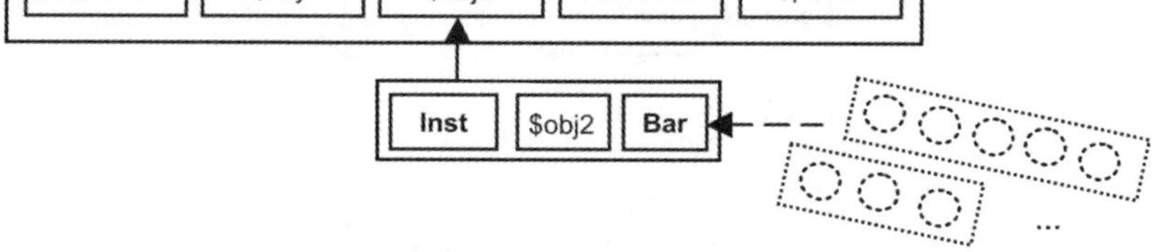

Figure 7. Goal representation of a construction step, qualified by three constraints.

Figure 7 shows the goal representation of the underspecified first construction step of the example dialogue presented in Figure 2. An arbitrary bolt (*$obj1*) has to be inserted into the center hole (*$port2*) of a bar (*$obj2*). However, when the human performs an incompatible action by putting a bolt in a wrong hole, *Max* is able to detect the violation of the center-hole constraint and to verbalize the reason (interaction move (8)). Refinements to this task representation, as they occur when the human interactant chooses to connect a yellow bolt with a three-hole bar in move (10), are then represented as variable bindings being effective throughout the plan context.

In Figure 2 (Move 11), *Max* explains the next construction step, which has a more complex structure. Its goal representation, which is subject to effective variable bindings, is shown in Figure 8. Because the first object variable (*$obj1*) is now bound to a specific yellow, slot-headed bolt (*Bolt-12*), *Max* uses a pointing gesture to refer to it. The second object (*$obj3*) is constrained to be a bar and not to be identical with the three-hole bar that has been used before (bound to *$obj2*). *Max* thus stresses this aspect by describing the object as "*another*" bar. Yet another constraint relating the lengths of the bars stems from *Max*'s long-term assembly knowledge base. It states that for a valid propeller, the rotor blades must have equal lengths. When told to perform the assembly action himself (12), *Max* is able to choose an appropriate bar as a second rotor blade where to insert the yellow bolt.

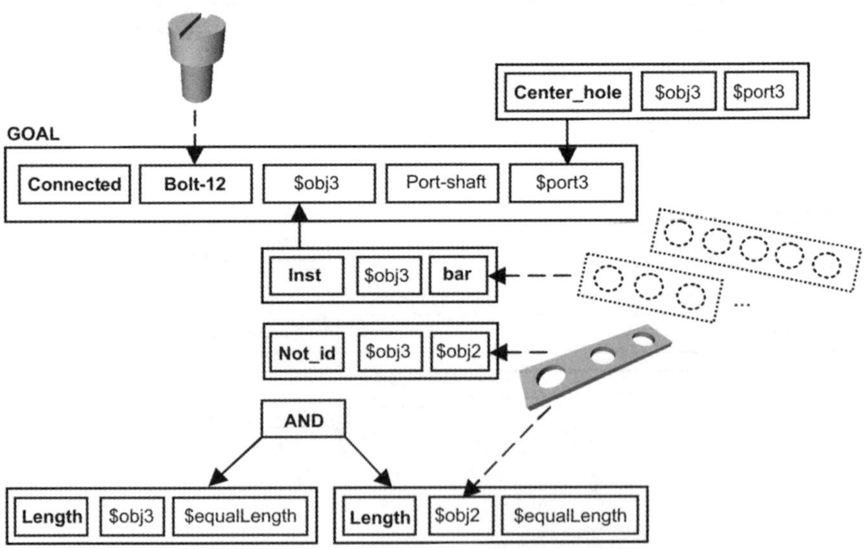

Figure 8. Goal representation of aligned second construction step.

5.3. Output planning

If the agent has the goal to achieve a certain state of the world, he will reason about which courses of action may lead to this goal. In result, he will formulate and aggregate situated plans that lead to the desired state of affairs. Each behavior that any of these plans incorporates may either be a communicative or a manipulative move. Both kinds of behaviors hence stand in a meaningful relationship to each other and can be carried out in a nested way when suitable. The decision is based upon the role that the agent currently fulfills. If *Max* is to act as the instructor – his initial role upon being asked by the human – he will verbalize the steps.

5.3.1. Planning communicative moves

When *Max* has decided to employ a communicative act, he has to decide *what* meaning should be conveyed and *how* to convey it in natural language, gesture, etc. In general, the behavior produced must be tailored to the agent's current role in the collaboration, expressing his beliefs and goals. It also must account for the current situational context including his interaction partner and the previous discourse. Thereby, real-time throughput is needed if the system is to seem natural, especially given other processing of input and output (Traum, Fleischman, and Hovy 2003). Generation methods that involve complex calculations are thus not appropriate.

In general terms, natural language generation starts with a communicative goal to be achieved and relies on various sources of knowledge. Among these are task and conversational competencies, a model of the addressee, and a discourse history (McTear 2002; Reiter and Dale 2000). The generation process itself consists of, first, selecting the content to be conveyed (*content selection*), secondly, structuring this content in *messages* that fit into and relate to ongoing discourse in meaningful ways (*discourse planning*) and, lastly, turning these messages into overt language and gesture (*sentence planning* and *realization*). In our approach, this process is an integral part of the agent's plan-based deliberations and is carried out naturally by dedicated plans when *Max's* mental attitudes decline him towards making an utterance. The communicative goal derives directly from the currently active intention on the agent's plan stack, e.g. to request the interaction partner to connect two objects: request.order "user" "connect" "Bolt_12" $obj3.

The goal of the generation process, then, is to determine all information needed for this communicative move to render it as a multimodal utterance.

Starting from a message (goal) as above, the general performative (action) is first derived directly from the type of the intended act (in our example request.order). *Content selection* then works to determine the information that specifies the parameters of the communicative act to concrete values and, if possible, refines the performative. *Discourse planning* determines the move's discourse function and the discourse segment (DSP) it is contributing to, both being derivable from the actual structure and ordering of the plans on the intention stack.

The final stage of output generation is to form a specific utterance that satisfies the intended communicative goal by fulfilling the corresponding action and conveying the selected content. Our approach to this is inspired by *systemic grammars* (Halliday 1985), which explicate the choices made in this derivation based on the functional aspects of a communicative act.

Our generator employs dedicated decision modules in a suitable order to model this generation process (Fig. 9). Each of these modules implements paradigmatic choices and results in realizations statements that are collected in an intermediate representation. The representation contains a central template node for the performative, along with nodes for the entities that play semantic roles in the respective event (e.g. action, object or attribute in the request template), thus laying down the constituents of the sentence.

By traversing the representation and accumulating the realization statements in the various nodes, the syntagmatic structure of the utterance is constrained. Such statements may concern the insertion, ordering, or conflation of grammatical functions (e.g. +Subject +Finite). For example, statements in our grammar cover subject-verb congruency and attribute-noun congruency, or state how the type of an object can influence the lexical item chosen for the associated verb. During *sentence planning*, the nodes are processed to build referring expressions, also considering gestures that can augment or even supplement the content of the verbal utterance. This includes deictic gestures that directly refer to entities in the environmental context as well as iconic gestures (as in utterance 15 of Fig. 2) that contribute visuo-spatial information. In our generation process, gestures can be stated either explicitly in terms of form features of the meaning-bearing phase, or by specifying a desired communicative function to fulfill (Kopp and Wachsmuth 2004). Currently, the latter mechanism is utilized to assign coverbal gestures, where the function is derived by the planner from the goal, action, and content of the interaction move. In addition, decisions are made whether to use an active or a passive form, e.g., depending on whether an agent entity is specified or not.

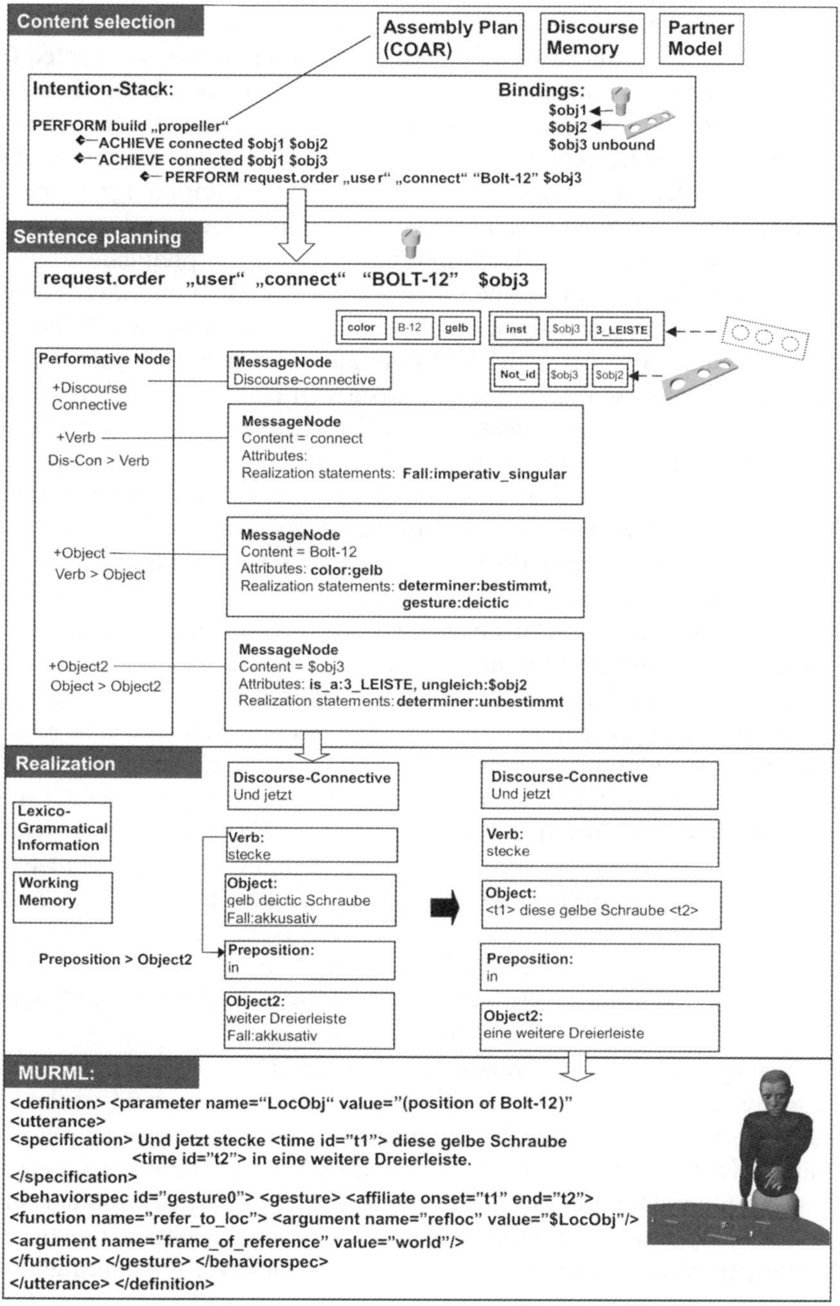

Figure 9. Workflow of generating a multi-modal (German) utterance

In the *realization* phase, the nodes are traversed again to choose a verbal item for each entity. This is done by retrieving words in their principled (not yet inflected) form from a lexicon. Additionally, the nodes are processed and filled with required lexico-grammatical information about the constituents (case, number, gender, determiner) in the form of further realization statements. For example, verb entries in the lexicon imply additional grammatical constraints to be met by the verb constituents. Likewise, subject-verb congruency leads to constraints entered in the finite verb's or predicate's realization statements. To account for the move's discourse function, *Max* is able to insert cue words into the template node to be prepended to the utterance. If the first communicative act is the first in a multi-step plan, e.g. the first construction step for an aggregate, the cue word will be "at first". If it is a successive step, the cue words consist of discourse connectives chosen dependant on the rhetorical relations between this utterance and the previous one ("then", "and now", "this time", "again"), and if it is the last step of a discourse segment *Max* will use "finally" or "at last".

Finally, the nodes are processed a last time to determine the final, inflected form of the lexical items and to combine them to a clause in accord with the realization statements. During this processing, gestures get adjusted to enclose the expressions they relate to. To this end, tags are used to state the start and end point of an accompanying gesture and are specified in an XML-notation. The generation process is able to create utterances in which a deictic gesture is employed to refer to an individual object, or an iconic gesture to depict a spatial relation (see Fig. 2). The complete multimodal utterance is then translated into MURML (*Multimodal Utterance Representation Markup Language;* Kranstedt, Kopp, and Wachsmuth 2002) and sent to the next level – realization of the overt behavior (see Sect. 5.4).

5.3.2. Creating turn-taking signals

When an interaction move is ready for being uttered, specific plans are invoked to find out which of the two interlocutors is currently holding the turn. If *Max* holds the turn or if the communicative act entails a turn-taking function value of *take-turn*, the agent performs the utterance right away, possibly interrupting the human interlocutor. If the agent is not the turn-holder, *turn-taking* achieve-plans are executed that first attempt to obtain the turn by producing predefined *wanting-turn* behavior, automatically adapting to the situation and only running until the goal relation is met (Leßmann, Kranstedt, and Wachsmuth 2004).

Figure 10. Max's behaviors for signaling wanting-turn and giving-turn

Likewise, if the agent decides to give up the turn after an utterance, respective behaviors are executed subsequently. Some examples of nonverbal turn-taking behaviors employed by *Max* are illustrated in Figure 10.

5.4. Output realization

The final step in output generation is to turn the planned interaction move into multimodal output behavior of *Max*. It starts out with information about the surface form, defined by a multimodal utterance tree out of textually defined words and possible gesture definitions in MURML, along with meta-information about the actual action and goal of the utterance. Organized as a pipeline architecture, it consists of two consecutive steps, *behavior augmentation* and *behavior realization*.

Behavior augmentation is meant to provide the XML specification, which only amounts to intended behaviors derived from communicative goals, with apposite nonverbal and paraverbal behaviors like intonation, eyebrow raise, head nod, or posture shifts. These behaviors do not encode explicit communicative goals, and are thus not conceived during output planning, but are essential to meaning as they underscore the central parts of the utterance. Behavior augmentation draws upon information about grammatical units (clause structure), information structure (theme and rheme), word newness, and contrast, each of which represented by dedicated tags in the XML tree. This tree is augmented with appropriate behaviors by applying each of an extensible set of generators to all of its nodes. Such generators are employed for gaze, intonation (specified in *GToBI* notation; Grice and Baumann 2001), eyebrow raises, and head nods. The information at disposal is thereby currently limited to clause structure and information structure.

The second step is to turn the multimodal utterance tree with its morphologically and phonologically-specified behaviors into synthesized speech and intonation, expressive gestures and other animations for *Max's* face and body, and to schedule them into synchronized multimodal output. For this task, we employ our *Articulated Communicator Engine* (Kopp and Wachsmuth 2004). It provides modules for the synthesis of gestural, verbal, and facial behaviors, and embeds them in an incremental process model that schedules and links their deliveries into synchronized, fluent utterances. It produces continuous speech and gesture in successive chunks, each of which being a synchronized pair of an intonation phrase and a co-expressive gesture. At that, synchrony between the modalities is achieved by timing the gesture and adjusting the duration of silent pauses in speech.

For the synthesis of gesture, *Max* has a kinematic skeleton (comprising 103 DOF in 57 joints) and is equipped with a module able to generate, in real-time on demand, all animations required to drive the skeleton as specified. Especially the latter is indispensable for the degree of situated behavior targeted in our work. Animation planning includes the allocation of body parts to perform a gesture with the expansion of complex movement constraints for symmetry or repetitions, and the preparation of co-articulation effects by planning gesture retraction to lead to an interim rest position when another gesture is about to follow. While all of these steps are still operating on the gesture specification in MURML, a final motor planning stage processes both the form definition originating from microplanning and the timing constraints set up during scheduling, and turns them into executable motor programs. That is, the motor planner seeks a solution to drive the kinematic skeleton for complete gestural movements that meet all form and timing constraints; see (Kopp and Wachsmuth 2004) for details on how computer animation techniques are employed to simulate unrestrained hand and arm movements.

6. Conclusion

We have presented the embodied conversational agent *Max*, who serves as a cooperative construction partner in assembly tasks. In the Virtual Reality environment in which the agent is situated, the human interactant engages with *Max* in a familiar face-to-face scenario. *Max* is able to deal with human conversational behaviors occurring in situated interaction like interruptions, turn-taking, incomplete references, interventions, multimodal input, and the anticipation of assembly action. But *Max* is not only able to deal with these behaviors on the perceptional side; he is also meets some of the expectations arising from his anthropomorphic appearance, namely, to generate natural conversational behavior himself. Running concurrently and in parallel, his perception, generation and reasoning processes lead to the production of multimodal utterances, active expression of turn-taking signals, and the intelligent management of construction tasks. The dynamic nature of the environment and the resulting partial predictability of discourse with the human interactant – combined with the overall need for knowledge, planning, communication, and acting – have led to the development of *Max's* cognitive architecture that connects deliberation based on a belief-desire-intention interpreter with fast reactive behavior.

Compared to the scenarios of other conversational agents, the collaborative assembly VR environment provides both *Max* and his human interaction partner with rich possibilities for interaction, bringing communicating and acting in the world closely together. This gain comes at the costs of less predictability and a harder manageability of the interaction. To account for the various aspects of such situated interaction, we arrived at a formal *interaction model* that characterizes the dimensions along which such situated interactions out of interleaving perception and action evolve. Part of this approach is to subsume both communicative as well as manipulative contributions to the interaction in order to allow the agent to handle both types of action in his cognitive architecture in a unified way. In summary, the setting of *Max* as a face-to-face communication partner in an immersive VR installation proved to be a very attractive environment for the study and simulation of situated conversational behavior, and it has helped us achieving a better understanding of how situated artificial communicators as targeted in the CRC 360 can be built.

References

Allwood, J.
1976 *Linguistic Communication in Action and Co-Operation: A Study in Pragmatics*. Gothenburg Monographs in Linguistics 2, Department of Linguistics. Göteborg: University of Gothenburg.

Anderson, J. R., and C. Lebiere
1998 *Atomic Components of Thought*. Hillsdale: Erlbaum.

Ardissono L., and R. Cohen
1996 Extending the role of user feedback in plan recognition and response generation for advice-giving systems: an initial report. In *Advances in Artificial Intelligence*, 109–120. Berlin: Springer.

Austin, J. L.
1962 *How to Do Things with Words*. Cambridge, MA: Havard University Press.

Becker, C., S. Kopp, and I. Wachsmuth
2004 Simulating the emotion dynamics of a multimodal conversational agent. In *Affective Dialogue Systems,* E.André, L. Dybkjaer, W. Minker, and P.Heisterkamp (eds.), 154–165. Berlin: Springer.

Biermann, P., and I. Wachsmuth
2003 An implemented approach for a visual programming environment in VR. In *Proceedings of the Fifth Virtual Reality Interaction Conference (VRIC 2003), Laval, France*: 229–234.

Blaylock, N., J. Allen, and G. Ferguson
2003 Managing communicative intentions with collaborative problem solving. In *Current and New Directions in Discourse and Dialogue*, Volume 22, J. van Kuppevelt, and R. W. Smith (eds.), 63–84. Dordrecht: Kluwer.

Bratman, M. E.
1987 *Intention, Plans, and Practical Reason*. Cambridge, MA: Harvard University Press.

Cassell, J., T. Bickmore, L. Campbell, H. Vilhjalmsson, and H. Yan
1998 Human conversation as a system framework: Designing embodied conversational agents. In *Embodied Conversational Agents,* J. Cassell, J. Sullivan, S. Prevost, and E. Churchill (eds.), 29–63. Cambridge, MA: MIT Press.

Chu-Carroll, J., and S. Carberry
2000 Conflict resolution in collaborative planning dialogs. *International Journal of Human-Computer Studies* 53: 969–1015.

Clark, H. H., and S. E. Brennan
1991 Grounding in communication. In *Perspectives on Socially Shared Cognition,* L. B. Resnick, J. M. Levine, and S. D. Teasley (eds.). Washington: APA Books.

Fink, G. A., C. Schillo, F. Kummert, and G. Sagerer
1998 Incremental speech recognition for multimodal interfaces. In *Proceedings 24th Annual Conference of the IEEE Industrial Electronics Society*, IEEE Computing Society (ed.), 2012–2017. Los Alamitos: IEEE.

Gratch, J., J. Rickel, E. André, N. Badler, J. Cassell, and E. Petajan
2002 Creating interactive virtual humans: Some assembly required. *IEEE Intelligent Systems* 17: 54–63.

Grice, M., and S. Baumann
2002 Deutsche Intonation und GToBI. *Linguistische Berichte* 191: 267–298.

Grosz, B. J., and C. L. Sidner
1986 Attention, intentions, and the structure of discourse. *Computational Linguistics* 12: 175–204.

Halliday, M. A. K.
1985 *An Introduction to Functional Grammar*. London: Arnold.

Huber, M. J.
1999 JAM: A BDI-theoretic mobile agent architecture. In *Proceedings of the Third International Conference on Autonomous Agents,* 236–243. Seattle: ACM Press.

Jung, B.
1998 Reasoning about objects, assemblies, and roles in on-going assembly tasks. *Distributed Autonomous Robotic Systems* 3: 257–266.

Jung, B., M. E. Latoschik, and I. Wachsmuth
1998 Knowledge-based assembly simulation for virtual prototype modeling. In *IECON'98 (IEEE),* 4: 2152–2157.

Kopp, S., B. Jung, N. Leßmann, and I. Wachsmuth
2003 Max – A multimodal assistant in virtual reality construction. In *KI - Künstliche Intelligenz* 4: 11–17.

Kopp, S., and I. Wachsmuth
2004 Synthesizing multimodal utterances for conversational agents. *Journal of Computer Animation and Virtual Worlds* 15: 39–52.

Kranstedt, A., S. Kopp, and I. Wachsmuth
2002 *MURML: A Multimodal utterance representation markup language for Conversational Agents.* Report 05/2002 of CRC 360 "Situated Artificial Communicators". Bielefeld: University of Bielefeld.

Larsson, S., P. Ljunglöf, R. Cooper, E. Engdahl, and S. Ericsson
2000 GoDiS – An accommodating dialogue system. In *Proceedings of NAACL Workshop on Conversational Systems,* 7–10. Seattle: ACL.

Latoschik, M. E.
2001 A gesture processing framework for multimodal interactions in virtual reality. In *AFRIGRAPH 2001, 1st International Conference on Computer Graphics and Visualization in Africa*: 95–100. Cape Town.

Lee, J., M. J. Huber, P. G. Kenny, E. H. Durfee
1994 UM-PRS: An implementation of the procedural reasoning system for multirobot applications. In *Conference on Intelligent Robotics in Field, Factory, Service, and Space (CIRFFSS),* 842–849. Houston.

Lemon, O., A. Bracy, A. Gruenstein, and S. Peters
2001 Information states in a multi-modal dialogue system for human-robot conversation. In *Proceedings of the 5th Workshop on Formal Semantics and Pragmatics of Dialogue (Bi-Dialog),* 57–67. Bielefeld: ZiF.

Leßmann, N., A. Kranstedt, and I. Wachsmuth
2004 Towards a cognitively motivated processing of turn-taking signals for the embodied conversational agent max. In *AAMAS 2004 Workshop on Embodied Conversational Agents - Balanced Perception and Action,* IEEE Computing Society (ed.), 57–64. Los Alamitos: IEEE.

Lochbaum, K., B. J. Grosz, and C. Sidner
2000 Discourse structure and intention recognition. In *A Handbook of Natural Language Processing: Techniques and Applications for the Processing of Language as Text,* R. Dale, H. Moisl, and H. Sommers (eds.), 123–146. New York: Marcel Dekker.

McTear, M.
2002 Spoken dialogue technology: Enabling the conversational user interface. *ACM Computer Surveys* 34: 90–169.

Pfeiffer, T., and M. E. Latoschik
2004 Resolving object references in multimodal dialogues for immersive virtual environments. In *Proceedings of the IEEE Virtual Reality 2004,* Y. Ikei, M. Göbel, and J. Chen (eds.), 35–42. Chicago: IEEE Computer Society.

Poggi, I., and C. Pelachaud
2000 Performative facial expressions in animated faces. In *Embodied Conversational Agents,* J. Cassell, J. Sullivan, S. Prevost, and E. Churchill (eds.), 29–63. Cambridge, MA: MIT Press.

Pollack, M. E.
1990 Plans as complex mental attitudes. In *Intention in Communication,* P. R. Cohen, J. Morgan, and M. E. Pollack (eds.), 77–103. Cambridge, MA: MIT Press.
1992 The use of plans. *Artificial Intelligence*, 57: 43–68.

Rao, A., and M. Georgeff
1991 Modeling rational behavior within a BDI-architecture. In *Proceedings of the International Conference on Principles of Knowledge Representation and Planning*, J. Allen, R. Filles, and E. Sandewell (eds.): 473–484. San Mateo: Morgan Kaufmann.

Reiter, E., and R. Dale
2000 *Building Natural Language Generation Systems*, Cambridge, UK: Cambridge University Press.

Rickel, J., and W. L. Johnson
1999 Animated agents for procedural training in virtual reality: Perception, cognition, and motor control. *Applied Artificial Intelligence* 13: 343–383.

Searle, J. R.
1969 *Speech Acts: An Essay in the Philosophy of Language*. New York: Cambridge University Press.

Sidner, C. L., C. Lee, and C. Kidd
2005 Engagement during dialogues with robots. In *Conversational Informatics for Supporting Social Intelligence and Interaction*. AISB 2005 Symposium.

Strayer, S., and P. A. Heeman
2001 Reconciling initiative and discourse structure. In *Proceedings of the 2nd SIGdial Workshop*, Denmark.

Traum, D. R.
1996 Conversational agency: The TRAINS-93 dialogue manager. In *Dialogue Management in Natural Language Systems (TWENDial)*, S. Luperfoy, A. Nijholt, and G. Veldhuijzen van Zanten (eds.), 1–11. Twente: University Press.
1997 A reactive-deliberative model of dialogue agency. In *Intelligent Agents III – Proceedings of the Third International Workshop on Agent Theories, Architectures, and Languages,* J. P. Muller, M. J. Wooldridge, and N. R. Jennings (eds.), 157–171. Berlin: Springer.

Traum, D. R., and F. A. Allen
1994 Discourse obligations in dialogue processing. In *Proceedings of the 32nd Annual Meeting of the Association for Computational Linguistics*: 1–8. Las Cruces: ACL.

Traum, D., M. Fleischman, and E. Hovy
2003 NL generation for virtual humans in a complex social environment. In *Papers from AAAI 2003 Spring Symposium on Natural Language Generation in Spoken and Written Dialogue.* 151–158. Palo Alto: AAAI.

Traum, D., and S. Larsson
2003 The information state approach to dialogue management. In *Current and New Directions in Dialogue.* J. van Kuppevelt, and R. Smith (eds.), 325–353. Dordrecht: Kluwer.

Traum, D., and J. Rickel
2002 Embodied agents for multi-party dialogue in immersive virtual world. In *Proceedings of the first International Joint Conference on Autonomous Agents and Multi-agent Systems* (*AAMAS 2002*): 766–773.

Voss, I.
2003 Conceptualisation of episodes in interactive virtual construction. In *HCI International 2003 Adjunct Proceedings,* C. Stephanidis (eds.), 185–186. Iraklio: Crete University Press.

Voss, I., and I. Wachsmuth
2003 Extending long-term knowledge on the basis of episodic short-term knowledge. In *Proceedings of the EuroCogSci03,* F. Schmalhofer, R. Young, and G. Katz (eds.), 445. Hove: Erlbaum.

Winikoff M., L. Padgham, J. Harland, and J. Thangarajah
2002 Declarative and procedural goals in intelligent agent systems. In *Proceedings of the* 8th *International Conference on Principles of Knowledge Representation and Reasoning (KR2002).*

Integrated perception for cooperative human-machine interaction

Christian Bauckhage, Gernot A. Fink, Jannik Fritsch, Nils Jungclaus, Susanne Kronenberg, Franz Kummert, Frank Lömker, Gerhard Sagerer, and Sven Wachsmuth

Abstract. Interpersonal communication is characterized by the amazing performance of human cognition. While talking to each other, humans unconsciously make use of their capability to interrelate different sensory impressions. Memorizing various perceptions and learning from our experience enables us to master unknown situations. Thus, interrelated perception is a key to flexible and cooperative interaction with the environment. Human-machine communication, in contrast, is up to now restricted by many constraints specifying the ways of interaction. Even sophisticated systems lack the flexibility and ease known from everyday communication. This article presents a perceptive system that integrates automatic speech processing with image understanding and has the capability to learn. The system is intended to be an intelligent interface of a robot that is verbally instructed to manipulate objects in its surroundings. By combining statistical and declarative methods for inference and knowledge representation this perceptive system reaches a performance which outranges ordinary human-machine interaction.

1. Introduction

Traditionally, most contributions to research in artificial perception concentrate on emulating human senses separate from one another. Sophisticated interactions between different sensory perceptions are widely neglected even though they are a characteristic trait of human cognition. Yet this approach is justified since most of the problems arising in branches like computer vision, spoken language processing or machine learning are of high complexity and still require domain dependent presumptions to be manageable. However, motivated by scientific progress and the ambition to handle complex cognitive tasks, integrating different modalities for automatic perception has gained attention nowadays (cf. e.g. McKevitt 1994; Sagerer and Wachsmuth 1999).

We will present a system comprising modules for digital image and spoken language processing which is intended to be the intelligent user interface of an *artificial communicator*. This term – defined in Fink et al. (1996) – characterizes a machine that performs visual and acoustic recognition tasks and is able to combine the resulting symbolic information. Based on inference from integrated information the machine can communicate and act. Users may talk to an artificial communicator in an everyday fashion. Finally, while communicating the machine is capable to extend predefined knowledge of its surroundings.

This contribution focuses on integrated processing of diverse signals in artificial communication. Although this work emerges from a research project also attended to psychologically or cognitive inspired perceptual front-ends for intelligent machines (cf. e.g. Ackermann et al. 1997; Braun et al. 1999; Heidemann et al. 1996; Rae and Ritter 1998) we will not emphasize these issues here. Likewise, we will not discuss robotics even though the project concerns robotic aspects of cooperative human-machine interaction as well. By means of two manipulators the entire system is able to act on surrounding objects so that true cooperation with the machine is possible (Jockusch, Walter, and Ritter 1997; Zhang, von Collani, and Knoll 1999).

Due to the overwhelming complexity of human cognition artificial communicating systems still must be adapted to particular domains. Nevertheless, machines of human like skills open up interesting perspectives: learning systems with sophisticated perceptual capabilities enable intuitive interaction even for inexperienced users and they easily adjust to new tasks. Therefore, artificial communicators seem to be the natural choice in applications like for instance service robotics (cf. e.g. Baker 1998; Mittal et al. 1998). Our system aims at intelligent support for flexible assembly. It is designed to enable the cooperative construction of objects like toy-airplanes or toy-trucks using parts from a wooden construction-kit for children. This scenario allows to study the problem of integrating different types of perception. Moreover, psychological phenomena of intuitive human-machine communication can be investigated. As we will show below, these issues are manageable, regardless of their algorithmic complexity. The techniques proposed in the following point out practicable avenues towards intelligent human computer interfaces.

Before we discuss our algorithmic approaches to intelligent systems, the next section illustrates how cooperative machines may benefit from perceptive capabilities. It presents an example indicating that automatic speech and image understanding facilitate intuitive operating of assembly cells. Section 3 illustrates the architecture of our system and the data flow between its interdependent components. In Section 4 our techniques to process spontaneous German speech are presented while Section 5 deals with computer vision aspects concerning our application. The integration of information obtained by speech and image processing is discussed in Section 6. A summary and some concluding remarks close this contribution.

2. A performance example

In order to emphasize the potential of intuitive human-machine interaction let us first consider an experiment carried out with our system. Besides introducing common problems in integrated speech and image understanding the experiment illustrated in Figure 1 characterizes the current performance of the system. The example reflects the systems competence in speech understanding, scene interpretation, and learning of new objects.

In Figure 1 every row of pictures shows: A view during an exemplary assembly process, a corresponding abstract representation, an instruction to initiate an assembly action, and the reaction of the system, respectively. The images of consecutive intermediate steps of the construction process depicted in the first column are labeled with the results from an object recognition process which maps symbolic identifiers to certain regions of an image. The virtual objects displayed in the second column are arranged according to rough estimates of the positions of objects detected in the scene (a detailed description of the visualization tool is given in Jung, Hoffhenke, and Wachsmuth, 1998). Whenever the instructions in the third column – it contains German expressions and their English translations – require the manipulation of an object the corresponding virtual object is highlighted in the fourth column. Finally, the lowermost image in this column shows a screenshot of an automatically detected assembly structure.

The course of this sample experiment is subdivided into five consecutive stages:

1. Initially, a couple of objects are spread arbitrarily within the sensory range of the system. Among the elementary parts there is an assembly for which a structural description is derived automatically. In order to start the process of construction the system is instructed to `"take the bar in front of the assembly"`. Note that the bar is indicated using a spatial relation so that processes of image and speech understanding have to be linked in order to identify the object specified by the user. As the perceptive system alone can not express its conclusions in terms of ac-

tions the representation of the scene is used to visualize the internal state of the system: the bar that corresponds to the instruction is highlighted.

2. Manually removing the bar from the scene results in the situation shown in the first image of the second row. In order to indicate that the system has noticed the disappearance of the bar and believes it to be grasped by a robotic manipulator the bar is virtually lifted up. Now the system is told

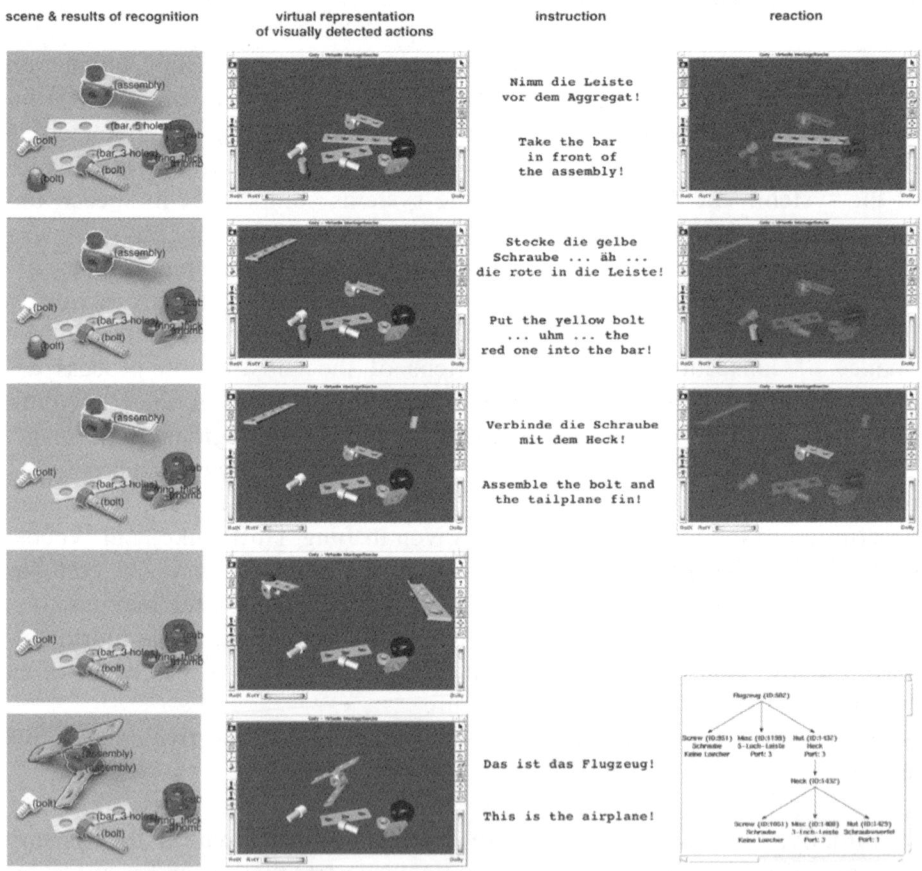

Figure 1. Visualization of the course of an experiment demonstrating integrated speech and image understanding. First column: the observed scene together with results of a visual object recognition procedure. Second column: a virtual representation of the observed scene. Third column: spoken commands to instruct the system. Fourth column: the corresponding reaction to the instructions of the user.

to "`put the yellow bolt ... uhm ... the red one into the bar`". Again, only image and speech understanding in combination can produce an accurate behavior. Additionally, a verbal correction which is a familiar phenomenon in spoken language has to be resolved correctly.

3. After the intended bolt was identified and manually removed from the scene its virtual counterpart is lifted up. Remember that the system is designed to support a two handed manipulator. However, there is no camera monitoring the manipulator so that it is impossible to observe object manipulations in detail. Consequently, at this stage of the experiment the system supposes the disappeared bolt to be in the second hand of the manipulator. Now the user tells the system to "`assemble the bolt and the tailplane fin`". Except of the acoustic model used for word recognition no knowledge of tailplane fins is modeled in the system. But since there is a complex object in the scene which could have an abstract meaning, the system concludes that the user is referring to the assembly. Due to this implicit name designation the structural description of the assembly is labeled as a tailplane fin and can be denominated accordingly in subsequent steps of the experiment.
4. Then, taking the course of the construction into account and using its knowledge of the dialog history, the system infers that the bar in the one hand of the manipulator has to be put onto the bolt in the other hand. This inference is logically consistent because there must be an empty hand that may grasp the tailplane fin. The systems conclusion is illustrated in the second image of the fourth row where the bolt and the bar are virtually put together and the assembly is lifted up. Note that the depicted mating relation of the bar and the bolt must not correspond to reality. It just visualizes the systems conception of what is going on.
5. In the final step of this experiment the user assembles all three objects and puts the resulting assembly back into the scene. By means of the procedure to recognize the structure of assembled objects together with knowledge of observed assembly operations the system generates an assembly plan and rebuilds the assembly virtually. Finally, reminiscent of our scenario the explicit information that "`this is an airplane`" causes the system to label the structural description respectively (see the lowermost image in the fourth column).

As this example underlines it is possible to instruct our system in a way that resembles interpersonal conversation. Generally, a user can refer to objects using their visual features or their relative position. Corrections may be used, natural pronunciation and hesitations do not disturb the speech understanding processes. Another feature not exemplified above is the capability to resolve ambiguities in spoken instructions by visually analyzing the surroundings. If an instruction can not be disambiguated the system is able to ask for further information or more detailed instructions. Thus, intuitive operating of the system is possible; if necessary one has to reformulate an instruction to achieve the desired action. This, however, can be done in a conversational manner and does not require special experience.

Our techniques to gain this integrated performance as well as the underlying concepts of system design and interaction are explained in the following.

3. System architecture

Architecture is one of the key issues in intelligent system design. Systems dealing with different types of signals being generated at different time scales require carefull organization of processing components to guarantee fast and consistent reactions. Well known approaches to this problem are for instance behavior-based realizations, agent-based concepts, or blackboard architectures (cf. e.g. Arkin 1998; Bradshaw 1997; Engelmore and Morgan 1988, respectively). Our system is based on both hierarchical and distributed representations of knowledge sources and thus cannot be categorized into one of these paradigms.

3.1. Module interaction

According to the perceptive capabilities our system consists of different components performing thc necessary computations. As shown in Figure 2 the individual modules are arranged as two tracks of speech processing and image understanding units converging in an integrating component.
Given an acoustic signal the left track starts with a speech recognition procedure. The corresponding results are transferred to an interpretation module whose results are used in a component controlling the dialog with a user.

In the image understanding track an object recognition procedure is used to recognize elementary objects of our scenario. Stereo image data allows to estimate the spatial position and orientation of detected elements. This information is monitored over time so that the system can determine if and how objects in its surroundings are moved. The memorized object data is passed on threefold: first, it is scanned by a process that detects and describes assembly structures. Secondly, it is used to detect basic construction actions. Thirdly, the memorized objects are sent to the module interrelating the perceptive modalities. In the component labeled *fusion* the assembly structures extracted from action detection and assembly recognition are fused yielding assembly plans that are stored in a database.

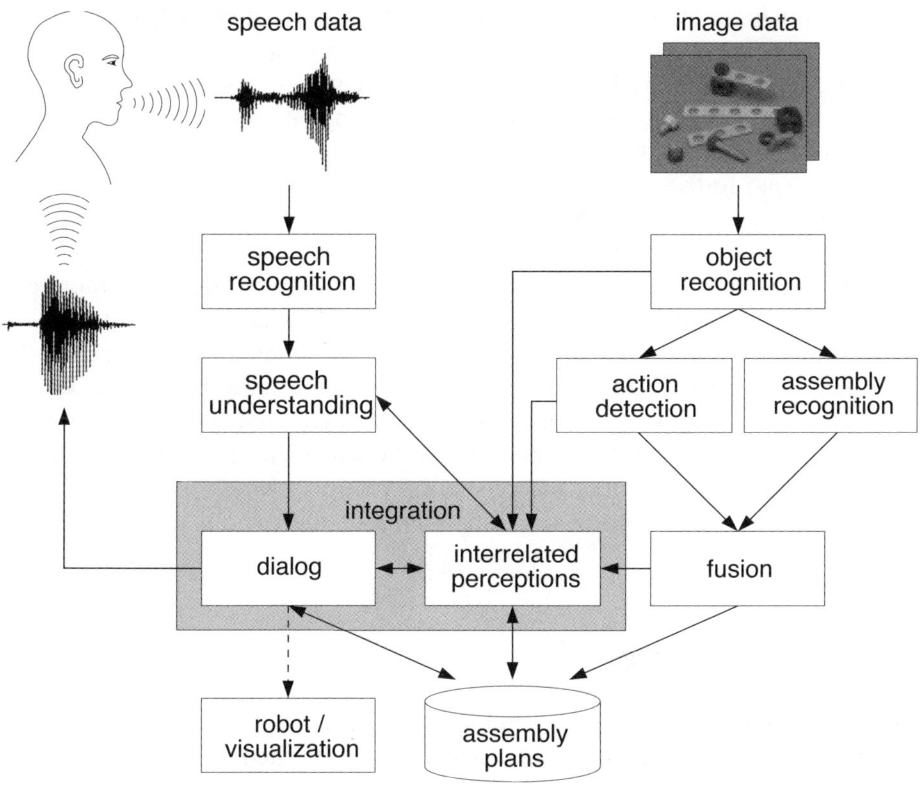

Figure 2. Module interaction in the proposed system architecture

Integration of different perceptive modalities is the main aspect of our system. Accordingly, the module that interrelates results from speech and vision processing plays a central role providing the system with related acoustic and visual information. The interrelation module uses the database to retrieve an intended assembly given an abstract name. Explicit and implicit naming of assemblies is realized via connections from the dialog module and the interrelation module to the database, respectively.

3.2. Distributed development environment

As an integrated architecture comprising many computationally demanding sub-tasks can never be realized in a monolithic system a distributed processing approach has to be adopted.

Although there are many concepts of distributed system design they all suffer from inherent limitations when applied to problems of multi-modal signal analysis. Therefore, a new and simple but powerful framework to integrate large distributed pattern analysis systems was proposed: DACS, the Distributed Applications Communication System (Fink et al. 1995).

A communication demon on each participating machine acts as a router for all internal traffic and establishes connections to demons on remote machines. Communication is based on simple asynchronous message passing with some extensions to handle dynamic reconfigurations of the system during runtime. On top of this elementary layer DACS provides some more advanced communication semantics like synchronous and asynchronous remote procedure calls and *demand streams*. The latter allow to set up the data-driven computations in the lower level vision and speech processing modules easily in just the same way as a producer-consumer interaction. Resources generated by some module can be accessed via a symbolic name transparently by any number of consuming modules which in turn can offer their processing results to other components of the overall distributed system.

4. Speech and language

Traditional approaches to speech understanding suffer from two severe limitations: first, speech understanding usually is subdivided into two processing steps, namely speech recognition yielding hypothesized word sequences and a subsequent interpretation of these results. Therefore, no influence of the linguistic knowledge on the recognition can be exploited. Secondly, in most systems the accepted language is rather restricted so that phenomena found in spontaneous speech are neglected in modeling and therefore inevitably lead to processing errors.

Our approach tries to overcome these limitations by using an integrated processing of *all* knowledge sources and an explicit modeling of relevant spontaneous speech phenomena on the acoustic as well as on the language level.

4.1. Integrated recognition and understanding

The principle idea of the proposed approach is to use a vertical organization of knowledge representation and integrated processing in order to overcome the drawbacks of the traditional horizontal architecture. The resulting tight coupling of speech recognition and understanding is shown in Figure 3.

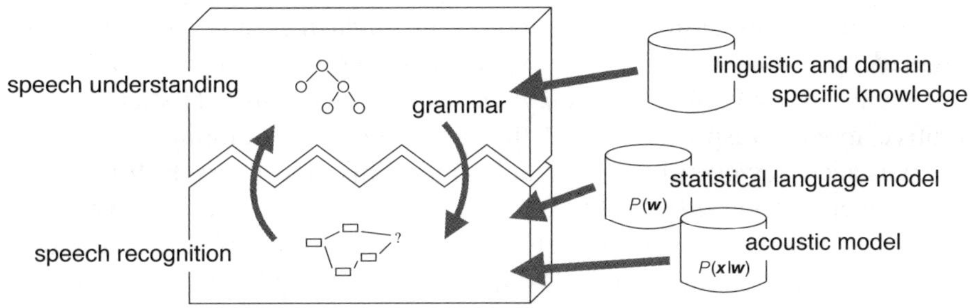

Figure 3. Overview of the integrated speech interpretation

The recognition process is directly influenced by the linguistic and domain-specific knowledge. Rather than hypothesizing isolated words only, hypotheses for domain-dependent constituents are generated that can easily be combined to form linguistic interpretations.

The proposed integrated architecture makes use of an enhanced statistical speech recognizer as a baseline module (Fink 1999). For developing recognition systems the overwhelming success of statistical methods within the past decade has established a quasi-standard approach. Its core technologies are Hidden-Markov-Models for describing acoustic events and statistical language models for providing estimates about word sequences likely to occur in a given domain. The goal of the recognition process is to find the word sequence $\hat{\mathbf{w}}$ that maximizes the probability of the combined statistical model given the observed acoustic data $\mathbf{x}$ according to:

$$\hat{\mathbf{w}} = \arg\max_{\mathbf{w}} P(\mathbf{w}) P(\mathbf{x} \mid \mathbf{w})$$

In the above equation $P(\mathbf{w})$ denotes the language model probability for the word sequence $\mathbf{w}$ and $P(\mathbf{x}|\mathbf{w})$ the probability of observing this word sequence as speech data $\mathbf{x}$ according to the acoustic model (cf. e.g. Jelinek 1997; Ney and Ortmanns 1999).

Though statistical language models are very successful in large vocabulary speech recognition they can not be used to convey linguistic structures of language and suffer from the need for huge amounts of training material. Especially for artificial domains as our construction scenario where domain specific data is scarce statistical language models can not demonstrate their full potential properly. Therefore, it is desirable to apply declarative language constraints, that can be specified by experts rather easily, in an equally robust manner as statistical ones during the recognition process. We developed a special coupling of a parsing component and the recognizer that enables us to exploit grammar restrictions in much the same way as scores provided by a statistical model. Experiments showed that comparable improvements in recognition accuracy can be obtained with statistical and declarative models respectively and that an appropriate combination of both improves accuracy even further (Wachsmuth, Fink, and Sagerer 1998).

However, it should be emphasized that this use of a grammar during the recognition process does not merely act as a special kind of language model. As speech understanding also relies on structures being built from sequences of word hypotheses an appropriate application specific design of the grammar can provide useful intermediate interpretation hypotheses directly. Therefore, the speech recognizer generates hypotheses about domain-specific constituents and not simply sequences of word hypotheses.

The higher-level analysis of these elementary interpretation hypotheses is performed within a semantic network using the ERNEST network language (Sagerer and Niemann 1997). From the baseline hypotheses semantic features are extracted and domain-specific interpretation frames are filled according to certain application dependent rules (Brandt-Pook et al. 1999).

As the integrated speech processing is embedded in a multi-modal environment it is highly desirable that results can be obtained already during the production of an utterance. Therefore, both the recognition and the understanding module process speech input *incrementally*. For the acoustic recognition a method for producing final recognition results with some delay to the time-synchronous processing was proposed in Fink et al. (1998). Incremental interpretation is then achieved by applying combination rules between internal semantic representations and domain-specific constituents as soon as these are hypothesized by the recognizer (Brandt-Pook et al. 1999).

4.2. Handling spontaneous speech phenomena

Humans interacting with multi-modal systems cannot be expected to always adhere to certain rules of communication. Therefore, in a robust system the speech processing modules have to be able to cope with spontaneous speech input which largely deviates from speech read from e.g. text prompts or used in a dictation task. Especially clear pronunciation, vocabulary limitations, and restrictions in language use can never be enforced.

Consequently, acoustic models for spontaneous speech phenomena as so called *human noises* (e.g. breathing or lip smacks) and hesitations (like e.g. `uhm` in the example of Fig. 1) are part of the recognition lexicon. Though there has been some progress recently, the detection of *out-of-vocabulary* words can still not be performed robustly on the level of acoustic recognition. Therefore, we employ a recognition lexicon which exceeds the one used by the understanding component but covers all lexical items frequently found in our corpus of human-human and human-machine dialogs.

In spontaneous German speech there are hardly any restrictions about the order of constituents within an utterance. Therefore, the grammar used jointly by the recognizer as a kind of language model and by the understanding component to build up semantic structures does not contain structural descriptions of complete sentences from the language fragment investigated. Rather only smaller domain-specific linguistic constituents are modeled that are allowed to occur in any order within an utterance.

Syntactic phenomena frequently found in spontaneous German speech are repairs and extrapositions in which information given in one constituent is specified or corrected by subsequent material. As mentioned above only domain specific constituents are derived without any restriction on their order. Consequently, it is necessary to resolve repairs and extrapositions by inferring the possible references between both participating constituents. The resolution of repairs and extrapositions is threefold: first, based on the syntactic structure of the utterance possible repairs or extrapositions have to be detected. Secondly, a suitable reference constituent must be identified, i.e. an antecedent constituent of the utterance which can be specified or corrected by the subsequent material. Thirdly, the antecedent utterance has to be re-interpreted due to the subsequent material. This final interpretation is derived by integrating the subsequent material into the reference constituent (Kronenberg and Kummert 1999b). An example of a correction is given by the second utterance of Figure 1. The integration of the correcting constituent `"the red one"` into the antecedent utterance `"Take the yellow bolt"` leads to the re-interpretation `"Take the red bolt"`. Not indented processing results can occur if this integration process adds contradictory information to the reference constituent. To avoid these overgeneralizations visual context information is integrated into the parsing process by using the techniques to interrelate different perceptions described in Section 6. The computational framework for the derivation of repairs and extrapositions is based on a LR(1)-parser and a unification grammar. Both, the LR(1)-parser and the unification framework, are modified to handle spontaneous speech (Kronenberg and Kummert 1999a). These modifications lead to a processing model which is robust to out-of-vocabulary words, to speech recognition errors due to morphologically similar words, and to deletions of function words.

5. Objects, assemblies and actions

It is widely agreed that sight is the most important of the human senses. Correspondingly, investigating computer vision has a long tradition in artificial intelligence research (cf. e.g. Ballard and Brown 1982). Using computer vision to monitor assembly, however, is scarcely explored by now and remains an interesting topic of research.

5.1. Object recognition in image sequences

Computer vision knows two principle approaches to object recognition. Appearance-based approaches like template matching, eigenspace projection, color histograms, or receptive field histograms work well on isolated objects or properly segmented images (cf. e.g. Schiele and Crowley 1996; Swain and Ballard 1991; Turk and Pentland 1991). But due to their global features they have problems with partially occluded objects and cluttered images. On the other side, feature-based approaches calculate essential local descriptors which should be invariant to affine and perspective transformations, to view point changes, or to different illumination conditions (cf. e.g. Mundy and Zisserman 1992; Reiss 1993; Wang and Healey 1996). The problem here is to find appropriate invariants which are sufficiently discriminatory to allow a reliable object recognition.

To recognize elementary objects of the construction-kit we use local features calculated on the basis of regions of homogeneous color. Therefore, a polynomial classifier maps the YUV-values of each image pixel onto one of the fundamental colors that may occur in our domain. Then regions of identical color are segmented and their boundaries are approximated by a polygon and appropriate features like compactness or eccentricity are calculated.

The recognition process uses explicit object models which are represented by the semantic network language ERNEST (Sagerer and Niemann 1997). Objects are modeled by their parts and are embedded in a specialization hierarchy. A bar, for instance, is a generalization of three-holed-bar. Each concept of the network has attributes like color or form parameters with admissible ranges for their values. To start the recognition process a rule based classifier calculates up to three competing object hypotheses for each image region (this is a simplified version of a hybrid approach combining neural networks and ERNEST; CF. Heidemann et al., 1996). The object hypotheses are stored in competing search tree nodes and are verified or rejected according to the structural knowledge represented in the semantic network subsequently. In this instantiation process restrictions for position, color, and shape are propagated in a model-driven way (Kummert et al. 1998).

Although this detection of objects is very efficient it is needless to process every image of a sequence that way. Usually, changes in subsequent images are small even if objects or the camera were moved. Features like position or shape may change but structural relations among parts of objects are preserved. Therefore, we use the structural information represented in structured instances of the semantic network as an expectation for the next image. This requires establishing temporal relations between analysis results. This is done by a memory process that computes matches between image regions through time (Kummert et al. 1998). Given such correspondences, previously generated structures are used to calculate bottom-up valid instances without any search effort. These efficiently calculated instances also reflect changes due to moving objects or an active camera. If new objects appear in the scene they are initially processed by the strategy outlined above, afterwards the propagation strategy can be applied.

In order to enable a robot to approach an object of interest (using the robot's hand camera for grasping), we realized a coarse but efficient 3D-reconstruction. Objects detected in stereo images are matched and based on calibration data a depth value for each object's center of mass is calculated. The orientation of an object is estimated by aligning the main axes of the detected objects and the main axes of corresponding models.

5.2. Recognition of assembled objects

Throughout the past decade there was extensive research in assembly modeling for sequence planning and monitoring. Familiar approaches rely on graph based techniques, on geometric modeling, or on semantic decompositions (cf. e.g. Chakrabarty and Wolter 1997; Homem de Mello and Sanderson 1990; Rabemanantsoa and Pierre 1996, respectively). Known approaches to assembly observation rely on geometric object models. Consequently, their recognition capabilities depend on particularly exact measurements as provided by laser-range-finders (Ikeuchi and Suehiro 1994; Miura and Ikeuchi 1998) or – if using vision – they are restricted to block world objects (Tung and Kak 1996). To accomplish visual assembly recognition in our scenario we use syntactic models to represent assembled objects. This approach is reasonable since mechanical assemblies are highly structured objects and it applies to any type of complex objects (Bauckhage et al. 2000).

A syntactic representation of bolted assemblies is based on the following considerations: a bolted assembly necessarily consists of a bolt and a nut. Optionally, these parts may fix some miscellaneous objects like bars or rings. All three components, however, are either given by elementary objects or by subassemblies. These observations lead to the cyclic model depicted in Figure 4.

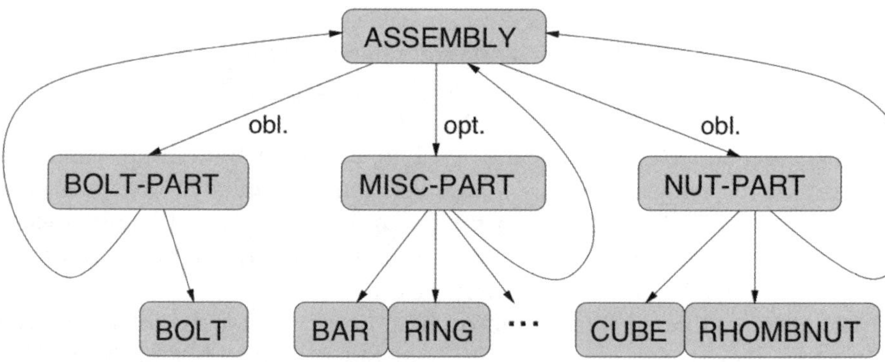

Figure 4. Recursive model of bolted assemblies: Bolt- and nut-part are obligatory components, the misc-part is optional. All three parts either consist of elementary objects or of assemblies.

Implementing this model as a semantic network using ERNEST, and analyzing clusters of detected elementary objects allows to derive structural descriptions of assembled objects as shown in Figure 5 (Bauckhage, Kummert, and Sagerer 1998). The structure in this figure describes the object called `"airplane"` assembled in the introductory example; it consists of a bolt, a bar and a complex nut which represents the `"tailplane fin"`. Moreover, examining the topological appearance of a cluster of objects yields detailed information about the mating relations among the objects. These relations specify which holes of a bar or a cube are occupied by bolts. Therefore, structural descriptions supplemented by mating relations enable the generation of assembly sequence plans (Bauckhage, Kummert, and Sagerer 1999). The system employs these plans to virtually reconstruct assemblies detected in an image (see second column of Fig. 1).

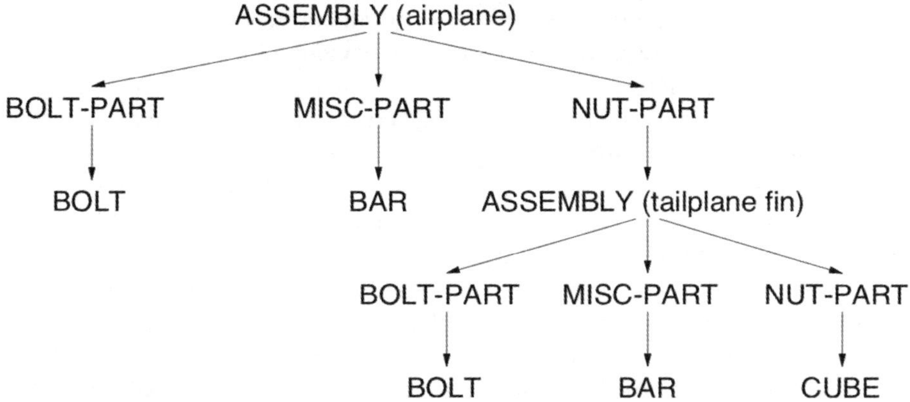

Figure 5. A structural description according to the recursive model in Figure 4. It describes the assembly constructed in the introductory example.

The performance in assembly recognition is influenced by two factors: if the input, i.e. results from elementary object recognition, is of poor quality, correct results simply cannot be produced. Furthermore, if the task is difficult, because, for instance, objects are perspectively occluded, wrong results are very likely. Figure 6 shows how the correctness of results depends on the difficulty of the task. To produce this figure 163 images of assemblies were categorized into 10 classes of difficulty. For some of the images the results from elementary object recognition were corrected manually so that in this experiment the input data always was correct. The difficulty of a task was assessed by a fuzzy function depending on the four parameters *number of visible parts in the assembly*, *number of visible bolts*, *mean number of adjacent objects*, and *mean degree of perspective occlusion*. Obviously, the correctness of results decreases with an increasing complexity (note that for difficulties of 0.0 and 0.9 no examples were in the test set). The next subsection presents a method to incorporate process knowledge in order to cope with this phenomenon.

5.3. Detection of assembly operations

The previously presented image-based recognition of assemblies reaches best performance if all single objects are visible and recognized correctly. Due to perspective occlusions these prerequisites cannot be guaranteed for all objects within a complex assembly. Consequently, incomplete assembly structures may be generated. Therefore, we developed a second method to extract assembly structures by observing the construction process leading to an assembly. As the visual observation of actions is computationally expensive and difficult, we currently use symbolic information about the temporal changes of objects, i.e. new objects being put into the scene and disappeared objects being taken out of the scene, to infer actions (Bauckhage et al. 1999). Therefore, our monitoring approach is independent from whether a human or a robot acts in the scene and can reuse results from object recognition that are available anyway since they are needed by other modules, e.g. assembly recognition. Integrating a visual action recognition would demand much more computational power without gaining substantial benefit except for actions which are independent of object changes (e.g. *Connect* action, see below).

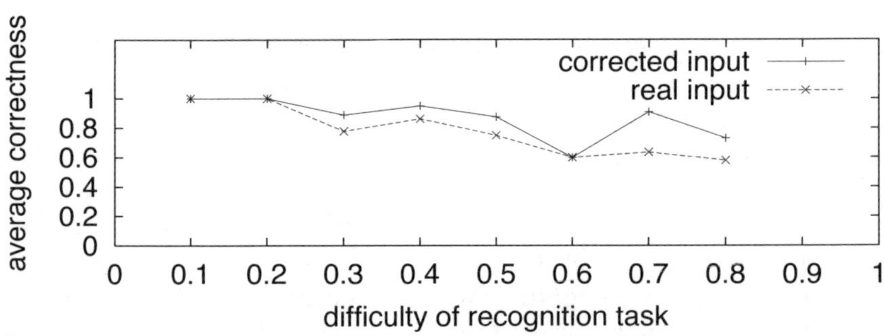

Figure 6. Correctness of the results yielded by the assembly recognition method measured by means of 163 examples from different categories of complexity

A two-hand model is used to reflect the actual contents of the hands which are usually outside the field of view. Based on the state of the two-hand model and information about new and disappeared objects the three relevant actions shown in Figure 7 can be inferred. Adopting the notation from planning literature the figure indicates the necessary preconditions to detect actions and the state changes of the two-hand model respectively.

The *Connect* action is not observable because assembling objects does not lead to new or disappeared objects in the scene. Therefore, this action can only be inferred if the next *Take* action has happened which lead to the disappearance of the next object.

Because our approach only uses symbolic information about new and disappeared objects to detect actions, we need to make the following assumptions:

- Each hand can hold one object or one (partial) assembly.
- Objects may only be put down in the visible scene.
- New objects may only be put into the scene if no similar objects are in the hands of the constructor.

Take X	
Preconditions:	hand: empty ∧ X on_table ∧ X -> disappeared
Effects:	hand: X ∧ ¬ (X on_table)
Connect X Y	
Preconditions:	hand_1: X (BOLT_PART) ∧ hand_2: Y (MISC_PART ∨ NUT_PART)
Effects:	hand_1: XY ∧ hand_2: empty
Put down X	
Preconditions:	hand: X ∧ X -> new
Effects:	hand: empty ∧ X on_table

Figure 7. The preconditions to infer actions based on symbolic changes of objects and the resulting effects on the two-hand model. The notation hand_1 and hand_2 indicates the two different hand states but does not denote a specific hand or manipulator.

After a sequence of construction actions has been detected one state of the two-hand model contains the structure of the assembly. While this information is quite reliable regarding the object types and their order in the constructed assembly, the connection details are unknown due to the missing visual observation. After placing the assembly back into the scene, the visual assembly recognition obtains a second assembly structure including connection details, but here some parts may be missing due to visual occlusion. By fusing the two assembly structures tiny objects which are occluded in the image of the assembly can be inserted into the final assembly structure as they are contained in the assembly structure from action detection.

6. Interrelated perceptions and dialog

In the two preceding sections we have presented the speech and vision modules of our system. These modules extract interpretations of utterances and structural descriptions of objects from the input signal. To perform construction tasks as introduced in section 2 a dialog with an instructor must be enabled and his verbal instructions must be executed. Therefore, links between the analyzed speech and objects in the scene must be established. In this section we describe two modules responsible for this, the *interrelated perception* and the *dialog* component.

6.1. Interrelating speech and vision

Linking language and vision has a history since the innovating work of Winograd (1973) and Waltz (1981). Jackendoff (1987) has postulated an integration framework based on the conceptual and 3-D vision level. Such classical approaches combine both perceptive modalities on a symbolic logical level which may be enriched by a complete 3-D representation of a recognized object. Current research aims at drawing referential links between speech and image interpretations on a level closer to the signal (Roy and Pentland 1998) and at using sophisticated models of uncertainty (Nagel 1999).

A multi-modal interaction scheme of an artificial communicator as described in this article has to take different kinds of uncertainty into account: categorical uncertainties, e.g. which object classes are called `"thick"`, which directions are called `"in front of"`, and perceptive uncertainties, e.g. erroneous classification results of the vision components or the speech recognizer. Therefore, all information provided by the speech and image processing modules is assumed to be generated by a stochastic process which is modeled by a Bayesian network (Wachsmuth and Sagerer 1999).

In order to compute the mapping between objects referenced in an instruction and objects perceived in the scene, we propose a multi-layered representation of the vision results. In Figure 8 an example of such a *scene graph* is shown. Two complementary aspects are represented in this scene graph:

1. An instructor of the system can denote an *intended object* (*IO*) by specifying qualities of the visual appearance of an object class, like type,

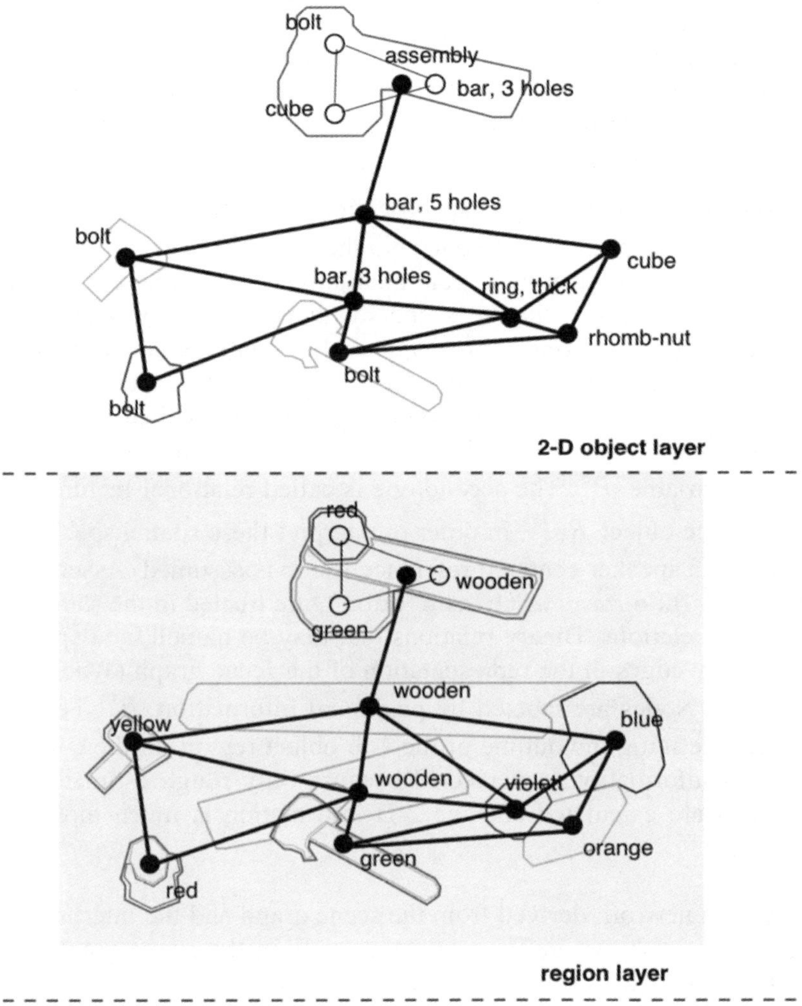

Figure 8. Multi-layer representation of the scene (see Fig. 1 first column). Nodes are labeled by object features. Edges define relations between objects which will be possibly references by a speaker. Note that there is a top down influence of the 2-D object layer on the definition of relevant regions which constitute a node in the scene graph. Bolts consist of a colored head and a wooden thread. Both regions are merged by the object recognizer and a color attribute is newly assigned. Assembled objects are defined by a merged region but do not have a color attribute. The subsumed elementary objects are represented in a subgraph associated with the assembly node.

color, shape, or size. In the scene representation, the same object class is described by a color attribute on the region layer and a type attribute on the object layer. Unknown objects are represented by a homogeneously colored region without a type label assigned. The verbal and visual observations are subsequently denoted by random variables: F_{ij}^{S} models the *j*-th quality of the *i*-th object specification in an utterance, and F_{kl}^{V} models the *l*-th feature of the *k*-th object in the scene.

2. Additionally, the instructor can qualitatively describe the spatial arrangement of objects in the scene by unary spatial propositions, like `"take the left one"`, or binary spatial relations between the intended object and the *i*-th *reference object* (RO_i), e.g. `"the bar in front of the assembly"`. The first one is subsequently called positional feature of the *i*-th object specification in an utterance and is denoted by a random variable P_i^S. The second one is called relational feature of the *i*-th reference object Rel_i^S. In order to interpret these spatial specifications, currently, a speaker centered reference frame is assumed. Assembly relations, like `"the bar with the cube"`, are treated in the same manner as spatial relations. Binary relations that may be named by a speaker are denoted by edges in the representation of the scene graph (Wachsmuth et al. 1999). Nodes are labeled by positional information P_k^V, i.e. the 2-D polygon defining the outline of the *k*-th object region. In the current system 3-D information is neglected because only rough estimates of 3-D positions are calculated and the 2-D information is much more precise and stable.

The Bayesian network derived from the scene graph and the interpretation of an instruction is shown in Figure 9. Any node in the scene graph and any object mentioned in an utterance correspond to a subnet in the Bayesian network which integrates all visual/speech evidences of the different layers. An additional random variable C_k^V is introduced which models all possible object classes of the *k*-th visual object in the scene. The edges of the graphical model are labeled by conditional probabilities which either have been estimated from data collected in psycholinguistic experiments (cf. Socher, Sagerer, and Perona 1998), $P(F_{ij}^S \mid C_k^V)$, from hand labeled test sets, $P(F_{kl}^V \mid C_k^V)$, or have been derived based on computational models (Wachsmuth et al. 1999), $P(Rel_i \mid P_{k_{io}}^V, P_{k_{ro}}^V), P(P_i^S \mid P_k^V)$.

"Please, take [the round red object]$_0$ left to [the short bolt]$_1$."

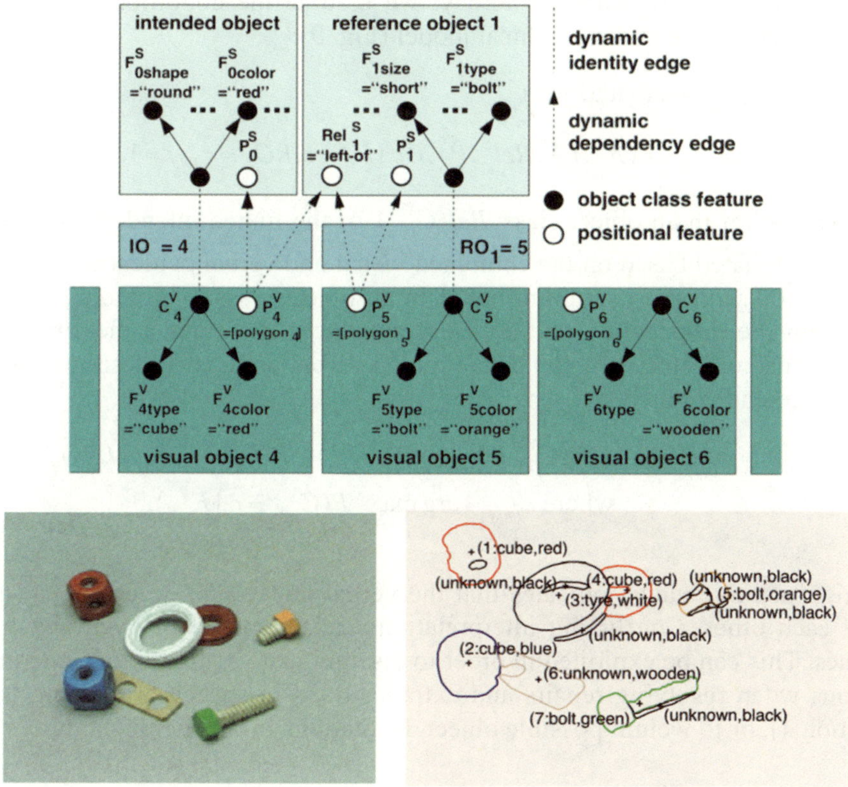

Figure 9. Graphical model of the probabilistic interaction scheme: the resulting mapping of a typical instruction and scene interpretation is shown. The red rim left to the orange bolt is wrongly classified as a cube. The bar obtained no type label and is interpreted as an unknown wooden object. Unknown black regions are assumed to represent shadows and are subsequently ignored. Due to the estimated conditional probabilities, the system knows that orange bolts are short, rims are round, and that rims are wrongly classified mostly as cubes. Therefore, it can infer the intended object correctly even though the decision is based on erroneous data.

The Bayesian network is evaluated in the following way (in order to simplify the notation of the following equations, variable names with *S* indices denote sets of random variables, e.g. $F_0^S = \{F_{0j}^S \mid j = 1 \ldots k\}$):

1. The most probable explanation, consisting of the intended visual object i and the used reference objects $r_1 \ldots r_m$, is calculated which is explaining the observed evidences. Thereby, we assume the conditional independencies shown in the graphical model (Fig. 9):

$$io^V = \arg\max_{i} \max_{r_1 \ldots r_m} P(F^S, F^V, Rel^S, P^S, P^V \mid IO = i, RO_j = r_j, j = 1 \ldots m)$$

2. The belief in an object class $Bel(C^V_{io^V})$ of the linked intended object io^V is calculated based on the combined visual and verbal evidences. A comparison with the maximum belief in an object class, which only results from the propagation of the visual evidences, provides a measurement for the consistency (*cons*) of the joined verbal and visual descriptions of the intended object.

$$cons(io^V) = P(C^V_{io^V} = c_{max} \mid F^V_{io^V}, F^S_0) - P(C^V_{io^V} = c_{max} \mid F^V_{io^V})$$
$$\text{where } c_{max} = \arg\max_{c} P(C^V_{io^V} = c \mid F^V_{io^V}).$$

A high positive value indicates that the verbal and visual descriptions support each other. Conflicting interpretations cause smaller or even negative values. This can be exploited in order to disambiguate contradictory interpretations when resolving repairs and extrapositions in speech processing (see Section 4), or to weight possible object denotations in the dialog module.

6.2. Dialog

In the last years, many spoken dialog systems have been developed in areas such as travel information service, conference registration, restaurant guide, or reservation service (c.f. e.g. den Os et al. 1999; Eckert et al. 1993; Rudnicky et al. 1999; Seneff and Polifroni 1996; Woszczyna et al. 1993). However, most of these systems are restricted to the utilization of speech input, so that no other perceptive modality can be exploited. In contrast to these approaches our dialog module must integrate utterances of the instructor, information of the visible scene, and messages from the manipulator to realize a natural, flexible and robust dialog strategy.

Our dialog module is realized within the semantic network language ERNEST (Sagerer and Niemann 1997) using the dialog model shown in Figure 10. The model is based on an investigation of a corpus of human-human and simulated human-machine dialogs. Every path through the model reflects one course of a possible human-machine dialog. The dialog starts with a greeting of the module and ends, if the instructor indicates the end of the assembly process. As an admissible sequence of the intermediate states is nearly unrestricted, the dialog behavior is very natural and robust (Brand-Pook et al. 1999).

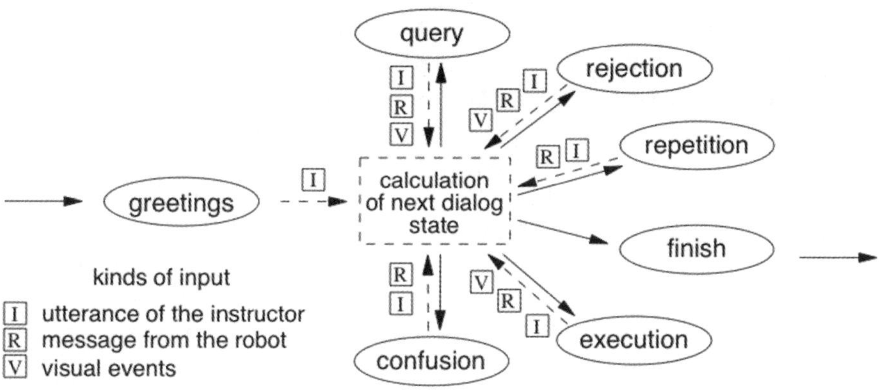

Figure 10. Model of the human-machine communication

State transitions are initiated if new information from the instructor or the robotics, if it is connected to the system, is available. Currently, we also integrate events from the action detection into the activation of state transitions. The box in the center symbolizes the state transition function, which analyses the new information and combines it with the current dialog context and information gathered from the integration module to select the next state.

In the state *query* the dialog asks for a more exact object denotation, if competing or uncertain results arrive from the integration module. Of course, the instructor is not forced to answer the question. As nearly every state transition is allowed, the instructor can give a completely new instruction. If the system should perform an action, e.g. grasping an object, and all necessary information is gathered the state *execution* is selected. If the robotic component is connected to the system, the analyzed representation of the action including the relevant objects detected in the scene are forwarded to this module. Otherwise the action is visualized as shown in the example in Figure 1. The bottom line of the system is to continue the dialog in every situation. This is realized via the states *rejection*, *repetition* and *confusion*. Actions which cannot be executed are immediately rejected. If the analysis of a verbal instruction failed completely, the dialog verbalizes this failure and asks for a repetition of that utterance. If the dialog has gathered completely contradictory information it expresses its confusion and asks for a totally new instruction.

7. Discussion

The joint processing of different perceptional modalities and the capability to learn are characteristic traits of human cognition. These capabilities shape the way we interact. Since machines usually lack these capabilities, human-machine interaction requires special experience and is rarely intuitive. Thus, human-machine interaction benefits from constructing intelligent systems with integrated perceptive capabilities.

7.1. Summary

We presented an artificial communicator designed to behave cooperatively in order to support flexible assembly. The system understands spontaneous German speech; integrating statistical speech recognition performed by Hidden-Markov-Models and knowledge based speech understanding overcomes the limitations of traditional speech processing. LR(1)-parsing based on a unification grammar allows to resolve repairs and extrapositions. Domain specific knowledge encoded in semantic networks enables to recognize objects and assemblies in image data. A rule based algorithm monitors basic assembly operations, fusing these with structural descriptions of recognized assemblies yields assembly sequence plans.

A Bayesian network integrates results from speech and image understanding. The system can learn names of complex objects, it applies robust dialog strategies, and can ask to resolve ambiguities. Due to this scheme of integrated signal processing, a user may refer to objects in the scene as he would do in interpersonal communication and intuitive interaction is possible. A virtual reality tool is used to visualize the system's conception of its surroundings. The different modules realizing all these features are organized as a distributed system, thus making it possible to exploit the computing power of workstation clusters to speed up processing.

7.2. Performance

Experiments have proven the usability of the system and justified our algorithmic approaches. While a quantitative evaluation of an integrated system is difficult, algorithms solving isolated tasks like speech understanding or object recognition can be rated easily. Separately evaluating the modules yielded a word accuracy of 71% for spontaneous speech recognition and a totally correct constituent accuracy of 61% and a partially correct constituent accuracy of 11%. Object recognition accomplishes 92% and assembly detection yields 80% correctness. For the interrelated perception component an accuracy of 87% was obtained. Further details on the evaluation can be found in Fink (1999); Wachsmuth, Fink, and Sagerer (1998); Brandt-Pook et al. (1999); Fink et al. (1998); Kronenberg and Kummert (1999a); Kummert et al. (1998). The module interactions and their processing times are described in more detail in Fink et. al (2006).

Beyond evaluating the accuracy and processing time of individual modules, however, no off-the-shelf technology is available yet to assess the overall performance of integrated systems with sophisticated perceptive capabilities. Some authors argue that experiments demonstrating complex systems running are sufficient to legitimate the applied techniques (Tung and Kak 1996). We adopt this point of view, since it corresponds to what is known as *end-to-end evaluation* (Bub and Schwinn 1996).

Table 1. Summary of experimental interactions with the system.

Experimental Setting				Results			
#Participants	#Objects in Scene	#Objects in Assembly	#Bolts in Assembly	Time[s] / # Subjects	# Instructions / # Subjects	# eff. Instr. / # Subjects	Success Rate
9	8	2	1	107	3.0	2.1	89%
8	10	2	1	81	3.0	2.2	100%
7	8	3	2	180	6.0	3.7	57%
8	10	4	2	216	8.6	4.8	88%
4	8	5	3	420	10.7	7.7	75%
6	10	6	3	503	15.8	10.0	83%
							average 82%

The visual and acoustic signals that must be interpreted in our scenario vary considerably. Objects are situated arbitrarily, the user is free to choose his instructions, and human-machine dialogs evolve randomly. Thus, every component of the system induces uncertainty to the interpretation of the surroundings. Erroneous results from lower level modules cause erroneous results in higher level modules. However, the system is capable to ask for details or for disambiguation if interpretations of visual and acoustic input are inconsistent. It can be interrupted or corrected if its reaction to an instruction was wrong. Thus, intelligent interaction between user and machine introduces flexibility to recognition: the goal of an interactive session with the system is still reachable, even if some symbolic interpretations are temporarily incorrect.

As illustrated in Table 1, this was verified experimentally. In 42 experiments, 9 naive but cooperative male and female participants instructed the system to perform assembly construction tasks of different complexity. The task complexity depends on the number of objects in the scene, the number of objects comprised in an assembly, and the number of assembled bolts, which indicates the number of rigid connections. The table shows the average time and number of instructions until the intended goal was reached or the user initiated a termination. Obviously, time and number of instructions increase with the task complexity. The number of effective instructions grows as well, where effective instructions are those instructions that lead to the desired result. A single effective instruction usually corresponds to a series of instructions as for complex tasks more corrections and disambiguations are necessary. An experiment was counted as a failure, if after the final step of interaction the system's concept of its surroundings was wrong. This usually happened when results from speech recognition and visual object recognition both were of poor quality. Failures were also due to vision conditions with perspective occlusions where assemblies could not be recognized correctly. In most experiments, however, the rate of successful interactions with the artificial communicator was satisfactorily high. Taking all different experiments into account the overall performance of the system amounts to 82% correct interactive sessions.

7.3. Transfer and improvements

The approaches to speech and image understanding described in this contribution have already been applied to other domains (Fink 1999; Sagerer and Niemann 1997). Currently we try to port all the modules introduced here to another domain. The goal is to realize a mobile communicator based on a commercial platform that navigates in an office environment and can be instructed similar to our current system. This of course requires to exchange the lexicon for speech understanding and the knowledge base for object recognition. More sophisticated approaches to object recognition might be necessary as well. We intend to adopt techniques of perceptual grouping and voting techniques for object recognition that already have been tested in the construction scenario and will be integrated into the current communicator (Braun et al. 1999; Schlüter et al. 2000).

7.4. Conclusion

Assessing the performance of an intelligent system must not be restricted to the evaluation of individual modules at certain points in time. Rating a sophisticated system rather has to consider how the machine performs from the beginning until the end of a session. By integrating different perceptive modalities, learning of name designations, and applying flexible dialog strategies our system is capable to reach a user's intended target. Thus, it meets the requirements we expect from cooperative human-machine interaction.

Acknowledgments

This work was supported by the German Research Foundation (DFG) within the Collaborative Research Center 360. We would like to thank the many visitors of our lab to whom we could demonstrate our system throughout the last years. The fruitful discussions we had on these occasions provided many valuable suggestions and inspired us to prepare this article. We would also like to express our gratitude to the people working in the neuroinformatics group and the artificial intelligence group and their leaders Helge Ritter and Ipke Wachsmuth who contributed greatly to the work presented here.

References

Ackermann, F., A. Maßmann, S. Posch, G. Sagerer, and D. Schlüter
1997 Perceptual grouping of contour segments using markov random fields. *Pattern Recognition and Image Analysis* 7: 11–17.

Arkin, R.
1998 *Behaviour based robotics*, Cambridge, MA: MIT Press.

Baker, K. D. (ed.)
1998 Vision-Based Aids for the Disabled (special issue). *Image and Vision Computing* 16.
Ballard D. H., and C. Brown
1982 *Computer Vision*. New York: Prentice Hall.
Bauckhage, C., J. Fritsch, F. Kummert, and G. Sagerer
1999 Towards a Vision System for Supervising Assembly Processes. In *Proc. Symposium on Intelligent Robotic Systems (SIRS'99),* 89–98.
Bauckhage, C., S. Kronenberg, F. Kummert, and G. Sagerer
2000 Grammars and Discourse Theory to Describe and Recognize Mechanical Assemblies. In *Advances in Pattern Recognition,* 173–182. Berlin: Springer.
Bauckhage, C., F. Kummert, and G. Sagerer
1998 Modeling and Recognition of Assembled Objects. In *Proc. Annual Conf. of the IEEE Industrial Electronics Society (IECON'98)*, 2051–2056.
1999 Learning Assembly Sequence Plans Using Functional Models. In *Proc. IEEE Int. Symposium on Assembly and Task Planning (ISATP '99)*, 1–7.
Bradshaw, J. (ed.)
1997 *Software Agents*, Menlo Park: AAAI Press.
Brandt-Pook, H., G. A. Fink, S. Wachsmuth, and G. Sagerer
1999 Integrated recognition and interpretaion of speech for a construction task domain. In *Proc. Int. Conf. on Human-Computer Interaction*, Volume 1, 550–554.
Braun, E., G. Heidemann, H. Ritter, and G. Sagerer
1999 A multi-directional multiple path recognition scheme for complex objects applied to the domain of a wooden toy kit. *Pattern Recognition Letters* 20: 1085–1091.
Bub, T., and J. Schwinn
1996 VERBMOBIL: The Evolution of a Complex Large Speech – to – Speech Translation System. In *Proc. Int. Conf. on Spoken Language Processing (ICSLP'96)*, Volume 4, 2371 – 2374.
Chakrabarty, S., and J. Wolter
1997 A Structure-Oriented Approach to Assembly Sequence Planning. *IEEE Transactions on Robotics and Automation* 13: 14–29.
den Os, E., L. Boves, L. Lamel, and P. Baggia
1999 Overview of the ARISE project. In *Proc. European Conf. on Speech Technology*, 1527–1530.
Eckert, W., T. Kuhn, H. Niemann, S. Rieck, A. Scheuer, and E. Schukat-Talamazzini
1993 A spoken dialogue system for German intercity train timetable inquiries. In *Proc. European Conf. on Speech Technology*, 1871–1874.

Engelmore, R., and T. Morgan (eds.)
1988 *Blackboard Systems*, Reading: Addison-Wesley.

Fink, G.A.
1999 Developing HMM-based recognizers with ESMERALDA. In *Lecture Notes in Artificial Intelligence, Volume 1692*, V. Matoušek, P. Mautner, J. Ocelíková, and P. Sojka (Eds.), 229–234, Berlin: Springer.

Fink, G. A., J. Fritsch, N. Leßmann, H. Ritter, G. Sagerer, J. J. Steil, and I. Wachsmuth
2006 Architectures of situated communicators: From perception to cognition to learning. In: *Situated Communication*, G. Rickheit, and I. Wachsmuth (eds.), 359–378. Berlin: de Gruyter (this volume).

Fink, G. A., N. Jungclaus, F. Kummert, H. Ritter, and G. Sagerer
1996 A distributed system for integrated speech and image understanding. In *Int. Symposium on Artificial Intelligence*, 117–126.

Fink, G. A., N. Jungclaus, H. Ritter, and G. Sagerer
1995 A communication framework for heterogeneous distributed pattern analysis. In *Int. Conf. on Algorithms And Architectures for Parallel Processing,* 881–890.

Fink, G. A., C. Schillo, F. Kummert, and G. Sagerer
1998 Incremental speech recognition for multimodal interfaces. In *Proc. Annual Conf. of the IEEE Industrial Electronics Society (IECON'98)*, 2012–2017.

Heidemann, G., F. Kummert, H. Ritter, and G. Sagerer
1996 A Hybrid Object Recognition Architecture. In *Artificial Neural Networks – ICANN 96*, C. von der Malsburg, W. von Seelen, J. Vorbrüggen, and B. Sendhoff (eds.), 305–310. Berlin: Springer.

Homem de Mello, L., and A. Sanderson
1990 AND/OR Graph Representation of Assembly Plans. *IEEE Transactions on Robotics and Automation* 6: 188–199.

Ikeuchi, K., and T. Suehiro
1994 Towards an Assembly Plan from Observation Part I: Task Recognition with Polyhedral Objects. *IEEE Transactions on Robotics and Automation* 10: 368–385.

Jackendoff, R.
1987 On beyond zebra: The relation of linguistic and visual information. *Cognition* 26: 89–114.

Jelinek, F.
1997 *Statistical Methods for Speech Recognition*, Cambridge, MA: MIT Press.

Jockusch, J., J. Walter, and H. Ritter
1997 A tactile sensor system for a three-fingered robot manipulator. In *Proc. IEEE Int. Conf. on Robotics and Automation (ICRA'97)*, 3080–3086.

Jung, B., M. Hoffhenke, and I. Wachsmuth
1998 Virtual Assembly with Construction Kits. In *Proc. ASME Design for Engineering Technical Conferences (DECT-DFM'98).*

Kronenberg, S., and F. Kummert
1999a Soft unification: Towards robust parsing of spontanous speech. In *IASTED Int. Conf. on Artificial Intelligence and Soft Computing*, 381–385.
1999b Structural dependencies between syntactic relations: A robust parsing model for extrapositions in spontaneous speech. In *ASRU: IEEE Int. Workshop on Automatic Speech Recognition and Understanding.*

Kummert, F., G. A. Fink, G. Sagerer, and E. Braun
1998 Hybrid Object Recognition in Image Sequences. In *Proc. Int. Conf. on Pattern Recognition (ICPR'98)*, Volume II, 1165–1170.

McKevitt, P. (ed.)
1994 *Integration of Natural Language and Vision Processing.* Dordrecht: Kluver.

Mittal. V., H. Yanco, J. Aronis, and R. Simpson (eds.)
1998 *Assistive Technology and Artificial Intelligence: Applications in Robotics, User Interfaces and Natural Language Processing.* New York: Springer.

Miura, J., and K. Ikeuchi
1998 Task Oriented Generation of Visual Sensing Strategies in Assembly Tasks. *IEEE Transactions on Pattern Analysis and Machine Intelligence* 20: 126–138.

Mundy, J., and A. Zisserman (eds.)
1992 *Geometric Invariance in Computer Vision*, Cambridge, MA: MIT Press.

Nagel, H.-H.
1999 From video to language – a detour via logic vs. jumping to conclusion. In *Proc. Integration of Speech and Image Understanding*. 79–100, IEEE Computer Society.

Ney, H., and S. Ortmanns
1999 Dynamic programming search for continuous speech recognition. *IEEE Signal Processing Magazine* 16: 64–83.

Rabemanantsoa, M., and S. Pierre
1996 An artificial intelligence approach for generating assembly sequences in CAD/CAM. *Artificial Intelligence in Engineering* 10: 97–107.

Rae, R., and H. Ritter
1998 Recognition of human head orientation based on artificial neural nets. *IEEE Transactions on Neural Networks* 9: 257–265.

Reiss, T., (ed.)
1993 *Recognizing Planar Objects Using Invariant Image Features*, Berlin: Springer.

Roy, D., and A. Pentland
1998 Word learning in a multimodal environment. In *Proc. ICASSP'98*, 3761–3764.

Rudnicky, A., E. Thayer, C. Constantinides, et al.
1999 Creating natural dialogs in the Carnegie Mellon communication system. In *Proc. European Conf. on Speech Technology*, 1531–1534.

Sagerer, G., and H. Niemann
1997 *Semantic Networks for Understanding Scenes*, New York: Plenum.

Sagerer, G., and S. Wachsmuth (eds.)
1999 *Proc. Integration of Speech and Image Understanding*. IEEE Computer Society.

Schiele, B., and J. Crowley
1996 Object recognition using multidimensional receptive field histograms. In *European Conference On Computer Vision (ECCV'96)*.

Schlüter, D., F. Kummert, G. Sagerer, and S. Posch
2000 Integration of regions and contours for object recognition. In *Proceedings of the 15th International Conference on Pattern Recognition*, Volume I, 944–947. Barcelona.

Seneff, S., and J. Polifroni
1996 A new restaurant guide conversational system: Issues in rapid prototyping for specialized domains. In *International Conference on Spoken Language Processing (ICSLP'96)*, 665–668.

Socher, G., G. Sagerer, and P. Perona
1998 Baysian Reasoning on Qualitative Descriptions from Images and Speech. In *ICCV'98 Workshop on Conceptual Description of Images*, H. Buxton and A. Mukerjee (Eds.)

Swain, M., and D. Ballard
1991 Color indexing. *International Journal of Computer Vision* 7: 11–32.

Tung, C.-P., and A. Kak
1996 Integrating sensing, task planning and execution for robotic assembly. *IEEE Transactions on Robotics and Automation* 12: 187–201.

Turk, M., and A. Pentland
1991 Eigenfaces for recognition. *Journal of Cognitive Neuroscience* 3: 71–86.

Wachsmuth, S., H. Brandt-Pook, G. Socher, F. Kummert, and G. Sagerer
1999 Multilevel integration of vision and speech understanding using bayesian networks. In *Computer Vision Systems: First International Conference*, H. I. Christensen (Ed.), 231–254, Berlin: Springer.

Wachsmuth, S., G. A. Fink, and G. Sagerer
1998 Integration of parsing and incremental speech recognition. In *Proc. European Signal Processing Conference*, Volume 1, 371–375.

Wachsmuth, S., and G. Sagerer
1999 Connecting concepts from vision and speech processing. In *Proc. Integration of Speech and Image Understanding,* 1–20. IEEE Computer Society.

Waltz, D.
1981 Generating and understanding scene descriptions. In *Elements of Discourse Understanding*, B. Webber and I. Sag (eds.), 266–282. New York: Cambridge University Press.

Wang, L., and G. Healey
1996 Illumination and geometry invariant recognition of texture in color images. In *Computer Vision and Pattern Recognition*, San Francisco.

Winograd, T.
1973 A procedural model of language understanding. In *Computer Models of Thought and Language*, 152–186. San Francisco: Freeman.

Woszczyna, M., N. Coccaro, A. Eisele, et al.
1993 Recent advances in JANUS: A speech translation system. In *Proceedings of DARPA Human Language Technology Workshop*, 211–216, Princeton: Morgan Kaufmann

Zhang, J., Y. von Collani, and A. Knoll
1999 Interactive assembly by a two-arm robot agent. *Robotics and Autonomous Systems* 29: 91–100.

Architectures of situated communicators: From perception to cognition to learning

Gernot A. Fink, Jannik Fritsch, Nadine Leßmann, Helge Ritter, Gerhard Sagerer, Jochen J. Steil, and Ipke Wachsmuth

Abstract. A characteristic feature of intelligent systems is the interaction of numerous processes in areas as perception, attention control, sensori-motor interaction, memory, reasoning, or speech understanding. While in the past the primary goal in building artificial cognitive systems was to realize a suitable number of respective partial functions, the focus in this area has recently shifted more and more towards investigating overall architectures for integrating a large number of heterogeneous partial skills to make them interact *intelligently*. The development of such architectural concepts is one of the main goals of the CRC 360. In this contribution, results for three partial demonstrators are presented, which focus on three central aspects of system integration: perception, cognition, and learning. These demonstrators have also been combined and work on a realistic level of complexity. Consequently, we believe that the concepts developed can contribute essentially to the research on architectures of artificial cognitive systems.

1. Introduction

Embodied cognition is playing an increasingly important role in various areas including the development of human-centered robotic systems, the modeling and testing of production mechanisms in cognitive sciences, or with regard to virtual humanoids in virtual reality scenarios. Cognition is also a central aspect of the research in the Collaborative Research Center (CRC) 360 which is devoted to communicative aspects of artificial systems in human-machine interaction. Our focus here lies on the development of artificial systems which are able to replicate the behavior and competence of natural communicators in relevant aspects. In view of the complexity of this task a limited basis-scenario is taken as the point of departure. In this scenario language, gestures, knowledge, planning, action, and sensori-motor activity of a human user and an artificial cognitive agent have to be coordinated with the goal to cooperatively solve a common construction task.

The artificial system has to be able to perceive its environment and especially its human interaction partner visually and acoustically and process the perceived information context sensitively and cognitively adequate – it has to perceive and act in a situated way. This requires the integration of perception, dialog participation, discourse knowledge, turn-taking behavior. But also the ability to generate a linguistic description of the current partial goal, the ability to formulate statements about its own perceptual status, and the ability to comment in general on ongoing actions beyond what is currently taking place are important in communication.

The implementation of such systems shifts the challenge from the solution of single partial problems to the level of the architecture: The development of efficient mechanisms for dynamic and incremental coordination within a wide spectrum of partial abilities becomes the key question. Here simple composite structures are rare. More often it is the case that essential partial functions cooperate with each other in a complex manner and are implemented in heterogeneous software and hardware environments.

Research on architectures for such systems is, therefore, inevitably placed between two extremes: on the one hand, the construction of idealized systems for an implementation as extensive as possible to facilitate the analysis of overall concepts, and, on the other hand, the development of systems which focus on their participation in a realistic real world situation. Our human ability to imagine actions and pictures in an *inner simulation* indicates that both poles have to be combined in order to implement artificial cognitive systems. This motivates the path taken by the CRC 360 to combine methods of modern VR-modeling, knowledge of cognitive architectures, today's possibilities of realizing perceptual components, and research in the area of situated machine learning in realizing three prototypical demonstrators in the areas of perception, cognition, and learning and to combine these in one human-machine-interface.

The first partial demonstrator contains a perceptive front-end-system in which visual perception, language processing and comprehension, as well as the integration of the visual and linguistic levels take place. We will focus particularly on the integrated processing of audio-visual sensory impressions. The basis for a robust multimodal human-machine-dialog is accomplished by using a close integration of processing steps as well as probabilistic means of fusing unimodal perceptual hypotheses into multimodal interpretative structures.

The second partial demonstrator contains a number of cognitively motivated factors. The presentation of an anthropomorphic "partner" to embody the already realized interactive and communicative ability lies at its center. A VR-approach was used as the basis for the realization to represent an agent which can move as naturally as possible, approximate human-like behavior within the dialog scenario, and has several output channels at its disposal. It can disclose information about its internal status using facial expression and body language. At the same time it can provide information about the construction procedure using verbal utterances. Control over this behavioral repertoire was realized in the form of a cognitively motivated architecture.

The third partial demonstrator focuses on situated learning. Robots will not leave their specialist role and become versatile aids in our everyday life before we have mastered the interaction of linguistic dialog, gesture, and visual demonstration necessary to instruct robots to perform certain tasks. The aim of the third partial demonstrator, therefore, is the development of a suitable learning architecture which enables a robot to observe actions, *imitate* these successfully, and – as a prerequisite – to establish and maintain a *common focus of attention* with its human partner. For the required multimodal communication with the user in this setting there have to be perceptive abilities at least in the areas of speech comprehension, active vision, and the interpretation of non-verbal cues such as hand gestures. Therefore this demonstrator relies on and is closely integrated with the other partial demonstrators, especially with regard to the components of perception and language.

All three partial demonstrators are based on a larger number of functional modules which were developed, evaluated, and optimized in the earlier phases of the CRC 360 (Bauckhage et al. 2001; Brandt-Pook et al. 1999; Kopp and Wachsmuth 2004; Steil et al. 2001; Wachsmuth and Jung 1996). Their availability allows for the possibility of assessing their workability on the level of more complex architectural concepts in concrete implementations. We believe that the partial demonstrators described in the following sections are important milestones along the difficult path towards more complex and comprehensive artificial cognitive systems, a path which offers many challenging research questions along the way.

2. Perception

The perceptually oriented prototype of an artificial communicator is situated in a construction scenario and supports the flexible combination of simple elements in a toy unit construction system to more complex entities: The instructions given by a human instructor allow for objects present in the working environment to be manipulated and combined into more complex units. These actions can be performed in a virtual scene representation as well as by the real manipulator of a robot.

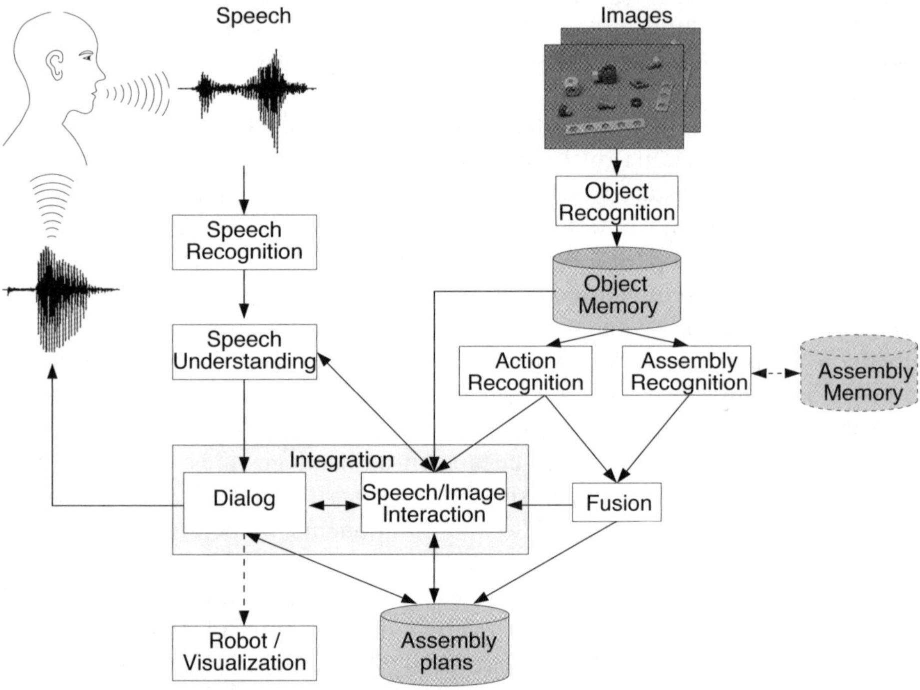

Figure 1. Modules and module interactions of the perceptive front-end

The architecture of the perceptually oriented partial demonstrator is depicted in Figure 1. It is made up of two main signal processing paths projecting onto one integrative component. In the strand depicted on the left-hand side the integrated recognition and interpretation of linguistic utterances takes place. This produces feature structures, which represent the meaning of domain specific constituents. Visual data are segmented and interpreted in the modules shown in the right-hand strand. These generate hypotheses about single objects as well as complex ones. The relations which are additionally obtained between these results over a period of time allow for the recognition of actions and construction plans for assemblies. The results of the image and language processing are merged in one module. This module uses Bayesian networks to calculate integrated interpretations. At the same time a state-based dialog component realizes robust strategies for the discourse and is responsible for the generation of questions for the system in case of incomprehensible or ambivalent instructions (Brandt-Pook et al. 1999).

The integration module, which brings together the results of the image and language processing and relates them to each other, plays a central role in this architecture. There is an interface between the dialog component and a database which stores combined structures extracted from images. Therefore, it is possible to introduce descriptions for assemblies under construction during the course of a construction dialog, in an explicit as well as implicit manner. In order to facilitate the testing of the perceptive front-end it is possible to replace the robotic component with a visualization module. This visualization module illustrates by means of virtual reality the current interpretations that the system has derived about objects and events in its environment.

2.1. Integrated speech and image processing

We use a speaker independent recognition system for natural language input to generate robust and flexible linguistic communication (Fink 1999). The recognition process is directly influenced by a partial parser which applies linguistic restrictions and restrictions given by the scenario on the hypothesized word sequences. As the instructor should neither have to rely on a specific command syntax nor on the use of specific object descriptions, the subordinate language comprehension modules have to work at a high level of *referential imprecision*. This does not result in simple word hypothesis sequences, which are normal for typical recognition systems, but in partial syntactic structures, e.g. object descriptions (*the red cube*) or spatial relations (*left of*) (Brandt-Pook et al. 1999).

Semantic networks which model domain specific object knowledge are employed in order to recognize elementary objects and assemblies of objects in image sequences (Kummert et al. 1998). At the same time a rule-based algorithm recognizes elementary construction operations. When the results from the overall recognition are fused, it is possible to derive construction plans for the combined objects visible. This leads to the acquisition of extensive knowledge from pictorial data about previously unknown complex objects (Bauckhage et al. 1999).

In general, the automatic integration of the results from the speech and image processing is impaired by various uncertainties such as faulty recognition results or the use of partial or unspecific object references. Our approach takes this into account by interpreting the integration of the various perceptual modalities as a statistic decoding process which can be modeled using Bayesian networks. More specifically, each object description which is recognized in a speech signal and every object that is recognized in an image is represented as an independent subnetwork. The individual model nodes represent linguistically describable or visually recognizable object features as well as possible relations between them. The statistical dependencies between the possible concrete feature values associated with these nodes represent relations between the linguistic descriptions and specific objects as well as between uncertainties and errors which occur due to the respective process of analysis. If there are such probabilities a network can be generated around an utterance about a scene and then afterwards be relaxed. The most probable mapping between the visually recognized objects and the spoken language description obtained from the speech signal can then be defined using the optimal *a posteriori* hypotheses about the appropriate relational node. As soon as these have been calculated, more inferences can be made, for example about the most likely probability of the class of objects determined (Wachsmuth and Sagerer 2002). This allows for the determination of whether an object and which object was named verbally.

2.2. Temporal behavior

The temporal behavior of all the modules was obtained for the technical evaluation of the system's efficiency as well as for the optimization of the system's reaction time. This data was analyzed and individual modules were optimized to ensure that the time between the instruction and the response is as short as possible.

The temporal behavior of the whole system for an instruction with an intended object and a reference object (*Take the tail left of the red bold*) is shown in Figure 2 as an UML-sequence diagram. The level of granularity corresponds to the modules shown in Figure 1. The figure clearly shows the asynchronous input modality language relative to the image processing loop as well as the asynchronous processing of these modalities. The average reaction time of about 500-850 ms needed by the system to generate answers depends on the number of objects involved in instructions.

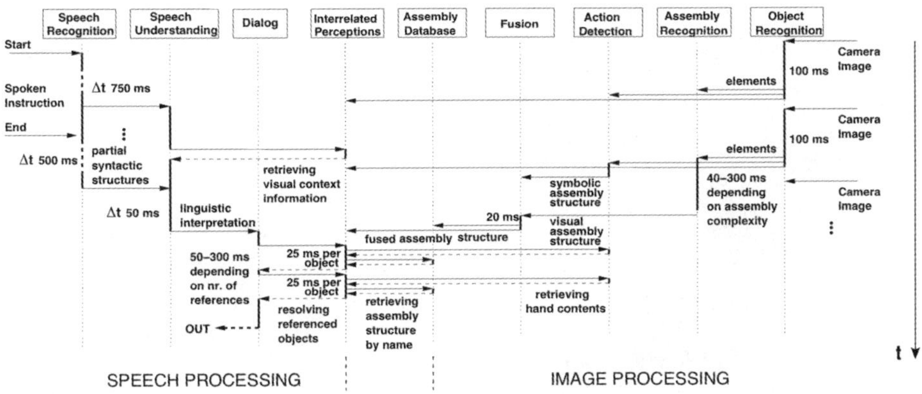

Figure 2. UML-diagram showing the temporal behavior of the modules of the perceptual front-end.

Not only the length of the system's reaction time but also the quality of the interaction between user and system is highly relevant. Extensive evaluative experiments were conducted in order to examine these aspects more closely. In these experiments naïve users had to try to solve simple construction tasks in cooperation with the system (Bauckhage et al. 2002). The results of the evaluation have shown that with the increasing complexity of the construction task and the increasing number and complexity of the user's instructions, the number of the system's questions also increases. The quality of the interactions deteriorates only slightly despite the large increase in the number and the length of the instructions. This means that the constructional goal is reached in most cases and that the whole system reveals a robust interactive behavior.

3. Cognition and embodiment

This section introduces a cognitively motivated architecture for a virtual anthropomorphic agent. The architecture provides a basis for an artificial communicator which concentrates on natural and direct interaction with the human partner. This approach not only pursues a concept for an artificial humanoid dialog partner, but also the development of a theoretical model for the integration of various different approaches of cognitive models to consolidate embodiment and cognition coherently. The architecture is applied in the anthropomorphic artificial communicator *Max* (Fig. 3) in a virtual reality scenario.

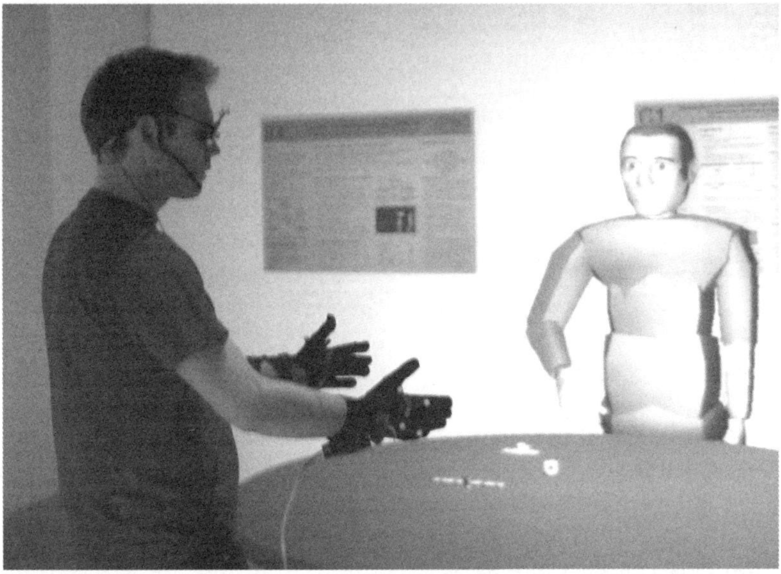

Figure 3. Interaction with the virtual anthropomorphic agent *Max*

It allows for dialogs with planned utterances as well as for spontaneous reactive utterances, such as turn-taking and feedback signals. In addition, there is the possibility of integrating different specialized planners in the process of communication, e.g. planners with knowledge about the construction of "baufix" airplanes and specialized memories, with, for example, dynamic conceptual models for aggregates (Wachsmuth and Jung 1996). The concept of communication is based on the speech act theory of Searle (Searle and Vanderveken 1985) and its extension to communicative acts as introduced by Poggi and Pelachaud (2000). The dialog system itself is plan-based. Communicative acts are represented as action-plan-operators. By this means, the cognitive component can be applied to both dialog and action planning. The representation of the movements of Max's body is achieved using real-time computer animation of a kinematical model (Kopp and Wachsmuth 2004).

3.1. Architectural structure

The core system conceived for the situated artificial communicator Max integrates symbol processing and behavior based approaches in one hybrid system architecture. The architecture is concerned with perception and reactive behavior, higher mental processes such as inferences, and planned actions, up to and including the integration of attention and motivational appraisal of courses of actions (using *desires*). Figure 4 is a sketch of the agent's architecture. The circle, which is divided into a *perceive-reason-act* triad, represents the internal processing of the agent and delimits it from its environment. The triple division emphasizes the coordination and the close interplay within the classic *perceive-reason-act* cycle. The direct flow of information between the sectors *perceive* and *act*, however, takes into account the fact that reactive behavior can evolve without previous deliberation or an involvement of the cognitive loop. Therefore, this approach can be characterized as a hybrid architecture which unites reactive and deliberative behavior in one structure.

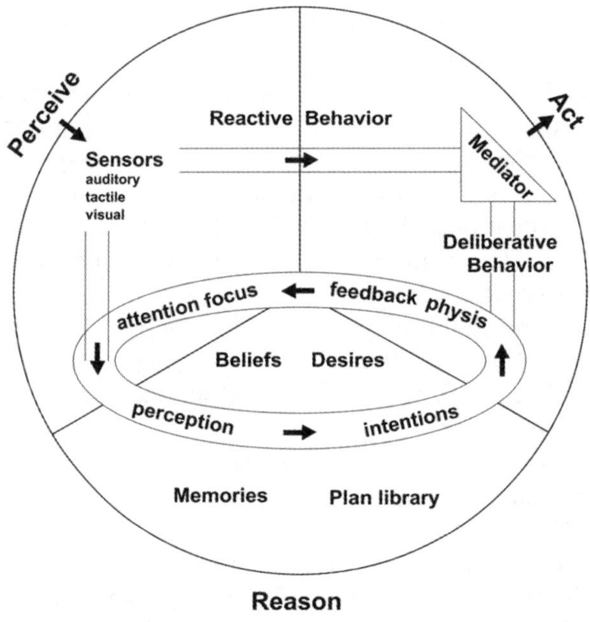

Figure 4. Structure of the cognitively motivated architecture.

The sectors *perceive* and *act* in the circle represent the body of the agent in the cognitive architecture. The agent is anchored in the environment due to its embodiment and operates in a close relation to the world. Furthermore, the body serves as a means for expressing multimodality (gesture, facial and emotional expression). Both sensory processing and the conduct of actions are characterized by the bodily characteristics of the agent. This is also taken into account in the choice of modality for actions to be executed.

3.2. Control flow

The perception, inference, and action components are realized as a concurrent line. There is parallel processing of the deliberate and reactive components. On the one hand, the sensory data can directly trigger reactive behavior, which operates quickly, on a lower level of abstraction and is characterized by a close coupling to the perception. Reactive types of behavior in the form of reflexes with high priority values can be used to provide immediate system reactions, such as avoidance behavior in the case of the threat of a collision. In the context of communication there are reactive behaviors as, for example, in turn-taking. In addition the reactive component takes over *secondary behaviors*, such as eye blinking.

On the other hand, there is the *cognitive loop*, which acts as a circuit in regard to the internal deliberative processing of the agent and depicts the interplay between the acquisition of data and the processing of information. Perception consists of the processing of perceived sensory data which is sensitive to the situational context rather than consisting of an inflexible acquisition of data. Cognition is not understood as an independent internal process but as a process which is linked closely to the body with a strong emphasis on the procedural component. The sensory data are the input for the cognitive loop and are filtered through *attention mechanisms*. By this, they can interact in the form of interpreted and analyzed perceptions with different specialized memories which may work on the basis of multiple representations. However, they store relevant facts on a high level of abstraction in a unified manner as *beliefs*, which represent part of the agent's working memory.

The kernel of the deliberative module follows the *Belief-Desire-Intention* (BDI) approach and builds on JAM (Huber 1999) and UM-PRS (Lee et al. 1994). Explicitly represented goals (*desires*), which can be activated by means of internal processing as well as from the outside, serve as the behavior triggering impulse. The formation of intentions in the cognitive loop is carried out by the BDI interpreter. It defines a current *intention* on the basis of the *beliefs* present, the agent's current desires and goals, as well as its alternative possibilities for action. The possible courses of action are represented in the form of plans. These plans are described by pre-conditions, context-conditions, attainable consequences, as well as a priority function.

On the one hand, the plan library consists of simple plans for converting simple actions directly into behaviors. On the other hand, dynamic and independent planners can be triggered if necessary for generating more complex plans to be executed. The overall priority of a plan is calculated using the priority of the *desire* which lead to its instantiation, an evaluation of the plan's competence in terms of its priority function, as well as other possible parameters. This overall priority competes with the priority of the existing plans. The one with the highest priority will become the current *intention* and has the chance to influence internal system variables and *beliefs* and to initiate behaviors, which will then compete inside the mediator for the access to the actuators.

Reactive and deliberate behaviors are both carried out by using behaviors and motor skills of different levels of complexity. It is the *mediator's* task to arbitrate between the behaviors by taking into account which of the modalities are inactive or already used within the scope of other behaviors. The basis for the decision made by the mediator consists of priority values, which express the urgency and relevance of a given behavior in a given situation and are calculated locally by the behaviors (Blumberg and Galyean 1995). As a result, action selection takes place both on the level of the cognitive deliberative formation of intentions, but also within the mediator on the level of the direct execution of actions. Not only the actively executed intention but also the currently competing behaviors are taken into consideration for the *feedback information*. The feedback of the completed actions and the agent's internal states influence the sensor system and perception in the form of *attention mechanisms* and conclude the cognitive loop. The loop emphasizes one of the central ideas of the architecture: A constant stream of information flows between the sectors and includes both the current sensory and actuator's information as well as the internal state.

3.3. Max as a construction partner

The experimental implementation realizes central aspects of the architecture and enables Max to explain the construction of different aggregates in response to the human partner's inquiries or to build aggregates in a cooperatively with her. This means that Max describes how "baufix" aggregates have to be connected according to his knowledge about the construction by using synthetic speech and employing various gestures. In this way he either explains the entire construction of an aggregate in step-by-step fashion or he only explains which is the very next step in the construction but leaves his partner to conduct the assembly. In order to perceive the human in the real world (movement, direction of gaze, gesture) tracked markers, data gloves, and a microphone, which sends the data to a speech recognizer, are used. Max provides feedback after the partner's action has been completed. If the construction was correct Max confirms this and continues giving explanations. If the action was wrong he revises it in the virtual environment and explains the procedural step in the construction anew.

Max uses situational knowledge from the COAR scene simulator (Wachsmuth and Jung 1996) to rate the success of actions. The COAR-description is updated with every step and contains information about the objects, their connections and further object features. In addition, Max is equipped with a simple visual-spatial perception, which is entered into a spatial memory. During the entire course of the dialog Max accounts for the dialog state and shows turn-taking behavior by speaking, for example, only when he has the turn. On the other hand, he can be interrupted at any time. Reactive behavior exists in the current version in the form of *secondary behaviors* which contribute to Max' lifelike appearance by using breathing movements and eye blinking. Above and beyond that, there is a behavior which fixes his gaze on his communication partner. If Max is not performing an action for which he needs visual control, he looks the human partner in the eye and follows him or her with his gaze. As soon, however, as Max starts explaining something, this behavior is overruled and Max fixates on the objects he is referring to.

4. On the way to situated learning

Recently the approach of *learning by imitation* has been discussed in order to make learning in cognitive systems feasible (Andry et al. 2001; Schaal 1999). The basic idea is to find a "role model" for a successful trajectory in the appropriate search area by means of the observations of the instructor. The third partial demonstrator, the artificial robotic system GRAVIS (Gesture Recognition Active Vision System) with perceptual, cognitive, as well as active vision and manipulation components, provides a suitable basis for the realization of this kind of situated learning. Figure 5 gives a schematic overview of the most important processing paths. The language processing modules and the attention mechanism supply the situational dialog information and the nonverbal (visual and gestural) information for the integrative module. The instructions that are recognized are transmitted to the attention mechanism, which, after renewing its focus, generates suitable commands for the robot control components (movement, grasping). Above and beyond that, there are further control functionalities integrated into the system. These are, for example, calibration functions for visual processing, the camera head, and "eye-hand"-coordination; more details can be found in (Steil et al. 2001; McGuire et al. 2002).

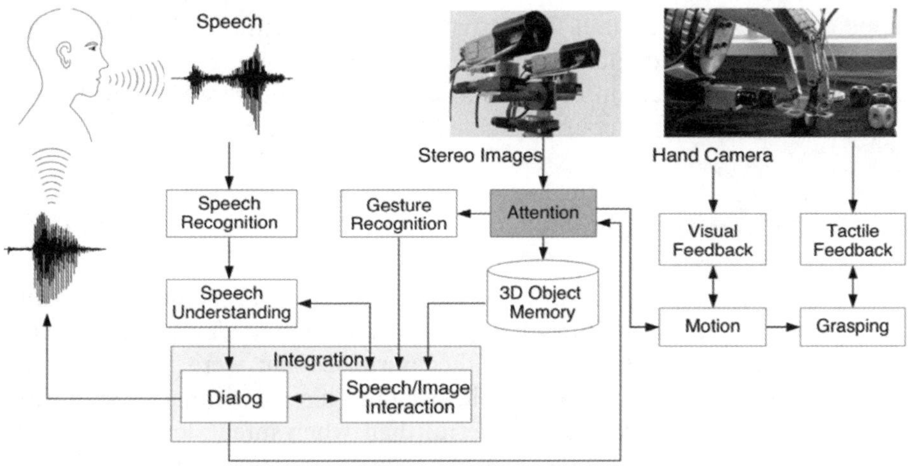

Figure 5. Schematic picture of the current active partial demonstrator

The grasping and manipulation is carried out by a standard 6DOF PUMA manipulator operated with the real-time RCCL-command library. It is additionally equipped with a wrist camera to obtain local visual feedback during the grasping phase. Grasping is carried out by a 9DOF dextrous robot hand developed at the Technical University of Munich. It has three identical human-sized fingers driven by an oil hydraulics system. The fingertips carry custom-built fingertip sensors to provide force feedback for control and evaluation of the grasp. To use one finger as a "thumb", the original hand design was changed by adding a palm and rearranging the fingers in a more human-like configuration (cf. also Fig. 7). An additional sensor matrix was fixed to this newly obtained palm. The matrix gives especially valuable feedback for power grips, and its resolution suffices to distinguish between the tactile profiles of different objects.

The vision hardware consists of a binocular active vision head with two 3-chip-CCD color-cameras, controllable pan, tilt, left/right vergence and motorized lenses determining focus, zoom and aperture, which combine to a total of 10 DOFs. For the real time processing of the stereo images a

DATACUBE-system is used, which processes images at a rate of 25 Hz in a pipeline architecture. An attention mechanism is employed for the integration of the different visual channels by choosing salient fixation points based on a summation of topographical feature maps (Steil et al. 2001). A holistic object recognizer, which is based on neural networks (Heidemann et al. 2000), makes hypotheses about the place and identity of objects within the scope of the camera around the current focus of attention. The information gained is put at the disposal of the image-language-integration component described in section 2.1 in order to classify those objects which are focused on repeatedly during the course of an explorative sequence.

4.1. Modularity and adaptivity

Many of the partial capabilities described above are implemented as functional modules in the architecture of the active partial demonstrator. They can usually be employed also for other purposes and were first developed and tested independently of the whole system. This means that used in isolation modules usually are more powerful than when integrated in the GRAVIS-system. The GRAVIS-system can use their capabilities only in restricted fashion due to its reciprocal dependencies, its less specialized hardware, and the often worse quality of input data.

A system, such as GRAVIS, which operates in the real world and interacts with a user, can be disturbed in many ways and can be impaired in its functionalities. In our case, most problems come from changing light sources, varying skin color, the appearance of unknown objects, and technical problems of the robot components. Above and beyond that, the architecture demands a robustness of the partial modules in many ways because the visual system, the robot arm, and the hand operate in only roughly calibrated coordinate systems; 3D-object positions and 3D-deixis are estimated using 2D-pixel coordinates and, therefore, all calculations are concomitantly imprecise. Therefore, it is a decisive requirement for the robust functioning of the entire architecture that local adaptivity already operates at the level of the individual modules and that local feedback be available during the execution of actions.

From a global view, learning and adaptivity is a complex phenomenon which is reflected in the numerous different proposals how to relate and implement its various aspects. In the present system, learning takes place at several time scales. At the slowest time scale learning methods are used in order to create initial system functions by off-line algorithms. Examples in the unsupervised training of the sensory front end of a neural-network-based object classifier and the supervised training of hand recognition modules. Such learning does not involve any behavior of the robot; instead, it permits the creation of important initial subsystem functionalities which would have been much harder to obtain by explicit programming alone.

The second *local refinement level* comprises those learning processes whose adaptive changes occur on-line, during (and based on) the actual behavior of the robot and refine its initial capabilities. Learning processes at this level are largely encapsulated in a single functional module, thereby allowing to strike a good balance between benefits and implementability. Typical examples in our system are subsystem calibrations (e.g. on-line color-recalibration of the visual attention and the object recognition), slow adaptation to changing environment conditions (e.g. "habituation" of the fingertip sensors, dynamic renormalization of the feature weights in the saccadic system with respect to the current feature statistics, continuous update of the skin color model, or forgetting factors in the object memory), and mechanisms to ensure that system variables remain well inside their operating ranges. This level can be considered as hosting most of the long-term plasticity of the system, and its algorithms can largely be based on ideas of statistical learning.

Finally, the third *situated level* addresses the challenge to make rapid (ultimately one-shot) learning feasible, which clearly poses a significant research challenge. In the context of the GRAVIS demonstrator this level is addressed within a paradigm of *situated learning for imitation grasping* (Steil et al. 2004) to enable the robotic system to carry out a variety of grasps of everyday objects, visually observing and imitating a human instructor who indicates useful grasp postures with his or her own hand.

4.2. Outlook for an integrated learning architecture

As pointed out in the previous section, to enable learning at the short time scale of the situated level will depend in an essential way on the interplay of several functional loops complementing each other (Fig. 6). Three such loops, *observation*, *internal simulation*, and *sensori-motor exploration*, can lead to a scheme that appears sufficiently powerful to enable fast situated learning.

The objective of the *observation loop* is to gain a promising action template in the sense of imitation learning discussed above. This requires robot capabilities to watch the environment, respectively the instructor, in order to

(1) extract relevant features, events, and chains of observed partial actions, (2) translate these from the observed to an intrinsic perspective, and (3) exploit them for forming an action template that is focused on promising regions of the a-priori very high-dimensional search space.

At a second stage the observed action template has to be improved further through an *internal simulation loop*, exploring possible actions in the vicinity of the observed template and selecting promising action candidates. At this stage model knowledge of and intrinsic perspective (e.g. about kinematical and sensor constraints of the actually used hardware) can be incorporated and merged with constraint information made available from the observation loop. In the current setting, the computational basis of this component is a dynamics based grasping simulation, allowing the application of reinforcement learning methods to improve the grasping strategy. This kind of *search space restricted reinforcement learning*, where the exploration of actions can be restricted to a neighborhood of the observed successful trajectory, is promising to reduce search spaces.

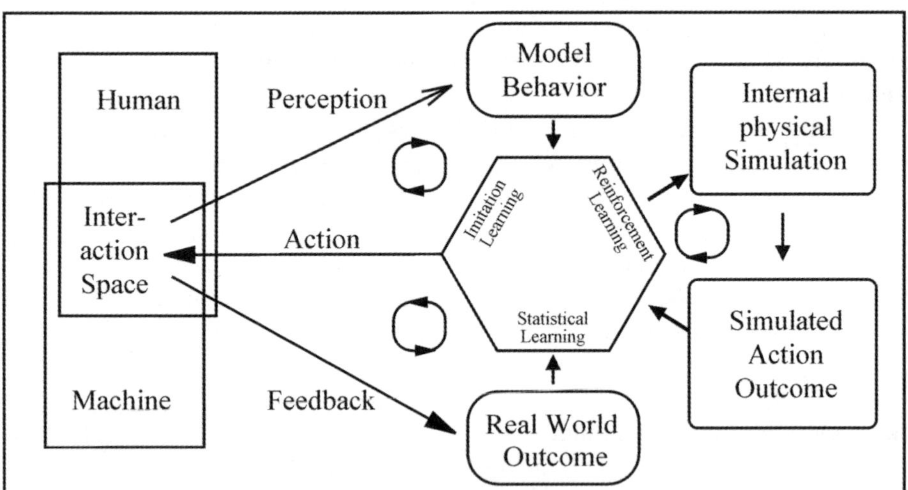

Figure 6. Multi-level learning architecture for realization of imitational learning

Finally, the third, *sensori-motor loop* is responsible for actually carrying out promising actions. Since the internal simulation model and its observation-based refinement can always only approximate the actual situation, actual execution of the action is faced with two alternative evaluation criteria: First, a maximization of knowledge gain with the consequence of risky actions, for instance near decision boundaries; second, a maximization of robustness with the consequence of conservative actions in maximal distance to decision boundaries, leading only to minimal information gain.

In summary, the *observation loop* acquires example actions from the instructor, while the *simulation loop* provides refinements and adaptation to the constraints imposed by the robot system. This changes robot learning into an interactive *situated learning* process, which uses speech and the multi-modal perceptual channels for an effective optimization of the system's exploration.

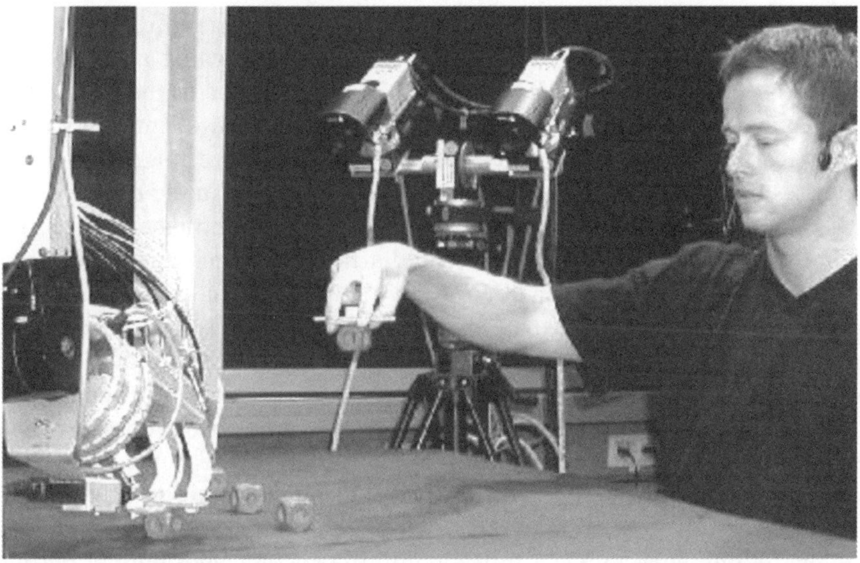

Figure 7. Imitation scenario: postures of the GRAVIS-system robot hand set in 'equivalently effective' forms using human hand gripping as a model.

5. Summary

The presented architectures integrate many capabilities to enable an intuitive situated communication of human users with an artificial cognitive system. Research on such architectures often suffers from implementing one of two extremes: large and powerful systems, which have grown over years but are inflexible and, on the other hand, small-scale idealized and simplified architectures too far away from real world requirement. In our Bielefeld CRC 360 we have met this challenge by developing three highly congruent partial demonstrators. They each represent one part of a larger artificial cognitive system which can still be surveyed while focusing mainly on one topic. They can be combined and maintain a realistic level of complexity throughout.

The perceptual partial demonstrator has the key tasks of combining language and vision and giving us important insights into how meaning is constituted and how robustness and natural situatedness grow. The cognitive partial demonstrator combines modern VR-techniques for realizing an anthromorphic agent with cognitive knowledge about the control of its behavioral components. This partial demonstrator is useful for investigating how and under which conditions multimodal feedback for the transmission of turn-taking signals or emotionality can be generated. The third partial demonstrator focuses on the important topic of situated learning in a robot system. We use this demonstrator to explore the combination of the visual attention mechanism, gesture recognition, and the integration of multimodal dialog for learning by imitation, i.e. the ability to perceive linguistic-gestural sequences of actions and to copy these in a suitable way in the robot.

All three partial demonstrators are designed to complement each other and in their combination realize a situated artificial communicator which can interact with a human partner in a largely natural way in an instruction scenario. The research strategy that has been followed so far has passed an important and difficult level of testing. The evaluation possibilities that have come out of this in the area of human-machine-interaction sequences will serve as a point of departure for the further research on the comprehension and learning of mechanical action on a cognitively higher level. And also – in the long-term perspective – they will contribute work towards portable, cognitively motivated architectures which can lead to high-level, task-oriented "alignment" between future cognitive systems and human partners. This would at least partly contribute to the aim of constructing intelligent systems.

Acknowledgments

We would like to thank all our colleagues in CRC 360, at the Faculty of Technology, and at the Faculty of Linguistics and Literary Sciences who have contributed to the development of the above described partial demonstrators. Our special thanks go to Elke Braun, Christian Bauckhage, Robert Haschke, Gunther Heidemann, Bernhard Jung, Stefan Kopp, Franz Kummert, Frank Lömker, Patrick McGuire, Frank Röthling and Sven Wachsmuth. – This reserach was funded by the German Research Foundation (DFG) as part of the Collaborative Research Center 360 "Situated Artificial Communicators".

References

Andry, P., P. Gaussier, S. Moga, J. P. Banquet, and J. Nadel
2001 Learning and communication via imitation: An autonomous robot perspective. *IEEE Transactions on Systems, Man, and Cybernetics* 31: 431–442.

Bauckhage, C., G. A. Fink, J. Fritsch, F. Kummert, F. Lömker, G. Sagerer, and S. Wachsmuth
2001 An integrated system for cooperative man-machine interaction. In *IEEE International Symposium on Computational Intelligence in Robotics and Automation*, 328–333. Banff.

Bauckhage, C., J. Fritsch, F. Kummert, and G. Sagerer
1999 Towards a Vision System for Supervising Assembly Processes. In *Proceedings of Symposium on Intelligent Robotic Systems*, 89–98. Coimbra.

Bauckhage, C., J. Fritsch, K. Rohlfing, S. Wachsmuth, and G. Sagerer
2002 Evaluating Integrated Speech and Image Understanding. In *Proceedings of International Conference on Multimodal Interfaces (ICMI)*, 9–14. Pittsburgh.

Blumberg, B. M., and T. A. Galyean
1995 Multi-level direction of autonomous creatures for real-time virtual environments. *Computer Graphics* 29: 47–54.

Brandt-Pook, H., G. A. Fink, S. Wachsmuth, and G. Sagerer
1999 Integrated Recognition and Interpretation of Speech for a Construction Task Domain. In *Proceedings of International Conference on Human-Computer Interaction, Vol. 1,* 550–554. München.

Fink, G. A.
1999 Developing HMM-based Recognizers with ESMERALDA. In *Lecture Notes in Artificial Intelligence*, Vol. 1692, V. Matoušek, P. Mautner, J. Ocelíková, et al. (eds.), 229–234. Berlin: Springer.

Heidemann, G., D. Lücke, and H. Ritter
2000 A system for various visual classification tasks based on neural networks. In *Proc. Int. Conf. on Pattern Recognition*, Vol. 1, A. E. A. Sanfeliu (ed.), 9–12. Barcelona.

Huber, M. J.
1999 JAM: A BDI-theoretic Mobile Agent Architecture. In *Proceedings of International Conference on Autonomous Agents*, 236–243. Seattle.

Kopp, S., and I. Wachsmuth
2004 Synthesizing multimodal utterances for conversational agents. *Journal of Computer Animation and Virtual Worlds* 15: 39–52.

Kummert, F., G. A. Fink, G. Sagerer, and E. Braun
1998 Hybrid Object Recognition in Image Sequences. In *Proceedings of International Conference on Pattern Recognition, Vol. 2*, 1165–1170. Brisbane.

Lee, J., M. J. Huber, P. G. Kenny, and E. H. Durfee
1994 UM-PRS: An Implementation of the Procedural Reasoning System for Multirobot Applications. In *Conference on Intelligent Robotics in Field, Factory, Service, and Space (CIRFFSS)*, 842–849. Houston.

McGuire, P., J. Fritsch, J. J. Steil, F. Röthling, G. A. Fink, S. Wachsmuth, G. Sagerer, and H. Ritter
2002 Multi-Modal Human-Machine Communication for Instructing Robot Grasping Tasks. In *Proc. Int. Conf. on Intelligent Robots and Systems (IROS)*, 1082–1089. Lausanne.

Poggi, I., and C. Pelachaud
2000 Performative facial expression in animated faces. In *Embodied Conversational Agents*, J. Cassell, J. Sullivan, S. Prevost, et al. (eds.), 155–188. Cambridge, MA: MIT Press.

Schaal, S.
1999 Is imitation learning the route to humaniod robots? *Trends in Cognitive Sciences* 3: 233–242.

Searle, J. R., and D. Vanderveken
1985 *Foundations of Illocutionary Logic*. Cambridge, UK: Cambridge University Press.

Steil, J. J., G. Heidemann, J. Jockusch, R. Rae, N. Jungclaus, and H. Ritter
2001 Guiding Attention for Grasping Tasks by Gestural Instruction: The GRAVIS-Robot Architecture. In *Proc. Int. Conf. on Intelligent Robots and Systems (IROS)*, 1570–1577. Maui, Hawaii.

Steil, J. J., F. Röthling, R. Haschke, and H. Ritter
2004 Situated robot learning for multi-modal instruction and imitation of grasping. *Robotics and Autonomous Systems* 47: 129–141.

Wachsmuth, I., and B. Jung
1996 Dynamic conceptualization in a mechanical-object assembly environment. *Artificial Intelligence Review*, 10: 345–368.

Wachsmuth, S., and G. Sagerer
2002 Integrated analysis of speech and images as a probabilistic decoding process. In *Proceedings of the International Conference on Pattern Recognition*, 588–592. Québec City.

A systems framework of communicative understanding

Hans-Jürgen Eikmeyer, Walther Kindt, Yvonne Rittgeroth, and Hans Strohner

Abstract. When communication partners try to construct shared interpretations of their verbal utterances or other information in an interactive way, they are engaged in an act of communicative understanding. Cognitive factors such as linguistic and world knowledge seem to interact intimately with physical and social factors in almost all phases of this process. We propose a theoretical framework which will be able to integrate most of these factors. We present a systems analysis of the various components and processes of communicative understanding in the beginning and specify these general ideas in three subsequent chapters by research on speaker, listener and emerging joint actions. We exemplify the proposed theory in three central fields: communicative strategies for understanding clarification requests, the role of inference in understanding, and perspective taking in referential communication.

1. Introduction

Communicative understanding is an interactive process, in which communication partners try to construct shared interpretations of their verbal utterances or other information. In general, this is achieved not only by means of their linguistic and world knowledge, but also by considering the information given by their physical and social environment. In communicative understanding cognitive, physical and social factors seem to interact intimately in almost all phases of the process.

The aim of this research is to develop a theoretical framework which will be able to integrate most of these factors. In the second part of the chapter, we present a systems analysis of the various components and processes of communicative understanding. In the third, fourth and fifth parts, we specify these general ideas by research on speaker, listener and emerging joint actions. We exemplify the proposed theory in two central fields: several communicative strategies for the securing of understanding such as clarification requests and perspective taking in referential communication. Finally, in the sixth part of this contribution, we present a systems analysis of understanding processes in task-oriented communication.

As we have shown in Eikmeyer, Kindt, and Strohner (2006), our research is based on an elaborate empirical and formal methodology, namely the grounded experimental simulative method. In that chapter, we exemplified this methodology by means of our research in the field of clarification requests. Complementary to that chapter, here we focus on the theoretical and empirical foundations of our research.

2. The systems framework

2.1. Cognitive systems

In cognitive science, a growing number of researchers agree with the integration of internal and external views on cognition. The notion of cognitive system refers not only to the processes inside the cognitive system, but also to the external relations with its environment.

For a definition of a system, we require five sets *X, Y, Z, f* and *g*. *Z* is a set of internal configurations of the system, which are called mental states. X is a set of objects outside Z, which are called input elements of the environment. *Y* is a set of objects outside Z, which are called output elements of the environment. *f* is a subset of the Cartesian product (Z x X) x Z, which is called transition relation. And *g* is a subset of (Z x X) x Y, which is called output relation. A system is called deterministic, if both f and g are functions, i.e. they relate to any ordered pair <z,x> in their domains exactly one element in their range as value.

Depending on the impact of the environment and their internal states, most systems change more or less. Systems with changing states are *dynamic systems*. In a deterministic system the change between the state z at time *t* and at time *t + 1* can bc described by means of the transition function

$$z_{t+1} = f(z_t, x_t).$$

The state change is a function of the original state at time *t* and the input X at that time. Of course, a system's state can be very complex and can be influenced by many components with emerging attributes. The output Y of a deterministic dynamic system may be computed with the output function

$$y_t = g(z_t, x_t).$$

At a closer look, the behavior of cognitive systems, which has been described in a global way by the transition and the output relation, combines many single processing steps specified by corresponding partial relations. Comparable to a game of chess, where the player has many different possibilities for choosing a move, the rules governing cognitive systems often allow for a margin of freedom in decisions for state transitions and output reactions. This tolerance can be strategically exploited to achieve certain goals. In such cases it makes sense to regard the system game-theoretically as consisting of two parts, a non-deterministic base system and a set of selection functions used as strategies. By this technique a very simple system theoretic concept of strategies can easily be set up. Moreover, cognitive systems can be conceived of as being built up by different subsystems or modules interacting in all kinds of ways. The specific interactions in a system thus create the specific properties of the system.

In order to understand the specific function of a certain system, it is helpful to differentiate between additive and emergent attributes of the system:

- Additive attributes are calculated from the sum of certain attributes of the subsystems, e.g. the total weight of a system can be calculated from the sum of the weights of its subsystems.
- Emergent attributes are totally new results of the interaction of the subsystems in a certain environment, e.g. if dynamite and fire are brought together, the emerging result is an explosion, which is not related to these two subsystems in isolation.

The notion of emergent attributes is particularly crucial for the analysis of cognitive systems. When a cognitive system is presented with certain stimuli, which response emerges and which mental state can be inferred on the basis of the responses? Depending on the already existing knowledge and motivation, the possible emergent responses can differ tremendously.

2.2. Communication systems

In communication, two or more cognitive systems interact by transmitting some information from one system to another. In most communication situations, the partners have at least a rudimentary knowledge of each other. Therefore, in communication systems, an additional component of mental states, i.e. partner-oriented knowledge, must be added to the units already existing. Partner-oriented knowledge contributes greatly to the probability of emergent responses of one or both interlocutors.

According to the systems framework, the dynamics in communication depends on the estimated relevance of the various input sources. For communicative understanding, these sources comprise especially the verbal information, the referential field, the communicative partner, and general conditions of the situation. On different occasions, these sources may differ in relevance. Consequently, one unit may dominate the other units and strongly influence their related knowledge, e.g. in some cases the partner-related knowledge may be so relevant that it overrides individual response strategies. This functional view of communicative understanding is in good agreement with the "good-enough principle" recently proposed by Ferreira, Bailey, and Ferraro (2002: 15) for the interaction of syntax and semantics: "The goal of the comprehension system might be to deliver an interpretation that is just good enough to allow the production system to generate an appropriate response; after all, it is the response that is overt and that determines the success of the participants' joint activity. An adequate theory of how language is understood, this will ultimately have to take into account the dynamic demands of real-time conversation."

In communication systems, three types of emergent actions can be differentiated: actions by the actual speaker, actions by the actual listener, and joint actions by both. In the following, we will present some of our data related to these three types. For each type, we first go into our observations on the communicative strategies of the interlocutors. After this, we discuss observations, which may shed some light on the cognitive processes of the communication partners.

3. Dynamics of communicative understanding I: The speaker

3.1. The communicative level

In task-oriented communication, the instructor tries to give relevant verbal information for task achievement to the constructor. In complex tasks, as in our experimental scenario, the contribution of the speaker may refer to specific aspects of task achievement, including the discourse itself, the actual state of the construction and the responses of the constructor. When problems arise, the instructors generally intensify their efforts in order to overcome the problems. In our transcriptions these strategies are clearly to be seen, in most cases several times. In the following, we present same examples of our data.

3.1.1. Discourse-oriented strategies

Some complex tasks, e.g. the construction of the "baufix" airplane in our experimental scenario, cannot be carried out in a single step. In this case, it is useful to make a plan for the complete instruction with global and local structures.

As to global discourse structuring, we frequently observed the following strategies:

- Final result: At the beginning of the instruction, a common strategy is to name the intended final result of the construction task, e.g. *We now are going to construct an airplane.*
- Main portions: Instead of clarifying the function of the whole object under construction, the speaker may give some information about its main portions, e.g. *First the wings, then the fuselage.*
- Simple things first: An efficient global structuring strategy is to pick out simple things first and difficult things later, e.g. *I guess it is easiest to start with the large parts.*
- Recollection: Some instructors try to remember how they managed to build up the airplane and use this recollection as basis for their instruction, e.g. *As far as I can remember, the fuselage is the most complicated part of the task.*

In contrast, the local level of discourse structuring mainly serves to clarify the functional or temporal relation between two construction actions. Some local structuring is explicit, some implicit:

- Connectors such as "after", "before" or "because" present explicit information about the type of relation between two actions.
- Unspecific verbs such as "fix" give less information about the relation between construction actions and objects compared to specific verbs like "screw".

3.1.2. Construction-oriented strategies

In addition to the structuring devices mentioned above, the construction itself is the main topic of the discourse. Several instructors checked the intermediate results by asking questions such as *Do you now have an object that looks like the wing of an airplane?*

3.1.3. Constructor-oriented strategies

Especially in rather complex task environments, the instructor should make comprehension as easy as possible for the constructor (Kindt 1998). Accordingly, we found several such strategies in our data:

- Reformulation: The reformulation of an utterance can give both more information and time for the comprehension processes of the constructor and thus can help him or her to understand the instruction, e.g. *Side by side, that is, in the second and in the third hole.*
- Negation: Negation can prevent the constructor from making certain probable mistakes (Jang 2003), e.g. *Take the yellow bolt with the name 'Lorenz Baufix' on it; that is, not the one with the slot.*
- Analogy: A good means for making the task simpler for the constructor is the use of analogies to already accomplished parts of the task, e.g. *Now the same procedure with the other wheel.*
- Comprehension control: In order to ascertain that the constructor did comprehend an utterance, the instructor can directly ask for feedback, e.g. *Do you understand?* This question helps to focus the cognitive effort on the meaning of the utterance and signals the constructor that understanding it is highly relevant for task accomplishment.

3.1.4. Problem-solving strategies

As we have shown in the previous sections, the instructors, by means of various strategies, including discourse-oriented, construction-oriented and constructor-oriented strategies, take care that many potential understanding problems can be avoided. Nonetheless, problems may occur at the various levels we distinguished. Problems can be caused by the speaker or the listener (Kindt and Weingarten 1984). In the following, we present some problem-solving strategies for discourse, construction and constructor problems.

- *Discourse-related problems:* In task-oriented communications in which both interlocutors are novices, word-finding problems often occur. In our data, we found many lexical ad-hoc constructions for the objects in the airplane scenario as *Fünferträger* (fiver bar) for a bar with five mounting holes. The "good-enough principle" (Ferreira, Bailey, and Ferraro 2002) is again relevant for the success of the created object names. If they lead to a better communicative understanding in the specific discourse situation, they are retained. If not, they are cancelled and replaced by other ad-hoc constructions. The German noun *Salmiakpastille* (*licorice lozenge*) is one such retained notion: It is applied to an orange rhombic wooden nut, although the word literally refers to some sort of candy; it is used because the wooden part and licorice lozenges both have a similar rhombic form. This is widely known as a Donnellan-phenomenon (Donnellan 1966).

- *Construction-related problems:* Sometimes the construction of a certain part of the airplane may prove to be too difficult at that point in time. As an efficient problem-solving strategy, the instructor can stop the construction of the critical part and restart with another part; e.g. *You'd better put away those cubes and forget the last construction step, and take <pause> uhm you haven't fixed these two long bars, have you?*
- *Constructor-related problems*: Giving an instruction does not always mean using a simple imperative construction. In fact, some instructors try to avoid imperatives because they are considered as impolite. In order to be polite to the constructor, instructors often produce modulated and complex instructions, e.g. N*ow you should put the wheels together, from these round red parts and the white rubber things*.

3.2. The cognitive level

With respect to *language production,* there has been an ongoing intensive discussion on its architecture and process dynamics over the last twenty years. Here, we want to address the means by which a speaker controls his own production and the techniques used in case a problem occurs.

In the influential model of Levelt (1989) one finds three instances where self-monitoring, i.e. an observation of the own production of a speaker, can take place. One such instance is a loop in the conceptualizer component, which controls the message construction. Not very much is known about the details of this process. Taking Levelt's perspective of the speaker as information processor, maybe not very much can be said, since the information to be processed stems from inside the speaker. An alternative view is proposed by Herrmann and Grabowski (1994), who regard language production as a regulation process, in which an utterance is an action transforming the actual state of a system into a target state. Thus, there is a speaker external reason for becoming active. Two more monitoring routes take (a) the phonetic plan constructed by the formulator module and (b) the overt speech signal as input into the speech comprehension system, which then feeds the parsed speech into the self-monitoring component mentioned initially.

Monitoring is a necessary prerequisite for the production *of self-repairs* as discussed by Levelt (1983). In this paper a well-formedness rule for self-repairs is formulated, which relates them syntactically to coordination structures, and a rich typology for self-repairs is proposed. However, the classification is both inhomogeneous and incomplete: some classes are defined syntactically, others semantically and quite a few of our data could not be classified within this framework. Especially the semantically defined subclasses are often not empirically separable. A uniform syntactic classification distinguishes bridging repairs and supplement repairs (Eikmeyer et al. 1999; Kindt and Laubenstein 1991). Going one step further, another necessary prerequisite for the production of a self-repair is the occurrence of a problem during the production of an utterance. This problem can either be a speaker internal production problem or a problem caused by the outer world, e.g. noise or the actions of other interlocutors.

A prototypical speaker's internal production problem are speech errors or "slips of the tongue". Dell's (1986) model shows that these errors are not random but highly regular, since a small number of error types appears on different linguistic levels, e.g. the word level, the morpheme level and the phoneme level. In the framework of the CRC 360, several contributions have been made in this research area, the most important one being the proposal of a completely connectionist language production model (as opposed to Dell's hybrid model; see Eikmeyer et al. 1999; Schade 1992, 1999; Schade and Eikmeyer 1998), which explains the formation of errors. Moreover, the model addresses planning processes covering both the aspects of 'what-to-say' and 'how-to-say-it', although it is limited to the production of referential expressions. A monitoring system and a repair strategy for the model have been proposed by Schade and Laubenstein (1993). This subsystem detects potential errors (but it does not check this effectively and does not try to reconstruct the source of the problem) and it reacts in an automatic way by a reset-approach in a system of cascaded processing levels.

Self-monitoring, speech errors and self-repairs are thus three important aspects of language production by which speakers try to control their production. Together, they seem to make up a resource-saving and automatic subsystem, which tries to prevent malfunctions or at least tries to limit the damage.

4. Dynamics of communicative understanding II: The listener

4.1. The communicative level

In task-oriented communication, the listener carefully has to check his or her understanding of the instruction. If the listener is not sure whether he or she got everything right, a clarification request is an effective strategy to obtain more information. In analogy to instructions by the speaker, clarification requests include discourse-, construction- and instructor-oriented strategies.

4.1.1. Discourse-oriented strategies

Requests for clarification can be formulated in many different ways. A major difference refers to the specificity of the requests (see Eikmeyer, Kindt, and Strohner 2006):

- Specific requests include specific information concerning the understanding problem, e.g. questions like *The red one?* or *The red one or the yellow one?* after the instruction *Take a long bolt.*
- Unspecific requests do not name a certain referential possibility. Usually the constructors open questions with, e.g. *Which color?* after the instruction *Take a long bolt.*

4.1.2. Construction-oriented strategies

Clarification requests may refer to different aspects of the construction, including the following aspects:

- Object type, e.g. *The red one?*
- Object position, e.g. *Does the bolt go on or under the bar?*
- Object direction, e.g. *Parallel or orthogonal?*
- Action type, e.g. *Do you want me to fix it?*
- Action result, e.g. *Should it look like the other wheel?*

The situational conditions in which these clarification requests are produced may also be very different. They may be more or less repetitions of instructions or influences by the constructor.

4.1.3. Instructor-oriented strategies

Our corpus contains some cases in which the instructor (I) could not answer a clarification request immediately. The constructors (C) then often used reformulation strategies (see below). This points to the cooperative attitude of the constructor, which is quite in parallel to the cooperative strategies pointed out in Section 3.1.3.

C: *Which way round? Does it matter?*
I: *What <pause> which way round?*
C: *Yes, is it a bit thicker on one side?*

4.1.4. Problem-solving strategies

Also in good agreement with the problem-oriented behavior of the instructor (see Section 3.1.4) are the problem-solving strategies of the constructor. In our data, strategies related to discourse problems, construction problems and instructor problems can be discerned:

– Discourse-related problems:

I: *And a thumb screw, no, two thumb screws.*
C: *Thumb screw, what is that?*

– Construction-related problems:

C: *Can't you start from the other side first?*
I: *Okay, let's start from the back.*

– Instructor-related problems:

I: *You must turn the cube, the blue one, there is a thread on the other side.*
C: *Yes, wait a moment.*

4.2. The cognitive level

Semantic inference is a central part of the general communicative dynamics on the cognitive level. According to the systems approach, semantic inferences may be strongly influenced by the communicative situation as well as by the partner-related knowledge. Specifically, we need to explain which conditions may activate certain inferences, which further internal conditions may influence these inferences, and what the partners may do to control the inference processes. However, before being able to discuss these processes, it is necessary to analyze the basic notions of meaning and inference (Kindt 2001a).

A theory of meaning creates the basic layer for a theory of inference. The minimal requirement for a theory of meaning is the idea, that in language understanding the listener assigns a semantic structure to an utterance which is continouously augmented and modified. This structure is part of the listener's mental state. The four kinds of propositions needed for the description and explanation of semantic affairs refer to (a) properties of utterances, (b) the relation between utterance parts and parts of the meaning structure, (c) properties of meaning structures, and (d) the relation between parts of the meaning structure and other mental states. Additionally, utterances which are regarded as sentences have to be assigned meanings which represent states of affairs. Finally, a notion of validity – as known from logical semantics – models a recipient's ability to decide if the state of affairs applies to the situation in question.

Inferences can augment a semantic interpretation, or they can constitute or establish it. Augmenting inferences correspond in principle to the logical notion of a theory- or context-dependent inference. In contrast, inferences constituting a semantic interpretation are needed to decide which semantic interpretation should be assigned to a part of an utterance in a context, and, consequently, they are to be located on a meta level. Since both types of inferences can be reconstructed by logical means, the gap usually claimed to exist by cognitive scientists can be bridged.

A basic question to be answered is how inferences are triggered and which procedures they adopt. As a result of an empirical analysis of repairs by Kindt (2001b) and in generalizing the Gricean ideas, one can assume expectations as to the correctness (quality), completeness (quantity), relevance and appropriateness (manner) of linguistic entities. These expectations can concern all linguistic levels. If in trying to understand an utterance one of these expectations is not satisfied, this can trigger solving the problem at hand with the help of an inference. In case expectations as to appropriateness or correctness are not met, inferences constituting an interpretation are drawn. Augmenting inferences, in contrast, are used where relevance and completeness expectations are not met. It is a fundamental shortcoming of the Gricean theory of implicatures that it does not say anything about the methods used for inferencing. Sometimes, inferences are induced by gestalt principles known from perception psychology. Mainly, inferences have to be seen in the context of schemes of everyday argumentation such as analogy, the Aristotelian topos of consequence (see 4.2.1. below), and the like.

In case a recipient does not succeed in arriving at a semantic interpretation which conforms to the expectations, in dialogical situations he can address the speaker, and the two of them can start a repair sequence for coordinating inferences. This is, however, a very resource-consuming way of solving the problem, but speakers can try to prospectively solve a possible problem by regulating inferences. A rather simple mechanism for the speaker is to formulate the inference to be drawn explicitly her- or himself. A more intricate mechanism would be to use lexical or phraseological formulations which conventionally lead to stable inferences. For more regulating techniques see Kindt (2001a, 2002).

4.2.1 Experimental study: Inference and actions

The study presented is the first step towards the goal to examine inference processes in an experimentally controlled manner. The inference processes in question are those drawn with the Aristotelian topos of consequence. This inference rule can be used to decide upon the expediency of actions. An action which is not regarded as expedient will not be carried out or taken into consideration. We started with simple inferences of consequence in a blocks world scenario where expediency is judged by the possibility to put an object on top of another one. In the experimental setting both unique and ambiguous referential noun phrases are used in order to refer to blocks as shown in Figure 1.

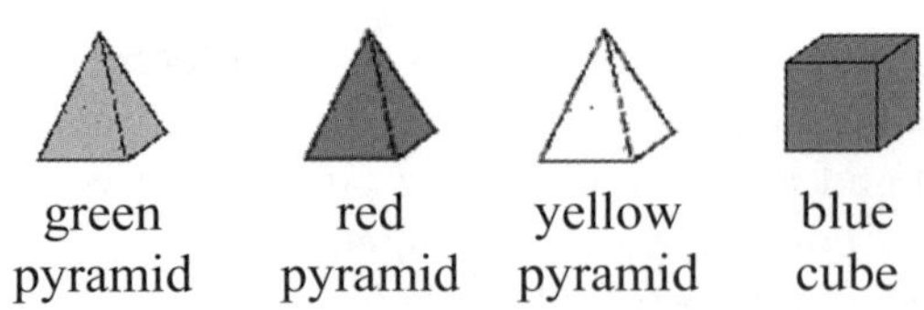

Figure 1. Objects in a blocks world

Imagine a participant in the experiment is instructed to *put the blue object on top of the yellow object*. In this case (case 1) the consequence that the action is not possible would be an inference based on the topos of consequence: A cube cannot be placed on top of a pyramid, because it will fall down. Thus, the action would not be expedient. If, however, the same instruction were to be given in a blocks world with two yellow objects, a yellow pyramid and a yellow cylinder (case 2), the instruction is ambiguous and an inference is needed to arrive at decision for one of the two actions. In weighing up the consequences of the two actions, the participant will decide upon the action leading to a positive, stable result. In our example the participant will thus take the blue cube ("placed object") and place it on top of the yellow cylinder ("target object"). This behavior is also a case of the application of inference following the pattern of the topos of consequence.

The participants in our computer based experiments had to carry out 40 such tasks. The participants were always shown one or two target objects with a color matching the one given in the instruction. There were never two objects with a geometrical form which would allow something to be placed on top of them. In addition to the cases 1 and 2 presented above, we created situations (case 3) with two target objects, for example two pyramids, of the color requested by the instruction, neither of which are able to have something put on top of them. In case 4 there was exactly one target object matching both color and form of the instruction. Moreover, there were two bins on the screen in order to put objects into them, if the construction could not be carried out as in cases 1 and 3.

The results of this preliminary study showed that, in the setting described above, in many cases the topos of consequence plays a role in the decision for an action. This can be inferred from the instructions leading to the expected reactions, as specified above. Concentrating only on these cases we could arrive at several results.

In cases 2 and 4 (at least one target object with the requested color and geometrical form) the decision for action is, on average, faster than in cases 1 and 3 (no geometrically suitable object). Geometrically unsuitable target objects, which nevertheless were of the color asked for, dramatically increased reaction times.

This time difference was not expected, since our processing assumptions were based on a sequence of the following steps: (a) find target objects matching the color, (b) check the geometrical form of the objects, (c) decide upon suitability or unsuitability (d) carry out action or report unsuitability. According to this sequence there should be no difference in processing an object with the correct color and form and one with the correct color and incorrect form. Since the participants of the experiment came to the decisions we had expected, the processing time for step (c) could make a difference: maybe it takes longer to come to the decision that something is impossible than it does that something is possible. It can be argued that more processing time is needed in the negative case because all possibilities have to be taken into consideration before the task can be carried out to the best of the constructor's ability.

In analyzing not only the cases leading to a correct result, but all cases, we found another instance of this effect. The blocks world objects were presented on the computer screen. The objects were meant to be three-dimensional objects, but were presented on a two-dimensional medium. Many participants preferred to stick to the words of the instruction rather than arrive at configurations which were possible on two-dimensional screens but not in three-dimensional reality. Thus, they applied a different criterion for actions which were capable of being carried out, but showed a behavior consistent with following the inference pattern of the topos of consequence in deciding upon which action to take. An interaction with other patterns for decision taking can, however, not be excluded.

5. Dynamics of communicative understanding III: Emerging joint action

5.1. The communicative level

5.1.1. Joint discourse-oriented strategies

In our airplane scenario, most of the construction objects are unknown to the interlocutors. Since it is necessary for a clear understanding of the instructions to agree on the referents of the intended actions, the interlocutors carry out joint endeavors for referent and local clarification. These efforts include the following joint strategies of negotiation of meaning:

- *Naming:* After a proposal for naming an object by one of the interlocutors, the other implicitly agrees to this proposal by also using the name, or explicitly by expressing his or her consent. If the partner is not fully convinced of the proposal, a negotiation problem arises (see below).
- *Explication of meaning:* Particularly with local prepositions, it is often unclear how the preposition should be understood. In many of these cases both partners cooperate in meaning negotiation, e.g. if the phrase "next to the block" is not quite clear, the other interlocutor may react with the more precise phrase "directly on the block".
- *Inference:* A third strategy of meaning negotiation refers to the consequences of the intended action. If the constructor wants to signal the

partner whether he or she correctly understood the instruction, he or she can react with an inference drawn from the instruction, e.g. *Then there is no bolt left.*

5.1.2. *Joint construction-oriented strategies*

In almost all phases of the construction process, the interlocutors try to assure one another that they have so far proceeded in the right way. They give information to one another as to how the airplane now looks and what has already been done: *Now you must have <pause> on top of that such a, such a <pause> such a long bar, then below that there, go those <pause> those which you already fixed at the end with the short bar, and below that also <pause> this free end of the short bar <pause> you got it?*

5.1.3. *Joint problem-solving strategies*

Throughout our experiments, the interlocutors demonstrated that they are excellent problem solvers. They did this by working hard to avoid problems and by engaging themselves intensively in solving any occurring problems. We outlined this in the sections 3.1 and 4.1. In addition, many pairs of collaborators proved also to be excellent cooperative problem solvers by using joint problem-solving strategies:

- *Division of labor:* If one partner detects a problem, the other immediately looks for a possible solution.

  C: *It does not work <2 seconds silence>*
  I: *You have to turn the bolt. I also tried to turn the other one*
  C: *I got it, you are right, it works*

- *Pardon:* A good strategy to evoke joint problem-solving efforts is begging one's pardon when a problem arises. A negative strategy would be to accuse the partner of causing this problem by making a mistake.

  I: *And they are both on the five hole bar*
  C: *No, I did ask you*
  I: *Yes, they have to be on the five hole bar*
  C: *Then one is in the first hole of the five hole bar and the other one is in the second hole*

I: *I told you, girl, I told you for sure, I took extra care*
C: *I believe you did not say it.*

- *Encouragement:* Encouraging the partner proved to be an excellent strategy for joint problem-solving.

I: *Then you have to take off the blue cube again...*
C: *Sh***
I: *and turn it this way. Yes, I did, that happened to me as well. It's not so bad*

- *Joint repair*: An obvious cooperative strategy is joint repair. In a joint repair effort both partners contribute in multiple steps to repair a problematic utterance.

C: *Oh, everything on top of one another?*
I: *Yes, yes*
C: *That is first the bolt, then the pink and then that plastic thing?*
I: *No, first the bolt, then the plastic thing, then the wheel and then the pink*
C: *Yes, as I said, the pink one after the wheel*
I: *Yes, after, yes, good"*

5.2. The cognitive level

Perspective taking is one of the essential prerequisites in task-oriented dialogues. If either of the communication partners refers to a certain object as being "in front of", "behind", "to the left of", or "to the right of" another object, their perspectives with regard to the object may be different. In this case, the problem must be considered by the partners at a certain moment and solved through the alignment of perspectives.

During the last few years, several theories have been proposed in order to explain the processes in perspective taking. The two-step theory (Keysar et al. 1998; 2000) focuses on the dynamics of communicative interaction. Accordingly, perspective taking proceeds in the following two steps:

- The first step comprises the interlocutors' subjective and highly automatic processing. This phase is essentially unrestricted by common ground knowledge of the interlocutors.

- The second step includes a controlled monitoring process, in which the perspective of the partner is taken into consideration on the basis of the common ground.

The two-step theory tries to separate the individual and shared levels in perspective taking. In the words of Keysar et al. (2000: 32), this furthers "the understanding of the mental processes that underlie conversation. Research in the field typically investigates comprehension from a macro-level approach and gives prominence to the assumption of shared perspective. Our micro-level investigation suggests that addressees tend to rely on information from their own perspective. Given that face-to-face interaction requires participants in conversation to act quickly, such a quick and easy comprehension strategy might be a crucial cognitive tool for a resolving ambiguity in conversation." In line with this, we investigated some of the micro-level dynamics of perspective taking in the field of task-oriented communication.

5.2.1 Experiment 1: Reaction time

Our study focused on the cognitive processes of perspective taking in a multi-phase picture-sentence verification task. Twenty student participants were presented with 24 different picture-sentence combinations (plus five warming-up trials) on a computer screen. Each picture showed a specific communication situation, in which the speaker explains the position of a certain object to the listener (Fig. 2)

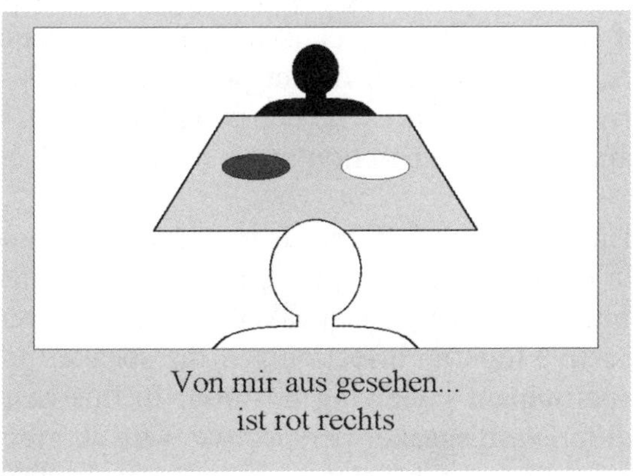

Figure 2. An example of the experimental stimuli

The pictures on the screen comprised written verbal descriptions of the intended object position. Two thirds of the sentences included an explicit statement about the perspective of either of the protagonists (e.g. *Von mir aus gesehen ist rot links*, which translates as *From my point of view, red is on the left*); one third of the sentences did not (e.g. *Rot ist links*, or *Red is on the right*).

The participants' task was to decide as fast as possible whether the utterance of the speaker in the depicted scene was correct or not. One group of participants worked according to the instruction "The speaker is always the black figure", the second group according to the instruction "The speaker is always the white figure".

Having defined the speaker in the scene, the procedure of the experiment comprised the following phases:

- *Phase 1: Alignment with speaker position:* In the first phase of the experiment, only the visual scene is presented on the screen. The critical factor is the position of the speaker (compatible vs. incompatible with the participant's viewing position). The dependent variable was inspection time, i.e. the participants had to push a button in order to signal that they had gathered enough information about the depicted scene.
- *Phase 2: Alignment with the verbally described perspective:* In phase 2, the first part of the verbal description (*Von mir aus gesehen* or *Von dir aus gesehen*) is added to the picture on the screen. The critical factor now is the verbal perspective (speaker's perspective vs. listener's perspective). Again, the dependent variable is inspection time.
- *Phase 3: Localization of intended object:* In the final phase, the verbal description of the intended object is added to the depicted scene. The critical factors are the physical object position (left vs. right hemifield) and the locative (*left* vs. *right*). The dependent variables include the number of errors and the choice reaction times for correct decisions.

In Phase 1, no inspection time differences between the two speaker positions were observed. In phase 2, there was a significant main effect of verbal perspective and an interaction between speaker position and verbal perspective: The verbal perspective took an effect only if the speaker position was compatible with the participant's viewing position. In this case, the inspection times in the condition with speaker perspective were shorter than the inspection times in the condition with listener perspective. In phase 3, the experiment also resulted in an interaction between speaker position and verbal perspective. When the speaker position was compatible with the participant's viewing position, the verification times from the speaker perspective were shorter than those from the listener perspective. When the speaker position was incompatible with the participant's viewing position, the results were inverted. In this last case, the error rate was also higher. In addition, the condition without information about the perspective of speaker or listener resulted in longer verification times and higher error rates than the two other conditions.

The results are compatible with the two-step theory of perspective taking. In Phase 1, the participants did not react at all to the occasion of taking the speaker's perspective. In Phase 2, the participants seemed to react to the verbal perspective only when their viewing position was compatible to that of the speaker. Only in Phase 3, when the participants were forced to react by means of a verification task, did they also react to the speaker on the other side of the table. In both cases, the reaction times were shorter when no perspective taking was necessary. The question, however, what exactly was going on during the longer reaction times, cannot be answered by the reaction time method. Therefore, in Experiment 2 the participants' eye movements were recorded during the whole experimental procedure.

5.2.2. Experiment 2: Eye movements

The inspection times as such did not indicate when in the course of processing people committed themselves to a particular perspective. They also could not provide direct evidence for any change of perspective. Recording eye movements while people are listening to verbal statements, however, can provide direct evidence for comprehension processes, in particular for reference resolution (Ferreira and Henderson 2004; Pomplun et al. 1997; Sichelschmidt 2005; Spivey-Knowlton et al. 1998). Above all, the question as to whether recipients already change perspective when hearing „from my point of view…“ (as said by a speaker at varying locations), or whether they rather wait until the end of the phrase can be answered by means of eye movement tracking (Avraamides 2003; Hanna, Tanenhaus, and Trueswell 2003; Li and Gleitman 2002). Therefore, we conducted a second experiment on perspective shift using eye gaze tracking (Sichelschmidt, Jang, and Koesling 2003).

Eighteen students participated in the experiment. They were all native speakers of German , they had all normal or corrected-to-normal vision, and they were randomly assigned to either a „Black is Speaker“ or a „White is Speaker“ group. During the experiment, they each had to verify 32 picture-sound combinations. The pictures showed a face-to-face dialog scene similar to that used in Experiment 1 (cf. Figure 1). In the present experiment, the colored spots were made harder to perceive by reducing their size and increasing their distance. The verbal materials were presented auditorily in order to let the participants focus their visual attention on the scene. In the present experiment, we used only two-phrase sentences such as *Von mir aus gesehen ist rot rechts* (*from my point of view, red is on the right*). During the experiment, we recorded the participants' eye movements using a video-based SMI EyeLink 1 tracker.

The following factors were systematically varied within cases (unless indicated otherwise):

- The speaker's position was either in the foreground (ahead) or in the background (opposite).
- The referent object was located either in the left or in the right hemifield.
- The perspective was verbally defined by either *von mir aus gesehen* (*from my point of view*) or by *von dir aus gesehen* (*from your point of view*).
- The locative used was either *links* (*on the left*) or *rechts* (*on the right*), rendering one half of the correct answers „true" and the other half „false".
- And finally, as mentioned above, the designated speaker was either Black or White throughout the experimental session (between cases).

As in Experiment 1, the trials were presented in a quasi-random order after a few warming-up trials. Eventually, 5035 relevant fixations from 548 correct trials were analyzed at three levels of granularity.

At the trajectory level of analysis, we found that the average reaction time (from the onset of the utterance until the participant pressed the key) amounted to 4622 ms. Since the duration of the sound files was 3500 ms, this means that, after the end of the sound file, the participants took about one more second to arrive at the correct decision. Furthermore, a structural comparison between the empirical eye movement trajectories and the theoretical trajectories, which represent the minimum of eye movements necessary for arriving at a decision, yielded an average Levenshtein distance of 2.1. This means that the empirical trajectories were substantially longer and more complicated than the theoretical ones. A qualitative analysis of the trajectory data showed that scanning strategies differed between individuals rather than between conditions. Altogether, the measures at the trajectory level of analysis seem to reflect the global difficulty of perspective alignment rather than local shifts of perspective – the more so since they were independent of conditions.

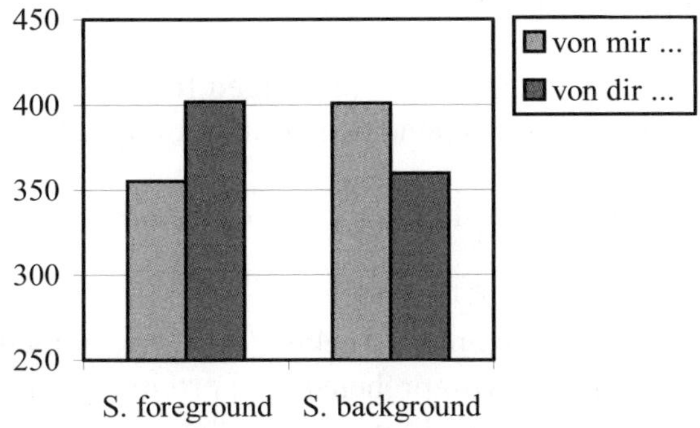

Figure 3. Mean fixation duration in ms

As to the fixations level of analysis, where fixations as the constituents of a trajectory are under study, the average number of fixations per trial – 9.2 to arrive at a correct decision – was also supportive to the view that perspective alignment is an intricate matter. The mean fixation duration was 377 ms. As a measure of local cognitive effort, fixation duration was determined by a significant interaction between „speaker's position" and „perspective":

- When the speaker was located in the foreground, the speaker's perspective (*Von mir aus gesehen*, or *From my point of view*) was easier to process in terms of fixation duration.
- When the speaker was located in the background, the addressee's perspective (*Von dir aus gesehen,* or *From your point of view*) led to shorter fixations.

Finally, at the synchrony level of analysis, the „voice-eye" lag was investigated. The Event Onset Asynchrony (EOA), that is, the onset of the first referent-directed fixation after the onset of a referring word, was different for different types of referring expressions. It was longest for the locative (*links* or *rechts*; i.e., *on the left* or *on the right*, respectively) at the end of a sentence (745 ms). It was shorter for the perspective specifier (654 ms) or the object specifier (684 ms). These values were independent of conditions.

Taken together, the second experiment on perspective shift in referential communication has shown that

- perspective taking can successfully be studied by means of eye movement tracking;

- perspective alignment is an intricate cognitive process guided by individual strategies;
- changes of perspective manifest in prolonged fixation duration;
- ease of perspective taking depends on compatibility with the participant's egocentric view;
- the process of perspective alignment is closely time-locked to the verbal utterance.

As to the first point, eye movement tracking is a proven method for the on-line investigation of speech comprehension (Ferreira and Henderson 2004; Trueswell and Tanenhaus 2004). In particular, the establishment of reference is a phenomenon that has received much attention lately. With the present experiment, we have successfully demonstrated that people's eye movements reflect the process of perspective taking in a rather direct fashion.

The second point is made clear by the relatively long time that people took in order to arrive at a correct decision. Obviously, a verification task on the locatives *links* (*left*) and *rechts* (*right*) is a cognitively demanding affair (Hörnig, Claus, and Eyferth 2000). The non-minimal trajectories that the participants have employed, and the individual differences, suggest that perspective updating is accomplished by means of a number of cognitive subprocesses, the interplay of which is to be investigated in more detail in further experiments.

The third point emphasizes the local, and on-line, character of perspective alignment. Unlike other eye movement parameters, such as the number of fixations, fixation duration reflects quite directly the cognitive effort which people make on the processing of the verbal element in question (Boland 2004; Joos, Rötting, and Velichkovsky 2003). The fact that any difficulties people encountered in the processing of locatives is manifested in fixation duration corresponds well with the view that language users, in the course of comprehension, incrementally construct a mental representation of the states of affairs described by the text.

The fourth point has some bearing on the nature of the cognitive processes involved in perspective alignment. The disordinal nature of the interaction suggests that the resource-consuming effects of perspective changes do not add up in time. Instead, perspective change is accomplished in a flip switch like fashion: If the last perspective taken is compatible with the primary deictic view, that is, the viewer's egocentric perspective, things are easy. If not, they're not. This finding once again emphasizes the importance of the egocentric frame of reference (Epley et al. 2004; Keysar et al. 2000; Marcel and Dobel 2005) as a starting point for the construction of a mental representation. It may also provide a clue to the question of why perspective in everyday communication is a source of misunderstanding: Language users may differ in their speed and their readiness to abandon their egocentric point of view.

Finally, the interval of 654 ms between the onset of the perspective specifier (*mir* or *dir*; or *my* or *your*, respectively) and the first fixation of the appropriate picture element indicates that participants utilize local referential information already during the processing of the first part of the utterance. The fact, however, that the EOA was independent of conditions provides an argument against the view that people analyze each and every referential expression to the full. If this were the case, the EOA would have been longer when the speaker's position were incompatible with the participant's egocentric view, than when the speaker's position and the participant's perspective were compatible. Rather the finding that the EOAs did not differ between these conditions is in line with current psycholinguistic theories which feature shallow processing (Ferreira, Bailey, and Ferraro 2002; Lockhart 2002; Mauner, Tanenhaus, and Carlson 1995): Language users proceed economically, in that they analyze expressions only to such an extent that it suffices, or is "good enough", to maintain mutual understanding.

6. Towards a systems theory of communicative understanding

In parts 3, 4 and 5 of this chapter we have shown that not only speakers and listeners individually contribute to a better understanding between the two partners, but this understanding is also significantly sustained by emergent joint actions. Both individual and joint responses include discourse-related, construction-related and partner-related strategies and, if needed, problem-solving efforts at the cognitive and communicative levels. As we have shown in the experiments on clarification request and perspective taking, the selection and dynamics of these strategies greatly depend on the situational and temporal circumstances.

6.1. The architecture of the system

Taken all together, we are now able to present the basic structure of a cognitive system that is able to perform the behavior observed. Starting from the systems framework outlined in Section 2, the knowledge units of the cognitive system should include individual and joint strategies. During the course of task-oriented communication, the proportion of the joint strategies should increase and the proportion of the individual strategies should decrease.

Figure 4 shows the structure of a cognitive system as a subsystem of a task-oriented communication system. The cognitive system is embedded in a situation, i.e. the functionally relevant parts of the physical and social environment. Situations can often be defined by the task, general social orientation, or conventional norms of the actual communicative event. However, the situation may not be seen as static. Often, it is highly dynamic and can change with every word during a discourse.

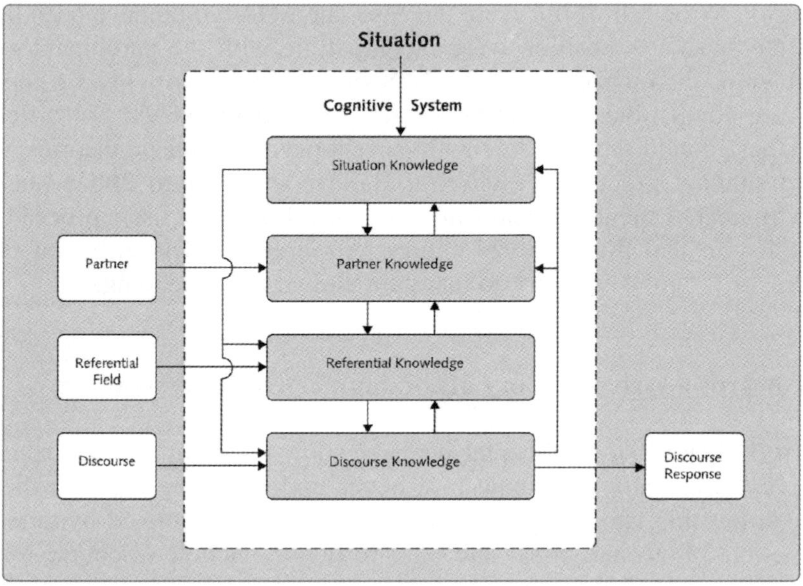

Figure 4. The internal and external structure of a cognitive system as subsystem of a communication system

For task oriented-communication, three components of the situation are particularly relevant, the partner, referential field, and discourse:

- Partners can vary in many aspects, including cooperativeness which is one of the most important characteristics in our experimental setting.
- The referential field may be easy to scan or difficult in terms of complexity or perspective.
- The discourse proceeds along the time scale and brings new information with every upcoming word.

Corresponding to the external influences, the cognitive system has special knowledge units to process these influences in order to produce an adequate discourse response comprising verbal and nonverbal behavior.

6.2. The dynamics of the system

As we already mentioned in part 2.3, we conceive of the dynamics of cognitive systems in communication as constrained-based, interactive and parallel. In doing this, we are in good agreement with many recent communication theories. The basic conflict, however, arises when the role of the partner knowledge in the communicative dynamics is to be clarified. Three theoretical positions have recently been discussed – the two-step theory (Barr and Keysar 2005), alignment theory (Garrod and Pickering 2004; Pickering and Garrod 2004), and situated activation theory (Brennan and Metzing 2004).

Whereas our findings in the perspective taking study are compatible with the two-step theory, the results in the clarification request study support the situated approach (Eikmeyer, Kindt, and Strohner 2006). However, the findings of the perspective taking study may also be explained by the situated theory, as this approach is broader and more flexible than the other two theories. Communicative understanding includes individual and joint strategies which vary according to situational demands as we have shown in the preceding sections 3, 4, and 5.

7. Conclusion

Communicative understanding is a central part of human social interaction. Research in many disciplines of social science has shown that in most cases social interaction is goal-driven and to a high degree partner and situation dependent. Communicative conventions and strategies, the personalities of the communication partners and the purpose of their interaction affect their mutual adaptation and their expectations for future interactions. In communicative understanding the impact of the social situation must be taken into account, not just as an additional factor but as a necessary basis and precondition for many cognitive and communicative processes.

"Given the complexities," Schober and Brennan (2003: 155) argue, "it seems naive to imagine that we can determine, across discourse context, and for a particular aspect of language use (say word selection in production), what sorts of adaptations always occur. Presumably the adaptations vary according to conversationalists' (chronic or momentary) attentional capacities, discourse goals, interest in taking their partner's perspective, and so on)."

Future research should focus on the combined effects of some of the factors mentioned by Schober and Brennan and demonstrated in our studies. The conceptual basis of this attempt is related to a systems view of alignment in communication. According to this view, communicative understanding is seen as a complex interaction of cognitive systems emerging in a more comprehensive social system with new capabilities. Some of the most important factors governing these systemic processes include task orientation, time course and transfer to novel situations:

- As goal directedness is a general feature of social actions, many communicative activities are performed to serve certain functions. Task orientation in human communication will influence verbal and nonverbal communication and other social behavior at different levels of the action hierarchy. In some cases, the interactions may not result in social convergence, but in misunderstanding and divergence. In addition, many communicative interactions rely on social problem solving in institutional settings (Giles, Coupland, and Coupland 1991).
- Communicative understanding consists of processes of different duration. The time course of processing words, utterances, conversation turns, and conversation sequences comprises various cognitive and emotional processes including conceptual priming, model construction, strategies, and expectations. Short-term discourse processes may be more automatic than long-term processes, some of which are highly controlled and thoroughly planned (Snyder and Stukas 1999).
- As present empirical research shows that communicative understanding is highly situation dependent, the problem arises as to how to handle the necessary transfer to novel situations in research and practical application. Recently, this crucial problem has been handled by closer consideration of the original situation (Anderson, Reder, and Simon 1996). In many learning contexts transfer of novel linguistic and conceptual knowledge is of great importance, e.g. in first-language acquisition (Tomasello 2003), second-language learning and language therapy (Ferguson 1999).

Considering the theoretical problems of research into situated processes of communicative understanding – what are the adequate methods and theories to deal with them? Taking the theoretical problems of research into situated processes of communicative understanding into consideration, the question arises as to what the adequate methods and theories for dealing with them are. A plausible methodological approach is the control and systematic variation of the most important situational factors according to qualitative and quantitative communication analyses. A plausible theoretical approach is to extend game theoretical concepts and apply them to cognitive and communicative phenomena. The starting point for such an approach (cf. Eikmeyer, Kindt, and Strohner 2006) is an input-output model for a language processing phenomenon, e.g. clarification requests. Such a model specifies a set of independent (input) and dependent (output) variables and the relations between them. This model has to be refined step by step with a growing set of intervening variables, which describes the internal structure in more and more detail. The structural refinement has to be accompanied by a specification of the transition and the output relation. The interplay of variables and relations has to be evaluated with respect to empirical data until, in the end, a full system theoretic analysis has been reached.

The resulting picture of communication will not only show the high flexibility of this type of social interaction but also, as converging evidence, some basic and general cognitive strategies, which may be relevant for many situations of human communication. To reach this goal, a close cooperation between empirical, theoretical, formal and simulative methods will be helpful (Eikmeyer, Kindt, and Strohner 2006).

Acknowledgements

We thank Kyung-Won Jang, Elke Prestin, and Gesche Schaffranietz for their effective support and fruitful discussions.

References

Anderson, J. R., L. M. Reder, and H. A. Simon
1996 Situated learning and education. *Educational Researcher* 25: 5–11.

Avraamides, M. N.
2003 Spatial updating of environments described in texts. *Cognitive Psychology* 47: 402–431.

Barr, D., and B. Keysar
2005 Making sense of how we make sense: The paradox of egocentrism in language use. In *Figurative Language Comprehension: Social and Influences,* H. L. Colston and A. N. Katz (eds.), 21–42. Mahwah: Erlbaum.

Boland, J. E.
2004 Linking eye movements to sentence comprehension in reading and listening. In *The On-Line Study of Sentence Comprehension: Eye-tracking, ERPs and Beyond*, M. Carreiras and C. Clifton, Jr (eds.), 51–76. New York: Psychology Press.

Brennan, S. E., and C. A. Metzing
2004 Two steps forward, one step back: Partner-specific effects in a psychology of dialogue. *Behavioral and Brain Sciences* 27: 192.

Dell, G.
1986 A spreading-activation theory of retrieval in sentence production. *Psychological Review* 93: 283–321.

Donnellan, K.
1966 Reference and definite descriptions. *Philosophical Review* 75: 281–304.

Eikmeyer, H.-J., W. Kindt, and H. Strohner
2006 System theoretical modeling on situated communication. In *Situated Communication,* G. Rickheit and I. Wachsmuth (eds.), 411–436. Berlin: de Gruyter (this volume).

Eikmeyer, H.-J., U. Schade, M. Kupietz, and U. Laubenstein
1999 A connectionist view of language production. In *Representations and Processes in Language Production*, R. Klabunde and C. von Stutterheim (eds.), 205–236. Wiesbaden: Deutscher Universitäts-Verlag.

Epley, N., B. Keysar, L. Van Boven, and T. Gilovich
2004 Perspective taking as egocentric anchoring and adjustment. *Journal of Personality and Social Psychology* 87: 327–339.

Ferguson, A.
1999 Learning in aphasia therapy: It's not so much what you do, but how you do it! *Aphasiology* 13: 125–132.

Ferreira, F., K. G. D. Bailey, and V. Ferraro
2002 Good-enough representations in language comprehension. *Current Directions in Psychological Science* 11: 11–15.

Ferreira, F., and J. M. Henderson (eds.)
2004 *The Interface of Language, Vision, and Action: Eye Movements and the Visual World.* New York: Psychology Press.

Garrod, S., and M. J. Pickering
2004 Why is conversation so easy? *Trends in Cognitive Science* 8: 8–11.

Giles, H., G. Coupland, and N. Coupland (eds.)
1991 *Contexts of Accomodation: Developments in Applied Sociolinguistics.* Cambridge, UK: Cambridge University Press.

Hanna, J. E., M. K. Tanenhaus, and J. C. Trueswell
2003 The effects of common ground and perspective on domains of referential interpretation. *Journal of Memory and Language* 49: 43–66.

Herrmann, T., and J. Grabowski
1994 *Sprechen*. Heidelberg: Spektrum.

Hörnig, R., B. Claus, and K. Eyferth
2000 In search for an overall organizing principle in spatial mental models: A question of inference. In *Spatial Cognition: Foundations and Applications,* S. O'Nuallain (ed), 69–81. Amsterdam: Benjamins.

Jang, K.-W.
2003 "Mach' das nicht..." Zur Verarbeitung negativer Handlungsanweisungen. Report, CRC 360, Bielefeld: University of Bielefeld.

Joos, M., M. Rötting, and B. M. Velichkovsky
2003 Bewegungen des menschlichen Auges: Fakten, Methoden und innovative Anwendungen. In *Psycholinguistik – ein internationales Handbuch,* G. Rickheit, T. Herrmann & W. Deutsch (eds.), 142–167. Berlin: de Gruyter.

Keysar, B., D. J. Barr, J. A. Balin, and J. S. Brauner
2000 Taking perspective in conversation: The role of mutual knowledge in comprehension. *Psychological Science* 11: 32–38.

Keysar, B., D. J. Barr, J. A. Balin, and T. S. Paek
1998 Definite reference and mutual knowledge: Process models of common ground in comprehension. *Journal of Memory and Language* 39: 1–20.

Kindt, W.
2001a. Neue Wege der Inferenzforschung. In *Sprache, Sinn und Situation,* L. Sichelschmidt and H. Strohner (eds.), 109–124. Wiesbaden: Deutscher Universitäts-Verlag.
2001b. Syntax und Pragmatik: Eine zu entdeckende Verwandtschaft. In *Pragmatische Syntax,* F. Hundsnurscher and F. Liedtke (eds.), 5–29. Tübingen: Niemeyer.
2002 Koordinations-, Konstruktions- und Regulierungsprozesse bei der Bedeutungskonstitution. In *be-deuten: Wie Bedeutung im Gespräch entsteht*, A. Deppermann and T. Spranz-Fogasy (eds.), 34–58. Tübingen: Stauffenberg.

Kindt, W., and R. Weingarten
1984 Verständigungsprobleme. *Deutsche Sprache* 3: 193–218.

Levelt, W. J. M.
1983 Monitoring and self-repair in speech. *Cognition* 14: 41–104.
1989 *Speaking: From Intention to Articulation.* Cambridge, MA: MIT Press.

Li, P., and L. Gleitman
2002 Turning the tables. Language and spatial reasoning. *Cognition* 83: 265–294.

Lockhart, R. S.
2002 Levels of processing, transfer-appropriate processing, and the concept of robust encoding. *Memory* 10: 397–403.

Marcel, A., and C. Dobel
2005 Structured perceptual input imposes an egocentric frame of reference – pointing, imagery, and spatial self-consciousness. *Perception* 34: 429–451.

Mauner, G., M. K. Tanenhaus, and G. N. Carlson
1995 Implicit arguments in sentence processing. *Journal of Memory and Language* 34: 357–382.

Pickering, M., and S. Garrod
2004 Toward a mechanistic psychology of dialogue. *Behavioral and Brain Sciences* 27: 169–226.

Pomplun, M., H. Rieser, H. Ritter, and B. M. Velichkovsky
1997 Augenbewegungen als kognitionswissenschaftlicher Forschungsgegenstand. In *Strukturen und Prozesse intelligenter Systeme,* R. H. Kluwe (ed.), 65–106. Wiesbaden: Deutscher Universitäts-Verlag.

Schade, U.
1992 *Konnektionismus: Zur Modellierung der Sprachproduktion.* Opladen: Westdeutscher Verlag.
1999 *Konnektionistische Sprachproduktion.* Wiesbaden: Deutscher Universitäts-Verlag.

Schade, U., and H.-J. Eikmeyer
1998 Modeling the production of objects specifications. In *Localist Connectionist Approaches to Human Cognition,* J. Grainger and A. Jacobs (eds.), 257–282. Mahwah: Erlbaum.

Schade, U., and U. Laubenstein
1993 Repairs in a connectionist language production model. In *Contributions to Quantitative Linguistics,* R. Köhler and B. Rieger (eds.), 79–90. Dordrecht: Kluwer.

Schober, M., and S. Brennan
2003 Processes of interactive spoken discourse: The role of the partner. In *Handbook of Discourse Processes,* A. C. Graesser, M. A. Gernsbacher and S. R. Goldman (eds.), 123–164. Mahwah, NJ: Erlbaum.

Sichelschmidt, L.
2005 More than just style: An oculomotor approach to semantic interpretation. In *Proceedings of 2005 Symposium on Culture, Arts, and Education,* J. C.-H. Chen, and K.-C. Liang (eds.), 118–130. Taipei: NTNU Press.

Sichelschmidt, L., K. W. Jang, and H. Koesling
2003 *Perspective alignment in referential communication.* Presented at the 12th European Conference on Eye Movements, 22 August 2003, Dundee.

Snyder, M., and A. A. Stukas
1999 Interpersonal processes: The interplay of cognitive, motivational and behavioral activities in social interaction. *Annual Review of Psychology* 50: 273–303.

Spivey-Knowlton, M., M. K. Tanenhaus, K. Eberhard, and J. Sedivy
1998 Integration of visuospatial and linguistic information in real-time and real-space. In *Representation and Processing of Spatial Expressions,* P. Olivier and K. Gapp (eds.), 201–214. Mahwah: Erlbaum.

Tomasello, M.
2003 *Constructing a Language: A Usage-Based Theory of Language Acquisition.* Cambridge, MA: Harvard University Press.

Trueswell, J. C., and M. K. Tanenhaus (eds.)
2004 *Processing World-Situated Language: Bridging the Language-as-Action and Language-as-Product Traditions.* Cambridge, MA: MIT Press.

System theoretical modeling on situated communication

Hans-Jürgen Eikmeyer, Walther Kindt,
and Hans Strohner

Abstract. This contribution introduces the *Grounded Experimental-Simulative Method* which is a result of research on situated communication. The method combines qualitative and quantitative communication analysis, both supported by an annotated corpus management and analysis system with controlled experiments. The empirical results lead to the formulation of theorems for system models with specified input, intervening states and output variables. Finally, these models can be simulated on a computer. The methodology demonstrates the significance of the methods used for empirical and formal analyses in the different branches of linguistics for an integrated system-theoretical development of models.

1. Introduction

This contribution presents a comprehensive methodology for empirical, theoretical, and simulative research in cognitive science. The starting point for this methodology is, on the one hand, the belief that theoretically and empirically backed research on the complex subject of natural language communication needs a systematic and interdisciplinary integration of methods. On the other hand, this kind of integration is possible only on the basis of a system theoretical conception of linguistics, which combines structural with procedural analyses (Eikmeyer et al. 2006).

The systems framework conceptualizes communication as the interaction of dynamic systems in a given situation using linguistic utterances. Our empirical setting consists of interactions during a construction task. In these interactions a constructor has to put together the model of an airplane while relying solely on the verbal instructions of the instructor. The verbal output of the instructor functions as input for the constructor and is processed in dependency of the external situation and the mental state. At the same time the constructor reacts to the input with his own output by making a construction and linguistic utterances.

As an example of methodology, a study on communicative understanding is chosen. The subject of investigation of this project are the verbal instructions in which the instructor and constructor undertake specific linguistic or mental activities in order to arrive at a successful communication. The specific goal of this project is a model of referential clarification requests in task oriented communication.

Which procedure seems most effective for reaching this goal? In extension to the usual experimental methodology in psycholinguistics and simulation methods in computer science, we conduct discourse analytical research in order to find ecologically valid hypotheses. Consequently, we talk about a *Grounded Experimental-Simulative Method*. The first step includes an extensive corpus on communication in which relevant phenomena can be observed.

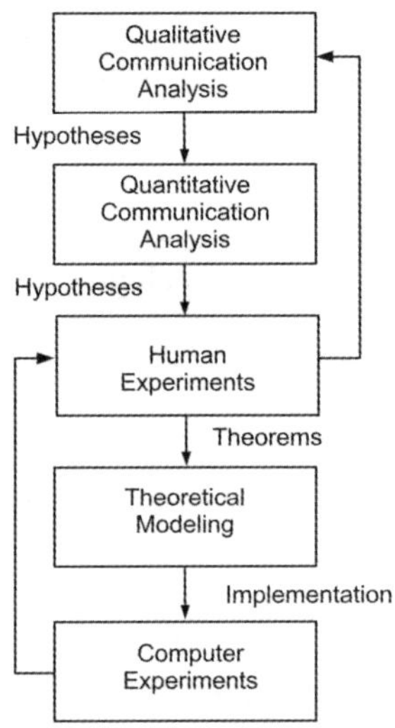

Figure 1. The Grounded Experimental-Simulative Method

Moving beyond the customary approach in qualitative communication analysis, the search for hypotheses is supported by quantitative methods using computer evaluation for corpora. As a computer evaluation needs an annotation system as a prerequisite, the respective contextual conditions and features must be identified using formal linguistic indicators.

The next step of the Grounded Experimental-Simulative Method is the use of experimental methods for checking the hypotheses found by the communication analyses.

It should not be assumed that a single experiment suffices in order to confirm or falsify the hypotheses tested. Very often it cannot be explained sufficiently to what extent the experimentally varying contextual conditions are responsible for the observed effects. Furthermore, often there are indications that there are other still unconsidered relevant factors. In such cases it can be useful to modify the hypotheses accordingly before conducting the next experiments.

The experimentally confirmed hypotheses are used in the next step, possibly also using the already available theories, in order to construct a theoretical model for the behavior of the system. Generally it can be assumed that not all relevant influential factors from the corpus or the experiments conducted are included or controlled. Therefore certain theoretically and empirically founded intervening variables are added to the model in order to arrive at an explanation of a wider scope. This allows for a generalization of the model.

The final step of the method is the computer simulation. It checks if the model constructed is sufficiently precise for a computer system running in real time.

2. Qualitative communication analysis

Research in communication analysis has shown that successful communication between interlocutors relies to a great extent on the interactive coordination of meanings. This is especially true for task-oriented communication, since specific goals have to be arrived at. Discourse analysis has identified a number of strategies speakers and hearers apply to achieve coordination (cf. Kindt 1998; 2002).

Usually, linguistic discourse research deals with corpora consisting of spontaneous speech. Such corpora have the disadvantage that the underlying tasks and the related communicative expectations vary and the parts taken over by the communication partners can be defined very differently. In order to allow for a higher comparability and a better generalization of the results of the analysis, it is useful to work with corpora elicited experimentally, under controlled conditions.

The twenty-two dialogues in the corpus of the Collaborative Research Center (CRC) were transcribed and then analyzed for communication strategies. Occurring problems were divided into problems of formulation and problems of comprehension.

This type of analysis shows regularities and certain dependencies which form the starting point for the formulation of hypotheses. The constructors (C) in the corpus, for example, very often use inferences introduced by the conclusive conjunction *so* (*also* in German) testing the instructors (I) and the degree of understanding, as shown in the following example:

I: *ja das wird dann – das ist jetzt das Heck von dem Flugzeug – das ist – das – äh Höhenruder.*
yes that will be then – this is now the stern of the airplane – this is – the – ehm elevator.

C: *mhm, – na also ähm ist das dann – quer dazu, | oder wie?*
mhm, – well so ehm is that then – crossways | or what?

I: *| ja, quer dazu.*
| yes, crossways.

Moreover, clarification requests were usually formulated as alternative questions using the conjunction *oder* (*or*), or in form of *wh*-questions using the question pronoun *welch~* (*what*), as the following two examples from the corpus show:

I: *sagen wir, den gelben, weil ich auch gelb habe und jetzt äh nimmst du dir noch eine von den kleinen roten Schrauben.*
say we the yellow since I also yellow have and now eh take you one more of the small red bolts

C: *eckig oder rund*
angular or round

I: *rund – nicht die Rauten*
round – not the rhombs

C: *mhm*
mhm

I: *und dann – nimmst du dir einen von diesen äh Würfeln mit den vielen Löchern drin.*
and then – you take one of these ehm cubes with the many holes in it.

C: *welche Farbe?*
what color?

I: *das ist eigentlich egal – wenn ich das richtig sehe, ja, kunterbunt durcheinander*
that is actually whatever you like – if I see that correctly, yes, motley

C: *okay*
okay

These examples indicated relatively soon that the number of referential objects to choose from is a relevant independent variable.

3. Quantitative communication analysis

3.1. Computer assisted analysis of linguistic corpora

The computer assisted analysis of linguistic data uses an annotated corpus of linguistic data as its search space. The core of this data is a transcription of the observed verbal behavior or speech. This information is enriched by additional information which characterizes selections of the verbal behavior in a purposeful and dependent way. An unlimited number of annotations can be attached to a stretch of speech. The analysis combines search facilities for both the core data and the annotations. With respect to the core data, a full text search with regular expressions is used in our system. It is more powerful than a string search since a regular expression describes not only a single string but a set of strings. Annotations, on the other hand, assign a finite number of properties to a selection of verbal behavior. The kind of information covered in an annotation is the central property and other properties are assigned by attribute-value-pairs, where the attribute subspecifies the aspect of the information given by its value.

3.1.1. Aim and functionality

If one wants to implement a software system for handling corpora of communicative interactions from an applied linguistics point of view, one has to consider the three following basic functionalities:

Transcription: This is the possibility to represent an interaction between two or more persons in a written form. Interactions include both verbal and non-verbal means. It also means that a representation of the language signal produced by the interlocutors is the core of the gathered data. It has to be ensured that arbitrary information can be added to the core data. The visualization of the data uses a score view with a number of voices for the interlocutor's language signal. Such a view easily codes the relation between an interlocutor and what she is saying. Moreover, it depicts overlapping speech.

Annotation: This is the possibility of adding meta information to the core data. This type of information is in no way limited with respect to what it is and how many perspectives on the core data it is representing. However, the meta information has to be formally structured to make it treatable for machines. We chose an attribute-value-based approach, i.e. all meta information is represented by attribute-value-pairs in which the attributes to be used have to be specified.

Analysis: All information of the corpus, including the language signals and all annotations, has to be accessible for an automatic mechanism which analyzes the data according to the user's requirements. These include full-text search as well as search for attributes, values, or attribute-value-pairs of annotations and combinations of both. All such queries are formulated in a special language.

From a purely practical point of view, the two following functionalities are nice to have:

Accessibility: All data has to be easily accessible for a group of researchers, and the system has to be accessible from different places and from any software platform. A web-based approach is optimal for these means.

Re-usability: All information of the annotated corpora has to be exportable in a suitable standardized output format in order to offer an interface to other systems. For practical reasons and based on the current state-of-the-art in text technology we chose XML as our export language.

3.1.2. Data model and technical aspects

A theoretical data model has to guarantee the formal integrity of the data. We needed a data model for a corpus which is a set of interactions. An interaction is represented by a directed acyclic graph. These graphs contain two types of nodes: those representing a single contribution of a speaker during the interaction – called text chunks – and those representing annotations.

Text chunks contain an ordered sequence of minimal elements. According to the language transcribed, these may be words, morphemes, phonemes, or anything else that might be suitable. All text chunks are related by their respective positions: they start somewhere in another chunk, mostly at its end, but possibly somewhere in the middle. An edge in the graph has this position as the value of its start-attribute. Overlapping speech is thus easily represented.

Annotations are coded similarly: they have two edges pointing to a text chunk and the start- and end-attribute of the respective edges to code the relative position of the annotation with respect to the text. Both types of node have a set of attribute-value-pairs attached to them. The set of admissible attributes has to be defined by the user.

Technically, the system uses a client-server architecture. User interaction happens via a web browser communicating with a dedicated web server using HTTP for a protocol. The CGI-interface starts PERL-programs which themselves communicate with a data base (for the persistent storage of the data) and a PROLOG-engine (for data analysis). The theoretical data model was mapped onto a relational data base scheme covering both the graph model and the attribute-value based information. In addition to algorithms for data handling, a transformation interface was implemented, which shows the language data in a score view with HTML (Fig. 2). A query language was designed for data analysis.

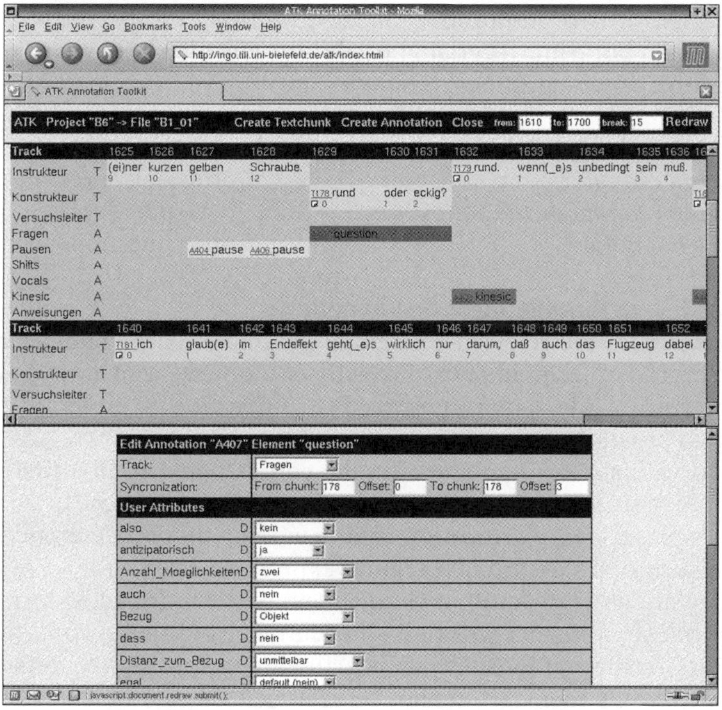

Figure 2. View of a software system for corpora of communicative interactions

3.2. The case of requests for clarification

In the framework of the CRC 360 we looked at how interlocutors can ensure that they understand one another. They can do so either in a prospective way when they (try to) make sure that no problem arises, or they can do so in a retrospective way when they already have a problem. In construction dialogues in which an instructor tells a constructor how to manipulate certain objects, a basic problem is to make sure that both talk about the same objects. In case of an object identification problem due to a lack of information on the side of one of the interlocutors, a request for clarification can be posed. Several strategies can be applied in such a case, but, based on eclectic analyses, we were able to formulate an initial hypothesis.

For its formulation we use the following terminology: Depending on the situation, a specific or an unspecific request for clarification can be formulated. Specific requests for clarification can be a proposal (a possible partial object description adding more information to the information already available) or a list of two proposals connected with *or*. Unspecific requests for clarification do not name a certain possibility. They are open questions, preferably in form of *wh*-questions. Examples are:

I:	*take a long bolt*	
C1:	*the red one?*	[proposal, specific]
C2:	*the red one or the yellow one?*	[list, specific]
C3:	*what color?*	[open question, unspecific]

This gives rise to formulating a first hypothesis.

Hypothesis 1: The relevant referential parameter is the number of possible reference objects: in case of exactly two objects a specific *or*-question is preferred, while a more unspecific *wh*-question is preferred for more than two possibilities.

In order to validate this hypothesis in the corpus one can, in a first step, apply a full text string search for the word *or* in order to identify all possible specific requests for clarification and annotate those occurrences which really are such cases. A full text regular expression search for *wh*-words (actually, they are *w*-words only in German and occur in inflected forms as e.g. *welcher, welche, welches*) will find all occurrences of these words and allow for the classification of those which actually are unspecific requests for clarification. Proposals like C1's cannot be searched for and thus have to be annotated as specific proposal. Therefore, simple search helps to find candidates for expressions of a special kind and annotate them accordingly.

Once the annotation has been performed, one can then search for annotated selections of speech:

- Show all specific requests for clarification
- Show all proposals
- Show all open questions asking for 'size', 'color', or 'length' information

Moreover, Boolean combinations of search patterns of the kinds mentioned above can be used.

Our results show that 80% of all requests for clarification found in situations with only one possible object are proposals, i.e. specific requests. This is a significantly higher percentage than that of all proposals. The specific lists with *or* are the preferred way of formulating requests for clarification in situations with two possible objects (66%). Unspecific requests, on the other hand, were found in differing proportions throughout the corpora (cf. Rittgeroth et al. 2001).

4. Experimentation on language use

As a crucial part of the Grounded Experimental-Simulative Method, experiments serve as a link between quantitative and qualitative communication analysis and the theoretical modeling part of the method.

4.1. Linking communication analysis to experiments

Communication analysis results in a rich description of the communicative processes going on in the intended research field. However, for theoretical modeling the information resulting from communication analysis is often too complex and too vague. What is needed is an evaluation procedure of the theoretical hypotheses which results from the interpretation of the observed behavior sequences. This evaluation procedure is contributed by the experimental method (cf. Sichelschmidt and Carbone, 2003). It includes the following steps.

Hypotheses. Clearly formulated hypotheses are one of the first steps towards theory building. Hypotheses are the result of communication analysis and a necessary precondition for precise experimentation. Hypotheses are formulated as declarative expressions linking two groups of variables pertinent to the research topic in the form of "If group A has property E1, then group B has property E2." Usually, the variable group A is termed the independent variable and B the dependent variable. In order to get the A-B relationship in a relatively undisturbed way, other variables C, which may influence it, have to be thoroughly controlled. Thus, hypotheses link dependent and independent variables.

Research design. On the basis of the selected hypotheses the research design spells out the variable types A, B, and C with respect to the experimental setting. If there is more than one variable in the independent group, a factorial design is given. Since in a factorial design the various interactions between the selected variables have to be considered, the number of variables should be restricted to a manageable size. Due to the risk of measurement interferences, the number of dependent variables also should be as small as possible. One of the most difficult experimental tasks consists in controlling the variable group C. If relevant variables are not included in the control, the design may end in an ecologically invalid situation which is not related to the authentic situation observed in communication analysis. Thus, the research design clarifies the relationships between the various variables involved in the research design.

Interpretation of results. The analysis of the experimental results yields answers to the question whether or not the results contradict the hypotheses. If the analysis confirms the hypotheses, one is justified to ask for possible generalizations of the original hypotheses and to ask for causal explanations. In cases in which the hypotheses have to be rejected some interpretational work has to be done. What are the possible reasons for the failure? They may be found in the underlying hypotheses or in the experimental design. A crucial part of the experimental method is to give some tentative answers and, even more important, to give some hints about how these problems can be resolved. The overall criterion for these suggestions is their compatibility not only with the experimental results but also with the observations during communication analysis. Thus, experiments give valuable insight into the mental processes underlying the observable behavior of the participants.

4.2. A sample experiment

In order to illustrate these functions of the experimental component, we will describe an experiment carried out as part of a larger research project (cf. Kindt, Strohner, and Jang 2002). Specifically in the present study, we put our focus on the influence of referential ambiguity and time pressure on question strategies. Our hypotheses, based on the theoretical approach of situated understanding (e.g. Kindt 1998, 2002), included in addition to the effects of a semantic factor (see Hypothesis 1, Section 3.2. above) also a pragmatic factor. Since in our experiment setting the cooperativeness of the participants is high, time pressure may increase their collaborative efficiency and thus strengthen their tendency to produce specific clarification requests:

> *Hypothesis 2:* Time pressure has a significant influence on the question strategy: The instruction to react as fast as possible results in more specific descriptions than no such instruction.

The experimental procedure consists of a game of cards between two persons: a confederate of the experimenter and a participant without knowledge about the experiment. The cards show arrays of four objects which can be combined in groups of two or three objects, e.g. two large hexagonal bolts, one small hexagonal bolt, and one small round bolt (see Figure 3). On each trial the confederate names a specific object in the array which the participant has to identify. If the confederate says *the small bolt*, there are only two alternative target objects. However, if the confederate says *the hexagonal bolt*, there are three alternative target objects. If the participant is not sure about the object intended, she or he is encouraged to ask a question for clarification. The type of this question for clarification is the dependent variable in the experiment.

The whole experimental procedure was tape recorded. In addition, the experimenter documented any potentially relevant behavior of the participants.

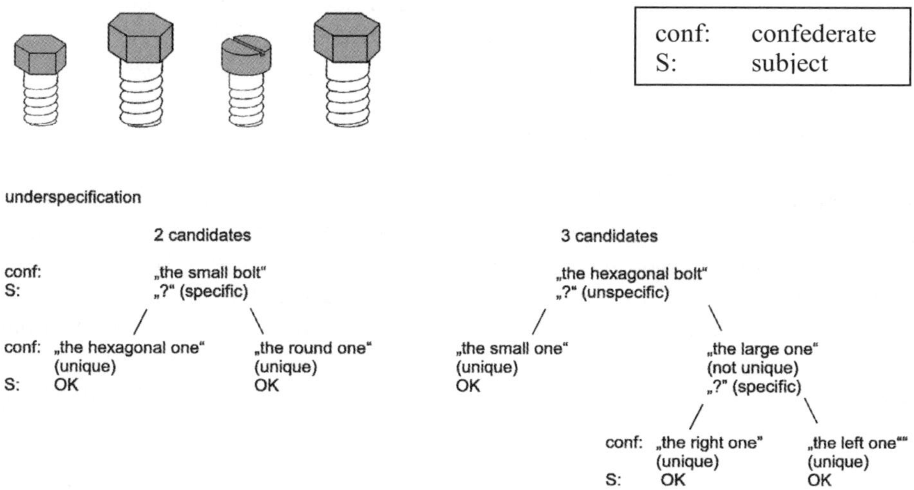

Figure 3. Construction of the experiment

The results (cf. Table 1) were in line with the two hypotheses given above. A referential field of two objects resulted in more specific questions (e.g. “Do you mean the hexagonal or the round one?”) than did a referential field of three objects. In this case, for instance, a preferred question was “Which one do you mean?” Equally, time pressure resulted in more specific questions. These main results of the experiment with human participants thus support the hypotheses 1 and 2 from above and they can be transformed into theorems which serve as an input for the theoretical modeling component of the method.

Table 1. Main results in absolute and relative frequencies of question types

time pressure	number of objects	other	unspecific	specific	sum
no	2	41 (19,5%)	64 (30,5%)	105 (50,0%)	210 (100%)
	3	42 (18,0%)	93 (39,9%)	98 (42,1%)	233 (100%)
yes	2	21 (11,2%)	48 (25,5%)	119 (63,3%)	188 (100%)
	3	30 (13,3%)	71 (31,6%)	124 (55,1%)	225 (100%)

These theorems are also compatible with the results of communication analysis of authentic questions for clarification in our corpora. Even in cases in which the results obtained from the corpora seem to be in conflict with the results from the experiment, a more finely grained analysis was able to show the relevance of the experimentally demonstrated strategies.

4.3. Linking experiments to theoretical modeling

Theoretical models consist of a logically consistent network of propositions. As already mentioned, experimental hypotheses are formulated to fulfill these requirements. The basis of experimental hypotheses is the conditional relation between the independent variables A and the dependent variables B with respect to the controlled variables C. Once established, the conditional relation or dependency between variables A and B can be interpreted in a more specific way: Often it raises the suspicion of a *causal* relation, thus exceeding the empirical facts.

Somewhat similar to the criticism of the term "causal" analysis is the explication of the term "mental" analysis. By trying to explain the confirmed relations between the independent and dependent variables, researchers rely on certain intervening variables which characterize internal states of the model. However, the important question is how to interpret these hypothesized structures or processes. Are they believed to be real instances of mental units or do they serve only a formal function in order to connect the input and output of the observed organism? Researchers have to be careful not to fall back onto the ideologically based positions of mentalism. One procedure generally agreed upon in the experimental community is to stick closely to the operationally defined independent and dependent variables. Anyhow, experiments serve as a valid heuristic basis for formulating well-founded hypotheses on mental structures and processes.

5. Theoretical modeling

The theoretical modeling component is the central link between the human and computer experiment components. A theoretical model integrates the experimentally confirmed theorems into a coherent system (cf. Eikmeyer et al. 2006), which relates the independent variables to the dependent variables. In most cases this is possible only if certain intervening variables between independent and dependent variables are constructed. These hypothetical instances and their functional relations form the creative part of the model and often give reason for critical discussions.

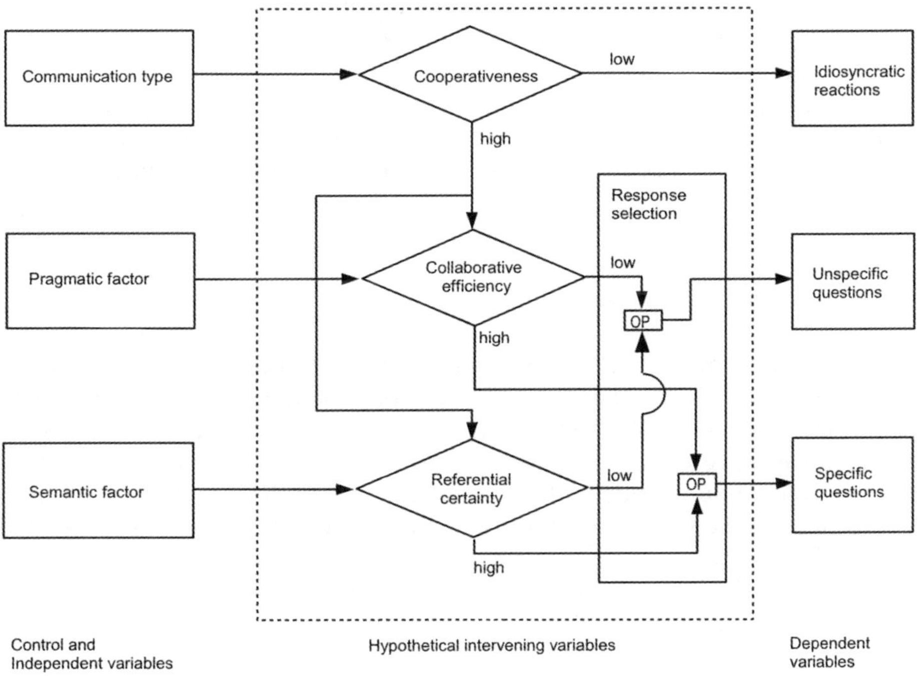

Figure 4. A simple model of the observed question strategies with its independent, intervening, and dependent variables and its main activation routes

In order to illustrate the theoretical modeling component we start our argumentation with a simple model of the described scenario for clarification requests. The model is given in the form of a diagram (cf. Figure 4), which is based on the two theorems resulting from the experiments on humans. This model has been made up in a way which is quite typical for models proposed in psycholinguistics and psychology, but diagrams like these ultimately rely on the interpretation of their readers. Such diagrams certainly have a high heuristic value, but we will propose a simplified input-output model (Section 5.1), which is explicit in the sense that it is formulated with mathematical concepts. This guarantees that the model can be subject to an evaluation leading to a refusal or the acceptance for the time being (cf. Eikmeyer 1983, 1988, 2003; Schade and Eikmeyer 1993). Modifications of this model are proposed in order to show that the model constructor has several degrees of freedom and to discuss ways to extend the model (Section 5.2). Finally, we derive a full quantitative model from the input-output model (Section 5.3).

Before we go into detail, we should make clear what it is that is to be modeled. In a dialogue two people communicate. Linguistic acts can be referential (i.e. they indicate which "thing" is being talked about) or predicative (i.e. one says something about a "thing"). A listener can be unable to understand a referential act in which case she/he will probably make a clarification request. The model shows the linguistic structure of this request by indicating whether it is a specific question, an unspecific question, or an expression of some other kind.

5.1. A simple input-output model

Variables in models have values, but the range of possible values has to be specified as well as the exact way of their combination. The values 'low' and 'high' used in Figure 4 can be meant to represent (a) two discrete values the variable can have or (b) values on a continuous scale ranging from a minimum to a maximum value with 'low' being close to the minimum and 'high' being close to the maximum. We will set out with the first proposal here and turn to the alternative in Section 5.3.

Basically, the assignment of values to variables in the framework of the model follows strict rules:

- The independent variables and the control variables take their values due to the experimental design.
- the intervening variables either receive their values directly from the independent or control variables, or combine values of intervening values.
- the dependent variables receive values from intervening variables or their combinations.

The model has three independent or control variables representing the experimentally controlled factors. According to the rules specified above, the values of the control variables have to be brought from the real world into the model. This happens usually by some arbitrary coding scheme, which, however, has to be strictly applied. We use combinations of characters as values which are chosen relying on mnemonic techniques:

– *Communication type.* Communication can occur in different forms. One relevant dimension for these forms is the cooperativeness: Political discussions are often very uncooperative, task-oriented communication is usually cooperative. This variable has two possible values: "to" means that the communication type is task-oriented, "nto" means that it is not.
– *Time pressure.* Psychological studies often have come to the result that cognitive processes change when time pressure is exerted on the participants of experiments. We manipulated this factor in the above mentioned experiment, because it is a productive source for gaining insight. This variable has two possible values: "tp" means that time pressure is exerted, "ntp" means that it is not so.
– *Number of objects.* Problems of reference are one of the most frequent sources for misunderstandings (Bazzanella and Damiano 1999). Incomplete or ambiguous referential noun phrases can lead to side sequences with clarification requests in case the referential field and the linguistic expression do not simply match. The relevance of this variable became clear already during qualitative communications analysis. This variable has two possible values: "3+" (three or more) means that there are more than two objects in the semantic field, which can be referents of the linguistic expression; "2" means that there are exactly two objects. This variable will be addressed again in Section 5.2.

The model uses three hypothetical intervening variables. We give a heuristic description of their role first and add a precise assignment of values afterwards. We use a numerical coding scheme for the intervening variables, since we want to express the output-relation with the help of mathematical formulae.

– *Cooperativeness.* Since a necessary precondition for a successful task-oriented communication is cooperativeness, this intervening variable dominates the whole interaction process. Only if the cooperativeness is high enough, the two variables 'collaborative efficiency' and 'referential certainty' can function in a predictable way. Otherwise, the results will be some other reaction. – 'Cooperativeness' has value "1", if the 'communication type' has value "to"; otherwise, it has value "0".
– *Collaborative efficiency.* If the participant tries to react cooperatively and there is a moderately high time pressure, he or she should select the most efficient question strategy. Undoubtedly, the most efficient strategy is to

ask a question which includes as much information as possible. In this case, the cognitive effort may be higher, yet the efficiency of the question will also increase. – 'Collaborative efficiency' has value "1" if 'time pressure' has value "tp", and value "0" otherwise.

– *Referential certainty.* If the referential field consists only of two possible objects, the related knowledge of these two objects and their critical differences should be very good. This referential knowledge is an excellent precondition for planning a specific question, e.g. in the form of "X or Y?" If the referential field consists of three or more potential objects, the knowledge is more diffuse and the preferred question strategy might be something like "Which one do you mean?" – 'Referential certainty' has value "1" if 'number of objects' has value "2", and value "0" otherwise.

Let us begin with making proposal (a) more explicit: For a model with two discrete values we need two discrete entities, let us call them 0 and 1.

Using two discrete values for the range of a variable has a direct impact on the Theorems 1 and 2 formulated above, since preferences turn into binary differences as shown below, where we indicated the textual changes for comparison (new text in italics after the older version). The same holds for all variables as there is no "more or less" any longer, but a "yes or no." The discreteness thus leads to an oversimplification.

> *Theorem 1* (oversimplified version): The relevant situational parameter is the number of possible reference objects: in case of exactly two objects a specific *or*-question is ~~preferred~~ *used*, while a more unspecific *wh*-question is ~~preferred~~ *used* for more than two possibilities.
>
> *Theorem 2* (oversimplified version): Time pressure has a significant influence on the question strategy: The instruction to react as fast as possible ~~results in more~~ *leads to* specific questions ~~than no such instruction~~, *while no pressure leads to unspecific questions*.

This is the exact meaning of the informal specification given in Figure 4 for an oversimplified model with discrete values. The two hypotheses also determine the values of the three dependent variables 'other reaction', 'unspecific question', and 'specific question'. The relations between all variables are described completely and in a formally explicit way by the matrix shown in Table 2. The inherent oversimplification has to be kept in mind.

The matrix specifies the eight possible combinations of values of the three independent variables in the corresponding rows. Since the dependent variables represent three mutually exclusive ways of behavior, only one of the three final columns can have value 1 in the same row, the others have value 0. Rows 1 to 4 cover Theorem 1 from above, rows 5 and 8 cover theorem 2. Rows 6 and 7 are not at all mentioned in Figure 4, but in line with the overspecification we do not assume a specific question (but see definition 2c below).

Table 2. Value matrix of a discrete model

Condition	Independent variables			Intervening variables			Dependent variables		
	Communication type	Time pressure	Number of objects	Cooperativeness	Collaborative efficiency	Referential certainty	Other reaction	Unspecific question	Specific question
1	nto	ntp	3+	0	0	0	1	0	0
2	nto	ntp	2	0	0	1	1	0	0
3	nto	tp	3+	0	1	0	1	0	0
4	nto	tp	2	0	1	1	1	0	0
5	to	ntp	3+	1	0	0	0	1	0
6	to	ntp	2	1	0	1	0	1	0
7	to	tp	3+	1	1	0	0	1	0
8	to	tp	2	1	1	1	0	0	1

Moreover, one can specify the values of the dependent variables by arithmetic operations with the values 0 and 1 ('*' indicates multiplication and '–' indicates subtraction. The names of the intervening variables are shortened in order to enhance readability in this and the following definitions).

Definition 1:

other reactions = 1 – *coop*
unspecific question = *coop* * (1 - *coll* * *ref*)
specific question = *coop* * *coll* * *ref*

However, Figure 4 tells us more than the story of the value combination (which it does not even tell in a very explicit fashion). Figure 4 is a flow chart diagram in which all variables appear as boxes: rhombic boxes are used for the three intervening variables mentioned in Table 2 and rectangular boxes are used for the others. The rhombic boxes are used in order to describe alternatives to be considered or decisions to be taken. All three such boxes have two possible outcomes. There are, moreover, small operator-boxes which indicate that some process is taking place. One could be inclined to interpret Figure 4 in such a way that a high value of 'cooperativeness' is propagated to 'collaborative efficiency' and 'referential certainty' in order to induce the consideration of alternatives. This interpretation, however, must be made explicit in addition to the input-output behavior. The same holds for the temporal relations between information flow and operations carried out: if they are important, they have to be spelled out explicitly.

5.2. Modifications of the simple model

Instead of using variables which can take one of two values only, as discussed above, one can equally well use a single variable with more values. In a variant of the model under discussion one could use a single dependent variable named 'linguistic reaction' with three different values, let us say 1, 2, and 3, where 1 would stand for some other reaction, 2 for an unspecific question, and 3 for a specific question. One can easily define this variable with the following equation:

Definition 2a:

$$\textit{linguistic reaction} = \\ 1 * (1 - \textit{coop}) + 2 * \textit{coop} * (1 - \textit{coll} * \textit{ref}) + 3 * \textit{coop} * \textit{coll} * \textit{ref}$$

The three terms added in this equation correspond to three dependent variables discussed above, each multiplied with a factor. Since exactly one of them has value 1 and the others have value 0, the desired result is arrived at by adding two zeros and one non-zero value. Using a few mathematical operations yields the shorter version :

Definition 2b:

$$\textit{linguistic reaction} = 1 + \textit{coop} - \textit{coop} * \textit{coll} * \textit{ref}$$

Both definitions will give the value 3 for row 8 of Table 3 and the value 2 for rows 5 and 6, and 7. Rows 1 to 4 have the value 1.

Moreover, it is not necessary to use only the natural numbers (0,1,2,3,...) as values. On can use real numbers as e.g. 0.0, 0.5 and 1.0 and define alternatively:

Definition 2c:

$$linguistic\ reaction = coll * 0{,}5 * (coll + ref)$$

This will yield value 1.0 in row 8 of Table 3, value 0.5 for rows 6 and 7, and value 0 in the other lines. Notice that this formula is the first one which connects two variables additively. This always indicates that there is no interaction between the two. This mirrors the fact that there was no tendency towards an interaction between the pragmatic and semantic factors. In oversimplified models this cannot be modeled directly.

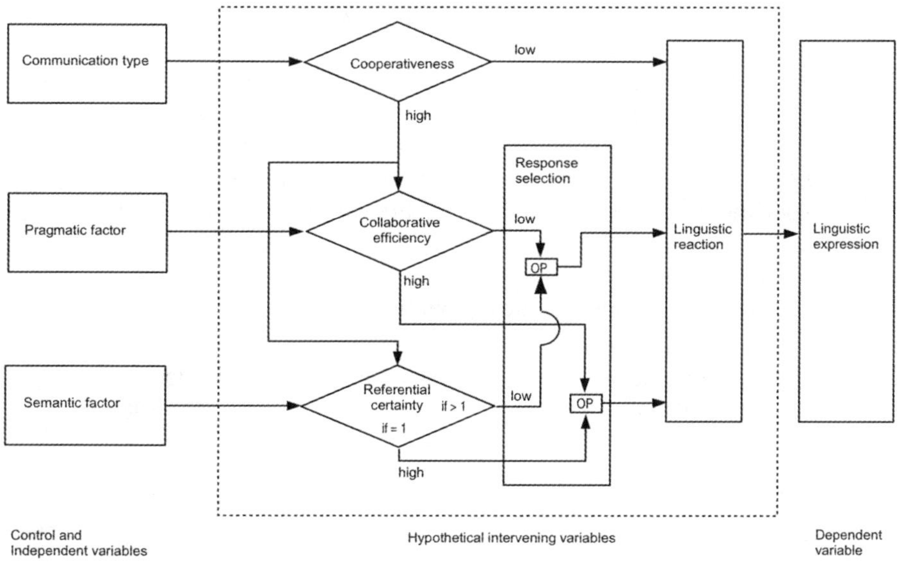

Figure 5. An elaborated model

Another variant of our model can be arrived at by specifying the substructure of a variable. The variable 'linguistic reaction', for example, can be replaced by a complete language production model. This approach will add lots of new intervening variables and a new dependent variable 'linguistic expression', which does not simply indicate the type of the linguistic reaction by a number, but specifies its wording explicitly. This would certainly be a challenging enterprise, but obviously too complex for this contribution (see Eikmeyer et al. 1999; Schade 1992, 1999; Schade and Eikmeyer 1998 for proposals). A graphical representation of this change and of another proposal discussed immediately below can be found in Figure 5.

Specifying the substructure of a variable can also be applied to other variables. The variable 'referential certainty' has been defined above indirectly by the number of potential objects one can refer to. Thus, there is some hidden 'intelligence' located in the different coding steps. This can be made explicit by defining the value of variable referential certainty directly by a conditional: as "low" or 0 if there are more than two objects to chose among, and as "high" or 1, if there are exactly two objects.

5.3. A continuous model

Experiments do not only lead to a description of the outcome of some sort of processing, they often result in absolute numbers of cases and percentages and the task of a model can be to approximate this distribution by an arithmetical law. Such a distribution has been presented above in Section 4.2., Table 1 as a result of an experiment on the form of questions in relation to 'collaborative efficiency' and 'number of objects'. The communication type in this experiment was not varied. For this reason the upper half of Table 3 is blank due to a lack of data.

Table 3. A continuous model for the distribution of reactions

Condition	Independent variables			Intervening variables			Dependent variables		
	Communication type	Time pressure	Number of objects	Cooperativeness	Collaborative efficiency	Referential certainty	Other reaction	Unspecific question	Specific question
1	no data								
2									
3									
4									
5	no data			0.80	0.20	0.20	0.20	0.30	0.50
6				0.80	0.20	0.80	0.18	0.40	0.42
7				0.80	0.80	0.20	0.12	0.25	0.63
8				0.80	0.80	0.80	0.13	0.32	0.55

In the columns for the independent and intervening variables of the lower half, the value 0.8 is used for a high degree of relevance of one of the variables and the value 0.2 for a low degree. This pair was deliberately chosen to start with. In the lower right-hand corner there is a replica of the percentages given in Table 1 as decimal numbers. Thus, the possible range for the values is the closed interval [0, 1].

The task is to approximate the values of each of the three dependent variables by a function or formula expressed with the help of the intervening variables. We thus want to arrive at three formulae as in Definition 1 above, but this time we ask for the probability of a processing result.

With respect to the variable 'other reaction', the old formula specified for the discrete case can still be used for Definition 3. The formulae for the two other dependent variables are in fact modifications of the formulae for the discrete case. The overlap is indicated with a bold print in Definition 3. The formulae for both questions are structurally very similar, as can be seen in the data in which both columns have an almost identical value in rows 5 and 6 and 8. Differences are reflected in the formulae by the large bracket after 'coop *': There is a negation and 'coll' subtracted in the formula for unspecific questions, while there is no negation and 'ref' subtracted in the other. Everything following this large bracket has to do with the relation of the value in row 7 to the value in row 6. In fact, the value in row 7 is higher in one case and lower in the other.

Definition 3:

$$\mathit{other\ reactions} = 1 - \mathit{coop}$$
$$\mathit{unspecific\ question} =$$
$$0.45 * \mathit{coop} * (1 + \mathit{coll} * \mathit{ref} - \mathit{coll}) + 0.3 * \mathit{coll} * (1 - \mathit{ref}) =$$
$$0.45 * \boldsymbol{\mathit{coop}} * \boldsymbol{(1 - - \mathit{coll} * \mathit{ref}} - \mathit{coll} \boldsymbol{)} + 0.3 * \mathit{coll} * (1 - \mathit{ref})$$
$$\mathit{specific\ question} =$$
$$0.8 * \boldsymbol{\mathit{coop}} * (1 + \boldsymbol{\mathit{coll} * \mathit{ref}} - \mathit{ref}) \quad + 0{,}42 * (1 - \mathit{coll}) * \mathit{ref} - 0.1$$

Definition 4 results from the application of simple algebraic laws to the formulae from definition 3. This definition shows the similarity and differences between the two variables in still another way.

Definition 4:

$$\mathit{unspecific\ question} =$$
$$0.45 * \mathit{coop} * (1 - (1 - \mathit{ref}) * \mathit{coll}) \quad + 0.3 * \mathit{coll} * (1 - \mathit{ref})$$
$$\mathit{specific\ question} =$$
$$0.8 * \mathit{coop} * (1 - \mathit{ref} * (1 - \mathit{coll})) \quad + 0{,}42 * (1 - \mathit{coll}) * \mathit{ref} - 0.1$$

The formulae specify polynomial functions, and the approximation is quite good, as is evidenced by the relative small absolute errors. The model values and the empirical data are contrasted in Table 4.

Table 4. Comparison of approximated and empirical data

Condition	Approximation			Error			Empirical data		
	Other reaction	Unspecific question	Specific question	Other reaction	Unspecific question	Specific question	Other reaction	Unspecific question	Specific question
5	0.20	0.33	0.50	0.00	0.03	0.00	0.20	0.30	0.50
6	0.20	0.35	0.40	0.02	0.05	0.02	0.18	0.40	0.42
7	0.20	0.26	0.53	0.08	0.01	0.10	0.12	0.25	0.63
8	0.20	0.33	0.50	0.07	0.01	0.05	0.13	0.32	0.55

An important difference between the discrete model and the continuous one is that for a model with two values 0 and 1 (or true and false) there is an algorithm which allows to construct a formula out of a table as the six columns on the right of Table 2. For the continuous model there is no such algorithm, but methods of numerical mathematics can be applied. Sometimes it even suffices to approximate by intelligent guessing and trial-and-error.

This discussion is by no means the end of the story. The model approximates the distribution of different kinds of linguistic reaction with a constant value 0.80 for 'cooperativeness' and four combinations of 0.2 and 0.8 for the two remaining intervening values. Nothing is known empirically about other combinations, but Definition 3 makes a theoretical prediction, which can be tested empirically in the next round of the methodological cycle shown in Figure 1.

6. Computer simulation

At this stage we have transformed the model into a formal system and now it has to be implemented as a computer program. We do this by following the guidelines proposed by Marr (1982).

A model is a reduced and simplified description of a section of reality (cf. Eikmeyer 2003). This can be characterized by the fact that the model highlights the essential aspects while it neglects the unessential ones. In addition to this relation the connection between a model and its theory has to be kept in mind. This connection can be better understood through the three levels of description proposed by Marr (1982) for information processing models. Such a process takes information as input and turns it into output. On the first level, a computational theory has to be specified, i.e. a theory which describes what the transition from input to output aims at and why this is suitable. The latter means the specification of the necessary and sufficient conditions of the transformation. These are based on empirical evidence of the process to be described. The second level of description asks for both the representations of the information assigned to the input and the output variables. Moreover, it requires the specification of an algorithm for the transition in the formulation of which the intervening variables play a central role. These two levels can be called the model. Marr's third level deals with the physical realization of the algorithm. If this realization is done by a computer, it is called a simulation.

The model shown in Figure 4 is an input-output system, in which the control and independent variables make up the input and the dependent variables make up the output to be specified on the first level. The intervening variables and their connections are used to formulate the algorithm for the transition from input to output. The results which the algorithm has to deliver are specified in either Table 1. Definition 1 specifies the formulae to which the algorithm can apply. Since the values for the input and the output have been specified and since the algorithm is sufficiently characterized, all requirements for the second level of description have been fulfilled.

Once a model has been specified, it has to be evaluated, i.e. it has to be found out, in what respect the model correctly describes reality and in what respect it is false. A computer simulation can be used as a tool for model evaluation. Tests can be repeated almost endlessly, all parameters can be modified, and new hypotheses or predictions can be derived. For a simple model, as the one discussed here, a spreadsheet program is all one needs:

- Enter the values for the columns of the intervening variables from Table 3 into columns A, B, and C, respectively.
- Enter '=1-A1' into field D1, copy it and paste it into fields D2 to D8.
- Enter '=A1*(A1-B1*C1)' into field E1, copy it and paste it into fields E2 to E8.
- Enter '=A1*B1*C1' into field F1, copy it and paste it into fields F2 to F8.

According to Popper (1971), falsifiability is a minimal requirement for scientific models. Marr (1982) claims that modeling has to aim at the specification of representations and algorithms. Johnson-Laird (1988, p. 52) further adds that "theories of the mind should be expressed in a form that can be modelled in a computer program."

7. Conclusions

The Grounded Experimental-Simulative Method can be looked at from several perspectives. We will start with a justification for it from a narrower linguistic perspective and then turn to the broader context of cognitive science in general.

The methodology proposed above tries to clarify which significance the methods used for structure and process analysis in the different branches of linguistics have for an integrated development of models. These methods are – in contrast to common appreciation and practice – not to be regarded as competitive but as complementary. Our project shows that the analysis of the structure of communication has to combine communication analysis (qualitative and quantitative) with grammar- and semantic-theoretical methods. At the same time, the relevance of postulated structures in language and communication can be backed up by process-analytic studies of the systems involved. In addition, psycholinguistic experiments might have little impact if they are not based on a differentiated fundament of linguistic theories.

The future development of cognitive science depends not only on progress in theory construction but also on methodological innovation. We need new methodological concepts and procedures which will contribute to a better integration of the cognitive subdisciplines. This paper presents one possible strategy of relating some of the disciplines to each other. Specifically, we propose that communication analysis, experimental research, and computer simulation cooperate in order to build up a new integrated method named Grounded Experimental-Simulative Method.

The core of this new approach consists of a close relation between human and machine experiments. The obligatory link between these two types of experiments results from precise theoretical models, which can be formalized in adequate computer programs. If the classic experimental-simulative method is applied to complex discourse, it must be grounded. The methods of communication analysis have to be included in order to relate the human experiments to ecologically valid discourse. Since authentic corpora are hard to analyze due to their complexity, computer assisted analysis of these corpora is added to the method.

The Grounded Experimental-Simulative Method is not only able to contribute to the methodological integration of cognitive sciences but can also form a basis for theoretical progress. If all authors in cognitive sciences could agree that good theories should be transformed into formal models, which are to be confirmed in human and computer experiments, then efficient criteria for theory testing would be available. In our opinion these criteria will be better met by systems analysis models than by other types of theory.

Acknowledgements

We thank Kyung-Won Jang, Elke Prestin, Yvonne Rittgeroth, and Gesche Schaffranietz for their effective support and fruitful discussions. We also thank Ingo Bax for implementing the computer system for handling corpora of communicative interactions.

References

Bazzanella, C., and R. Damiano
1999 The interactional handling of misunderstanding in everyday conversations. *Journal of Pragmatics* 31: 817–836.
Eikmeyer, H.-J.
1983 Procedural analysis of discourse . *Text* 3: 11–38.
1988 Simulation. In *Neue Technologien und Medien in Germanistik und Deutschunterricht,* N. Oellers (ed.), 51–56. Tübingen, Niemeyer.
2003 Simulative Methoden. In *Sprachproduktion,* T. Herrmann, and J. Grabowski (eds.), 51–70. Göttingen, Hogrefe.
Eikmeyer, H.-J., W. Kindt, Y. Rittgeroth, and H. Strohner
2006 A systems framework for communicative understanding. In *Situated Communication,* G. Rickheit, and I. Wachsmuth (eds.), 379–409. Berlin: de Gruyter (this volume).
Eikmeyer, H.-J., and U. Schade
1993 The role of computersimulation in neurolinguistics. *Nordic Journal of Linguistics* 16: 153–169.
Eikmeyer, H.-J., U. Schade, M. Kupietz, and U. Laubenstein
1999 A Connectionist View of Language Production. In *Representations and Processes in Language Production,* R. Klabunde, and C. von Stutterheim (eds.), 205–236. Wiesbaden: Deutscher Universitäts-Verlag.
Johnson-Laird, P. N.
1988 *The Computer and the Mind. An Introduction to Cognitive Science.* London: Fontana.

Kindt, W.
1998 Konzeptuelle Grundlagen einer Theorie der Verständigungsprobleme. In *Verständigungsprobleme und gestörte Kommunikation,* R. Fiehler (ed.), 17–43. Opladen: Westdeutscher Verlag.
2002 Koordinations-, Konstruktions- und Regulierungsprozesse bei der Bedeutungskonstitution: Neue Ergebnisse der Dynamischen Semantik. In *be-deuten. Wie Bedeutung im Gespräch entsteht,* A. Deppermann, and T. Spranz-Fogazy (ed.), 34–58. Tübingen: Stauffenburg.

Kindt, W., H. Strohner, and K.-W. Jang
2002 Rückfragestrategien bei referentieller Ambiguität: Ein Beispiel von Bedeutungskoordination im Diskurs In *Prozesse der Bedeutungskonstruktion,* I. Pohl (ed.), 357–374. Frankfurt: Lang.

Popper, K.
1971 *Logik der Forschung.* Tübingen: Mohr.

Rittgeroth, Y., S. Birkemeier, K. Poncin, and W. Kindt
2001 *Rückfragen als Strategie zur Verständigungssicherung.* Report 2001/05, CRC 360. Bielefeld: University of Bielefeld.

Schade, U.
1992 *Konnektionismus: Zur Modellierung der Sprachproduktion.* Opladen: Westdeutscher Verlag.
1999 *Konnektionistische Sprachproduktion.* Wiesbaden: Deutscher Universitäts-Verlag.

Schade, U., and H.-J. Eikmeyer
1998 Modeling the production of object specifications. In *Localist Connectionist Approaches to Human Cognition,* J. Grainger, and A. Jacobs (eds.), 257–282. Mahwah: Erlbaum.

Sichelschmidt, L., and E. Carbone
2003 Experimentelle Methoden. In *Psycholinguistik. Ein internationales Handbuch,* G. Rickheit, T. Herrmann, and W. Deutsch (eds.), 115–124. Berlin: de Gruyter.

Index of names

Subject index

■ The Yearbook of South Asian Languages and Linguistics

Edited by Rajendra Singh

2003. 316 pages. Paperback.
ISBN 3-11-017580-0

2004. viii, 281 pages. Paperback.
ISBN 3-11-017989-X

2005. viii, 279 pages. Paperback.
ISBN 3-11-018618-7

WWW.MOUTON-PUBLISHERS.COM

South Asia is home to a large number of languages and dialects. Although linguists working on this region have made significant contributions to our understanding of language, society, and language in society on a global scale, there is as yet no recognized international forum for the exchange of ideas amongst linguists working on South Asia.

The *Yearbook of South Asian Languages and Linguistics* is designed to be just that forum. It brings together empirical and theoretical research and serves as a testing ground for the articulation of new ideas and approaches which may be grounded in a study of South Asian languages but which have universal applicability.

Each volume of this yearbook has four major sections:

I. Invited contributions consisting of state-of-the-art essays on research in South Asian languages.

II. Refereed open submissions focusing on relevant issues and providing various viewpoints.

III. Reports from around the world, book reviews and abstracts of doctoral theses.

IV. A forum for dialogue; critiques; comments and discussions; reports on research activities; and conference announcements.

In the words of the Editor-in-Chief, 'other than excellence and non-isolationism, we have no agenda and no thematic priorities.' This pioneering yearbook will interest all those in the fields of sociolinguistics, language studies, grammar, literature, and sociology.

W DE G
Mouton
de Gruyter
Berlin · New York